The American Marshall Plan Film Campaign and the Europeans

A Captivated Audience?

Maria Fritsche

Bloomsbury Academic
An imprint of Bloomsbury Publishing Plc

BLOOMSBURY
LONDON · OXFORD · NEW YORK · NEW DELHI · SYDNEY

Bloomsbury Academic
An imprint of Bloomsbury Publishing Plc

50 Bedford Square
London
WC1B 3DP
UK

1385 Broadway
New York
NY 10018
USA

www.bloomsbury.com

BLOOMSBURY and the Diana logo are trademarks of Bloomsbury Publishing Plc

First published in 2018

British Library Cataloguing-in-Publication Data
A catalogue record for this book is available from the British Library.

ISBN: HB: 978-1-3500-0933-2
       ePDF: 978-1-3500-0934-9
       ePub: 978-1-3500-0935-6

Library of Congress Cataloging-in-Publication Data
A catalog record for this book is available from the Library of Congress.

Cover image © Bert Hardy/Picture Post/Hulton Archive/Getty Images

Typeset by Integra Software Services Pvt. Ltd.
Printed and bound in Great Britain

To find out more about our authors and books visit www.bloomsbury.com.
Here you will find extracts, author interviews, details of forthcoming events and
the option to sign up for our newsletters.

For Jakob

Contents

List of Figures   viii
List of Tables   x
Acknowledgements   xi
List of Abbreviations   xiv

Introduction   1
1   Visualizing the Marshall Plan   21
2   By Europeans – for Europeans: Local Film Production   47
3   The Cold War as Text and Context   73
4   US Policy into Film: Productivity   99
5   US Policy into Film: European Integration   129
6   Filmmakers and Information Officers as Cultural Transmitters   157
7   Audience Reception   181
8   Distribution and Exhibition   205
Conclusion   229

Filmography   241
Notes   255
Sources   306
Bibliography   310
Names and Film Title Index   328
Subject Index   332

List of Figures

1.1 *Men at Work*: The Marshall Plan sends men back to work   28

1.2 *A Ship Is Born*: Masculinity and manual labour are inextricably linked   28

1.3 Boys as instigators of change in *Project for Tomorrow, Story of Kaula* and *Hansl and the 200,000 Chicks*   33

1.4 The power of film in *Concerning Dairy Production*   34

1.5 *Village without Water*: The lack of water has locked the Italian village into poverty   41

2.1 Canted camera frames in *Tomorrow We Live* illustrate Italy's turmoil   56

2.2 (a, b) 'For the jobless, new jobs. For the despairing, new heart!' (*Land of Apulia* and *Village without Words*)   57

2.3 Destruction of land in *The Jungle that Was* signalizes progress   63

2.4 *Hugo and the House of Europe*: Rebuilding Europe requires close cooperation   67

3.1 *Men and Machines* in support of the defence effort   82

3.2 *The Smiths and Robinsons* do their bit to protect Britain from a communist attack   83

3.3 Where liberalism dwells ... (*As the Young Ones Sing*)   88

3.4 Visualizations of the communist danger in *Without Fear*   92

3.5 The censored newspaper scene in *All My Ships* that sparked American concerns of communist propaganda   97

4.1 *Productivité* illustrates the benefits of productivity   101

4.2 Removal of trade barriers brings prosperity to everyone (*The Shoemaker and the Hatter*)   111

4.3 *Silkmakers of Como*: Easing the tension between the old and the new   112

4.4 Turning unproductive land into fertile soil in *Land Redeemed, Rice and Bulls, The Village Tractor* and *Bull's Eye for Farmer Pietersen*   114

4.5 Electricity frees up manpower in *The Invisible Link*   115

4.6 *Yusef and His Plough*: Young Yusef's entrepreneurial spirit serves his community well   116

4.7 Happy pigs thanks to scientific farming (*The Streamlined Pig*)   118

4.8 The milk's journey from cow into milk powder in *The Extraordinary Adventures of One Quart Milk*   120

4.9	Variety is troublesome: *Marketing*	122
5.1	The mapping of Europe in *The Marshall Plan at Work* and *The Changing Face of Europe* series	135
5.2	Is Europe Christian or Muslim – or both? (*The Hour of Choice*)	136
5.3	*The Hour of Choice* presents the Europeans as diverse, but tied together by the same values	137
5.4	In *E comme Europe*, young Europeans meet at the river Rhine to celebrate the European idea	140
5.5	Children learn the benefits of peaceful collaboration in *Let's Be Childish*	142
5.6	The ship as promise of revival in *Henry's Story* and *Provence*	143
5.7	Fishermen in the North Sea – trailblazers for a united Europe in *Shoot the Nets!*	145
5.8	'Behind each ship lies a country' – the ship as a symbol of recovery in *A Ship Is Born*	146
5.9	The ship as a symbol of hope in *Village without Words*	147
5.10	The MP clears the blocked waterway and connects what belongs together in *Corinth Canal*	150
5.11	The experience of war has tied the Europeans together (*Somewhere to Live*)	152
5.12	*Breakthrough*: Men return to work at Aura thanks to the ERP	154
6.1	The limits of international understanding. This scene from *As the Young Ones Sing* gave the film officer reason for concern	174
7.1	*Talking to the Italians* offers a glimpse of the audience at an open-air MP film show	182

List of Tables

1.1   Chronological development of MP film production, based on a sample of 167 MP films   23

2.1   Breakdown of MP film productions by country, based on a sample   50

Acknowledgements

The Marshall Plan was scheduled to take place over a four-year period. This book project has exceeded that duration by far, though I am forced to conclude that its impact is likely to be somewhat less momentous!

The American efforts to promote the European Recovery Programme in post-war Europe have occupied many years of my life. It has been a demanding and, at times, a very difficult, experience, but also one that has been consistently instructive and illuminating. I want to take the opportunity to express my gratitude to a number of people who supported this project and helped bring it to completion. My first thanks must go to my esteemed colleague Hans-Otto Frøland who gave me the impetus to begin this project. I would also like to thank the Norwegian Research Council whose generous funding has allowed me to immerse myself in the topic and to pursue my research across Europe and the Atlantic. During my project, I have spent lengthy periods of time at different research institutions and universities, and have profited in many ways from academic debate with colleagues and from a great many inspiring seminars and talks. For their hospitality, I would like to thank: the German Historical Institute in Washington, DC, which also funded a lengthy research stay at the National Archives; the University of Southampton and colleagues from the Film Studies Department, especially Tim Bergfelder; the Centre for Contemporary History (ZZF) in Potsdam, in particular Christoph Classen and Jürgen Danyel and their team; the Forschungsstelle Zeitgeschichte (FZH) in Hamburg; and, last but not least, its neighbouring Institute for the History of the German Jews, especially Beate Meyer and Björn Siegel, who took me under their wing.

In my research and writing I was dependent on the help and specialist knowledge of experts. I am especially indebted to Linda Christenson, and her husband Eric, for their generosity, kindness and hospitality. Linda unstintingly shared her materials as well as her vast knowledge of the subject, connected me to other experts in the field and showed an unending and infectious enthusiasm for the topic. I would also like to express my gratitude to Anne Bruch, Regina Longo, Jeanpaul Goergen, Marianne Thys and Verena Weber for generously sharing their materials with me and for offering priceless information. I am particularly grateful to Heiner Ross in Hamburg, who gave me access to his large collection of documents and books on the Allied re-education efforts. For their invaluable advice I thank Gérard Bossuat, Günter Bischof, Heide Fehrenbach, Frances Lynch, Frank Mehring, Mette Peters, Ramón Reichert, Justin Smith, Matthias Steinle, Thomas Tode and Wolfram Kaiser.

A pleasurable consequence of undertaking an empirical study of such broad geographical scope was that it involved research visits to archives and libraries in various countries. I am thankful to the knowledgeable archivists, librarians and colleagues who went out of their way to help me navigate their archival holdings, or who provided me with film prints, materials or contacts. I would especially like to thank: in Austria, Karin Moser from the Filmarchiv in Vienna; in Belgium, Alain Goossens and Valéria Musio from the Cinémathèque de la Fédération Wallonie-Bruxelles in Brussels, and Bert Musial, head of the audiovisual library of the European Commission; in Denmark, Karin Bonde Johansen, Palle Petterson and Lars Ølgaard from the Det Dankse Filminstitut in Copenhagen; in France, Sandra Willmott from the OEEC Archive and Library, Pierre Chantreuil and Kane Hamedine at the CNC, Brice Amoroux at INA and Vivien Richard at the Archives Nationales – Pierrefitte in Paris; in Germany, the incredibly helpful staff of the library and document archive of the Deutsche Filminstitut in Frankfurt am Main, Beate Dannhor, Christiane Eulig, Uschi Rühle and Svetlana Sikora; Angelika Voß-Louis, Karl Otto Schütt and Dorothee Mateika at the library of the Forschungsstelle für Zeitgeschichte in Hamburg, and Babette Heusterberg at the Filmarchiv of the Deutsches Bundesarchiv in Berlin. In the Netherlands, I was very well taken care of by Bas Agterberg and Bert Hogenkamp at Beeld & Geluid in Hilsversum, and by Rommy Albers and Piet Dirkx at EYE in Amsterdam. Thank you also to Catherine Cormon, Frank Kessler, Mette Petters, Jan Willem de Vries and particularly to Vera Weber for helping with my research in the Netherlands. Thank you to Tone Føreland from the Nasjonalbiblioteket in Mo in Norway, and to the many archivists and staff at the US National Archives in College Park, MD, for responding to all my queries.

This book had a long gestation period. The fact that I finally brought it to completion owes much to the support of several people. Special praise should go to Anne Bruch, Christian Cargnelli, Mario Daniels, Sue Harper, Katja Seidel and Kristian Steinnes, who invested considerable amounts of time and energy reading and commenting on drafts of chapters. Your critical and thoughtful feedback has been invaluable. Thank you also to my friend Birgit Johler, who shared with me the pains and pleasures of the writing process during several retreats in the beautiful Austrian countryside. For gently ironing out my stylistic glitches and being enthusiastic about the Marshall Plan, I thank my friend

Daniel Weston. I also owe a special thank you to my wonderful proofreader Jeremy Lowe for accompanying me through the last stages of the book with great patience and encouragement. I would like to extend a thank you to the two referees for offering fair and helpful criticism on my book proposal and manuscript, and to my editors at Bloomsbury Publishers, Rhodri Mogford and Beatriz Lopez, for supporting me throughout the publication process, and for insisting on strict deadlines!

Finally, I would like to express my gratitude to all my friends and my family for their practical and emotional support. However, the greatest thank you of all goes to Jakob Schindegger, who has showed incredible patience and good humour throughout the project. Thank you for your support, your encouragement and your love. This book has been with me ever since we met, and it is yours, as much as it is mine.

List of Abbreviations

BA	Bundesarchiv (Germany)
BFI	British Film Institute
BPC	British Productivity Council
CGT	Confédération générale du travail (communist-led French trade union confederation)
CIA	Central Intelligence Agency
CIC	Community Information Councils (Greece)
CNC	Centre national du cinéma et de l'image animée (France)
COI	British Central Office of Information
DFI	Deutsches Filminstitut, Frankfurt
EANPC	European Association of National Productivity Centres
ECA	Economic Cooperation Administration
EIU	British Economic Information Unit
EPA	European Productivity Agency
ERP	European Recovery Program
EYE	EYE Filmmuseum, Amsterdam
FRG	Federal Republic of Germany
GARIOA	Government and Relief in Occupied Areas (Germany)
GPO	General Post Office (UK)
HICOG	High Commission(er) for Germany (US)
IMS	International Motion Picture Service (US)
INA	Institut national de l'audiovisuel (France)
MFU	Ministeriernes Filmudvalg (film committee of the Danish government)
MOI	Ministry of Information (UK)
MP	Member of Parliament
MPEA	Motion Picture Exchange Association
MSA	Mutual Security Agency
NA	National Archives, Kew (UK)
NARA	National Archives and Records Administration (US)
NATO	North Atlantic Treaty Organization
NPC	National Productivity Centres

OEEC	Organisation for European Economic Co-operation
OMGUS	Office of Military Government U.S. in Germany
OSS	Office of Strategic Services (US)
RG	Record Group
SGCI	Secrétariat général du Comité interministériel pour les questions de coopération économique européenne (France)
UN	United Nations
UNRRA	United Nations Rehabilitation and Relief Administration
US	United States
USIA	United States Information Agency
USIE	United States Information and Education Exchange
USIS	United States Information Service

Introduction

The Marshall Plan (MP), or European Recovery Programme (ERP) as it was officially called, occupies a central place in popular historical memory. The third episode of the well-known CNN documentary series *The Cold War*, first aired in 1998, is entirely devoted to it.[1] It presents the case of a Marshall Aid-sponsored scheme that provided American mules to impoverished Greek farmers to illustrate how the ERP sought to revive the European economy. The documentary producers combined archival footage with oral history interviews to illustrate how the programme worked. The footage shows a Greek boy and his grandfather applying for a mule. After several months' waiting time, they receive information that a ship with a load of mules has arrived from the United States. The Greek farmers initially struggle to control the large, temperamental animals. But the boy handles them with sensitivity, and manages to team the large mule with his small, scrawny donkey. The documentary's narrator, the British actor Kenneth Branagh, notes the symbolism inherent in the scene: the powerful American mule helps the weak Greek donkey to plough the field and consequently increase agricultural output. What neither the narrator nor the film credits mention, however, is that the archival footage is actually a clip from the propaganda film *The Story of Koula* (1951), produced to promote the MP to Europeans. The CNN documentary thus turned propaganda into historical evidence – an example of filmic recycling that, while highly questionable, nevertheless helped to secure the longevity of these 'Marshall Plan films'. The example shows that the films are not lost and forgotten, but still shape our memory and knowledge of the MP.

This book tells the story of the MP films. It analyses and compares their production, distribution and reception in various parts of Europe, establishing how the Americans used them to secure political, economic and cultural influence in Europe. It explores the problems the Americans experienced in the process, and discusses the reactions of the European audiences. In expanding the hitherto predominantly national focus of studies on this topic, this book examines how

US policies and strategies were influenced by the different national political and cultural contexts in which the films were produced and disseminated. Like the United States, Europe was not a homogenous entity, even though some US policymakers envisaged it as such. It was a diverse conglomerate of nation states and regions that responded very differently to the US propositions. In analysing the films' role within the MP and within the wider context of the Cold War, this books aims to illuminate the complex process of cultural transmission and the use of films as tools of propaganda.

The passing of the Economic Cooperation Act of 3 April 1948, which launched the ERP, also kick-started the propaganda campaign for the MP. It was a campaign on a vast scale, covering seventeen European countries and making use of all media available. Apart from films, radio broadcasts and exhibitions, it used newspapers, leaflets and posters to disseminate the message. Film was considered the most persuasive medium of information, and played a key role in the MP propaganda campaign. Between 1948 and 1954 around 200 films were produced to promote the MP to European audiences. The films, mostly short documentaries, were exhibited in regular cinemas before the main feature, as well as screened non-commercially in schools, union halls, country inns and clubhouses, and even outdoors in village squares. To make the films more effective, US strategists hired European filmmakers to produce them: this was film propaganda made by Europeans, for Europeans. Thus, the MP films were also the locus where the interests and aims of different actors collided: US policymakers, US information officers, European filmmakers and European audiences. By examining the films in the context of policy and strategy discussions, this book also explores the tensions between the actors, and assesses their respective influence on the films' form and content.

Why Marshall Plan propaganda?

The ERP was one of the largest economic aid programmes in history. Named after Secretary of State George C. Marshall, it is often simply referred to as the Marshall Plan. It was Marshall who presented to the public the US government's intention to provide economic assistance to war-torn Europe to revive their economies. In the now famous speech at Harvard University on 5 June 1947, Marshall invited the European governments to come together to work out the necessary financial requirements and measures to rebuild the European economy.

Marshall's proposal to replace the temporary relief programmes with long-term economic assistance was as much politically as economically motivated. The MP, though by no means a coherent plan when it was announced, followed in the footsteps of the Truman Doctrine, which President Truman had put before US Congress only a few months earlier. In promising American support to all democratic nations threatened by totalitarian regimes, the Truman Doctrine demonstrated the US government's intention to take on a more active role in the world. Truman's speech is often interpreted as the final departure from US isolationism, which was confirmed by Marshall's offer.

The rationale behind the MP and the Truman Doctrine was the same: to use economic instruments to achieve security for the United States. Never again should the world experience an economic collapse and the rise of authoritarian regimes that had so nearly brought it to the brink of destruction. The US policymakers took their lessons from the failure to secure Europe's lasting economic recovery after the First World War. They saw in the ERP a means to restructure post-war Europe economically and politically so as to revive global free trade, which was considered the basis for a secure economic and political future. In strengthening the liberal-capitalist system, the MP would also help to contain Soviet power and curb the influence of European communist parties.[2]

Marshall's offer was extended to all Europeans, including the Soviet Union and its satellites in Eastern Europe. However, the US government rightly expected that the Soviets would refuse to participate. Although initially interested, the Soviets were unwilling to accept the terms of the ERP, as these gave considerable power to the United States and advantaged the US dollar.[3] The MP and the Soviet rejection of it thus deepened the division of Europe.

While many European governments eagerly took up the proposal, trying to reach agreement over the details and conditions proved complicated. The ERP built on the principle of self-help and required the European nations to cooperate. Seventeen European states participated in the ERP: Austria, Belgium, Denmark, France, Greece, Iceland, Ireland, Italy, Luxembourg, the Netherlands, Norway, Portugal, Sweden, Switzerland, Turkey, the United Kingdom and West Germany (originally as the Anglo-American Bizone and the French occupation zone); also included was the Anglo-American zone of the Free Territory of Trieste, which was under UN control until 1954. They established the Organization for European Economic Co-operation (OEEC) on 16 April 1948. By signing the OEEC Convention, the member states committed themselves to cooperating with each other – a first step towards European integration. The national representatives in the OEEC decided (together with the Americans) over the allocation of Marshall Aid and coordinated the implementation of the economic reforms that the ERP requested – but with limited success. In addition, each state also had to enter into a bilateral agreement with the US government. The United States thus gained considerable influence over the economic policies of the European governments, which caused much dissatisfaction in Europe.[4] But it was not only European scepticism that needed to be overcome. The US government also had to convince the American taxpayers to extend long-term financial aid to the Europeans before it could launch the programme. It managed to achieve its goal through a propaganda campaign that highlighted how the MP would serve national interest.[5] Finally, on 3 April 1948, ten months after Marshall had informed his audiences about the government's willingness to extend economic aid, US Congress passed the Economic Cooperation Act. It created the statutory framework of the ERP and granted a total of over $13 billion in financial and material aid to Europe, to be paid out over a period of four years.

The ERP's stated goal was to assist the participating states in reviving their economies so that they would become 'independent of extraordinary outside economic assistance' by summer 1952.[6] Its measures aimed at boosting industrial and agricultural production, stabilizing their finances and currencies, and facilitating intra-European trade and exchange through closer cooperation and the removal of trade barriers and tariffs. Marshall Aid served as the lever to pressure the European governments into reforming their fiscal, economic and trade policies and modernizing their industries according to modern US standards – though with varied success. Some European governments successfully evaded US demands for economic or fiscal reform, exploiting the spectre of communism to win concessions.[7] Although keen to obtain financial and technical assistance from the United States, the European governments were also under pressure from their electorate. The communists, who denounced the MP as a covert instrument of American imperialism, were not the only ones who were critical of the participation in the ERP. Many Europeans feared, not without reason, that the reforms the Americans demanded would affect them negatively.

Even before the MP was launched, US strategists expected that it would encounter a certain degree of resistance, as had been the case in the United States. Yet, without the broad support from the European workers and the public in general, the economic and fiscal reforms deemed necessary to revive European economy could not be implemented. Since a publicity campaign had managed to garner popular support for the Economic Assistance Act at home, the Marshall Planners concluded that also the success of the MP in Europe relied on an effective information programme.[8] 'Information' was deemed necessary to counter the communist attacks against the MP. Furthermore, it should persuade the Europeans that the ERP provided the only solution to the economic problems their countries faced, and presented the key to Europe's security and lasting peace. Finally, it was meant to convince the Europeans of the superiority of the US liberal-capitalist model and its ability to guarantee higher living standards and lasting economic growth.

Film was, in the eyes of the US strategists, a particularly useful medium to rally European support. First, because film, unlike a newspaper or a radio broadcast, provided a multisensory experience, and was therefore considered to have a deeper impact.[9] Second, it enjoyed broad popularity and worked for audiences of all ages and different cultural backgrounds. Third, film granted access to those who could not be reached through most other media: the illiterate and little educated.

The propaganda campaign for the MP started in summer 1948 and was conducted under the aegis of the newly established Economic Cooperation Administration (ECA). An independent government agency, the ECA had its European headquarters in Paris and country missions in each of the states that participated in the ERP. An Information Division was in charge of developing propaganda policies and strategies. A number of subunits, including a film unit, were tasked with producing and disseminating information material through the country missions. In October 1951, in the wake of the outbreak of the Korean War, the ECA was abolished. The newly established Mutual Security Agency (MSA) continued the MP propaganda campaign from January 1952 until summer 1953, when the agency was shut down. MP film propaganda was then handed over to the newly established US Information Agency (USIA), which organized the distribution of MP films and brought ongoing film projects to completion.

The Marshall Plan film campaign: Scope and aim of the study

Albert Hemsing, the last head of the ECA/MSA film unit, provided an account of the film unit's propaganda work for the MP. Less a scholarly study than an insider's view of the organization of the film programme, it provides a rare glimpse into the organization's strategies and practices.[10] For, while the MP has been the subject of intense scholarly debate, resulting in a plethora of books and articles, scholarship has predominantly focused on the economic and political aspects of the MP. Although the interest in the role of the MP as producer and transmitter of culture has grown over recent years, we still know too little about the use of culture within the MP and the European responses to that.

Most research on the MP propaganda programme has adopted a national approach and focused on a single nation state. David Ellwood has led the field with his pioneering studies on the implementation and reception of the MP in Italy; he was also the first to investigate the role of MP films.[11] The important work of Regina Longo and Paola Bonifazio demonstrating the convergence of interests between the ECA and the Italian film industry and government have made Italy the best-researched case so far.[12] Comparatively little is known about the propaganda campaign in the other sixteen European countries that participated in the ERP. Brian McKenzie has produced a fine study on the ECA's promotional activities in France, but his focus is not on film.[13] Richard Kuisel's illuminating analysis of the French responses to the influx of American culture addresses the MP and its publicity efforts only in passing.[14] While the American 're-education' programme in West Germany has attracted considerable scholarly attention, relatively little research has been done on ECA's propaganda campaign for the MP, which always played second fiddle to the military's re-education programme. The German historians Frank Mehring and Hans-Jürgen Schröder have contributed some articles that explore the thematic and visual aspects of MP films that were shown in West Germany.[15] Ramón Reichert has done the same for Austria.[16] Reinhard Wagnleitner has examined the US propaganda strategies in Austria, yet without specifically considering the role of the ECA. A few other works have addressed the role of MP films and the involvement of filmmakers in other national contexts, but not in depth.[17]

Shifting the geographic focus to the United States, Elisabeth Heffelfinger has shown how the MP films were recycled for US television to rally domestic support for the government's interventionist politics, though the US authorities were actually prohibited by legislation from doing so.[18] Much broader is the approach taken by Gabriele Clemens, Anne Bruch, Jeanpaul Goergen and Thomas Tode. Rich in fascinating detail, their recently published voluminous study compares films by various national and transnational European sponsors to illustrate discursive and visual patterns in the filmic representations of Europe.[19]

Many aspects of the MP propaganda campaign and its role in transferring American norms and values remain unexplored: this goes both for the production and distribution of MP films in other countries than those named above and for the transnational exchange of films across European borders. Although the ECA propaganda strategists pursued a policy of locally organized film production and distribution, most films were earmarked for European-wide distribution, for reasons of efficiency as much as for garnering popular support for the idea of a united Europe. This raises important questions concerning a film's exportability and the issue of intra-European cultural transfer.

The role of the filmmakers themselves, and that of the US information officers and their influence on the film, has also hitherto hardly been addressed. To fully understand the films and their meanings, we need to know more about who decided on their form, content and message. Another considerable gap in the research concerns the important field of reception: we know very little about who the audiences were, in what context they saw the films, how they responded to them and how these responses fed back and possibly influenced the policies and the propaganda effort of the United States. Lastly, the MP films themselves demand closer scrutiny, especially regarding their often neglected visual and aural aspects, including their adaption for export to other countries.

This book combines analysis of the national and local with a broader transnational – and transatlantic – perspective. It illuminates differences and similarities between the different countries and sheds light on the tensions between the European project that the Americans promoted and the national self-assertions with which Europeans responded.[20] Apart from closely analysing visual form, content and meaning of almost 170 MP films, the book explores how the filmmakers and supervising information officers tailored the film programme, and discusses their influence on ECA policies and propaganda strategies.

In investigating the American propaganda efforts in different cultural, political and socio-economic contexts, this book hopes to enrich our knowledge of the complex workings of cultural transfer. It also aims to add new insights into the history of the early Cold War. By analysing the use of MP films as cultural weapons, it illustrates how the struggle for spheres of influence was fought on the ground, and what roles the Europeans played. In addition, it discusses how the political, economic and cultural dynamics in the different European countries shaped the MP film campaign. Scholarship on cultural diplomacy and Americanization has pointed to the obstacles the United States encountered in its attempts to export its products and culture to post-war Europe. The ECA, too, struggled to sell the MP's policies and its inherent American ideals to the Europeans. Confronted with scepticism and even outright resistance, the ECA was forced to adapt its vision for a future Europe to make it more palpable to Europeans.[21] But while the ECA was able to coerce European governments to implement reforms by threatening to withhold financial assistance (although with varying success), the propagandists could not force audiences to watch a film. Instead, they had to attract and hold their attention by adapting the films and their messages to the audience's interests. The findings show that the information officers largely operated through trial and error and acted much more pragmatically than the official ECA rhetoric suggests. If needed, they even ignored their own government's policy goals, which illustrates the variety of interests that existed within the Truman Administration.

The book addresses four central issues. The first concerns the medium of film and the visual and narrative strategies it employed: How were MP policies translated into moving images? Which arguments did the films convey? How did the form and content of the films change over time, and why? The second cluster of questions focuses on the role of the US information officers and European filmmakers as cultural transmitters: How much freedom did the information officers and the filmmakers have in determining policy goals and strategies? Who exerted influence, and on which levels? And whose interests did the films promote? The third issue concerns the recipients of MP propaganda, using audience surveys and opinion polls to find answers to the following questions: Who were the target audiences, how did they respond to the MP films and how did their reactions differ in the various regions of Europe? How did the reactions and interests of the European audiences influence American strategies and policies? The fourth group of questions addresses the external influences on the MP film programme: How did the local context influence, complicate or facilitate the production, distribution and reception of MP films? How did the Cold War discourse reverberate in the films and shape the ECA's propaganda strategies and film policies? In what way did the US government's political and strategic interests, and the shift of US foreign policy after the outbreak of the Korean War, impact the MP film campaign?

Theoretically, the book is situated in the field of Americanization studies. Americanization has in the past often been equated with cultural imperialism, representing those at the receiving end as passive victims of America's cultural or economic might. Such a view has long been abandoned: it is now usually understood as a process of transfer and adaptation of American – or what is considered to be American – products, culture, norms and practices.[22] Like similar studies that examine the projection of influence between national cultural spaces, I operate with the concept of cultural transfer. While MP propaganda did not export culture in its narrow meaning, it used cultural tools to promote American socio-economic standards and values, which were not only perceived, but also sold as part and parcel of, American culture. The concept of transfer is not one-directional, but a process of interaction that *can* result in cross-cultural fertilization. Cultural transfer, or 'cultural transmission', highlights selective appropriation, adaptation or rejection by those at the receiving end.[23] Still, even though the concept ascribes agency to the 'recipient', it should not be misunderstood as a process of exchange between equal partners. In the realm of institutionalized propaganda especially, the transfer has a clear direction.[24]

The partial lack of sources and the limitations of my own 'womanpower' made it impossible to investigate the implementation and reception of the MP film programme in all seventeen countries. I, therefore, chose to focus on specific countries, while ensuring that all European regions were represented. The decision over which countries to include was based on the availability of records, their strategic importance, as well as the level of propaganda activities. France, Greece, Italy and West Germany thus take centre stage in the book. These states were of highest strategic importance to the United States, not least because of the strength of their communist parties and/or their geographic proximity to communist-ruled territories. Turkey, Denmark and the Netherlands have been included to illustrate specific aspects of the film campaign. Austria, Norway and Britain are analysed, but feature less prominently in this book. Only few records exist on the US propaganda efforts in Belgium and Ireland. Belgium had no funds for information activities, meaning that the neighbouring Dutch mission organized the dissemination of films in Belgium. Ireland did produce one MP film, but I was unable to unearth any records that document the production, distribution or reception of MP films in the country. Consequently, these countries are mostly addressed in the context of discussions of policies and strategies. Iceland, Luxembourg, Portugal, Switzerland and Sweden were of low strategic importance to the United States. They had (virtually) no information budget and thus experienced only very limited propaganda activities.

The book adopts a qualitative approach and combines the close reading of textual records with film analysis. Around 170 MP films (out of a total of around 200) form the core of this analysis. I accessed them through (film) archives – many films are held by the US National Archives – and partly through online platforms.[25] The MP films are of varying lengths, between 3 minutes and 35 minutes, mostly in black and white, and predominantly documentary films.[26] To obtain information on filmmakers and the production of film, I conducted research in various European film archives and libraries where I was granted access to film catalogues, film reviews and press reports, as well as some films. Unfortunately, production materials, scripts and correspondences relating to MP films are scarce, as the production companies and filmmakers seldom deemed them important enough to keep.

To investigate the policy planning, production, distribution and reception of the film campaign, I accessed the vast repository of the US National Archives (NARA) at College Park, Maryland, which hold the records of the US agencies that were engaged in promoting the MP in Europe. I investigated the records of the information offices of the ECA/MSA, the US military and civilian administration in West Germany (OMGUS and HICOG), the US State Department, as well as the US Information Service (USIS) and its successor, the US Information Agency (USIA). These archival materials comprise a large variety of documents, such as policy papers, guidelines, conference minutes, memoranda, telegrams and letters, mission activity reports and country studies, audience surveys and opinion polls, distribution statistics, film print orders, contracts and some film and dubbing scripts. Although the records also contain documents from European institutions and individuals that were engaged in MP propaganda, they largely reflect the US side of the operation. Despite being contractually obligated to promote the ERP in their countries, most European governments left the task to the ECA country missions. It is for this reason that I was not very successful in finding documentation about the European involvement in the propaganda effort at the European archives. Hence, while the textual sources at hand tell us, though often only indirectly, about those at the receiving end of propaganda, they give a predominantly US perspective on the MP film campaign. This inherent bias does not limit the value of the sources. However, the often self-promoting writings require careful and critical analysis to distinguish between different layers of meaning and identify zones of conflict where the exchange between the Europeans and the Americans became most visible.

Most people involved in the propaganda campaign are no longer alive. Luckily, scholars before me have conducted interviews with filmmakers and ECA officials which I was able to use. These interviews prove to be a particularly valuable resource, as they provide information about the practices of film production and distribution, or about conflicts that did not find their way into the written records. Of course, oral history interviews with spectators would have provided invaluable insights into the reception of MP films, but the time frame and scope of this book did not allow such an extension of the research.

The subject of this book spans many fields and disciplines: the history of the MP, the Cold War and European integration; film history; transnational history; the fields of Americanization and cultural diplomacy; propaganda; and cinema and reception studies. Conducting a study with such a broad scope is bound to disappoint experts in the various fields. This book is neither an economic history of the MP nor a political history of the Cold War. My aim has been to bring together different perspectives and to combine different sources in order to shed light on the cultural dimensions of the MP and the Cold War, and to explore the encounters between Americans and Europeans via the production and viewing of the films. In tracing the trajectory from policy into film, and by comparing the implementation of the US propaganda effort in different European countries, I am taking a step into a fascinating field of cultural and social history. It will hopefully encourage others to follow and to fill the gaps I leave behind. But this book comes with another caveat. It does not – and cannot – provide a definitive answer to the question whether the US propaganda effort had an impact and changed European attitudes towards the MP or America's involvement in Europe. Instead, it casts light on the tensions surrounding the MP film propaganda campaign, bringing into relief the various clashes and convergences of interests.

'Propaganda' versus 'information'

Throughout this book, I use the term 'propaganda' interchangeably with 'information' to describe the American efforts to convince the Europeans of the benefits of the MP and its underlying principles. Propaganda is a loaded term that is often associated with manipulation and deception.[27] US policymakers and strategists traditionally referred to their propaganda activities euphemistically as 'information' in an effort to dissociate the United States from propaganda's 'totalitarian application and wicked connotations'.[28] I, however, employ the term propaganda in its neutral meaning as the 'dissemination of information … to influence public opinion'.[29] My understanding of it is defined by the sponsor's intention to persuade and not by the 'truthfulness' of the arguments it puts forward.

American MP propaganda pursued two main aims, which were closely connected: one was to *explain* the aims of the ERP or its measures; the other was to *persuade* the European spectators to accept its arguments as truths. The explaining aspect is particularly strong in MP films promoting the policy of productivity. They are similar in style and purpose to the genre of educational film, which provides instruction by visually describing a process or phenomenon. Unlike educational films, the MP films always carry an unambiguous ideological message that seeks to persuade the viewer of the superiority of the liberal-capitalist model.[30]

Propaganda has been used for many centuries. It was for the first time during the First World War that the US government (as well as other governments) made systematic use of modern media to rally their people behind the war effort. The US Committee on Public Information, which also conducted propaganda abroad, later came under fire for having deliberately spread false information during the war. Propaganda, nevertheless, blossomed in the interwar years, both in the field of business advertising and in the marketing of government policies. The boom of modern mass media and the expansion of the economy gave birth to the new field of public relations and the profession of the advertising expert.[31] The pioneer in public relations Edward Bernays, who worked for corporate business as well as governmental agencies, advocated the use of propaganda in democracies. He considered propaganda a legitimate and even honourable means 'to focus and realize the desires of the masses'.[32] Bernays operated on the understanding that the general public had a limited understanding of the complexities of the world, which made it vulnerable to the wrong kind of manipulation. This was a sentiment shared by the influential journalist and political writer Walter Lippman, who suggested that the government educate the public and 'manufacture' consent to safeguard modern democracy.[33] Also in interwar Europe, propaganda as practice became widely accepted in the realms of politics and business. John Grierson, the father of the British documentary school, was an avid advocate, and convinced the British (and later the Canadian) government to sponsor films to educate the public.[34] However, the term became increasingly associated with the authoritarian regimes of Hitler, Mussolini and Stalin, and their skilful use of modern media to manipulate the masses.

After the United States entered the war, the Roosevelt administration established the Office of War Information (OWI) in 1942. While the American public, unlike the public relations and advertising experts, remained suspicious of propaganda, it accepted its need during wartime. However, once the war was won, it withdrew its support for the government's use of propaganda, as it seemed irreconcilable with the American ideals of liberalism and democracy. The OWI was dissolved in 1945. Some political figures, such as Secretary of State George Marshall, called for the continuation of 'information' activities abroad in order to counter the influence of communist propaganda. Their voices remained unheard until the Soviet–American relations rapidly deteriorated in 1947. The growth of communist parties in post-war Europe caused alarm in the US government and turned the tide of public opinion towards governmental involvement in propaganda overseas.[35] According to the MP historian Harry Price, 'Many Congressmen who tended to look askance at conspicuous publicity within the United States by a governmental agency took a different view of ECA publicity abroad.'[36]

The passing of the Smith-Mundt Act in 1948 presented a major turning point in America's stance on propaganda and cultural diplomacy in peacetime. It provided the legal basis for the overseas information programmes of the ECA and USIS. Still, the government sought to dissociate itself from the use of propaganda – if not in practice, then in name. Thus, officially the US authorities continued to refer to their propaganda activities abroad as 'information'. Unlike the communist enemy, which spread lies, the US agencies claimed to disseminate objective and factual information to educate and inform the people. The emphasis on 'information' was, of course, mere embellishment. Unofficially, the information officers used the terms information and propaganda interchangeably to describe their activities.

Three US agencies were already conducting information activities, when the ECA Information Division entered the European scene in summer 1948: the Office of Military Government of the United States (OMGUS) in Austria and Germany, the CIA and USIS. The propaganda activities of these agencies suggest that the MP information campaign was part of a wider American effort to export its culture, products and sociopolitical ideals to strengthen America's status, influence and economic power.[37]

OMGUS administered the US zones of occupation in post-war Germany and Austria. Its information department conducted a large-scale re-education programme to 'denazify' the citizens who lived in the US occupation zone.[38] For this purpose, it organized cultural and educational programmes that promoted American liberal values and taught democratic skills. It established newspapers and radio stations that employed natives and returning émigrés with the aim of furthering the free exchange of information and publicizing American culture and economic achievements. Over time, the US informational activities expanded into all three West German occupation zones. Film played a crucial role in the OMGUS's efforts to inculcate the Germans with American civic ideals.[39] However, the early practice of compulsory screenings of documentaries on Nazi atrocities was soon abandoned, as the films failed to 'shock' the Germans into reflection on their crimes. The OMGUS film officers replaced the 'atrocity films' with educational films that no longer spoke of German guilt but held up the United States as a model of a liberal-democratic society.[40] The US military government held a powerful position in West Germany, and also controlled the field of information. The ECA information office, which was set up in summer 1948, thus struggled to gain a foothold. Although the situation improved after OMGUS was dissolved and replaced with the High Commissioner for Germany, the ECA information office in West Germany continued to play second fiddle.

Another agency that was involved in propaganda activities overseas was the Central Intelligence Agency (CIA), created by the National Security Act in 1947. Established amid growing concerns over Soviet power, the CIA's main aim was to combat communism through the gathering of intelligence, but also through supporting anti-communist organizations of all types.[41] It subsidized cultural activities and publications that were deemed useful in the effort to undermine communism. The CIA stood behind outwardly private initiatives, such as the National Committee for a Free Europe created in 1949, and the Conference for Cultural Freedom, founded in Berlin in 1950, for which it mobilized non-communist left-wing intellectuals, writers and artists. It operated the radio station Radio Free Europe in Munich, which employed Eastern European refugees to broadcast information across the Iron Curtain.[42] The CIA was also granted access to MP funds to finance the activities of non-communist trade unions in Europe and beyond.[43] But, unlike the other US agencies operating in the field of overseas information, the CIA operated covertly and did not engage openly in propaganda.

The US Information Service (USIS) was perhaps the most important US agency in the field of information. USIS emerged from the OWI and the Psychological Warfare Branch (PWB), which, towards the end of the war, had established offices in Italy and France following the advance of the Western military; these came to be called USIS from 1945 onwards. Working now under the auspices of the State Department, USIS was tasked with promoting American culture and society and garnering support for US foreign policy. USIS offices operated reading rooms and libraries that distributed information and hosted cultural events.[44] They also sent out mobile film units to tour the countryside. USIS was most active in Italy, where it, early after the war, cooperated with local authorities to screen US-produced information and entertainment films to project a positive image of the United States. Severe budget constraints, however, limited USIS activities, until the passing of the Smith-Mundt-Act of 1948 put it on a stable legal basis.[45]

USIS was the ECA's main partner in the field of information, but also its competitor. The two agencies were legally obliged to coordinate and support each other's activities. Their information offices were often located in close proximity.[46] But working side by side on the same territory, targeting the same people, inevitably led to rivalries over their respective areas of influence. Since it was the ECA country mission that distributed the MP funds, the ECA became the prime contact for the national governments. This meant a painful loss of privilege for the US ambassadors, who had hitherto solely represented America's interests abroad.[47] The tensions between the ECA and the State Department and its foreign representatives trickled down to the lower levels and affected the relations between the local ECA and USIS information offices. In some countries, conflicts erupted over policy questions and respective areas of influence, as well as over diverging views on how to conduct an effective information campaign. Despite an 'information "peace treaty" between USIS and the ECA',[48] as the vice-head of the ECA Information Division jokingly called it, the relations between the two agencies remained tense until the two institutions gradually merged from 1952.

The number of US agencies conducting information programmes in post-war Europe illustrates how the United States tried to secure its influence abroad. It did so through various means: cultural activities, mass media and exchange and (re)-education programmes were employed to influence public opinion; in addition, technical and financial assistance as well as covert subsidies to anti-communist European governments and trade unions helped to forge strategic alliances. These programmes complemented and sometimes duplicated each other. Also their objectives partly overlapped: The information agencies of USIS and OMGUS were primarily concerned with projecting a positive image of the United States and promoting US liberal values in order to curb support for authoritarian ideologies. The CIA's covert propaganda activities were intended to strengthen the anti-communist forces. Meanwhile, the ECA's information campaign, at least ostensibly, sought to win popular support for economic modernization and free trade. So, how does MP propaganda fit into America's efforts to expand its political and cultural influence overseas?

The purpose of MP propaganda and the Marshall Plan

What was the function of MP film propaganda? The MP information campaign was embedded in the MP, and has to be understood in relation to it and its purpose.

For a long time, historians considered the MP as an effort to save post-war European economy from collapse – a narrative that was in line with the official version of the MP. By providing desperately needed economic and technical support, the MP sparked or at least accelerated Europe's economic recovery. According to this view, the ERP was an important factor in powering the economic boom that Europe experienced in the 1950s. The British historian Alan Milward questioned this interpretation, opening a fruitful debate on the purpose and impact of the MP. Milward and his supporters disputed the idea that the West European economy was in such a bad shape that its survival depended on American intervention. He argued that US intervention was politically motivated and designed to secure political influence in Western Europe.[49] Another school of thought, with Michael Hogan as its chief proponent, locates the MP in the ideology of liberalism that understands free trade as promoter of freedom and peace. Hogan argued that the rapidly deteriorating economic situation in Europe prompted the US government to intervene with a rescue programme. The aim of the liberal Marshall Planners was to avert economic collapse and 'to remake Western Europe in the likeness of the United States' in order to produce a new economic order that would result in lasting economic and political stability at home and abroad.[50] Robert Pollard emphasized the aspect of security. He interpreted the MP as an outcome of the early Truman administration's goal to ensure security through economic means. The MP was in his view motivated by the desire to revive international trade in order to foster security (predominantly, but not only, for the United States), rather than strengthen world capitalism or fight communism.[51]

While historians agree that the US government used Marshall Aid as a lever to pressure European governments into enacting fiscal and economic reforms,[52] they strongly disagree over whether the MP was 'necessary' for Western Europe's economic recovery. Milward challenged the received wisdom that the MP played a decisive role in Europe's recovery, pointing to evidence that many West European economies were already growing strongly when the decision to intervene with an economic programme was taken. Milward also disagrees with the interpretation of the economic crisis of 1947, arguing that it was actually caused by the speedy economic recovery of some countries, which resulted in an increase of imports from the United States and a subsequent payment crisis.[53] The German historian Werner Abelshauser, too, insisted that the MP played virtually no role for West Germany's swift economic revival. Instead, Abelshauser argued, it was the modernization, rationalization and expansion of industrial production under Nazi dictatorship, especially in the last war years, which formed the foundation for West Germany's economic boom.[54] Hogan and others rejected these claims, insisting that the MP had been crucial for Europe's successful economic recovery – not so much because of the injection of financial aid, but because it enabled the US government to restructure and modernize the European economy. They also suggested that America's offer to provide long-term assistance provided a much-needed psychological boost to the Europeans who saw little hope for betterment.[55]

To understand the emergence of the ERP, we need to look at the two historical moments that influenced the decision for the MP: the economically and politically turbulent interwar period and the emerging Cold War. The economic depression and the growth of authoritarian regimes in the 1930s led to a breakdown of free trade and gave rise to economic protectionism, which further fuelled international tensions. Already at the time, economic experts and policymakers pondered how such developments could be averted in future. In August 1941, US president Franklin Roosevelt and British prime minister Winston Churchill met to discuss the political situation and a post-war international system. The meeting resulted in the Atlantic Charter, in which the two powers expressed their commitment to ensure safety and peace for all nations, to liberalize international trade, to improve labour and living standards and to work for the abandonment of the use of force. At the height of the Second World War, leading economic experts and government officials from forty-four nations convened at Bretton Woods in summer 1944 to negotiate a new international financial order for the post-war world. The conference reached the conclusion that the key to lasting peace and security lay in the revival of the multilateral trading system. It reflected an idea that was central to liberal ideology, namely that free trade would generate freedom and peace. The conference established the International Monetary Fund (IMF) and the World Bank to facilitate international trade through the convertibility of currencies. The fact that the Soviet Union refused to ratify the final act or join the IMF and World Bank foreshadowed the emerging divide that would be further deepened through the MP.[56]

The other historical moment was the Cold War: as already mentioned, the Truman Doctrine and the MP were born amid growing tensions with the Soviet Union and Western fears of Soviet expansion. The MP built on the premise that a thriving market economy was the best vaccine against totalitarian (communist) ideologies,[57] which threatened security and peace, and, not least, the position of the United States as global power. The belief was that economic growth would translate into higher wages and better living conditions, which would encourage people to embrace democracy and withdraw their support for communist parties. Formulated as an economic aid programme, the ERP was designed to restructure the European political and economic order along liberal principles. The US government used Marshall Aid to strengthen centrist forces and to pressure European governments to undertake reforms. The underlying goal was to create a bloc of allies that were united by similar economic, political and social values.[58]

However, as the Cold War escalated, economic means seemed no longer sufficient to secure US power and security. The Berlin Crisis, the detonation of the first Soviet nuclear bomb in August 1949, the victory of the communists in China in October 1949 and the invasion of communist North Korean forces in South Korea in summer 1950 led the Truman administration to reconsider its approach. The economic approach was eventually replaced with a policy that sought to achieve security through military might. The creation of NATO in April 1949 can be read as an indication that the proponents of a more forceful, military approach began to gain the upper hand. The conclusion of the Mutual Security Act in October 1951 finally prioritized military assistance over economic support.

The context from which the MP emerged illustrates the intertwining of economic and political motives. While the aim was to strengthen the power of the liberal-capitalist states and to weaken support for communism, the latter was not the only adversary. As it turned out, the Europeans' reluctance to modernize represented a far greater obstacle to America's restructuring efforts.

Making a case for liberal capitalism was by no means easy in post-war Europe. Persistent high unemployment, widespread poverty, severe housing shortage, rising prices and low wages, with no signs of improvement in sight, gave strength to the communists' criticism of the liberal-capitalist model. Even though unemployment and destitution were not the only reasons why the communists in Greece, Italy or France had a large following, as many US policymakers believed, the communist promise to end unemployment and material want by abolishing the unfair division of wealth certainly resonated with the frustrated.[59] MP propaganda thus had to convince the European public that the liberal-capitalist model, or rather the regulated, mixed economies many European post-war governments favoured, presented the only viable solution to the existing problems. The films had to demonstrate that the Western welfare state model based on liberal market principles was a superior alternative to the socialist planned economy.

Like the MP, the MP films were ostensibly concerned with promoting economic recovery and modernization. These goals were, of course, imbued with ideological values and tied to the US government's strategic and political goals. By presenting the MP as essential for economic recovery, by claiming that lasting growth and security could be achieved only by implementing the principles of liberal market economy and by subtly pointing to the United States as protector of Europe, the films left no doubt about which path Europe had to take if it did not want to end in another war. While the films skirted the issue of communism in an effort to appear objective, communism was always present through its absence, and by this absence confirmed the liberal West's economic and moral superiority.

The Marshall Planners' aim to align European with US interests and thus create a bloc of shared economic, political and cultural values proved far more complicated to realize than envisaged. The difficulties the propagandists experienced in the course of this effort forced them to continuously re-evaluate their strategies and adapt their messages in order to be heard. However, the American propagandists' complaints about the widespread scepticism towards the MP and American intervention in Europe should not distort our view. It is worth remembering that Marshall's proposal to provide economic assistance was eagerly taken up by the European governments and (at least initially) welcomed by many Europeans. Geir Lundestad coined the term 'empire by invitation' to describe how European governments encouraged the United States to extend its influence in Europe in exchange for economic assistance and security. Reeling under the effects of war, many European governments pressed the United States for assistance to alleviate their enormous economic and social problems. Also the creation of NATO was strongly driven by European governments, who were anxious for US military protection amid growing concerns over the Soviet leadership.[60] The MP was by no means imposed on the Europeans, but rather served the entangled political, economic and strategic interests of both the US and Western European governments. The often contradictory responses of the Europeans to the MP and to MP propaganda, which emerge in the following chapters, have to be evaluated in this context.

The story of the MP film campaign is divided into two parts. The first part of the book is devoted to the films and the organizational, political and cultural contexts in which they were produced. It examines how the US policymakers sought to win acceptance for their goals, and how their policies were translated into imagery. The second part focuses on the actors in the film campaign: the US information officers and European filmmakers who were involved in the formulation and dissemination of the filmic messages, and those at the receiving end – the European audiences. Assuming that most readers have never seen a 'Marshall Plan film', I begin this book by explaining what the audiences actually saw when they watched a MP film. Chapter 1 thus analyses the films' visual and narrative strategies to promote the MP and also discusses how the films were adapted to different national contexts. Chapter 2 examines the ECA's practice of producing films locally, and considers how the sociopolitical conditions and infrastructure in the various countries impacted these 'national' film productions. Chapter 3 situates the MP film campaign in the context of the Cold War, asking how the escalation of the conflict with the outbreak of the Korean War and the subsequent shift of US foreign policy towards rearmament influenced the MP films and the film campaign. Chapters 4 and 5 investigate the visual representation of two key policies of the ERP, namely productivity and European integration. They explore the meaning of these policies, and analyse the discursive and visual strategies employed to promote these subjects. Chapter 6 shifts the focus from the films to the actors – the US information officers and European filmmakers – and explores their role in the policy planning and production process. It explains how their similar backgrounds and cosmopolitan outlook positioned them in between cultures and aligned their interests. Chapter 7 takes up the complex issue of reception, and outlines the varied responses of the European audiences to the MP and MP films, as well as the efforts of the propagandists to gauge the opinions of their viewers. Chapter 8 examines the exhibition and distribution of MP films in different European countries. It illustrates how national and local politics, infrastructure, cultural traditions and relations with other agencies influenced the dissemination of propaganda. The concluding chapter addresses the complex question of impact. It discusses the role of MP films in the wider context of Americanization and the US efforts to project its culture onto Europe, looking specifically at the role of Hollywood.

1

Visualizing the Marshall Plan

Paul Hoffman, the head of the Economic Cooperation Administration (ECA) and a businessman himself, argued that running the ECA without a strong information department would be 'as futile as trying to conduct a major business without sales, advertising, and customer-relations departments'.[1] Hoffman had taken part in the vigorous publicity campaign that had preceded the conclusion of the Economic Cooperation Act of 1948 in an effort to rally American taxpayers' support for the Marshall Plan (MP).[2] The success of this effort convinced US policymakers that the implementation of the European Recovery Programme (ERP) needed a propagandistic underpinning. Hoffman suspected that the MP did not sell itself on its own merits. Europeans needed to be told how the MP would benefit them. There was also the concern that, because America's European allies would have to wait a long time before seeing any visible improvements from the application of Marshall Aid, this could fuel frustration and resentment towards the United States, and thus be grist to the communist mill. A propaganda campaign for the MP should thus convince the sceptics of the honourable intentions of the US government, reassure the doubtful that the reforms were necessary and persuade the impatient that 'the good life' promised was just around the corner.

The question of how the MP films addressed these objectives is the topic of this chapter. It explores the themes and arguments of the films and analyses the visual and narrative forms through which they were expressed with the aim of identifying the MP films' rhetorical and stylistic patterns and their meaning. To provide the necessary context, I begin with a brief overview of the organization and quantitative development of MP film production.

The organization of MP film production

How much importance US policymakers assigned to propaganda is illustrated by the fact that in 1951 almost a third of the US staff at the ECA European headquarters in Paris were working for the Information Division.[3] Established in early summer 1948, the Information Division was in charge of all aspects of MP propaganda in the seventeen European states (plus the Free Territory of Trieste) that participated in the ERP, organizing and overseeing the production of films, radio broadcasts, leaflets, press material, posters and exhibitions. The Information Division was made up of a number of subunits, each of which dealt with a specific medium or aspect of the publicity effort. The largest of these branches was the Special Media Section, which used up most of the Division's budget.[4] It was divided into a Film Unit, on whose role this book focuses, a Visual Information Unit, which dealt with brochures and exhibitions, and a Radio Unit. There was also a News Writing Section, a Photo Section and a Research and Analysis Section. A Field Branch coordinated the information work in the country missions and liaised with the Department of State and the US Army on the use of their facilities.[5]

In each of the participating states, the ECA set up a country mission to oversee the distribution and implementation of Marshall Aid. The structure of the ECA Paris was replicated in the country missions. Therefore, each mission had an information office in charge of producing and distributing information throughout its host country. At its peak in 1951, over 1,000 people – 224 Americans and 782 Europeans – were working for the MP information programme across Europe.[6] The size of each local information office varied. Countries that the US government considered to be of high strategic importance would typically have a large information office that employed several US information officers and a number of local staff. The Italian information office in Rome was the largest, being the only office with a separate film section. Smaller missions would only have one US information officer who, with a couple of local support staff, would be responsible for the whole spectrum of information work, including film, press work, exhibitions and publications. In countries that were either very small or of little strategic importance, such as Luxembourg or Switzerland, the field of information was handled by the US Information Service (USIS) at the US embassies.

From summer 1948, when the Information Division became operational, to the end of 1954, when the last MP film was released, the Information Division produced about 200 MP films. It is difficult to give a more precise number, as film copies and production materials have been lost and films have been wrongly catalogued. Linda Christenson, who meticulously researched distribution catalogues and archive holdings to compile the comprehensive online Marshall Plan Filmography, provides information on 262 separate titles.[7] However, her list also includes some films that were produced by other US governmental agencies. The recently published voluminous study on film propaganda for a united Europe, edited by Gabriele Clemens, estimates the number to be higher, at around 300, but presumably applies a broader definition of 'Marshall plan film'.[8] From my own extensive evaluation of the existing literature, distribution catalogues and archival holdings I came to the same conclusion as Al Hemsing, the last head of the film unit, who estimated that the ECA/MSA Information Division produced about 200 films.[9] I analysed almost 170 separate titles for this book, mostly in the English version. In a number of cases I also accessed versions in a second or even third language for comparative purposes.[10]

When analysing the development of film production, it has to be kept in mind that the stated year of release does not tell us how much time passed from the drafting of the first concept to the approval of the final version. Even though a number of MP films were fairly uncomplicated compilation documentaries that could be completed quickly, others involved lengthy preparations, travel or repeated shootings; also, practical difficulties or political complications could protract production times, as the following chapters illustrate. Neither does the year indicate when the film actually reached audiences; many films were produced in one country and then exported to other European countries, which again was a time-consuming process: commentaries needed to be translated and recorded, rights for distribution had to be cleared and prints made before a film was ready to be shown in another country.[11] It usually took at least one year before a MP film entered distribution outside the country of production, and often more.[12]

The output of MP films in the early phase of the propaganda film campaign was low, as Table 1.1 indicates. It took a long time to set up functional information offices at the country missions. The massive increase in output in 1950 reflects the fact that many of these offices had started producing films in 1949. In

Table 1.1 Chronological development of MP film production, based on a sample of 167 MP films

Year of release	Number of MP films
1948–49	13
1950	74
1951	37
1952	22
1953–54	21
Total	**167**

addition, the Information Division had set up a separate film unit in Paris in summer 1949 to plan, coordinate and oversee the production and distribution of films in the different countries. This boosted the output, also because the film unit started to commission its own film projects. Another reason for the sudden hike in film productions was that the ECA had intensified its propaganda efforts from autumn 1949 after coming under strong domestic pressure to produce visible results.[13]

However, after the exceptionally high output in 1950, the number of MP film releases dropped to 37 in 1951. Figures then steadily declined from 24 in 1952 to 21 films in the last two years of the programme. The decrease can largely be ascribed to the shifts in US foreign policy. With the outbreak of the Korean War, the US government changed the focus of its foreign policy from economic reconstruction to defence. As result, the ERP was replaced with the Mutual Security Programme, through the Mutual Security Act of October 1951. Although the economic assistance programme continued in reduced form under the new Mutual Security Agency (MSA), which replaced the ECA at the end of 1951, the priorities – and with it also the goals – of the MP information programme changed.

Shortly after the switch from the ECA to the MSA, the local information offices at the European country missions underwent another organizational restructuring. From summer 1952 onwards they were gradually merged with USIS, although they still operated under the title of the MSA.[14] The policy shift and two waves of reorganization affected the information work: not just in terms of cuts in budget and information personnel,[15] but also in terms of morale.[16] The MSA and USIS were dissolved on 1 August 1953, and their information programmes were transferred to the newly created US Information Agency (USIA). The closing of the ECA/MSA film unit in October 1955 marked the end of this MP film campaign that had consumed considerable energy and finances.[17]

Development of function, themes and narratives

Not merely the output of MP films, but also their function changed over time as result of policy changes and organizational restructuring. What had been their function in the first place? MP films, as Al Hemsing, the last head of the film section, pointed out, 'had to serve several masters – 18 country missions, our information chieftains at headquarters, and the quite different purposes of ECA and MSA. Officially, the MP film campaign was launched 'to give Europeans the facts and figures on Marshall Aid … to stimulate industrial and agricultural productivity, and to promote the idea of a European community'.[18] Hoffman saw, as mentioned earlier, MP propaganda first and foremost as an advertising tool to instil in Europeans a desire for the US socio-economic model, and thus weaken the appeal of the communist model. To his next in command, the European representative of the ECA Averell Harriman, propaganda's key purpose was to counter what he saw as false communist allegations about the MP, and misrepresentation of American motives. Harriman, former US ambassador to Moscow and self-proclaimed 'premature anti-Communist',[19] explained to his information officers in January 1949 that they were 'engaged in a "battle of ideas" with the Cominform'. He encouraged them to make 'bold and imaginative use' of counterpart money (the funds that financed most MP information work) to combat communist propaganda.[20] The terms of the ERP, however, prohibited the ECA from conducting 'political' propaganda.[21] The officers in charge of film policy preferred a more subtle tone anyway and sought to avoid any statements that might be interpreted as political to strengthen the films' credibility.

So, how did the MP films reconcile these different, though partly overlapping, interests? What form did filmmakers employ to persuade Europeans not only of the benefits of economic modernization, but also of the superiority of the underlying liberal-capitalist ideology? Given that modernization of production, increase of output and free trade were key goals of the ERP, the MP films predominantly engaged with economic issues. Comparing the film programme of the USIA with that of the ECA, Richard Dyer MacCann felt that the latter films dealt with more rewarding subjects: 'Outward change, physical development, mechanical processes – these are natural subjects for the motion picture.'[22] Indeed, the field of economic reconstruction and technical modernization, which was at the core of the MP and MP propaganda, presented excellent opportunities for documentary filmmakers to promote progress through process. Documentary was the preferred form for MP films, as much for the subjects it dealt with – the real, material world and its people – as for its claim to be closer to reality.[23] Moreover, documentary film had since the 1930s been widely used for informational and educational purposes. It was, at least for the proponents of the influential British school of documentary, 'conceived and developed as an instrument of public use'.[24]

The MP documentaries took many different forms: newsreel-type compilation documentaries, so-called expository documentaries with authoritative commentaries, ethnographic-style reportages or travelogues and poetic documentaries that foregrounded the aesthetic rather than the informational. The 'father of documentary' John Grierson might have classified many of these as 'lecture films' and not as 'documentaries proper' in the artistic sense, but for our purposes they can all be assigned to the broad category of 'documentary'.[25]

Only a few MP films were fictional, in that they deployed professional actors to enact a fictional story. The Irish *The Promise of Barty O'Brien* (1952), for example, depicts the struggle of a young Irish man who is locked in a bitter conflict with his stubborn old father, who is opposed to electrification. The father is eventually converted to the new way of thinking while his son is abroad attending an ERP-sponsored training programme in electrical engineering. The ECA also produced nine animation films – a fictional format that was hugely popular with audiences. Animation held a wide appeal, and crossed linguistic and cultural barriers effortlessly. Furthermore, abstract concepts such as productivity, European cooperation or the dollar gap could be conveyed more easily through animated graphs. The great disadvantage of animation was its very labour- and time-intensive production, which explains the relatively small number of MP animation films.

The early phase of MP propaganda

The above quote by Richard Dyer points to the dominant subjects that MP films engaged with. Yet while the films display some strong thematic continuity, new themes emerged over time and were given more emphasis.

The central themes of the first MP films are the rebuilding of infrastructure, the modernization of factories, the creation of jobs and the fertilization of barren land. The only exception is the short animation *Story of a Rescue* (1948), which was the first MP film to be distributed across Western Europe.[26] Combining tableaus with animated figures, the film explains how the recovery programme works and illuminates the role the United States, the European governments and each individual European play in it. *Story of a Rescue* was also unique in that all other films completed in 1948 and 1949 were Italian productions, while *Story* was produced by the French animation studio Les Gémeaux for the Information Division in Paris. Since the bulk of the early MP films was made by Italians for Italians, the narratives and visuals emphasize national contribution to the recovery effort. The films foreground Italian initiative and self-help – not solely to fuel national pride or to promote the American value of entrepreneurism, but also to foster a sense of ownership among viewers. From its inception, the ERP was designed as a joint American-European effort that demanded the active contribution of the European countries; it rested on the ideal of self-help, expressed through the slogan 'help the people help themselves'.[27]

The early MP films illustrate the process of recovery and highlight the achievements made through the application of Marshall Aid and the Italians' own efforts. European integration and free trade, although key policy goals, are only addressed in passing. The importance of cooperation and exchange is, for example, expressed in the image of the crates of oranges being shipped to Northern Europe and Canada in *Liquid Sunshine* (1949), or through the narrator in *Men at Work* (1948/49), who explains that the graduates of a training school for waiters in Como will soon work in Paris, London or New York. The dominant theme of the films, however, is economic recovery. In every corner of the land, it seems, there are men busy digging, building, producing. Roads and aqueducts are being built, buildings erected, land ploughed and fertilized, stones hewn in quarries, ships unloaded, produce packed, machines operated, ships constructed. The high level of activity is almost contagious. The documentary *Railroads* (1948/49) depicts the reconstruction projects along the damaged rail line between Civitavecchia and La Spezia; the speed of the train that reconnects the two cities symbolizes the speed of economic reconstruction in Italy. The vast scope of the rebuilding effort is illustrated by the choice of locations. They range from the revival of salt production and the building of water supplies in Sicily (*Trip to Sicily*, 1948/49) and in the south-eastern region of Puglia (*Village without Water*, 1949), to northern Italy and its zinc mining industry in the Bergamo region (*Zinc Valley*, 1948/49) and to Maniago, the town famed for its handcrafted knives (*Handicraft Town*). The message the films convey is that the ERP fuels growth and modernization everywhere. The coverage of different regions is also meant to reassure audiences that Marshall Aid is divided fairly. The films thus promise a solution to post-war Italy's two most pressing problems, the economic North–South divide and the high rate of unemployment, especially in the South. Yet while they seek to spark a spirit of solidarity and unity, they also, as Paloa Bonifazio argues, reinscribe the division into a wealthier, industrialized North and a poor, rural South. The northern Italians are presented as entrepreneurial and productive, whereas the southerners are depicted as impotent subjects, helplessly locked in poverty until Marshall Aid-funded programmes come to their rescue.[28]

The MP narratives present the ERP as the spark that revives the Italian nation. Infrastructure, factories and shipyards are rebuilt, and with them the strength and self-confidence of the Italian men who return to work. The focus on manual labour and traditionally male jobs draws a direct connection between work and

Figure 1.1 *Men at Work*: The Marshall Plan sends men back to work.

masculinity: positioned amid welding sparks and pounding machines, the men are reinstated to their positions as producers and providers (see figure 1.1). Unemployment, only alluded to in *Men and Work* but central to *Aquila* (1949), undermines a man's masculine identity and makes him receptive to totalitarian ideology and other vices. By sending men back to work, the ERP and the Italian government fulfil a moral obligation that restores their dignity as head of the household. At the same time, this ensures the country's prosperity and security, as men with secure jobs are less susceptible to the promises of communism, as, for example, *Handicraft Town* illustrates.

The visual representations of gender remain fairly stable; also later MP films depict male protagonists predominantly in action, customarily engaged in physical labour. Men and work are presented as inextricably linked (see figure 1.2). Male employment is assigned a symbolic function, and indicates the good health of a society and a nation. Male industry signifies stability and prosperity, whereas male idleness – which MP films ascribe to external circumstances – spells

Figure 1.2 *A Ship Is Born*: Masculinity and manual labour are inextricably linked.

danger for the nation's future. The MP's promise to improve the lot of the 'little man' by creating jobs through economic reconstruction and modernization was also a promise to reinstate the man and the nation to their 'rightful place' – in the family and in the international community.

Working women, though not completely absent from the MP films, are situated at the margins. It is truly a man's world in the MP films.[29] A few films, such as the Greek *Return from the Valley* (1950) or the Italian *The Miracle of Montecassino* (1950), show women working in the rubble, rebuilding the country. But these films depict instances of post-war crisis, and present women's hard labour as a temporary measure. Others allow a brief glimpse of women tending the vegetable garden or repairing fishing nets. When with the outbreak of the Korean War the ECA intensified its efforts to boost industrial productivity, more women begin to enter the films. The British documentary *Over to You* (1951) and the MP film *Men and Machines* (1951) – the latter being the only MP film directed by a woman, the British director Diana Pine – show female workers at conveyor belts or machines.[30] In general, however, the later MP films, if they represent women at all, depict them as housewives and consumers who reap the fruits of male labour. Because the films grant much less space and screen time to women than to men, they suggest that the rebuilding of Europe and the production of economic growth has been, and will be, an entirely male affair. The MP narratives thus reinforce two dominant views of women and men: first, that women's work is primarily devoted to the basic sustenance for their families, and is thus not gainful, and second, that the important, productive work is done by men. This consequently justifies the attention and power given to men. Two value systems, slightly at odds with each other, are promoted in the films: liberal economic ideas contrast with the essentially conservative concepts that affirm the traditional division of gender roles into male breadwinner and female caregiver.

The later phase of MP film propaganda

Recovery and rebuilding remain staple themes in MP films, although they gradually move to the background. In later productions, images of ruins juxtaposed with newly constructed buildings often serve as reminders of the successes achieved through the application of Marshall Aid. The documentary *The Village that Wouldn't Die* (ECA France 1950) tells, through the eyes of a French housewife, the story of the rebuilding of a Normandy town that was completely shattered by Allied bombing. *Island of Faith* (ECA Netherlands

1950) describes how Marshall Aid helped the people in the Dutch province of Walcheren to rebuild the dykes that were destroyed during the war. *Somewhere to Live* (ECA 1950), the third episode of the *Changing Face of Europe* series, addresses the acute housing shortage in Europe as a result of widespread war destruction (see Chapter 5).

Also new themes emerged as the ERP entered its third year and film production expanded. In autumn 1949 the ECA decided, under pressure from US Congress, to intensify its efforts to increase Europe's productivity. Agricultural modernization thus became a key theme in MP films. *Victory at Thermopylae* (ECA Greece 1950), *Land Redeemed* (ECA Italy 1950), *Rice and Bulls* and *Renaissance Agricole* (both ECA France 1950) all report on successful soil reclamation projects in Greece, Italy and France, respectively. *Bull's Eye for Farmer Pietersen* (ECA Netherlands 1950), *Story of Koula* (ECA Greece 1951) and *Yusef and His Plough* (ECA Turkey) promise an increase in crops through the mechanization of farming, whereas *The Streamlined Pig* (ECA Denmark 1951) and *Bigger Potato Crops* (ECA Austria 1950) promote new scientific breeding and farming techniques. Another theme introduced into MP films around 1950 was the production of (hydroelectric) power and its role in fuelling industrial and agricultural production. Since electricity crosses borders easily, the subject also helped to make a case for European integration (see Chapter 5).

Even as US foreign policy underwent a radical shift from economic reconstruction to defence following the outbreak of the Korean War in summer 1950, economic modernization and productivity remained key themes. In fact, the film unit intensified its efforts to promote productivity, but moved into the industrial realm. To allow the European governments to finance the military build-up, they needed to drastically increase their exports and therefore had to produce more, and more efficiently. The productivity films encouraged standardized mass production and economic modernization (see Chapter 4).

Perhaps the most notable change resulting from the escalation of the Cold War was the significant increase in narrative references to security, expressed by frequent calls to 'strengthen the free world'. But these slogans often appear rather formulaic, because there is an imbalance between the medium and the message: the Cold War rhetoric is only aurally, not visually expressed. Surprisingly few MP films directly engage with the issue of defence, or denounce the communist enemy. One of them is the British documentary *The Smiths and the Robinsons* (ECA UK 1952). It rallies support for the re-established British Home Guard and seeks the consensus of the British public to continue the government's austerity programme in order to cover the increase in defence spending. The films

European Labor Day and *Without Fear*, both produced in 1951, are singular in that they openly condemn communism, a strategy the MP films otherwise avoid. The film unit also produced a series of 24 half-hour episodes with a clear anti-communist slant under the title *Strength for the Free World*.[31] Yet the series, mostly composed of footage from existing MP films and presenting the MP as a successful weapon against communism, was only screened on US television from 1952 to 1953, and never entered distribution in Europe.[32]

Narration and visual style

The films, as we have seen, showcased Europe's economic rebuilding and recovery, highlighted the successes achieved through Marshall Aid and promoted agricultural and industrial modernization in order to increase productivity; they eulogized hard-working men and praised the European efforts to further the process of recovery. How did the films visualize and frame these themes?

Narration

Many MP films have a classical three-act structure of problem description, application of remedy and demonstration of success. Some films outline the problem through a few establishing shots overlaid by a narrator's explanatory description, whereas others devote up to a third or even half of screen time to illustrating the problem. The before/after structure is reversed in films such as Ferno's *Island of Faith*, which begins with an illustration of successful recovery, then jumps back in time to remind the audience of the bleak situation that existed before the MP and finally returns to the reassuring present. This classic cause-and-effect narrative made a convincing case for the need for Marshall Aid and the benefits of its application.

A second group of documentaries takes a more observational form. These films do not show a development from problem to solution, but instead focus on an ongoing process of building or production. Since these films often assemble very similar scenes, and thus lack innate drama, they rely on commentary, soundtrack or visual aesthetics to engage the audience and give meaning to the images. In the Italian documentary *A Ship Is Born* (1951), the solemn commentary spoken in the rich baritone voice of Frank Gervasi, the head of the Italian information office, lends measured pathos to the scenes depicting the immense efforts of men constructing a ship. The film also uses colour to great effect. Since colour films were still a rarity in Italy, the Italian country mission hoped to trigger greater interest by its use in this film.[33]

The witty voice-over and sound effects in the French *The Extraordinary Adventures of a Quart Milk* (ECA France 1951) gives the factual account of milk powder production the necessary zing to keep the audience interested, and deflects from the film's propagandistic purpose. Poetic documentaries such as Herman van der Horst's city symphony *Houen Zo!* (ECA Netherlands 1951) or Arne Sucksdorff's *The Living Stream* (ECA Scandinavia 1950) chiefly convey meaning through skilful montages of visually impressive scenes and sounds that convey a mood rather than an explicit message.

The aim of propaganda film is to persuade the audience to accept a specific point of view. The MP films pursued many agendas, both economic and ideological. Yet at their most basic level, they sought to convince Europeans that the ERP had saved Europe from collapse, and that it was accomplishing what it promised to do. Most MP narratives present the MP as a timely rescue from deep economic turmoil. If the Americans had not offered help to the Europeans, then the situation in Europe would have deteriorated further, possibly – the implication was – resulting in famines, social upheavals and war. The MP, the argument went, represented the only solution to the European crisis. It built the foundation for economic growth and future prosperity, and thus guaranteed stability, peace and freedom. In order to give substance to this promise, the films often illustrate the necessary steps that need to be taken towards lasting recovery: modernization and rationalization of production, closer European cooperation through liberalization of trade and free movement, and improved industrial relations – the latter by including 'free', that is, non-communist, trade unions in the industrial decision-making process. The MP films were thus not merely promotional, they were also educational, in that they explained how change is produced.

Since the propagandists claimed to present objective and factual information, the MP films sought to appeal to the spectator primarily on the basis of rational argument. Animated or coloured maps of Europe were used to visualize the political and cultural unity of Europe – and to demarcate it from communist Eastern Europe. Graphs and maps were a popular device to suggest factuality, visual evidence of scientific 'truth'.[34] Scenes showing scientists, engineers or medical doctors attested to the validity of the film's argument simply by their presence as corroborative experts. A variation of the use of 'expert testimony' was to tell the story through eyewitnesses: commentaries spoken in the first person accompany the MP documentaries *Breakthrough* (ECA Norway 1950),

I Went Back (ECA UK 1950) and *Return from the Valley* (ECA Greece 1950). The virtual (or, in the case of *I Went Back*, actual) presence of a witness added authenticity and a human dimension.

However, the interest of audiences gradually waned as an increasing number of films illustrating details of economic reconstruction, production processes and agricultural modernization entered circulation. Audiences and country missions began to demand more entertaining information films. Particularly popular with the audiences were so-called human interest stories: these documentaries resemble fictional films in that they follow a – usually young and male – protagonist through his struggles and success. *Hansl and His 200,000 Chicks* (ECA Austria 1952), *The Story of Koula* (ECA Greece 1951), *The Story of Mahmoud* (ECA France 1952) and *Yusef and His Plough* (ECA Turkey 1951) all feature an entrepreneurial boy who eagerly embraces the opportunities the MP offers while the elderly observe him with scepticism. The boy's idealism and entrepreneurship are rewarded, to the benefit of the whole family or local community (see figure 1.3). Hansl becomes a veritable mass producer of chickens, Koula and Yusef increase the crops of their respective fathers' fields and Mahmoud returns to his Moroccan village as a skilled tractor mechanic.[35] Their stories are largely told on the visual level, which makes them easy to understand; it also strengthens the argument, as the 'visual evidence' seemingly speaks for itself. What is more, this form of narration invites the spectator to identify with the main protagonist, and thus triggers and retains the spectator's interest.

A documentary that effectively combined all these strategies to make a convincing and interesting story was an Austrian film carrying the rather prosaic title *Concerning Dairy Production* (ECA Austria 1954). The documentary features an old-fashioned Austrian dairy farmer as its main protagonist, who rejects as modern nonsense the advice of a visiting expert to modernize his cowshed according to the newest scientific research. Promptly, his grandchild

Figure 1.3 Boys as instigators of change in *Project for Tomorrow, Story of Kaula* and *Hansl and the 200,000 Chicks*.

falls ill of tuberculosis, the result of the contaminated milk from his cows. The farmer ruefully visits the expert's office in town to ask for his help. The expert pushes him into a film screening room next door, where a number of men watch an animation film, presumably the US short *Barn Ventilation and Clean Milk*.[36] Initially reluctant, the farmer is soon absorbed by the film, which explains, through animated graphics and an educational voice-over, how unclean stable conditions breed harmful bacteria and thus contaminate the cows' milk (see figure 1.4). By using the film-in-film device, the documentary underlines its impartiality and leaves it to the animation to convey the main argument. Immediately converted by the power of the visual demonstration, the farmer rushes home to start renovating his cowshed. When the agricultural expert visits the farmer at the end of the film, he finds a healthy grandchild and a content grandfather; but, most importantly, he sees a cowshed modernized according to the newest scientific guidelines.

One of the strengths of the documentary is its presumed authenticity: the protagonists speak the local dialect, and the farmer displays the manners and attitudes typical of a member of his group. The camera pretends to be complicit with the audience, who witnesses the stubborn farmer being converted. Yet it

Figure 1.4 The power of film in *Concerning Dairy Production*.

forces their attention, just like the farmer's, onto the film that is being screened, and persuades them to accept the 'scientific truth' by illustrating the immediate effect of the implementation of changes.

Titles and credits

A film, however, does not start with the first establishing shot: it begins already with the opening titles. The film titles and opening credits are an important part of the narration, as they manage audience expectations. The titles of the MP films are either descriptive and fairly prosaic (*Bigger Potato Crops!* or *Village without Water*) or poetic, such as *City out of Darkness* (Es wurde Licht), *Treasure of the Rhone* (L'Or du Rhône) or *Victory at Thermopylae* (Vittoria alle Termopili). Often, the titles suggest educational content, or promise an interesting reportage about a foreign country. Significantly, the opening credits usually make no reference to the MP or give an indication of the film's actual propagandistic purpose. Exceptions to the rule were the centrally produced MP film series *The Marshall Plan at Work* (ECA 1950) and the ECA newsreel series *ERP in Action* (ECA 1950). Moreover, most MP films – or at least the archived versions – do not name the sponsor, the ECA/MSA, again with the exception of the above-named film series. Instead, they customarily open either with the name and symbol of the distributor or the production company, or directly with the title of the film, followed by the names of the cinematographer, composer, editor and, finally, the director.

It is, of course, possible that references to the ECA/MSA were inserted into the opening titles at a later stage, when the copies for distribution were produced. Yet, considering that the film officers favoured a subtle approach to propaganda, as the following chapters illustrate, this is unlikely. A report by the Italian information unit confirms this assumption. Discussing the distribution of MP films, the report explains that the Italian audiences were presented with films that 'appear to them as a normal production telling an ECA story but not identifiable as overt ECA propaganda'.[37] The audiences were often unaware that what they were seeing was a 'Marshall plan film'. In many cases, the spectators might have grasped the film's agenda in the course of watching the film. However, they would not necessarily make the connection to the United States (or to the ECA/MSA as film producer), since other national or international agencies also produced films on the MP, or on economic modernization more widely.

Omitting the sponsor from the opening credits was just one of the MP film unit's tactics to heighten the film's credibility and make the audience more receptive to its message. Because the propagandists feared that highlighting US generosity might arouse anti-American sentiments, rather than gratitude, they sought to downplay American involvement. The film unit had to strike a fine balance between fulfilling its objectives of convincing the Europeans of the benefits of the MP and promoting the honourable motives of the United States, and the need to downplay the extent of America's role, which could alienate audiences if it seemed excessive. For this reason, the film unit claimed to 'tolerate no more than one reference to ERP, American aid, or the Marshall Plan in a one-reeler, nor more than three references in a two-reeler'.[38]

Again, there were exceptions: many early Italian MP films praise America's generosity and make ample use of the ERP logo to indicate that it was Marshall Aid that sparked economic growth and created jobs and house-building all over Italy. The Italian information office was obviously keen to counter communist promises of a better society and thus drew attention to the United States as the instigator of real change. British MP films did not shy away from mentioning the United States either; however, they tended to emphasize the reciprocal relationship between the United States and Britain and present the two countries as equal partners. In the majority of MP films, however, the presence and role of the United States can be inferred only from the strategically placed ERP logos, or from the use of terms such as modernization or productivity, which are imbued with the meaning of 'America'.

The need for restraint also explains another characteristic of MP films, namely the almost complete absence of visual or verbal references to communism or the Soviet Union. This absence is all the more conspicuous given that the information films produced by USIS or by the US military government in West Germany display less restraint in this matter.[39] The avoidance of such 'political' references in MP films was strategic: to fulfil the claim of being objective, the MP films had to appear apolitical in form and content. The propagandists at the Information Division also feared that an open engagement with communist arguments would give publicity to the communists, and thus put the Americans on the defensive. The MP films' focus on economic themes can also be considered as a strategy to deflect from America's geostrategic and political aims, as economic reform and modernization were widely perceived as apolitical instruments.[40] Films demonstrating an increase in output through mechanization or rationalization gave the viewer little cause to suspect political motives.

The escalation of the conflict with the communist powers following the outbreak of the Korean War gradually undermined the film unit's strategy of avoidance. Still, the communist enemy remains elusive in the MP films. The audiences of course knew – and were expected to know – what this 'speaking silence' addressed: the communist 'other', which, even if not named, mentioned or represented in any form, was present through its absence. It served as an invisible point of reference against which the American ideal of liberal capitalism, symbolically present through Marshall Aid and ERP reforms, was measured – and extolled.

Visual style

The films' main subjects are the material world, which is associated with transport and the production of power, goods and crops. Open natural and urban landscapes, as well as industrial settings, feature prominently in MP documentaries. The world that the MP films present is made up of harbours, roads, railways, dams and building sites, of power stations, factories and furnaces, of machinery and conveyor belts, and of excavators, bulldozers, tower cranes, tractors and mechanized ploughs. The myriad of shipyards, industrial plants and building sites – all populated with industrious workmen – set the scene for action. More importantly, they are themselves visible proof and agents of change: constantly expanding, growing or producing. And where the industrial settings provide the background for almost feverish activity, the vast natural landscapes, another staple element of the MP film, are emblems of continuity. The wide shots of long stretches of land reassure the spectator that the old continues to exist; at the same time, the images hold the promise of a better future without hunger or poverty, as the barren landscapes and swamps are turned into fertile fields.

The filmmakers' love of open landscape settings determined the framing and composition of shots. Therefore, the most frequent shots in the MP films are extreme long and very long shots combined with medium shots and close-ups, designed to concentrate the spectator's attention onto human action. The long-distance shots accentuate the expanse of the natural or industrial vistas, and thus underline the scale of the ERP operation. In order to concentrate the spectator's attention onto human action, the filmmakers combined these very long shot sizes with medium shots and close-ups. The medium shots, which capture large parts of the human body, usually from the knee or hip upwards, are close enough to identify a person, yet far enough away to show his or her immediate surroundings and movements. This shot size enables the cinematographer to illustrate human interaction with the environment: a worker operating a machine, a farmer cutting the wheat, an educator standing in front of his pupils.

Often, medium shots are used to demonstrate the workings of machines and the process of production, bringing the viewer close enough to the object to understand its function. Close-ups finally help to draw the viewer's attention to a technological detail, or to an object with symbolic meaning, such as a handful of grain signifying the success of agricultural modernization. Close-ups of (usually male) faces are also used to elicit an emotional response from the audience. Through close-ups, the spectator is able to witness the sorrow and worries of people suffering from the economic crisis and then their joy over the reopening of a factory or the provision of clean water. This virtual proximity fosters identification with the figures on screen, making the audience more willing to accept the underlying argument of the film.

The cinematographers reached for the tool box of documentary iconography to create dramatic effect: low-angle shots of enormous steel frames reaching into the sky, or shots of glowing furnaces spilling streams of gleaming white, molten metal, signify industry, economic recovery and growth. While the sponsors and filmmakers purported to persuade the audience on the strength of objective argument, they had to appeal to emotion to achieve maximum effect. Iconic images were employed to evoke feelings and thus make the audience more receptive to the message. Visual symbols allowed the filmmakers to convey a message without spelling it out: the symbolic image of the unloading of Marshall Aid goods from a steamer was so often used that it became an icon of the MP. Stop signs or closing boom gates as metaphors for the separation of Europe feature frequently. Motifs, such as the ship or the river, helped to create a sense of communality and connection, and thus bolstered the argument for European integration (see Chapter 5).

Sound and music

In the films, visual appeals to emotion achieve their full effect only in combination with audio. Sound – as sound effects, musical score or the modulation of a narrator's voice – is a key element for producing atmosphere and triggering an emotional response. Diegetic sound effects, such as the driving rhythm of a machine, the hammering of tools or the whistle of a factory horn, create a sense of realism. Of crucial importance is also the music that accompanies most documentaries, usually in the form of an orchestral score. A few films, such as *Village without Words* or *Aquila* (both ECA Italy 1950), rely entirely on the interplay between music and imagery to illustrate the despair of the poor and unemployed, as well as the upswing set in motion by the arrival of Marshall Aid. The musical score structures the narrative: it gives rhythm to the narration and adds drama by accelerating or slowing the pace of the film, or by accentuating certain scenes. Music can echo or underscore the movement of the film, from problem description to solution, by ascending from darker minor to lighter major scale, inevitably punctuating the arrival of ERP goods with crescendos.

Perhaps the most dominant sound in the MP films is the voice of the narrator. Off-screen narration was the accepted standard for documentaries at the time, and widely used. The off-screen commentary or voice-over substantiates the visual argument, or, in the case of those quickly produced compilation films that assembled different stock footage, gives coherence and meaning to the visuals. This non-diegetic commentary fulfils three important functions: first, it delimits the many potential meanings of the images; second, it adds weight to the film's argument, as the narrator often performs the role of an all-knowing yet invisible authority; third, the narrator's mode of speaking structures the narrative, injects rhythm, modulates the pace and appeals to the emotions.

The practice of adding a voice-over was informed by the conviction that the images, which potentially carry many meanings, needed to be 'explained' so that the viewer would understand the intended message. Off-screen narration was also used to underline the film's credibility, since the commentator typically takes the position of a seemingly impartial observer. Later, the use of the voice-over came under attack, not least because the narrator often adopts an authoritative or pedagogical tone. Critics likened the (usually male) off-screen narrator to a seemingly all-knowing voice-of-God, which dominates the visuals and guides the spectators' interpretations of the images.[41] More recently, film scholars such as Stella Bruzzi have come to the rescue of the off-screen narration. Bruzzi argues that a voice-over only draws attention to the fact that all documentaries represent an interpretation of facts, with the voice-over being only 'the most overt and blatant kind' of interpretation. Her argument that 'a strong voice-over rarely renders the truth contained within the image invisible'[42] was also forwarded by earlier media consumption studies which sociologist and film theorist Sigfried Kracauer conducted on behalf of the US State Department in Southeastern Europe and the Middle East in 1952. Kracauer reported that the film audiences there were so captivated by the imagery that they would pay little attention to the commentary.[43]

While the influence of the off-screen narrator was perhaps not as strong as the film producers expected, it certainly could add to (or sometimes reduce) the enjoyment of the spectator. The Norwegian information officer returned the

French MP documentary *The Jungle that Was* (1950) to the film unit, citing the reason that he was unhappy with the 'most unsatisfactory' commentary spoken by a narrator who 'raises his voice at the most awkward places, and makes sad incidents sound funny'.[44] The Danish information office was equally dissatisfied with the Danish synchronization of the same film, and criticized the lacklustre reading style and heavy accent of the narrator.[45] The narrator needed to have the right accent. If not, the audience might reject the whole film: the Dutch information officer refused to distribute *Story of a Rescue* in the Netherlands on the grounds that the narrator had a strong Flemish accent 'much resented by the Dutch' (the Dutch synchronization was made in Belgium).[46]

There existed many practical reasons for the use of a voice-over. For one thing, whereas a film without a commentary had to be composed carefully in order to tell a coherent story, a film producer could assemble disparate shots and tie them together by using a voice-over, which greatly reduced the time needed for filming and editing. Moreover, the film officers, who often wrote the commentaries themselves, were able to exercise a considerable degree of control over the picture this way, without interfering in the filmmaking. Last but not least, it enabled the ECA to tailor the film to the preferences of different national audiences, since a commentary could be easily and inexpensively changed, as the following case study illustrates.

Film translation – the role of the commentary

In general, the translations of the commentary were true to the original, except for minor adaptations. In some cases, however, commentaries differed considerably, as a comparison of the English and French version of *Village without Water* (1949) demonstrates.[47] The documentary, with the original title *Paese senz' aqua*, directed by the Italian Giuliano Tomei, was produced for the Italian country mission in 1949. Shot in black and white, it tells the story of a poor town in an arid part of southern Italy. For decades its inhabitants have suffered acute water shortage, and, as a consequence, poverty and deadly diseases. After numerous failed attempts to alleviate the situation, technical assistance provided through the ERP finally brings relief and connects the town to a clean water supply.

The film (see figure 1.5) opens with a slow pan over a barren, hilly landscape, accompanied by a slow piano tune in a minor key, which sets the mood for the film and illustrates the sense of despair that has settled upon the people. The land, scattered with a few skeletal trees, lies deserted in the sun, except for two sheep grazing on the few tufts of dry grass. Some empty straw huts and abandoned farming tools suggest

Figure 1.5 *Village without Water*: The lack of water has locked the Italian village into poverty.

a human presence. A cutaway shot brings into view rows of simple, whitewashed stone houses that cling onto a steep, rocky hill. The narrator sets the scene in southern Italy and explains that the situation in this town is representative of thousands of other Italian towns suffering from severe drought. A cut to a lone mule-cart trekking up a steep slope illustrates how the town's inhabitants are trying to cope. The cart carries a barrel with drinking water to the town, but 'not much, not enough to slate the thirst of 3000 people'. The commentator's mention of thirst is corroborated by a cut to a drinking glass into which wine is poured. The camera has now moved into the town; zooming out from the wine glass it brings into view two middle-aged men sitting in front of a tavern.

It is at this moment that the English and the French version, until now more or less identical, diverge. While the narrator remains silent in the English version, the French commentator talks throughout the next sequences.[48] He poses questions, interprets the images and then provides explanations. As the camera shows a boy entering the scene, the narrator asks why he disturbs the two men, who indulge quietly in the delectable wine. He suggests that it must be urgent business. As the camera follows the group of three, who walk to a town square where groups of dark-clad villagers stand waiting, the narrator explains that the men are pallbearers, and have been fetched because typhoid has claimed another victim and the corpse has to be taken to the funeral. As the procession of mourners moves on, the camera cuts to another square, where a woman hauls a bucket from a well. Zooming into the inside of the bucket, the camera reveals murky water with specks of dirt on the surface – the cause of the typhoid. The filmic problem description is concluded by a quick succession of short scenes that illustrate how the lack of water has locked the locals into poverty and despair.

Unlike the French narrator, who describes the scenes and the hopes and despair of the people in detail, the English commentary is much sparser. It leaves the audience to draw its own conclusions from the imagery. Here, the viewer learns of the typhoid deaths only as the two pallbearers enter the house and the narrator mentions the frequent typhoid outbreaks. Because the commentator remains largely silent, the musical score is given more prominence, and adds a tone of sobriety to the moving images. Both scenes build up suspense; but while the English version leaves the viewers in the dark as to what might happen, the French commentary takes the audience by the hand, asking directing questions, which it answers immediately. The English version requires a greater familiarity with visual language, whereas the French version leaves little room for individual interpretation. The insistent commentary makes the French version more diverting. The English version's long silences and solemn tone of voice, on the other hand, heighten the depressing mood conveyed by the imagery. In both films, the key message is the same; yet the different voice-overs alter the emotional colouring of the films. The information officers seemingly felt that the audiences in France (and, quite possibly, other Mediterranean countries) needed more guidance – and perhaps a more uplifting tone. The English (and perhaps other Northern European) viewers, on the other hand, might have found such a directive style too intrusive.

A distinct MP film style?

When analysing visual form, the question arises whether the MP films display a specific or unique film style. Are the MP films different from other sponsored information films produced at the time? And if so, in what way? The European filmmakers brought with them their individual approach and aesthetic style, and the films consequently carry their signature. At the same time, however, they had to meet the sponsors' formal requirements regarding the subject, message or length of film, which limited the possibilities of artistic expression.[49] Any attempt to identify a 'typical' MP film style is bound to lead to overgeneralization. The MP films certainly display similarities in themes, settings, narratives and mode of narration. However, this visual style is not specific to MP films, but refers back to other cinematic traditions brought in by the filmmakers who made them.

One of the most interesting features of the MP film programme is that the ECA/MSA commissioned European filmmakers for the film projects.[50] The decision to hire Europeans was based on the assumption that they were more familiar with European audiences, and would thus make more effective films. This view was echoed by European directors, such as the young Austrian filmmaker Georg Tressler, who made at least eight films for the ECA/MSA. Tressler was initially hired as an operator of a mobile film unit to bring US information films to rural Austria. His job brought him into close contact with the farming population and convinced him that, in order to have an impact, information films had to be tailored to the specific interests and horizon of the audience.[51] However, there were other reasons why the ECA preferred European filmmakers for the job: first, it helped to downplay US involvement, thus heightening the films' credibility,[52] and second, it was meant as a symbolic gesture to demonstrate that the Americans put their trust in the Europeans. The first head of the film section, Lothar Wolff, believed that the ECA's hiring policy attested to America's liberalism, for 'European producers ... were allowed by their American supervisors in ECA's motion picture section to tell the Marshall Plan story in the style most appreciated by their fellow Europeans'.[53]

The directors were not, however, 'European', but national filmmakers from different European countries. The country missions that produced MP films usually hired nationals of the country they operated in, with some notable exceptions. The question is, then, whether these locally produced MP films display elements of a unique 'national' style. Can we perhaps even consider them as products of a national cinema?[54] The case of Italy is perhaps the most useful to discuss this issue, since the Italian information office produced the highest number of MP films of all country missions, and commissioned only Italian filmmakers. Although some Italian MP films show an engagement with the Italian cinematic Neorealism style, their visual and narrative form are not distinct from other, non-Italian productions. The film *Aquila* (1950), for instance, is a documentary in the Italian Neorealist tradition. It depicts the plight of an unemployed Italian worker who is unable to provide for his family, and who, frustrated by his hopeless situation, steals a box of chocolates for his son. The camera in *Aquila* follows the desperate protagonist on his job search through the city of Trieste, which still carries the scars of the past war. Like similar Neorealist dramas, it exposes the hopeless situation of many poor Italians. However, it does not leave it there, but adds a happy ending: the protagonist, captured by the police for his theft, is pardoned, and finds a job in the refinery that is being reconstructed with Marshall Aid. He escapes poverty not by his own efforts, but by the helping hand of the Americans. Paola Bonifazio has convincingly argued that *Aquila* merely borrowed the Neorealist form and used it for a different ideological end.[55] The film's aim is not to shine a spotlight on the social problems that beset post-war Italy, but to convey an unequivocal political message. By contrasting marching workers with red flags and a communist agitator speaking on a town square with the practical help provided by the Americans, the film implies that the communists only talk and fuel social unrest, while the Americans act to actually improve the lives of the poor.

Even though some Italian MP documentaries show an engagement with national cinematic style, such as Neorealism, others do not. In fact, if we compare the MP films made by different European filmmakers, it is impossible to identify a specific 'national' style. The national element in MP film lies not in the form, but mostly in the content: the choice of subject, settings and protagonists, as well as in the occasional references to national culture and traditions. One reason why the MP films lack a distinct national style was the sponsor's aim and the film unit's editorial oversight: even though the ECA allowed for great diversity of form, the terms of their commission resulted in a certain standardization of argument. Another reason was that the documentary filmmakers who made the MP films were much less rooted in national cinematic cultures than producers of commercial fiction film. The documentarists, as Chapter 6 illustrates, were part of the same cinematic tradition: the Soviet montage cinema of the 1920s and, in particular, the British documentary movement of the 1930s, whose films and writings exerted considerable influence on the work of documentary filmmakers.[56] In fact, European documentary filmmakers emerged from much the same documentary traditions as their American and Soviet counterparts, and therefore their films display visual codes that are similar to American and Soviet productions.[57] Moreover, the documentarists were often cosmopolitan. Relying on public or private sponsorship for their films, documentary filmmakers had to be mobile to acquire a job, and this again fostered exchange between filmmakers.

The shared cinematic traditions of documentary filmmakers and their mobility explain why the MP films can also not be classified as typical 'European' films. Al Friendly, who headed the Information Division in Paris in 1949, was, however, convinced that the approach of European filmmakers was different. In a congratulatory note to the head of the information unit in Rome, Friendly singled out the MP documentaries *Handicraft Town* and *Village without Water* for special praise, and admitted to have learnt a great deal from these films: 'I guess it's I that have changed from a year ago. Now I like, and realize the necessity for, a much slower pace in movies for European audiences. I also like the very subtle and gentle references to ERP, where once I was urging the blatant, blunt approach. Now I can't stand it.'[58] Yet, while Friendly was certainly right that European movies were generally slower than Hollywood films,[59] the pace of American and European documentaries was similar. Friendly, himself a journalist and not a film expert, might have used as a point of comparison the hard-hitting, fast-paced American wartime propaganda documentaries. Compared with these, the MP films had indeed a more measured tone, and were not so overtly propagandistic. This, however, was a result of the ECA's film policy and of editorial oversight rather than an expression of a unique European style.

The MP films are not a monolithic bloc, but a diverse cluster of films. At the same time, they show thematic, narrative and visual similarities, which were a result of the films' assigned functions as well as editorial direction. The MP films were products of a collaborative process that involved a number of contributors from both sides of the Atlantic: first, the policy makers at ECA/MSA and State Department level, who set the targets and thus formulated the frame of the film campaign; second, the European directors, cinematographers, writers, editors and composers who played their part in the production of the film; third, the film officers at the Information Division in Paris who commissioned the film, sometimes wrote or revised the commentary script, supervised the production and gave the final approval; and finally, the US information officers working on the ground in the different countries. The latter often instigated film projects and were, to varying degrees, involved in selecting the filmmakers, drafting the scripts and giving the films their final form. The next chapter will take a closer look at these country missions and the practice of local MP film production in order to establish how local sociopolitical conditions, as well as the US government's strategic interests, shaped the output of films.

By Europeans – for Europeans:
Local Film Production

The ECA pursued a policy of European-centred film production, which took a two-pronged approach: contracting European filmmakers and producing films locally. The role of the information offices at the country missions was to initiate and oversee the production of MP films, and to hire, whenever possible, local filmmakers. Such a strategy seemed practical (the films could address local and national problems), economical (the film campaign was primarily funded by national counterpart funds) and more effective (European audiences preferred national film productions). However, the filmic output of the country missions varied greatly; it was influenced by the economic and political conditions, the existing infrastructure for film production, the grade of competition or cooperation between different agencies, and especially the availability of financing, which again correlated to a country's geopolitical importance.

The strategy of local film production

The decision to produce the MP films in the countries that participated in the MP presented the Information Division and its film unit with a number of challenges. One was the question of film exports. The politics of efficiency demanded that the locally produced MP films be distributed across Europe – to fill the high demand for information films and to give the MP the utmost publicity. The MP films were also meant to foster a European identity, and thus win over Europeans to the idea of unification. Yet how could these national films be made appealing to audiences in other European countries? Resolving the tension between national cultures and a European culture was not easy. This problem had already occupied representatives of the European film industries in the 1920s, who had attempted to build up a European counter model to Hollywood, envisaged as a 'vibrant pan-European cinema industry' with an integrated market. The project 'Film Europe' was not just motivated by the desire to curb the dominance of the Hollywood film industry; it was also a response to the growing concerns about a perceived Americanization of national and local (film) cultures in Europe.[1] The advocates of a Film Europe discussed how national culture could fit into or overlap with a wider European culture. What style, narratives or themes would speak to audiences in different parts of Europe?[2] The ECA film unit, though recognizing the difficulties of meeting the interests of national as well as European audiences, never discussed this issue in depth; instead, it addressed the problem in a quite haphazard way, by trial and error.

One aspect of this ad hoc approach was the hiring of filmmakers. At the outset, the principle of supporting locally initiated productions meant that the country missions usually contracted local filmmakers. However, because of a perceived or real lack of experienced – or politically trusted – filmmakers, the film unit occasionally hired non-natives for national film projects. Thus, British filmmakers shot the films for the country mission in Turkey, while the 'Greek' projects were divided between Italian and Dutch filmmakers. It seems that the information officers did not see this hiring practice as contradictory to their conviction that films were best made by filmmakers who knew their audience. Even though most information officers were quite aware of Europe's linguistic and cultural diversity, they approached Europe more or less as a single, coherent entity – as the old world in contrast to the new world. The film unit's 'working philosophy' to produce films 'by Europeans exclusively for Europeans' illustrates this perception of Europe as a culturally homogeneous continent.[3] From this perspective, it made little difference whether British or Italian filmmakers filmed a given documentary, since any European was presumably still closer in mentality to another European than an American was. They might have been correct in this: even though non-natives made the films for the Greek mission, they were still very popular in Greece, as Chapter 7 illustrates.

As the propaganda operation expanded and the demand for films grew, this approach to film production prove ineffective. The Information Division urged the country missions to contract more film projects, or to submit ideas for films to speed up production.[4] Yet, with the exception of the very active Italian country mission, the missions were unable to deliver a sufficient number of films to meet the high demand. Setting up information offices at the different country missions was a time-consuming affair, which meant that considerable time passed until the first film productions were launched; moreover, some local information offices lacked the funds, expertise or ambition to initiate film projects; bureaucratic procedures and a lack of coordination between the headquarters in Paris and the country missions caused further delays.[5]

As a result, the ECA film section, set up in summer 1949 as a subunit of the Information Division in Paris to plan, coordinate and oversee film production and distribution in Europe, decided to take on a more active role and, from 1950 onwards, started to turn out its own films. The bulk of these took the form of series, such as *The Changing Face of Europe* (1950–1951), consisting of six episodes, and the two twelve-part series *The Marshall Plan at Work* (1950) and *ERP in Action* (1950); later it also produced *1-2-3: A Monthly Review from Europe* (1952–1954), consisting of twelve episodes. These were all distributed commercially across Europe. The then head of the film unit, Stuart Schulberg, explained in late November 1950 that the plan was to produce fewer films, which were, however, 'sharper and more to the point'.[6] The film unit commissioned mostly films that adopted a transnational angle and tackled themes that the local productions did not cover sufficiently. Whereas the local productions framed the MP in a national context, the film unit's series highlighted the links between the European countries, making a case for European integration and, at a later stage, mutual defence. Importantly, the centrally produced documentaries were meant to complement, not replace, the productions by the country missions.

Organization and financing of MP film production

Nonetheless, the country missions continued to produce more films than the film unit in Paris, although there were considerable differences in output, as Table 2.1 illustrates. The Italian country mission was by far the most productive, followed by the missions in France, West Germany, the United Kingdom and Greece. At first glance it may seem that a country mission's film output directly reflected its strategic and political importance to the United States. Therefore, US propaganda efforts prioritized European countries with powerful communist parties, such as Italy and France, or that were situated in close proximity to communist territory, such as Greece, West Germany or Austria. The small number of films produced points to the limited strategic importance of Ireland and Sweden, while Iceland, Portugal and Switzerland produced no films. Yet, the filmic output was also influenced by other factors, in particular the availability of funding (which itself was linked to strategic interests, as we will see).

Table 2.1 Breakdown of MP film productions by country, based on a sample

Sponsoring country mission	Output
Austria	8
Denmark	5
France	15
Greece	7
Ireland	1
Italy	28
Netherlands	5
Norway	2
Scandinavia (Sweden, Norway, Denmark)	1
Trieste	2
Turkey	5
UK	7
West Germany	9
Total local production	**95**
ECA/MSA film unit	72
Total	**167**

Financing of MP propaganda

The information activities were largely financed through the so-called counterpart funds. The ERP operated on the principle of self-help: this meant that the European recipients had to match the Marshall Aid grants with contributions of equal value in their own currency. Thus, European governments would use Marshall Aid to obtain goods, raw materials or machinery from the United States and sell them to their respective industries. The earnings were paid into special accounts, known as counterpart funds. These funds would then, in consultation with the ECA mission, be used to finance the rebuilding and modernization of national infrastructure and industry. Five per cent of these counterpart funds were reserved for the ECA to pay for the cost of administration, which included expenses for public relations or information.

The size of a country mission's information budget was determined by the share of aid a country received, but also its type. Marshall Aid was paid out in the form of grants or loans. Only aid in the form of grants generated counterpart funding. Consequently, countries with large grants accrued large counterpart funds, which in turn expanded their country mission's budget for information. The bulk of Marshall Aid – $11.7 billion out of a total of $13.2 billion – was paid out as (non-repayable) grants: either as so-called 'grants in kind', in the form of goods, machines or raw materials, or as financial assistance. The rest of Marshall Aid constituted loans that had to be paid back. The typical ratio of grant to loan was 90 to 10. There were exceptions: all Marshall Aid to Austria ($677 million) and Greece ($706 million), for example, took the form of non-repayable grants. The deals for Ireland and Portugal were much less advantageous: 70 per cent of Portugal's very meagre aid package was made up of repayable loans and Ireland's aid was 87 per cent loans.[7] Belgium's allocation in the first year or the ERP contained virtually no grants because of the country's large gold reserves and rapid industrial growth.[8]

Apart from the disadvantage that aid in the form of loans had to be paid back with interest, the economic stimulus was much reduced, as loans did not produce counterpart funds. A small counterpart fund also meant a much-reduced budget for information activities. Thus, ECA information offices in countries that received a high payout had considerably more money at their disposal than those that received smaller grants. It was for this reason that the country mission in Belgium did not produce its own films.[9]

Great Britain, France, Italy and West Germany were among the most favoured recipients of Marshall Aid. In addition to its substantial loan of $3.75 billion, which Britain had already received through the Anglo-American Financial Agreement of 1946, the ECA allocated to Britain another $3.2 billion of Marshall Aid, of which 2.8 billion were non-repayable grants.[10] France received over 2.7 billion and Italy a little more than 1.5 billion. West Germany's share of Marshall Aid was 1.4 billion in loans, two-thirds of which were later converted to non-repayable grants through the London Debt Agreement of 1953.[11] In addition, West Germany received a total of $1.62 billion through the GARIOA programme, the Government Appropriation for Relief in Occupied Areas administered by the US Army. GARIOA aid, paid out between 1946 and 1950 mostly in the form of deliveries of food, fertilizer, seed and gasoline, also generated counterpart funds.[12] The US military government in Germany and its civilian successor could thus dispose of a generous information budget.[13] Some participants in the ERP, such as Switzerland or Sweden, did not receive (or require) any direct financial aid, but profited from the reduction of intra-European trade barriers.[14]

Although the declared aim of the ERP was to help European countries out of deep economic crisis, aid was not allocated solely on the basis of the graveness of the economic situation or the extent of war destruction. Just as important was the country's strategic and political importance to the US government and, to some extent, the negotiation skills of the European representatives. Thus, Turkey ($225 million), Ireland ($147 million) and Portugal ($51 million) received comparatively small allotments – only tiny Iceland, with a $29 million aid package, received less.[15] The small share for Portugal and Ireland can partly be explained by the fact that these were countries at the periphery, and of little economic and strategic importance. In Ireland's case, her wartime neutrality and strong domestic opposition to the MP, even from parts of government, may have played a role.[16] Turkey, on the other hand, was of strategic interest insofar as it gave the Western powers access to the oil-rich Middle East. However, the US government saw no need to lend extensive support to the largely agricultural Turkish economy, since it had already provided Turkey with $100 million in military assistance in March 1947. The ECA thus granted Turkey only $33.8 million of Marshall Aid in the first year.

The information budget and other factors influencing film output

The 5 per cent of a country's counterpart funds placed at the disposal of the ECA country missions paid for the salaries of the local staff, rental of office space and accommodation for the American mission personnel. It also covered most of the expenses of the local information offices, such as costs of paper and film stock, printing or dubbing services, and the fees of the film crews (but not the salaries of the US information staff or the costs of distribution).[17] If the 5 per cent was not used up, as was often the case in countries with large grants, the remaining balance could be invested in 'special projects'.[18] It emerged later that these special projects also included the secret funding of European trade unions or the sponsoring of anti-communist demonstrations by the CIA.[19] The surplus funds of one country could also be used to pay for information materials that were distributed in other ERP countries.[20] Al Friendly, director of the European Information Division in 1949, proudly remarked to his colleague at the US military government in Germany that the budget at the disposal of the Information Division and its units was 'generous – in short very big'.[21] The film section alone disposed of an annual budget of about $5 million in counterpart funds from the country missions.[22] The commissioned filmmakers were thus able to work without financial constraints; as the Austrian filmmaker Georg Tressler pointed out, 'There was plenty of money, and so the problem was just determining how to spend it'.[23]

Whether a local mission produced more or fewer films was influenced by the size of local counterpart funds, which correlated with the strategic importance of the recipient country, by the ECA's policy aims as well as by the power relations between headquarters and local information offices. While the Italian information office in Rome operated highly independently from Paris, the film unit exerted more control over the other information offices. Had it been up to the local information officer Emerson Waldman, for example, the mission in Norway would have produced more than just the two documentaries *Breakthrough* (1950) and *Nation on Skis* (1951). But Emerson's idea for a film on the activities of the Norwegian communist party was shelved. Though there is no further documentation on this film project, a letter by Waldman suggests that it was the film section that dragged its feet, presumably because the film did not fit into the ECA's objectives for 1949.[24] Another planned documentary on the 'natural economic tie-up between Norway and Italy' came to nothing in the end.[25] Here, it was the head of the powerful Italian information unit, Frank Gervasi, who advised that the script be rewritten and additional research undertaken, which presumably never happened.[26]

Another special case was Great Britain. Although Britain was the recipient of the greatest amount of Marshall Aid, as well as being one of Europe's largest countries with a population of around 50 million, the output of the British mission was comparatively small. While the ECA film unit in Paris employed many British filmmakers for its film series, the ECA country mission in London produced, relative to the country's size, comparatively few films. The main reason for this was that the British themselves undertook the bulk of publicity work for the MP, leaving the US information officer Joseph Evans with an 'easy job'.[27] The propaganda effort for the MP was largely carried out by the British Central Office of Information (COI) and the Economic Information Unit (EIU, a publicity unit within the Treasury).[28] The EIU had been set up by the British government in summer 1947 to inform the British people about the economic situation and the government's recovery programme. With the start of the ERP, the EIU created a separate subunit, the ERP Information Office. The head of the EIU explained its high investment in MP propaganda by pointing to the fact that it was impossible to publicize the government's reforms separately from the MP, as the MP was 'an element in, and a condition of, a general recovery programme'. The ECA information office worked closely together with the EIU, but its role was largely advisory: it proposed ideas and made suggestions (or requests), while the EIU realized the projects. The costs were shared.[29] Thomas W. Wilson, who set up the ECA information unit at the country mission in London and worked there until 1949, was impressed with the staff of the EIU and their efforts to educate the British people about the economic problems and the needed shifts in attitude. He remarked that 'all I had to do was suggest to them what I thought would be a good idea, and they did it. I did very little directly in the way of information activity.'[30]

The few films that the British country mission did produce were primarily concerned with the issue of industrial modernization and exchange. Three of these celebrated the benefits of productivity (see Chapter 4), while the others took stock of the progress achieved. *Report from Britain*, featuring the American actor Jackie Cooper and his wife travelling through Britain, lauded the British recovery effort and good Anglo-American relations. The documentary *I Went Back* (1950) also sent an actor on a journey: the British Leo Genn travelled to the continent to evaluate Europe's economic progress. *Adventure in Sardinia* (1950), an adapted and re-edited version of a documentary originally produced for Shell, depicted an UNRRA programme to extinguish malaria in Sardinia.[31] The topic of *The Hour of Choice* (1951), directed by Stuart Legg, promoted the European idea by convincing the Europeans of their shared cultural heritage.

The British example illustrates how the cooperation of a national government, or the lack thereof, could boost or hinder the propaganda effort on behalf of the MP. The following will examine more closely the film production in four countries, in order to establish how the political and economic context, the make-up of the national film industries as well as the presence of other US agencies shaped the output of MP films. Italy, France, Greece and West Germany are rewarding case studies on the grounds of their strategic importance to the US government, whereas Turkey illustrates how conflicts between the ECA and a national government could affect the propaganda effort.

A prolific producer: The case of Italy

The country with the highest output of MP films was undoubtedly Italy (see Table 2.1). By the end of 1949, the Italian mission, the only one with a separate film unit, had already completed twelve films. Led by the experienced Andrew Berding, the information office in Rome had a talented and energetic information team at hand: John Secondari, head of the film unit, and Frank Gervasi, who succeeded Berding as chief of the information office. They were described as exceedingly ambitious, and also had excellent connections to the Italian film industry.[32] Yet it was not solely the information officers' ambition that turned the Italian country mission into such a prolific producer of MP films; it also profited from the structures the US military had established on their advance through Italy. During liberation, the US army had occupied the famous film studio Cinecittà and engaged Italian filmmakers to produce information films for the Allied Control Commission. In addition, the State Department's US Information Service (USIS) had opened libraries and reading rooms that ran cultural programmes and organized film screenings.[33] In the run-up to the Italian government elections in April 1948, the US government pulled out all the stops to prevent the victory of the Italian Communist Party, including a publicity campaign in support of De Gasperi's Christian Democrats, for which the State Department joined forces with Hollywood studios.[34] The established structures and networks served Berding well when he opened the ECA information office in Rome in summer 1948. At the end of 1948, while the information offices in other countries were still trying to find their footing, the Italian mission was already turning out its first films.

Wally Nielsen, deputy head of the Information Division in Paris, found 'nothing but pleasant surprises' during his visit to Rome in spring 1949, though he was slightly uncomfortable with the information unit's strong autonomy, and with 'the slight tendency in Italy to view the Paris Information Office more with tolerance than dependence'.[35] But, since the Italian information office continued to impress the headquarters in Paris, it retained a high degree of autonomy throughout the operation.[36] Already in March 1949, Berding reported the completion of the fifth documentary *A Piece of Coal* (Un pezzo di carbone). Another film, *Two Counts* (I due 'conti'), had meanwhile been awarded the prize for excellence by the Italian government.[37] By the time the Information Division in Paris set up its own film section, the Italian information office had already been working for a year, and had produced a dozen films.[38] This fact added immensely to the standing of the Italian information team and enhanced its role in shaping the ECA's film policy. The Italian information office was keen to expand its influence, and, as we will see, became closely involved in film production for the ECA missions in Trieste and Greece. At the same time, it closely guarded its own territory against 'intruders': when Gervasi found that the Irish filmmaker Julian Spiro was shooting some scenes on land reclamation in Italy for the British-produced *The Changing Face of Europe* series, he demanded that the film unit Paris immediately stopped the filming.[39]

The Italian documentaries produced during the first one-and-a-half years focus on the reconstruction and modernization efforts across Italy. The choice of subject reflected the ECA's policy goals of the first year, which prioritized the rehabilitation of the infrastructure and transport facilities, the revival of agriculture and the generation of power.[40] The films highlight the industry of the Italians, and present male labour as guarantor of the nation's future. *Trip in Sicily* (Viaggio in Sicilia), for instance, illustrates the reconstruction efforts and economic developments in Sicily. *Two Counts* depicts the rebuilding of the Italian mercantile fleet at the shipyards of Genoa, Monfalcone and Naples. *Zinc Valley* (La valle del zinco) details the expansion of a zinc mine in the Bergamo region, and demonstrates the production process from initial mining to final product.

The title *Men at Work* (Uomini al lavoro) is illustrative of the topic it promotes. The film informs audiences about ERP-sponsored reforestation programmes and requalification projects that bring thousands of Italian men into employment. By showcasing working men (see also Chapter 1), the documentary celebrates male industry and conveys optimism about Italy's future. *Tomorrow We Live* (Dobbiamo vivere ancora) uses to great effect the language of noir cinema – with its canted camera frames, use of shadows and fast editing – to illustrate the disconcerting effects of economic crisis (see figure 2.1). Here, economic balance is symbolically restored through the surgery that saves the life of an injured worker; the recovery of balance is also expressed visually, as the camera regains its equilibrium.

The themes in later Italian film productions remain largely the same: the documentary *Cotton* (Cotone, 1950) illustrates how Marshall-Aid-sponsored cotton imports revive the cotton industry and create jobs. The rebuilding of transport and infrastructure is the subject of *A Ship Is Born* (Nave in cantiere, 1951) and *The Appian Way* (Via Appia, 1950). *Land Redeemed* (Bonifiche, 1950) and *Land of Apulia* (Apulia, 1951) promote ERP-financed land reclamation and irrigation projects and their positive impact on Italian society: 'For the jobless, new jobs. For the despairing, new heart' (*Land of Apulia*) (see figure 2.2).

Figure 2.1 Canted camera frames in *Tomorrow We Live* illustrate Italy's turmoil.

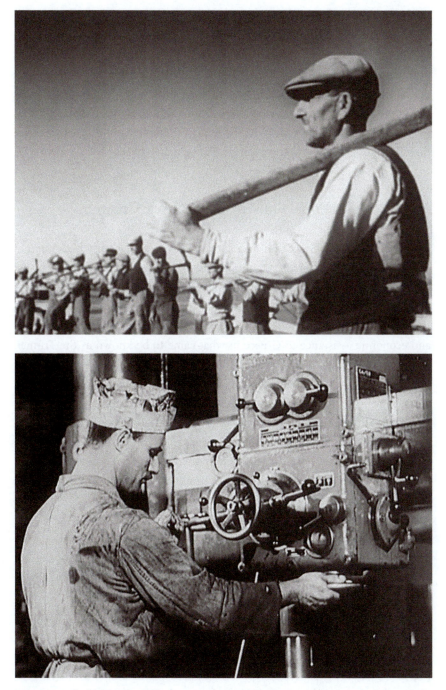

Figure 2.2 (a, b) 'For the jobless, new jobs. For the despairing, new heart!' (*Land of Apulia* and *Village without Words*).

New themes introduced were the expansion of hydroelectric power in *Hidden Power* (Lardarello, 1950) and the construction of housing in *Life and Death of a Cave City* (Matera, 1950). *Silkmakers of Como* (ca. 1951) promotes modern mass production – a subject most other MP films avoided. Resistance against industrial mechanization and standardization was strong in Italy, coming both from the powerful communist trade unions and from the traditional Italian industry, which was dominated by family-run enterprises. The Italian information office therefore thought it best to leave the issue of productivity alone.[41]

'National films' by non-natives: Greece

The ECA mission in Greece produced, relative to its size, a fairly high number of MP documentaries. Greece's economy and society had been ravaged by brutal Nazi occupation and a subsequent bloody civil war, which was still ongoing when the ECA set up its mission in Athens in summer 1948. In March 1947, President Truman persuaded the US Congress to extend substantial military and economic assistance to Greece in what came to be known as the Truman Doctrine. By supporting the authoritarian, right-wing Greek government in its fight against communist opposition, the United States hoped to keep Greece in the Western camp and prevent the Soviet Union from expanding its influence. Only one year later, the aid package was further replenished with Marshall Aid and a technical assistance programme that helped to rebuild and modernize the Greek economy. As in Italy, the motive for providing economic aid was based on the belief that by reducing poverty and unemployment, popular support for the communists would dwindle.

However, the communist-led partisan army, which was locked in a violent conflict with the government's military, enjoyed broad sympathy among the population for its previous fight against the Nazi occupiers.[42] One of the key challenges for the ECA mission in Greece was thus to win the trust of those people who opposed the right-wing government and were therefore highly suspicious of Western involvement. The fact that the Greek affairs were 'mainly run by us' (i.e. the US government), as Franklin Dixon, Officer of Greek Affairs at the Department of State from 1948 to 1951, admitted, did not help to improve the popularity of the United States.[43] The US agencies that conducted propaganda in Greece therefore sought to convince the Greeks that the MP was not motivated by strategic interests, but was intended to rebuild the Greek economy to improve the lives of the ordinary people. The generous aid package, which made many

US officials feel that 'we were Santa Claus to Greece',[44] could then be exploited by the ECA to sway the opinion of those many Greeks who were longing for economic betterment and peace.

The production of the first MP films in Greece started only in late 1949. During a visit to Greece in September 1949, the head of the film section, Lothar Wolff, encouraged the information officer at the Athens mission, Dowsley Clark, to submit ideas for films that showed the application of Marshall Aid. Four of Clark's ideas were selected: soil reclamation and rice growing in central Greece, the repatriation of Greek refugees, the reconstruction of a town called Naoussa and the reopening of the Corinth Canal.[45] Secondari, the head of the film unit in Rome, 'offered his assistance in supervising editorial and production problems'.[46] He suggested David Kurland, an American filmmaker who owned a production company in Rome, for the project; Kurland travelled to Greece to inspect several cities and develop the film projects.[47] In the end, however, the film unit hired him for only two projects. The other two were assigned to the Dutch-born filmmaker John Ferno, who had a production company in Paris.

Why were all these films, paid for by the Greek mission, made by foreigners? One reason was that the Greek film industry was recovering very slowly from the war. It struggled with shortages of materials and finances and suffered from restrictions of movement and strict government censorship.[48] Still, there was artistic talent available. The Greek information officer Clark, who had seen – and admired – a Greek film produced by Finos Films, suggested the company to produce a dramatic MP film for the Greek audience.[49] The Paris film unit – and the Italian information office – obviously had different plans. The next Greek film project – a dramatized story about the friendship between a boy and an imported American mule with the title *The Story of Koula* – was assigned to another foreigner, the Italian director Vittorio Gallo.[50] Another Greek film, *A Doctor for Arkadnos* (1951), went to Ferno, the film unit's favourite candidate. Regina Longo pointed to a conflict between the film section in Paris and the Italian film officer Secondari, who had ambitions to make a career in the film business, and thus sought to land the Greek projects for 'his' filmmakers in order to build up his network in the Italian film industry.[51] But there were also practical reasons: since only documentaries produced by Italian filmmakers could be shown in Italian cinemas, he was keen to expand the number of Italian-produced MP films.[52]

The 'Greek' documentaries focused almost exclusively on the rebuilding efforts of a war-shattered society. Ferno's *Doctor for Arkadnos* (1951) depicts Marshall Aid-sponsored programmes to fight malaria and expand medical care facilities;

the documentary never entered distribution in Greece, however, as health officials at the Greek mission objected.[53] Kurland's *Victory at Thermopylae* (1950) tells of a rice-growing project on a barren, salty plain made possible by Marshall Aid with the assistance of American agricultural experts. *Corinth Canal* (1950) used the clearance and reopening of the Corinth Canal, a vital waterway for Greece, to illustrate the recovery of Greece. The film unit acquired captured German footage that showed the destruction of the Canal by the German troops – rare luck indeed, which allowed the director Ferno to juxtapose German destruction with American rebuilding efforts.[54] Sometimes, local conditions or strategic interests delayed filming. Kurland's other film, *Mill Town* (1950), documents the rebuilding of the textile industry in the Greek town of Náoussa. Initially, the documentary was planned to show the revival of the town's industry sparked by the delivery of machinery for building an American textile mill. In reality, five months after the machines had arrived, the boxes were still unpacked, and the script had to be adapted.[55] Ferno's *Return from the Valley* (1950), about the repatriation of Greek refugees, was also postponed. In order to provide the necessary drama, the Greek information officer Clark decided to wait until spring to shoot the film, when thousands of refugees were expected to return to their homes.[56]

Ferno's films *Return from the Valley* and *Corinth Canal* are true *motion* pictures. His camera travels on a ship through the Corinth Canal, and accompanies refugees climbing up the hills to their former homes. Here, the movement itself is depicted as a success, whereas Kurland's *Mill Town* projects the idea that the full accomplishment will be realized in the future. The two filmmakers put a different emphasis on the theme of reconstruction. Both take an event as a starting point to illustrate the rebuilding of Greece, but for Kurland the delivery of machinery marks the beginning of a much larger rebuilding process, whereas Ferno's film depicts the return of the refugees itself as an important accomplishment.

Many stumbling blocks: France

After Italy, France was the most active producer of MP films. The French mission operated in a context that was very similar to Italy's: like Italy, France was a country with a large, rural population, a deeply split political landscape and a predominantly traditionally organized but weak industrial economy. France suffered from high unemployment and inflation, which fuelled social unrest. The French Communist Party enjoyed considerable support among the population, not least due to its connection to the *Résistance* under Nazi occupation, and was able to rally large numbers of workers through its trade union confederation *Confédération générale du travail* (CGT).[57]

Yet, compared to Italy, a country of similar size and of similar strategic importance to the United States, the French information office produced considerably fewer films. Film production was also much slower to develop, for a number of reasons. One was that the French mission prioritized other media at the beginning of the MP campaign. Cinema attendance in France was much lower than in its neighbouring countries, and fewer people had access to a cinema (see Chapter 8).[58] Another factor behind the lower output was that film production was tightly controlled by the French government. Film producers had to go through complicated bureaucratic procedures to acquire a shooting permit and raw stock.[59] Paradoxically, the French mission's geographical proximity to the ECA headquarters in Paris – they were located only a few blocks from each other – also had an adverse effect on its output. Having the Information Division at the headquarters in the vicinity worked to the disadvantage of the mission's information office. Partly this was because the ECA did not consider the staffing of the information unit at the French mission to be a priority, since the information experts at the headquarters were just around the corner. In addition, the people from headquarters were 'constantly interfering' in the work of the French mission's information office, as Helen Kirkpatrick remembered, who took over as head of the French information office in October 1949.[60]

The propaganda efforts of the French mission were further complicated by the political and societal climate in which the mission operated. The information officers struggled in particular with the vocal opposition of the French communists and of the communist-led CGT, which occasionally extended to active obstruction of the mission's propaganda efforts (see Chapter 8).[61] Many within the ECA and the State Department believed that the people's sceptical attitude towards the MP and the United States was largely on account of the communists' media campaign against the MP. The French government was no help; as in other aspects of the ERP, it was in fact resistant to the demands of the ECA.[62] Although contractually obligated to promote the ERP, the French government made no attempts to counter the communist allegations or to highlight the benefits of the MP, which infuriated the country mission in France.[63]

The ECA information office brought up the matter repeatedly with the French Foreign Ministry and the interministerial committee, Secrétariat général du Comité interministériel pour les questions de coopération économique européenne (SGCI), created on 25 June 1948 to liaise between the ECA, the Organization for European Economic Co-operation (OEEC) and the French ministries. Explaining that the US Congress was alarmed by the negative public opinion in France, and that it was threatening to withhold payments, the information office reminded the French of their obligation to publicize the MP. Nevertheless, the French government seemed deaf to the repeated demands of the ECA, and countered that if it promoted the MP, the French public might react negatively. However, in November 1948, the head of the SGCI, Robert Mitterrand, conceded that it might be in France's own interest to advertise the MP to its citizens. If the task of advertising the MP were left to people unaccustomed to French sensibilities, he warned his government, they might easily hurt French national pride and thus achieve the opposite effect. Mitterrand advised investing a limited sum in promoting the MP in order to prove to the ECA that the French government was willing to stick to the agreement.[64] Eventually, the government agreed, but instructed to advertise it only discreetly, 'le plus discrètement possible'.[65] According to Chiarella Esposito, the government feared being accused of acting as American puppets.[66] The French historian Gérard Bossuat explains the French government's unwillingness as being a complex mixture of ignorance regarding the importance of propaganda, national pride and concern that showing too much support for what the public perceived as a US initiative would destroy the fragile cohesion of French society.[67]

Faced with an unwilling French cabinet and strong pressure from Washington to show visible improvements in attitude, the ECA Information Division and the information office at the French mission joined forces: twelve completed MP films in 1950 are evidence of the intensified propaganda effort. The films address a broad variety of themes. They focus on power generation, the modernization and expansion of agricultural production, the revitalization of shipping and trade, the provision of housing and European cooperation. *Treasure of the Rhone* (L'or du Rhône) and *Liquid Force* (Force liquide) document the construction of massive hydroelectric power stations, for instance, and the documentaries *Renaissance agricole*, *Provence – terre de peuplement* and *Rice and Bulls* (Riz et taureaux) highlight achievements in the agricultural sector through the mechanization of farming, irrigation projects and the desalting of land for rice growing. The films address the farmers' fear of the reforms by promising the peaceful coexistence of tradition and modernity. Three MP films deal specifically with the effects of war and the rebuilding efforts financed by Marshall Aid: *The Village That Wouldn't Die* (Ce village ne voulait pas mourir) depicts the rebuilding of a town in Normandy that was destroyed by Allied bombing; *Henry's Story* (Une histoire d'Henri) is a dramatized story of the revival of French shipping on the river Rhine with prefabricated barges provided by the United States; *Liberty* (Liberté), finally promotes transatlantic relations by reporting on how the confiscated German ocean liner *Europa* was converted into the French passenger ship *Liberté* to carry passengers across the Atlantic.

Two of the French documentaries are set in the French colonies – a reminder that the application of Marshall Aid was not restricted to European soil. The European colonial powers Belgium, France, Great Britain, Portugal and The Netherlands were allowed to invest Marshall Aid in their overseas territories. The ERP-sponsored modernization of transportation and the expansion of agriculture and mining benefited both Europe and the United States: the Europeans could reduce their dollar debt by exporting raw materials from the colonies to the United States, while the United States gained access to colonial markets and important strategic materials. Almost 10 per cent of the Marshall Aid to France was thus channelled into the French territories in Africa.[68]

The two films released in 1950 document the modernization of the French colonies and highlight its benefits to the colonial subjects. *The Story of Mahmoud* (La fugue du Mahmoud), originally planned as part of a whole series of films on North Africa, shows the mechanization of farming in Morocco.[69] *The Jungle that Was* (Le Niger) documents the building of a dam on the Niger and the deforestation of the savannah to produce arable land to cultivate cotton and rice. Both films display a colonial attitude in that the African people are presented as the grateful recipients of Western knowledge and expertise. Traditional villages and customs as well as forests have to make room for modern dams, streets and large tractors, which serve as signifiers of progress (see figure 2.3). The films resemble the Turkish MP films, in that the mechanization of agriculture and the education of the young are presented as guarantors of economic growth and rising living standards.

Figure 2.3 Destruction of land in *The Jungle that Was* signalizes progress.

The French foreign ministry was closely involved in the planning of these film projects, and obviously had the final say on the choice of filmmakers. In view of the government's general reluctance to engage in propaganda, the foreign ministry's keen interest in this matter is surprising. Presumably the French government saw in the films a means to strengthen its position as a colonial power by illustrating its efforts to improve the lives of its colonial subjects.

Even though the French government became more supportive of the MP film campaign, the ECA still encountered serious bureaucratic hurdles if it involved foreign staff or production companies. When, for example, the Paris film unit contracted the British production company Wessex Films to film some scenes for *The Changing Face of Europe* series in France,[70] the company's application to import camera equipment was rejected. Therefore, it had to apply for project clearance to the French Ministry of Labour and then to the Centre National de la Cinématographie, which demanded that the English crew be duplicated by a French crew, thus doubling the costs. The French country mission was furious about these impositions. In the end, a liaison officer from the French Ministry of Information was ordered to resolve the conflict between the parties involved, and he obviously succeeded.[71]

Taking a back seat: The MP film in West Germany

Although a country mission's output of MP films is generally a reliable indicator of its strategic importance for the United States, this equation does not work in the case of West Germany. For the United States, West Germany merited special attention, for reasons of its Nazi past, its role as instigator of two world wars, its proximity to Soviet-controlled East Germany, and – not least – its industrial power. The US policy towards Germany underwent a decisive shift from a punitive to a more productive approach that considered the rebuilding of Germany as essential to prevent a collapse. When developing the MP, the US policymakers reached the conclusion that integrating Germany into a European network was essential to boost Europe's economic recovery, but also to curb Germany's power and allay the fears of her neighbours, in particular France.[72]

Yet despite Germany's strategic and economic importance, the ECA country mission to West Germany produced even fewer films than its French neighbour. The main reason for this comparatively low output was the power of the US military government (OMGUS), which administered the American occupation zone in West Germany. The head of OMGUS, General Lucius Clay, had undertaken considerable efforts to build up West Germany economically, against early US policy and against pressures from the other Allied powers. An advocate of a fair treatment of Germany, Clay fought hard to ensure that the German Bizone was not disadvantaged in the allocation of Marshall Aid, even if this brought him into opposition to the ECA.[73] The conflict between OMGUS and the ECA was, as Thomas Schwartz has outlined, largely a result of different views on Germany's future. Clay was opposed to the integration of West Germany into a European network, fearing that it would delay Germany's own economic recovery.[74] His unwillingness to cooperate with or yield any of his powers to the newly established ECA country mission in Frankfurt reverberated right down to the lower echelons, to the detriment of the ECA information office.

The OMGUS Information Services Division was the ECA information office's counterpart in Germany. Its main task was to 'de-nazify' Germans through a programme of re-education. Through mass media and cultural and educational programmes, the Germans should be taught democratic skills and the values of liberalism and tolerance. For this purpose, OMGUS established several radio stations, such as RIAS in West Berlin and Radio Rot-Weiss-Rot in Austria. To influence public opinion, as well as to export US journalistic practices, OMGUS sponsored magazines and newspapers, such as the *Neue Zeitung*, which was written by German emigrants.[75] Children and youths were singled out for special attention; educational films and discussion groups were intended to help 'cleanse' the children's minds of Nazi ideology and establish democratic structures from the bottom up.[76]

In July 1947, OMGUS had created a documentary film unit under the leadership of Stuart Schulberg, who would later transfer to the ECA. Over the span of two years, it produced fifteen documentaries.[77] While the main function of OMGUS films was to teach civic values, it also promoted the MP. *Me and Mr. Marshall* (1949) tells the story of an ordinary German, Hans Fischer, young and unemployed like many of his contemporaries. Hans finds a job in the Ruhr coal mines and, recalling the hardships of the early post-war years, attests to the ability of the MP to revive production and improve living conditions across Europe.

Like Hans, the ECA information unit in Frankfurt struggled to find its footing. It suffered from a shortage of staff, and received little support from OMGUS. In May 1949, the chief of the Information Division in Paris, Al Friendly, complained to the European head of the ECA that the 'army jerks' in charge of the information programme in West German zones gave the new ECA information officer, Walter Ridder, a hard time.[78] One month later, little had changed in what was now the newly established Federal Republic of Germany: 'The German information situation is in a nebulous and unhappy state,' wrote Friendly.[79]

The fact that the ECA Information Division headhunted Stuart Schulberg, the head of the OMGUS documentary unit, for its film section could be seen as a move to strengthen the position of the ECA information office in West Germany. The situation improved when OMGUS was replaced by the civil administration of the High Commission for Germany (HICOG) in September 1949. The ECA mission now came under the authority of the US High Commissioner, John McCloy, former World Bank president, who acted in the double capacity of High Commissioner and ECA mission chief.[80] Officially, the ECA information office remained independent. In practice, it cooperated very closely with HICOG's Information Services Division – so much so that most film production was undertaken by HICOG's Motion Picture Branch, which produced about eighty shorts between 1949 and 1952. While HICOG films displayed some thematic overlaps with MP films, their aim and form were different. HICOG productions were unambiguously pedagogical, and used case studies to contrast ideal democratic behaviour with negative representations of citizens who had no civic commitment.[81]

The films of the ECA information office, on the other hand, pushed for industrial modernization and European integration, while at the same time pointing to the helping (and protecting) hand of the United States. *Smoke* (Blauer Dunst, 1950) documents how the Americans came to the rescue of the German cigarette industry – and the German smoker – by providing 93,000 tons of Virginia tobacco worth $450 million through the ERP, to the detriment of the Turkish and Greek tobacco industry.[82] *Hides for Tomorrow* (Häute für Morgen, 1950) reports on how the ERP aided the recovery of the German leather industry. The humorous documentary *We and the Others* (Wir und die Anderen, 1951) makes a case for European integration by contrasting the progressive openness of the past with the current restrictiveness in Europe. How come, it asks, that in a modern, industrialized society, border controls and import duties hinder the freedom of movement that is needed for the economy to grow? *Hugo* (1952), a humorous cartoon series consisting of six episodes, each three minutes long, features a satirical German figure named Hugo who learns the benefits of European cooperation (see figure 2.4). The series boosted the output of the German mission considerably, but was actually produced outside Germany by the Dutch animation studio of Marten Toonder and his international team: the British animator Harald Mack as director, and the Danish animators Bjørn Ring and Bjørn Frank Jensen.[83]

Figure 2.4 *Hugo and the House of Europe*: Rebuilding Europe requires close cooperation.

Unmistakably anti-communist were the messages conveyed by the documentaries *City out of Darkness* (Es wurde Licht, 1950) and *Air of Freedom* (Berliner Luft, 1951), the latter a co-production with HICOG. Both present West Berlin as a modern 'showcase of the West', vibrant amid Soviet-controlled territory.

Why did the German information office not make a greater effort to produce films promoting the MP to the Germans? One reason for the low output was that the US information staff had little trust in the talent and political reliability of German filmmakers. In a joint conference, the HICOG information officer Convery Egan described the 'absence of talent' in the German film industry as a key problem.[84] As late as 1951, American film experts analysing the situation in West Germany complained that 'few if any qualified screenwriters' could be found.[85] And while Schulberg, as head of the ECA film unit, did not reject the use of German filmmakers altogether, he advised close guidance.[86] A second reason was that there was no shortage of information films that promoted US policies: OMGUS and its successor HICOG were highly prolific film producers, and the State Department saw little reason why the ECA should have its own information unit in West Germany. Peter Rathvon, producer and former president of the large Hollywood studio RKO Pictures, who inspected the US film operations in West Germany on behalf of the State Department's USIS in March 1951, strongly recommended a concentration of propaganda efforts. In his report, Rathvon addressed the problem of duplication and the 'senseless competition for the services of qualified local documentary producers'.[87] Rathvon was probably right that too many agencies were competing for the attention of the German audience: apart from HICOG and the ECA, NATO and various national governmental agencies were also producing information films.[88] Moreover, many MP films produced in other countries were shown in Germany. In the last quarter of 1952, only four out of fourteen MP films in commercial distribution were German.[89] A third explanation for the modest output was that most West Germans, though sceptical of the American occupier and its foreign policy, welcomed the ERP and supported its key policy goals for economic and political reasons. Since the Germans were able to observe at close range the developments in communist-ruled East Germany, they needed less convincing of the benefits of European integration and a close alliance with the United States.[90]

Cultural differences: Turkey

From the outset of the ERP initiative, Turkey ranked low on the ECA's priority list, which was also reflected in the allocation of Marshall Aid: in the first year, Turkey's share was a meagre $35 million in loans.[91] Accordingly, no Turkish MP films were produced before 1951. Neither the US government, the ECA nor the OEEC considered Turkey's economic situation serious enough to warrant substantial assistance. Turkey had not suffered heavy damage during the war, and its level of industrial development was, in the eyes of the Americans, too low to make it suitable for high investment. Turkey, which Machado described as 'chronically disappointed' about the allotments it received,[92] tried to pressure the US government into increasing its allocation by pointing to the military burden it had to shoulder to protect the rest of Europe. The US government and the OEEC, however, were reluctant to expand Turkey's share, and argued that Turkey misunderstood the purpose and aims of the MP.[93] The escalation of the Cold War, however, bolstered Turkey's position. The Turkish government managed to convince the United States that it deserved more economic assistance, as it spent half of the national budget on military defence to protect the West against the Soviet danger.[94] Already by the second year of the ERP, the allocation to Turkey was more than doubled to almost $72 million, half of it as a non-repayable grant.[95]

As Turkey gradually turned into an indispensable ally in the fight against the communist enemy, the stance of the Information Division towards it also changed. In May 1949, Waldemar Nielsen presented Turkey as 'the newest and strangest element in our whole operation,'[96] but left the propaganda efforts largely to USIS. One year later, the situation had changed. In order to help the Turkish government pay for its enormous defence costs, the Turkish country mission was encouraged to produce several films that encouraged the expansion of production. Turkey had no film industry, which is why the film unit in Paris contracted the British production company Clarke & Hornby in summer 1950, initially for four documentaries to be filmed on location. Clarke & Hornby produced them speedily, and completed the films by October 1950, receiving a contract for another two films. Before the films could enter distribution, however, they needed the approval of the Turkish government. But this turned out to be more difficult than expected.

Since Turkey was primarily an agricultural country, ECA policies aimed at expanding agricultural production. The export of wheat, in particular, was supposed to help Turkey to finance the upgrade of its outdated military.[97] The largest chunk of Marshall Aid, almost 60 per cent, went into the agricultural sector, and specifically into the purchase of farming machinery, such as tractors or combines, as well as the education of farmers.[98] These targets are reflected in the subjects of the MP films the Turkish ECA mission produced. The documentary *Yusef and His Plough* (Yusuf ve Sabani, 1951) promoted the iron plough as a means to cultivate more land. The film *The Village Tractor* (Köy Traktörü, 1951) used the large-scale importing of Marshall Aid-sponsored tractors as a starting point to educate the Turks about the use of farming machines. *Turkish Harvest*, completed in 1952, was essentially a compilation of scenes from the previous two films. The fourth film, titled *Control of Water* (Suyun Kontrolü), on the building of massive dams to store water for irrigation, never entered distribution, as a result of a change to Turkey's and the ECA's irrigation policy.[99]

All of the films are set in the vast, barren landscape of central Turkey. Life is still very traditional in these environs: people live off the land, tilling the fields, and grazing their cattle and sheep. After work, the men sit together, drinking tea, playing board games and chatting. The documentaries depict a patriarchal world where the elderly men make decisions, the young ones take orders, while the women work in the garden and the house. But modernity has found its way into these villages: in *Yusef and His Plough*, it is a radio broadcast that announces an ERP-programme promoting the use of iron ploughs, and in *The Village Tractor* a visiting expert who informs the villagers about a new Marshall-Aid-sponsored tractor scheme. The films appear more educational than promotional, with the narrator carefully explaining the application process for the farming machinery programme, or the importance of keeping the motor of the tractor cleaned and oiled. Their aim is to encourage agricultural modernization – a goal shared by the Turkish government, which was keen to rescue the largely rural population from their 'backwardness'.

Yet opinions on how these goals should be promoted were divided. When the films *Yusef and His Plough* and *The Village Tractor* were shown to representatives of the Ministry of Agriculture in April 1951, they responded with 'howls of dismay'. The Turkish government officials criticized the commentaries, which had apparently been written by a native speaker with little knowledge of the right agricultural terms. Moreover, they disapproved of the image of Turkey the films presented. The English producer Philip Mackie, who attended the screening as a representative of the film unit, summed up the problem: 'The government wants to show Turkey as modern or beautiful or both.' But neither of the films fulfilled these expectations. Mackie felt that the Turkish criticism was not really aimed at the films, but at the US government and the ECA: 'Now the Turks are literal-minded; more important, they are hypersensitive; most important, relationships between ECA and the Turkish government, and relations between ECA-information and the Turkish official information set-up, are pretty delicate just now.'[100] The Turkish government considered Marshall Aid as compensation for its massive military spending and willingness to defend the West against communist aggression, and therefore felt constantly rebuffed by the meagre payouts it received. The ECA and the OEEC, in turn, criticized Turkey's refusal to 'play by the rules', and its failure to present correct information or to keep deadlines. The Turkish government did not negotiate with the ECA and the OEEC but went straight to the US government, which caused frictions.[101] The MP thus 'turned into a point of grievance and misunderstanding' for both sides, which also affected the relations between the ECA information officers and Turkish officials.[102] The examples illustrate how political tensions impacted on the work of the propagandists, though cultural differences and the ECA's lack of understanding of Turkish society certainly aggravated the conflict.

Although the film unit implemented the requested changes, its hope that the films could be quickly released was dashed. In June 1951, the Ministry of Agriculture and the Turkish Press Bureau requested additional changes to *The Village Tractor*: the boy had to be chosen for his ability (and not for being the mayor's son, as in the original) if the film was to reflect the new social order in Turkey. The Turkish officials also wanted the narrator to emphasize that the farmers should decide 'in a democratic fashion' about the use of the village tractor, as conflicts had erupted over these machines.[103] The ECA film unit tried to smooth the relations by agreeing to all changes. Nevertheless, the film unit's diplomatic prudence in its dealings with the Turkish authorities irritated the British film producers Clarke & Hornby. They had been hindered from completing their assignment, and had received no payment due to the Turkish objections. In a letter dated 7 July 1951, Dennis Clarke complained about the long delay and the fact that the film unit cited bad weather (which may have been used metaphorically) as reason for the delay: 'I am a little puzzled as to why in correspondence your organisation has referred to "bad weather" causing delay; as you know, this is not a fact.'[104] In the end, the film unit in Paris agreed to financially compensate the British producers. It sent the film officer Nils Nilson to Turkey 'to clear up all pending matters and obtain final approval for the entire series of six films'.[105] Nilson, however, could only win European distribution rights for three of the six films.[106]

The examples of Turkey and France show how clashes of interest between national governments and the ECA, often exacerbated by a lack of cultural sensitivity, complicated the MP propaganda effort. Conflict was by no means restricted to the United States and its European partners. In West Germany, the ECA found itself in competition with the US military administration that controlled the field of information, which impeded the production of MP films. In the case of Greece, two external ECA branches – the Italian information office and the Paris film unit – were competing with each other; here, however, the rivalry proved conducive to the film output of the Greek mission. The British country mission's harmonious relations with the British information outfits benefited the overall propaganda effort of the MP, but it did not act as an incentive to the mission's film production. Italy held a unique position in the MP film campaign. The fact that the Italian information office was able to build on established structures and networks, and its good fortune in having a very ambitious and enterprising information staff, can at least partly explain why it became such a prolific producer. What distinguishes the country missions analysed here from others is that they all, with the exception of Turkey, had access to a very generous information budget. There was a direct correlation between the size of Marshall Aid allocation (and thus the budget for informational purposes) and a country's strategic importance to the US government. This also explains why countries at the northern or southwestern periphery produced few or no MP films. The Cold War and the superpowers' fight for spheres of influence thus also shaped the production of MP films, as well as the films themselves, as the following chapter illustrates.

The Cold War as Text and Context

Jessica Gienow-Hecht reminds us that the Cold War did not produce the social conflicts and controversies over economic modernization that characterized the early Cold War in Western Europe, but rather gave shape to these discourses.[1] The Cold War represented the setting and impetus for the MP, and consequently influenced the form, content and function of the MP films. In the following I want to examine how the political and economic developments during this pivotal period, and especially the outbreak of the Korean War and the American responses to it, framed the film policies and propaganda strategies of the ECA.

The Cold War and the MP

Secretary of State George C. Marshall's offer of 'friendly aid in the drafting of a European program',[2] which later became known as the Marshall Plan, was preceded by two major events: the announcement of the Truman Doctrine in March 1947 and the Moscow Conference of the four Allies, which ended on 24 April 1947. On 12 March 1947 US president Harry Truman convinced the US Congress to grant economic and military aid to Greece and Turkey, warning of the threat of communist expansion. Britain had informed the US government earlier that, due to its own dire economic situation, it could no longer afford to support the monarchical Greek government, which was locked in a violent conflict with the left-wing opposition. In his speech, Truman set out his proposal for a new interventionist policy that promised assistance to all democratic countries threatened by totalitarian forces. The second major event was the Moscow Conference, at which the foreign ministers of the four Allies met to discuss the economic rebuilding of Germany and the question of reparations. The conference gave expression to the rapidly deteriorating relations between the Soviet Union and the Western powers.[3] After weeks of discussion, George

Marshall returned to the United States without having reached an agreement on the future of Germany. The US government interpreted the 'unwillingness of the Soviet authorities' to revive the German economy as a deliberate attempt to destabilize Europe, which firmed up its resolve to act.[4]

Marshall's speech at Harvard on 5 June 1947 was a demonstration of support, but also one of strength. The fact that the Truman Doctrine and the MP were launched so closely together illustrates that America's willingness to respond to European pleas for economic help grew proportionally with increasing tensions between the United States and the Soviet Union. However, the US government did not just offer economic aid to win alliances against the communist enemy. US foreign policy was also shaped by the liberal conviction that the multilateral trade system needed to be revived to produce security. Economic assistance provided the means to restructure Europe economically and politically, with the aim of strengthening the liberal economic system and the position and security of the United States.

In the very early period of the Cold War it was primarily the governments of Greece, Italy and France that economically benefited from America's growing concerns about the communists. In Greece, it was the ongoing civil war that fuelled Western fears of communist expansion, as the Greek government's opponent, the communist-led Democratic Army, was supplied by communist Yugoslavia and Bulgaria. The $300 million that US Congress granted to the right-wing Greek government in March 1947 to support its fight against the communists would rise to 2 billion by 1953.[5] Strikes and (at times violent) mass demonstrations plagued France and Italy throughout 1946 and 1947. The French and Italian governments seemed incapable of remedying the causes of social unrest: the shortage of food and housing, high unemployment and inflation. They accused the communist parties, who played a leading role in the protests, of exploiting social and political instabilities; also many US policymakers saw in the European communist parties simple Soviet stooges, who were ready to instigate a revolution on Stalin's word.[6] To strengthen the anti-communist, centrist governments that had established themselves in Italy and France in May 1947 after ousting their communist partners, the United States provided direct financial aid and loans as well as covert funding through the American Federation of Labor and the CIA to ease the economic strain.[7]

The Truman Administration believed in the power of economic means to achieve security. It considered a strong economy as an effective remedy against the spread of communism, since unemployment and destitution were believed to be the breeding ground for authoritarian ideologies. Economic aid provided the lever to encourage European governments to undertake economic and political reforms to stimulate lasting economic growth and free trade. Moreover, it also served as an instrument for forging strategic alliances with anti-communist forces that would strengthen the position of the United States and the Western capitalist world.

The 'birth' of the MP coincided with the earliest escalations of the Cold War. Marshall's announcement followed in the footsteps of the Truman Doctrine and the failure of the Moscow Conference. Just as the first Marshall Aid deliveries began to reach Europe, the world witnessed the first major crisis between the Western and Soviet powers. On 24 June 1948, the Soviets, who were occupying Eastern Germany, blocked all routes that connected West Berlin to the western occupation zones. With the blockade, the Soviets were protesting the currency reform, which had entered into force in the three Western zones on 20 June 1948. The Soviet military governor, whom the Western Allies had officially informed about their decision two days earlier, denounced it as a violation of the Potsdam agreement and interpreted it as move to seal the division of Germany. The Western Allies were well aware that the introduction of a new currency in the Western zones would essentially split German into two separate countries.[8] By replacing the virtually valueless old Reichsmark with a new currency in which people trusted, the Western Allies succeeded in boosting production and eliminating the black market. Together with the currency reform, the provisional government of the German bizone also lifted the rationing and price controls on most goods and thereby reinstated the free market.[9] The Soviets reacted strongly to this move, cutting off the West Berliners from all supplies from Western Germany. Yet the Soviets' show of strength, intended to pressure the Western Allies to revoke the reform, met a resolute response: only two days after the Berlin blockade began, the Americans and British mounted an air lift on a massive scale, supplying the citizens of West Berlin with the essential goods for the next eleven months. Stalin lifted the blockade in May 1949 – a political and moral victory for the Western Allies. The ERP thus began amid the first major showdown between the United States and the Soviet Union. It was also prematurely ended by another confrontation – the Korean War.

The outbreak of the Korean War in June 1950 escalated the conflict between the two superpowers over spheres of influence and sparked a massive arms build-up on both sides. The shift of US foreign policy from economic reconstruction to defence was, however, already underway before North Korea invaded South

Korea. The detonation of the Soviet Union's first atomic bomb on 29 August 1949 and the victory of the communist revolutionaries in China in October 1949 had given America cause for concern over the growing power of the communists. The State Department's Policy Planning Staff warned President Truman on 7 April 1950 that the Soviet leadership was demonstrating efforts 'directed toward the domination of the Eurasian land mass', and was planning to destroy 'the integrity and vitality' of the United States. Its secret report advocated a more aggressive containment policy. The US government should, it suggested, expand the conventional and nuclear arms arsenal in the United States and Europe and prioritize military over economic assistance in order to deter the Soviets from launching an attack.[10]

Not everybody agreed with this course of action. Prominent critics, such as the new Secretary of State Dean Acheson and the head of the ECA Paul Hoffman, continued to advocate political and economic measures. They held the opinion that America's security was best protected by strengthening the European economy, by fostering European integration and by closer transatlantic relations. Their voices were soon silenced when in June 1950 North Korean forces, backed by the Soviet Union and communist China, invaded South Korea, whose government relied on US support. The invasion of South Korea triggered the policy shift which parts of the Truman Administration had been deliberating for some time. The communist attack confirmed American and European fears of a mighty communist bloc out to destroy the 'free' Western world. Many felt that a Soviet attack on European soil was the logical next step of communist expansion. The Truman administration responded to the threat with a massive increase in defence spending and expansion of the military. During the Korean War, military spending almost tripled, from 5 per cent of GNP in 1950 to more than 14 per cent in 1953.[11] The US government also encouraged Western Europe to build up and modernize its military defences. For this purpose, US Congress expanded the Mutual Defence Assistance Programme in October 1950 and allocated another $4 billion to its allies.[12] The outbreak of the Korean War also provided the impetus that turned the transatlantic alliance of NATO, which existed only on paper, into an actual defence force. The United States expanded its military presence in Europe – by 1953 there would be 244,000 US military personnel stationed in Western Europe – and appointed General Dwight D. Eisenhower, the Europeans' favoured candidate, as the supreme commander of the new NATO forces in December 1950.[13] This was an important signal: NATO was now an effective defensive alliance, and united Europeans and North Americans against the Soviet Union.

The impact of the Korean War on the ERP

The military build-up and the massive increase in defence spending threatened the continuation of the ERP. Hoffman and his allies were able to convince US Congress to continue providing economic assistance to the European governments in order to help them pay for the costs of the military build-up and to secure a certain standard of living to ensure social peace.[14] The leadership of the ECA argued that this support was essential because the financial strain of rearmament would weaken the fragile European economies, destabilize societies and strengthen the proponents of neutralism in Europe. Even so, despite the continuation of the ERP, many European governments struggled with the increase in military spending, which represented a huge burden on their budget and dollar reserves.[15] They delayed implementing economic reforms and often resorted to social spending cuts, which added to the growing dissatisfaction of the European public over sharply rising commodity prices, inflation and unemployment. The MP, which promised economic growth and jobs, higher living standards and peace, was losing credibility.

The passing of the Mutual Security Act by US Congress fifteen months after the outbreak of the Korean War brought about decisive changes for the MP and its information campaign. ECA officials warned that this shift of emphasis from economic to military security would threaten what the MP had achieved so far and thus weaken Western Europe's defence against communism. Truman sought to placate his critics. When signing the bill on 10 October 1951 he promised that the new Mutual Security Programme would continue to further the MP's aim 'to restore the productive power of the war-shattered countries', as well as improve the welfare of the people by investing in health and education.[16]

The new Mutual Security Programme brought together under one umbrella the various overseas assistance programmes: the ERP, the Mutual Defence Assistance programme of 1949 and the 'Point Four'-programme that provided technical assistance for developing countries. The Mutual Security Programme allocated $7.48 billion as 'military, economic, and technical assistance to friendly countries to strengthen mutual security and individual and collective defences of the free world'.[17] However, only slightly more than 1 billion was labelled as economic assistance, allocated according to the provisions of the Economic Cooperation Act of 1948. The main part – more than 5 billion dollars – was earmarked for military assistance and reserved for the European NATO members.[18] The rest was distributed among America's Asian allies. The name change, from European Recovery to Mutual Security, was programmatic. The Mutual Security Act downgraded the ERP to a complementary role in support of rearmament.

The act also abolished the ECA. Its responsibilities and powers were transferred to the newly created Mutual Security Agency (MSA), which started operating on 1 January 1952. The new agency was tasked with developing programmes 'designed to sustain and increase military effort'.[19] It also assumed many of the ECA's original duties, including the promotion of free enterprise, competition and productivity, as well as the strengthening of non-communist labour unions. Yet the MSA, with the former European Representative of ECA Averell Harriman as its director, never achieved the powerful status of its predecessor. Since it was not given charge over the whole budget of the programme, but only administered the already reduced economic assistance budget, its influence over European governments (and other US agencies) was weakened.[20] Moreover, the nature of the ERP changed. Whereas previously it had been a programme that was, at least ostensibly, designed to revive European economies, it was now put into the service of building up defence.

These changes also affected the MP information programme. While most information personnel transferred from the ECA to the new MSA, which continued the campaign, the programme's future was uncertain. Immediately after the passing of the Mutual Security Act in October 1951, the film unit had to start cancelling planned film projects due to budget cuts.[21] Some country missions, now operating under the MSA, discontinued producing MP films altogether.[22] From summer 1952, the US government gradually consolidated its overseas information programmes. Though nominally still working under the title and leadership of the MSA, the information offices at the MSA country missions were integrated into the US Information Service (USIS). In August 1953, both agencies were abolished, and replaced with the newly established US Information Agency (USIA).[23]

The merger with USIS, the ECA's former competitor in the field of information, was very unpopular with the ECA/MSA information staff. It resulted in a larger workload as a consequence of staff reductions and budget cuts. New administrative procedures and the stricter regulations of the State Department curbed the freedom the ECA information officers had previously enjoyed, and complicated the hiring of filmmakers.[24] The staff's frustration over the long-winded bureaucratic procedures, in some cases disagreement with the new focus on defence, and uncertainty about the agency's future, affected both the morale of the information staff and the production of MP films. A growing number of information officers jumped ship.[25] The MP information campaign was thus just as much affected by the organizational restructurings as by the shift in US foreign policy.

Adapting to the policy change: MP films and the Cold War

But how did the escalation of the Cold War affect the ECA's film policies? How did the US government's move to make military security a priority influence the content and form of the MP films?

At an information officers' conference in Paris in early December 1950, less than six months after the outbreak of the Korean War, the head of the Information Division's Special Media Section, Eugene Rachlis, used the term 'in-between period' to describe the context in which the ECA Information Division was operating. He informed his colleagues that 'nothing has yet firmed up' with regard to policy, but that the political situation in the East and in Europe pointed to a redirection of information policy. Rachlis predicted that in the near future 'it is likely that ECA information will stress military security', and that anti-communism 'will be even more stressed than it has been' – although this was not very much at the time.[26] Rachlis's address suggests that as 1950 turned to 1951, promoting defence or rearmament was not yet a priority for the ECA. No explicit guidelines were formulated on how to promote these issues nor how much emphasis they should be given.

Stuart Schulberg, head of the film unit, explained at the same conference that he saw no need to alter the film unit's strategies. Schulberg reasoned that the MP films should continue to talk 'in terms of things European, Western, or free and democratic' in order to increase their impact with European audiences. Directed at the critics who felt that the MP did not do enough to curb communist influence, he argued that a movie stressing a free and democratic spirit was 'more effective than an anti-Communist film per se'.[27]

Nevertheless, in spite of the fact that by the end of 1950 no decision had been taken to adapt the film policy to the US government's prioritization of defence, a change was taking place. New themes and new slogans started to emerge, and some MP films shifted to a more aggressive rhetoric. The change occurred only gradually: first, because film production was a lengthy process, and second, because the future, and future direction, of the ERP remained undecided for some time. Not before early summer 1951 did the information officers learn that the ECA would be replaced by a new agency by the end of the year. And so, although the economy remained a priority in the information campaign of the ECA and its successor, it came under increasing pressure to promote the defence effort and alert the Europeans to the threat of communist aggression.

How MP films 'fought' the cultural Cold War

If we look at the MP films that were completed after the outbreak of the Korean War, we find, first of all, a strong continuity in the MP's main themes of economic reconstruction and modernization. Significant is the strong push for industrial productivity. The US government's aim to build up the European military forces gave urgency to the ERP productivity programme, as the next chapter illustrates: to pay for the additional costs, Europe needed to drastically increase its exports, and thus produce more.

Alongside this continued economic focus, new themes emerged. The most evident change is the increasing frequency of slogans that call for the strengthening and defence of the 'free world'. The narrators now often remind European audiences of the need to unite, or to increase their strength so that they can defend their freedom against the – unnamed – enemy. These references to defence or military security are usually restricted to the aural level. Changing the commentary was, of course, the easiest way to adapt the films to the change in policy. The MP imagery, like before, is preoccupied with economic modernization and reconstruction and seldom displays any references to defence.

Another noticeable change was the emergence of films that promoted the need for rearmament. Even though their number is relatively small, the fact that they were produced at all is significant. The question that concerns us here is how these MP films responded to and intervened in the Cold War. How did the films convince the Europeans of the need to build up their military? Which discursive and visual strategies did the films employ to support the US defence effort?

Promoting the need for defence

The Cold-War-induced policy shift from economic assistance to rearmament presented the information personnel with new challenges. Promoting defence was not an easy task, since there existed considerable opposition to rearmament in Europe. The military build-up strained the budgets of European governments and resulted in a drastic increase in commodity prices and inflation, along with shortages of raw materials and cuts in social spending.[28] These developments reflected badly on the MP and fuelled anti-American sentiments. Public discontent was growing, and erupted in demonstrations and strikes in France, Italy and Austria. This in turn gave rise to concerns over social instability and growing support for communist parties.[29] A survey conducted in 1952 showed that Europeans were strongly sceptical of US military policies and concerned about the rearmament of Germany.[30] Many Europeans feared that the build-up of NATO and the rearmament programme were preludes to another war. In the Netherlands, it was particularly housewives and the 18–25 age group that were opposed to the military build-up.[31] In West Germany, a growing peace movement and increasing numbers of people with 'strong neutralist tendencies' opposed Germany's planned integration into a European defence system.[32] And the Austrians, who suffered from a pronounced 'fear of war', were deeply unconvinced by US foreign policy, despite their 'widespread distrust of the Russians and Austrian communists alike', as one report noted.[33]

Out of fear of producing negative reactions, and thus undermining the MP's whole propaganda effort, the film unit largely evaded the issue of defence. Among the few films that did address the issue are *The Smiths and the Robinsons* (1952), *The Hour of Choice* (1951) and the fourth episode of the six-part series *The Changing Face of Europe* (1951), titled *Men and Machines*. The theme of *Men and Machines*, incidentally the only MP film directed by a woman (Diane Pine), is industrial productivity. It illustrates the advantages of modern mass production, while reassuring the audience that traditional European craftsmanship will remain important. The documentary ends with a minute-long scene underscored by a military march, showing a tank conducting a set of moves on a stretch of land. This final scene appears somewhat disconnected from the rest of the film, as the thematic jump from modern production methods to the military is so sudden. The narrator seeks to establish a link between the film's main theme and the call for rearmament, arguing that Europe must direct a portion of her newly gained prosperity to the purpose of defence to ensure 'a good life for all her people'. The final scene, however, raises doubts whether the film really managed to rally support for the defence effort or alleviate the Europeans' fear of war: it concludes ambiguously, with a cut from the tank to a young boy on a tractor (see figure 3.1). The boy smiles into the camera before driving into a field, leaving the viewer wondering if he will soon be driving a tank, or will remain a farmer.

Figure 3.1 *Men and Machines* in support of the defence effort.

Men and Machines implies that Europeans need to make material sacrifices to safeguard Europe's future. More directly spelt out is the request in the British *The Smiths and the Robinsons* (1952). The film, which 'tells in terms of real people the story of Great Britain's contribution toward mutual peace and security', was aimed primarily at a British audience, but was also considered for Europe-wide distribution.[34] Produced and written by Philip Mackie, who worked for the Film Division of the British Ministry of Information, it seeks to explain and win consent for the British government's decision to continue the austerity programme.[35] The new Conservative government, which had won the election in October 1951 at least in part due to middle-class dissatisfaction with Labour's austerity policies,[36] was actually compelled to continue some of Labour's public-spending and rationing programmes. The new British government sought to pay for the costs of the military build-up by restricting consumption and increasing exports. This provoked considerable frustration, especially among these same middle classes who were longing for an end to rationing and price controls. In the election, the Conservative Party had also promised to re-establish the Home Guard to defend Britain against invasion or communist insurrection. However, once in power, it struggled to recruit a substantial number of volunteers, and so the obvious motivation behind the making of *The Smiths and the Robinsons* was to encourage the British to join the Home Guard.[37]

The Smiths and the Robinsons is a fictional film, but it is interspersed with archival footage to lend it a documentary feel. It tells the story of two English middle-aged, middle-class couples living next to each other in semi-detached houses in London. They are frustrated about rationing, and each regards its neighbours with envy for the privileges they enjoy. By comparing the two couples and revealing their frustrations, the narrative highlights their similarities. At the same time, it demonstrates ideal behaviour: although they grumble, the couples accept the material sacrifices as reasonable. In the end, they even join the Home Guard to show their commitment to the country. Mr. Smith and Mr. Robinson dig up their old uniforms and, with a mixture of baffled amusement and pride, train to cope with the emergency of an attack (see figure 3.2).

The two main characters were played by the popular actors Richard Massingham and Russell Walters, who had starred in many humorous government-sponsored information shorts on health or traffic-safety issues during and after the war.[38] Massingham and Walters also played the leads in the thematically very similar *What a Life!* (1948), produced by the British government, which encouraged the British public to look at the bright side of the austerity programme.[39] But *What a Life!* approached the issue in a much more ironic manner than *The Smiths and the Robinsons*.[40] While in *What a Life!* the British post-war gloom drives the two protagonists into attempting a (failed) suicide, Mr. Smith and Mr. Robinson behave in a much more balanced way. The Smiths and the Robinsons are presented as the British nation incarnate – critically minded, but never unreasonable; affable, but never intrusive; used to a certain standard of living, but always prepared to contribute and sacrifice their desires for the greater good.

Figure 3.2 *The Smiths and Robinsons* do their bit to protect Britain from a communist attack.

While celebrating the British commitment to the cause, the film downplays the negative effects of the government's austerity politics, and presents the rationing of goods as an inconvenience rather than real deprivation. The film seeks to evoke the spirit of the Blitz through its opening scene, which depicts a training drill (see figure 3.2). This suggests that the threat of invasion is having a positive effect, as it rekindles the spirit of solidarity that saw the British through the previous war: Robinson offers Smith a ride in his car to the military exercise, for example, and Smith invites the Robinsons to watch television. *The Smiths and the Robinsons* ends on a positive note: it presents a community of values that stands strong against an attack. And by insisting that solidarity, and the resolve to defend the British values espoused in the film, are sufficient bolsters against a threatening enemy, the film de-problematizes the issue of rearmament.

More importantly, and by extension, it makes light of the threat of nuclear war. It does this by inserting a televised address delivered by the British war hero Field Marshall William Slim, who insists that a strong voluntary force would deter the Soviet Union from launching a nuclear attack. Moreover, by drawing parallels to the Second World War and the Nazi bombing campaign, the film excludes possible alternatives to rearmament. Instead, it presents Britain and the Western world as being under immediate danger from an enemy that is not amenable to reason. In this scenario, the British government's decision to withhold material comforts from its population in order to invest in the expansion of its military appears not only reasonable, but also necessary.

Apart from *Men and Machines* and *The Smiths and the Robinsons*, only two other MP films promoting defence were produced. *NATO: Power for Peace* (1952) and *School for Colonels* (1952) promote the creation of NATO and illustrate the training of international staff officers. These films were co-productions with NATO, however, and the records suggest that the MSA contributed 'with nothing more than approval and financing'.[41] The overall strategy of these films was to establish a causal relationship between communism and rearmament. By describing the enemy as unreasonable or irrational, the films present the pooling of forces and a military build-up as the only solution to deterring the communists from attacking the 'free' Western world.

Illustrating the danger of communism

A second category of film that emerged after the outbreak of the Korean War supported the defence effort by highlighting the danger of communism as an ideology. Up to the outbreak of the Korean War, MP films shied away from an open engagement with communism, although the communist system had always served as the invisible point of reference. The film unit's strategy of avoidance was informed by the wish to keep up the pretence of providing apolitical information, but also by the fear that any engagement with communist arguments might give publicity to the communist cause.

It is important to note that the escalation of the Cold War did not reverse the film unit's strategy, but rather eroded it. Slowly a new type of MP film emerged that sought to disparage the communist enemy: *Air of Freedom* (1951) merely scoffs at communism and 'exposes' communist East Berlin as backward by contrasting it with modern West Berlin. Completed in the same year, the films *European Labor Day* and (particularly) *Without Fear* have a much more alarmist tone, presenting the West as under immediate danger of an attack. The anti-communist *Three Cities* (1952), a documentary on three cities situated in close proximity to the Iron Curtain (Berlin, Trieste and the Greek city of Naoussa), was televised in the United States only as part of the *Strength for the Free World* series. *Whitsun Holiday* (1953), which compares how people spend their Pentecost weekend in 'free' Western Europe with those in strictly regulated communist East Berlin, never entered regular distribution.[42]

All these openly anti-communist MP films frame communism as a threat – to peace, to prosperity or to Western liberal values. To counter the widespread European opposition to the US rearmament policy, the films sought to expose the enemy's intent to destroy the 'free' world. Figures of authority speak out, just as in *The Smiths and the Robinsons*, confirming that the threat is real. In *European Labor Day* and *Whitsun Holiday*, the filmmakers went so far as to edit in archival footage produced by the communists to make the danger seem real and pressing. Taken out of context, the images of marching masses on military parades in Moscow and Labour Day rallies in East Berlin conjured up fears of war. And by presenting the communists as forming a rigid, unthinking mass that marches in lock step, the films insinuate that the enemy cannot be reasoned with.

What all MP film narratives have in common is their dichotomist worldview – a view that divides the world into two mutually exclusive parts, in which the liberal-capitalist Western world occupies a superior position as guarantor of freedom, prosperity and peace. Whereas most films show only this 'free' world, *Air of Freedom* (1951) allows a glimpse on the other world. *Air of Freedom*, a co-production of ECA West Germany and the US civil administration of West Germany HICOG, compares the liberal West with the communist East. The compilation documentary is set in the divided city of Berlin, a centre-point of the Cold War and a city of high symbolic significance. Situated amid communist-controlled territory, West Berlin is presented as the showcase of liberal capitalism, and as visible proof of Western superiority. The film's title refers to the Berlin-based US radio station RIAS (Radio in the American Sector) which broadcasted news and music – signifiers of free speech – to Berliners and the people of East Germany.

The film takes the opening of the German Industry Exhibition in West Berlin in October 1950 as its starting point to illustrate the revival of German industry as well as the success of the modern US economy. *Air of Freedom* is the only MP film that directly compares the living standards of the capitalist and communist worlds, remarking with satisfaction that many East Berliners flock to the industry's fair in West Berlin to marvel at the Western products. Indeed, more than half of the 750,000 visitors to the exhibition in the newly erected George Marshall House crossed over from East Berlin.[43] The fair's most popular attraction was an exhibition titled 'America at Home', a demonstration of a modern American suburban family home made of prefabricated elements serving to showcase the high living standards of the American worker. It was overrun by curious visitors.[44]

Air of Freedom presents West Berlin as a modern city that is recovering from the war and has weathered the Soviet blockade, thanks to Marshall Aid and the US/British airlift. The bulging shelves, modern cafes and hip nightclubs of West Berlin exude promises of prosperity and individual freedom – and lure people from the East into the West. The film illustrates the political division of Berlin by juxtaposing scenes of West Berliners busily rebuilding their city with shots of drab East Berlin, including a Soviet tank and a war monument. The breezy operetta tune of *Berliner Luft* (Berlin Air), the unofficial hymn of Berlin, accompanies the hustle and bustle in West Berlin. In contrast, the music takes on a more sombre tone whenever the commentator speaks of East Berlin.

A short scene accentuates this contrast between the industrious, flourishing 'shop window of the West' and dreary, Soviet-controlled East Berlin. It shows a group of men behind a brick wall doing exercises on a high bar in a courtyard. The commentator, who in the previous remark has denounced the Soviet radio station for spreading its 'messages of hate' to West Berlin, locates this scene in East Berlin. He scoffs that 'the men of the Red Army dutifully practice their communist flip-flops', thereby contrasting the productive, capitalist West with the unproductive, communist East. The narrator's sarcastic reference to 'communist flip-flops' mocks Stalin's sudden reversals of policies. The men in the courtyard are presented as mindless puppets that simply re-enact Soviet politics through their gymnastics exercises. The footage gives no indication that these men are really Soviet soldiers (they seem to be in civilian clothes), or even that they are in East Berlin; but the narrator's description turns it into a fact, and assigns negative meaning to the images.

The commentary's taunting tone and sarcastic remarks do not fit in with the film unit's policy of avoiding open confrontation with communism.[45] Can the anti-communist slant be attributed to the influence of HICOG, which co-produced the film? The fact that no information can be found on the film's director, scriptwriter or editor suggests that no filmmaker was involved, but that the documentary was compiled by the information officers themselves. The film had a short lifespan, as the film's topicality soon made it look outmoded. Only one year after release, the film was relegated to the appendix of the MSA Catalogue of Documentary Films, filed in the category of films for which 'the general demand is not such as to justify a listing in this new issue'.[46]

Air of Freedom sought to disparage the communist enemy by comparing the standards of living between the East and the West. *As the Young Ones Sing* (Wie die Jungen Sungen, MSA Austria 1954), one of the last MP films to be released, presents the liberal-capitalist world as culturally and morally superior to the communist world.[47] The title of the film is a reversal of a popular German saying that children follow the example of their parents (Wie die Alten sungen, so zwitschern auch die Jungen). Tressler's film presents the children as role models for the older generation, a narrative strategy that a number of MP films employed. *As the Young Ones Sing* promotes international understanding and cooperation. It mixes professional Austrian actors with staff and pupils of the French international school *Lycée français* in Vienna, which had just moved into a new building. The camera follows the Viennese girl Gerti during her first days at school, illustrating the pains of social exclusion as well as the pleasure of finding new friends. Showing great sensitivity to the way children perceive the world, the film illustrates how Gerti is overwhelmed by the many new faces and the French language, which is alien to her, finding solace only in the companionship of another outsider, an African boy, Boula.[48] Over time, however, she becomes a fully integrated member of the international community.

The film matches the subjective view of the children with an outsider's view by including a side story of two Austrian school inspectors who visit the school. A French teacher guides the visitors through the building and explains the school's humanist principles. The figure of the guide, who points out certain aspects and interprets what the visitors see, fulfils the function of a narrator. One visitor acts as a representative of the audience: he asks questions, reflects on the information and draws the intended conclusions, as the following scene illustrates. At the end of their tour, the group of three stops in front of a large map of the world that is decorated with numerous pins representing the different national origins of the pupils. The teacher's argument that the large number of pins attests to the broad popularity of the school's ideals is met by approving noises from one of the visitors, who studies the map with great interest. The camera takes the perspective of the man's gaze, using an over-the-shoulder shot to direct the attention of the viewer to those parts of the map that he is presumably looking at: Western Europe. This space is densely covered with pins – a manifestation of Western Europe's liberalism. The visitor turns his face towards the teacher without altering his position and concludes: 'Very nice. But a pity that not all nations use this opportunity.' What he means becomes immediately clear as he leaves the frame, thereby revealing an empty space that shows the territory of the Soviet Union (see figure 3.3). The lack of pins designates the communists' disregard for Western liberal values. To ensure that the audience understands the message, the camera, underscored by a musical crescendo, zooms in on the map, leaving the audience to contemplate the meaning of the emptiness of the vast, communist-controlled space in the East and the high density of pins in Western Europe. Thomas Tode interprets this camera movement across the map as an 'invitation to improve relations with the neighbours.'[49] In my view, it is a rather heavy-handed propagandistic gesture that contrasts strangely with the otherwise subtle humorous tone of the film, which makes a persuasive argument for the ideals of internationalism and cooperation. For the film's main message is essentially humanist; it argues that differences in skin colour or language are only superficial. Yet, while the film seeks to demonstrate that linguistic or cultural differences can be bridged easily, it presents ideological differences as insurmountable.

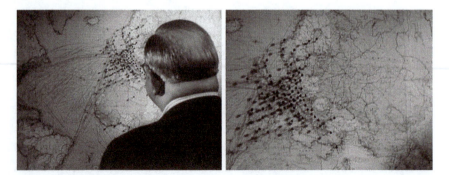

Figure 3.3 Where liberalism dwells … (*As the Young Ones Sing*).

Cold War controversies

The above illustrates how the escalation of the Cold War and the shift in US foreign policy put the ECA film unit under pressure to take a political stand and adopt a more forceful, overt approach. This, however, created considerable unease among the film policy planners. There had never been agreement on how ERP policies should be promoted. Differences of opinion existed between the Information Division and people outside the organization, between the Paris film unit and the local information offices, and between Americans and Europeans. Now, with rising Cold War tensions, disagreements over aesthetic and/or technical issues began to acquire a political meaning. How these disagreements played out in practice is illustrated by the following two examples: a dispute surrounding the British animation *Without Fear* over how to represent the communist enemy and a scandal over the employment of 'communist' filmmakers in Denmark that brought the Danish ECA mission 'embarrassing publicity'.[50]

Visualizing the communist threat in *Without Fear*

The dispute over the animated film *Without Fear* (or *Way for Europe*, as *Without Fear* was originally called) was basically over technical issues, but reflected the film unit's profound unease in engaging openly in political propaganda. The film's purpose was to outline the difference between a unified Europe achieved by totalitarian methods and one created by free association.[51] *Without Fear* is much more serious in tone than the humorous cartoon *The Shoemaker and the Hatter*, which was produced around the same time and was meant to rally support for the European idea by promoting free trade. The original draft envisaged a film that would make Europeans 'Europe-conscious'. It should convince them of the need for economic cooperation to 'protect Western Europe's traditional freedom'.[52] The final film, however, did not meet the sponsors' expectations, since it conjured up a sense of danger that left Europe looking rather exposed.

When Philipp Stapp, the film unit's executive producer, and himself an animator, received the first version of *Without Fear* in November 1951, he was greatly displeased. He felt that 'the visual treatment of the totalitarian sequence overpowered the rest of the film', giving the spectator 'an impression of strength in totalitarian government, which, obviously, we did not wish to convey'.[53] He also criticized the 'crude and jerky' human figures and technical blemishes. The animations were created by the London-based animation firm Larkins

Studio, under the direction of German-born animator Peter Sachs. Stapp had initially wanted to contract the British animation studio Halas and Batchelor, best known for George Orwell's adaption of the anti-communist *Animal Farm* (1954). However, Halas and Batchelor were already occupied with making *The Shoemaker and the Hatter*, and Stapp therefore approached Larkins. London was the centre of animation at the time, and both Sachs and the Hungarian John Halas were Jewish emigrants who had first-hand experience of authoritarian regimes. The film unit trusted them to make convincing arguments against totalitarianism and for Western liberalism.

However, the film unit's cooperation with Larkins Studio was fraught with difficulty, and led to what the Information Division's deputy head described as a 'minor *contretemps* between the Information Division and some filmmakers in London'.[54] Despite the film unit's dissatisfaction with the version Larkins delivered in November 1951, it could not demand changes on grounds of aesthetic differences. It therefore decided to amend the original commentary, and asked Larkins to rerecord and rescore parts of the film.[55] This only led to further complications, and eventually to a full-blown conflict. Stapp accused Larkins Studio of having delayed productions for months through long, tortuous discussions over the script, of not keeping to deadlines and finally of delivering material of inferior technical quality.[56] Larkins rejected these criticisms, arguing that the diversions were caused by the ECA's 'realignment of approach', which resulted in amendments to the script and to the contract which had been concluded in autumn 1950. Larkins also accused the film unit of delaying the production given that Stapp, dissatisfied with the originally approved commentary, had written a new narration and demanded that the film be rescored and rerecorded with a full orchestra in the final stages of production.[57] Stapp defended his position, arguing that changes to the script became necessary to align it 'with policy changes which came about as a result of the Corean [*sic*] war'.[58] The dispute was ended only on the advice of the Office of the General Counsel. The European head of the MSA, Paul Porter, informed Larkins that nothing could be 'gained by either of us through prolonging a controversy about opinion'.[59] Stapp and the new head of the film unit, Nils Nilson, grudgingly agreed terms and paid for the film, despite their dissatisfaction with the final product. What exactly did the film unit object to in the film? And what did they do with the final product they had purchased, but disliked?

What appears on the surface to have been a conflict over aesthetic and technical questions was actually a difference of opinion over how to convey a political message. *Without Fear* frames European integration in terms of defence against communist aggression. The narrative is divided into three parts: the first and last part focus on Europe, and set out the need for European cooperation, and the middle part illustrates the threat of communism. The introductory sequence presents a modern, productive and peaceful Europe, depicted using still images of rural and urban landscapes; these are populated by human silhouettes representing different sectors of society: male builders on scaffoldings, a farmer and his wife cultivating the fields, a girl skipping rope. But the promise of a prosperous Europe is undermined by what the narrator identifies as a problem: the existence of national borders. A map of Europe showing gulfs between the different states, accentuated by animated, red-dotted lines, visualizes these national divisions. Boom gates that criss-cross the screen underline the message that national barriers hinder the free trade of goods, food, work and power. Europe, the off-screen commentary argues, could provide for all if it would only make free use of its wealth and skills. Bright colours and a friendly, yet factual voice-over set the tone for this first part.

This contrasts sharply with the next sequence, which opens dramatically to sounds of marching drums and blurred, blue and red shapes fading in from the black background. Consistent with the dark undertone of the whole sequence, the commentary has a menacing tone. It warns of the dangers Europe faces; 'a new voice' is heard that 'threatens to mould Europe in its own pattern', which the narrator identifies as the voice 'of the all-powerful totalitarian state'. A musical crescendo introduces the visuals, which give shape to this 'voice'. A spreading net of red veins emerges from the dark and threads quickly towards the top of the screen to end in what appears to be an outstretched arm, the index finger of its hand pointing towards the sky. Zooming out, the camera reveals the outline of an enormous black silhouette against a glowing red background – the personification of totalitarianism. The narrator warns that the communist promises of unity and equality merely disguise the aggressive communist scheme to gain power: the communists smash national barriers and reorganize farms by force. The film displays the inhumanity of totalitarianism in a series of visually similar scenes that illustrate how it suppresses the freedom of individuals. Its pointing finger signifies the dogma that allows no dissent. The shape is echoed in the sharp bayonets of faceless armed men, the accusing fingers of informers and the gun barrels of the guards who arrest the victims (see figure 3.4).

To alert the spectator to the dangers of totalitarian methods, the animators deployed a colour scheme that consists largely of black and red, with red illustrating communist aggression and black symbolizing the joyless life under totalitarianism. The metaphor of animated red veins that quickly spread across

Figure 3.4 Visualizations of the communist danger in *Without Fear*.

the landscape is used several times to vividly capture the subversive character of communism. The veins permeate barriers, but also crawl across idyllic landscapes and spread under villages and farms until they come to a halt in a glowing red factory. The visual message is unambiguous: communism breeds in the factories, not in the countryside.

The third and concluding part, clearly set off from the middle part, soothes the emotions with a tender flute melody and a landscape in pastel blues and greens. Suddenly mild in tone, the commentator eulogizes the freedoms 'every man' enjoys in the West, including the freedom to voice political dissent. The sequence also showcases Europe's diversity as characteristic of Western liberalism: by panning over large tableaus that show groups of individuals of different ages, classes and genders (but not races) in different social settings and activities, the camera constructs an idyll of social harmony.

Only twice does the commentator come back to the issue of communism: in one instance, he points to it as an internal threat, the result of poverty and unemployment. This threat, the narrator claims, can be countered by a strong economy, achieved through free trade and cooperation. In another instance, the film warns of the external danger of communism through a blunt visual metaphor: a map of Europe, drenched in golden sunshine, is overrun by a dark, red-coloured wave from the East that turns into shapes of marching soldiers. The film concludes with silhouettes of muscular men joining hands in front of a yellow-blue sky, to re-emphasize that Europeans must unite to withstand a communist attack. This final scene shows that Europeans defend their freedom by peaceful means, hands held in unison – as opposed to the communists, who either work subversively or attack Europe with military might. Yet, perhaps, simply joining hands might not be enough to fight off the 'red hordes' that attack Europe? By summoning the spectre of a communist attack, the film thus implicitly legitimizes the idea that Europeans must make efforts to build up their military defences.

Unlike other MP films, which present the European project as a genuine liberal Western idea, *Without Fear* actually takes up the communist calls for unification in order to expose communist visions of European unity as a sham. Its use of intense colour contrasts, ominous visual metaphors, a dramatic musical score and a forceful, at times cynical, commentary lend *Without Fear* a threatening tone that makes no claim to objectivity. *Without Fear* is in many ways an atypical MP film. Not only is its aggressive tone strangely at odds with the film unit's otherwise more subtle propaganda strategies; its argument for European unity as a deterrent against communist aggression is also weakened by the lurid and powerful description of the communist enemy, which threatens to overbalance the message.

Considering the film unit's dissatisfaction with the film, it is surprising that it entered distribution at all, even though it did so only with considerably delay. In May 1952, the film unit cancelled the foreign language versions for which Larkins had initially been contracted, citing the 'unusually unpleasant nature' of discussions with Larkins as a reason.[60] By the beginning of 1953, *Without Fear* had still not been distributed.[61] The country missions were sceptical; the Icelandic mission refused to dub or show the film in Iceland, presumably because it did not want to upset the delicate relations between the country's right and left-wing camp.[62] The information office in West Germany wanted to commission an audience study before making a decision. The policymakers in West Germany were concerned that the film's animated images were too sophisticated or 'too frivolous' for a general audience. They also worried that for the West Germans, who were largely anti-communist and in favour of European integration anyway, the film might be to 'too obvious and repetitious'.[63] West Germany's US civil administration HICOG thus commissioned an extensive audience study consisting of audience observation, questionnaires and interviews in a German town in Nord-Rhine Westphalia in 1953. The film was screened to a 400-strong cinema audience after the main feature, *Don Camillo and Peppone*, a hugely popular Italian comedy about a dispute between a feisty Catholic priest and a hot-tempered communist mayor. The pairing with the comedy certainly helped to give *Without Fear* a favourable reception. The researchers were pleased to report that that the animation film was 'not too subtle or difficult for the average movie goer', and that the majority had understood that it promoted a united Europe. Most spectators answered in the affirmative when asked whether films like *Without Fear* were important to alert the people about the communist menace. Still, about one-fifth did not like the abstract imagery and loud colours, and 16 per cent of the moviegoers found the film too propagandistic, with one commenting: 'Such propaganda measures make people sore.'[64] The really interesting aspect of this study was not so much the audience response (or its interpretation by the sponsor), but the fact that the study was commissioned. It demonstrates that the information officers were profoundly uneasy about conducting overtly political propaganda.

'Communists and Marshallfilms'[65] – Cold War controversy in Denmark

Profound unease also led to another incident, this time one in which the Danish press raised the question whether the ECA was actually colluding with communists. While the information offices were used to attacks from the communist press, they were surprised to find themselves suddenly lumped in the enemy's camp. The controversy in Denmark illustrates how the ECA information officers did not just engage in the cultural Cold War discourse, but sometimes found themselves at the receiving end.

In summer 1950, the ECA country mission in Denmark was caught up in a flurry of domestic Cold War hysteria. It started when an editorial in a Danish newspaper suggested that the ECA was hiring communist filmmakers. The news produced a minor controversy, no more than a storm in a teacup, but which, according to the local information officer, 'fell on us like a ton of bricks'.[66] To describe the skirmish surrounding the production of MP films as a 'small Danish off-shoot of McCarthyism', as one commentator has put it, is certainly an exaggeration, but the episode shows how the Cold War in this instance gave shape to a domestic skirmish that interfered with the production of MP films.[67]

The ECA cooperated closely with the Social Democratic government to strengthen the weak Danish economy by boosting productivity – initially with little success. Danish agriculture, one of the most important fields of exports, suffered especially badly from the post-war slump, currency devaluation and trade restrictions.[68] To support the Danish government in its efforts to implement reforms, the film unit agreed to make six to twelve films that promoted Danish economic progress. In January 1950, a contract to that purpose was concluded between the ECA and the Danish Government Film Committee, MFU (*Ministeriernes Filmudvalg*).[69] The government had set up the MFU in 1941 to produce documentary shorts promoting governmental labour programmes intended to ease unemployment; it remained an important governmental sponsor of informational films after the war.[70] The contract assigned the MFU the role of producer with the right to select the film teams, while the ECA financed the films and retained the right of final approval. After further deliberation, it was decided to install a three-man supervisory team to ensure that the initial six films, shot at a cost of 70,000 Danish kroner each, conformed to the policies of the Danish government and the ECA.[71] The supervisory team consisted of one representative each of the ECA, the MFU and the *Statens Filmcentral*, the film department of the Danish Education Ministry.[72] The Statens Filmcentral was represented by its director, the film critic Ebbe Neergaard, who became the main supervisor of the film projects. Neergaard, though never a member of the communist party, was known to be sympathetic to the communist cause.[73]

Production began in February 1950, but was from the beginning impacted by 'internal Danish film quarrels' as well as rapidly growing tensions between the ECA and the Social Democratic government over the implementation of ERP policies.[74] The MFU had selected noted Danish filmmakers for the MP films. Among them were Jørgen Roos, who directed the MP documentary *The Streamlined Pig*, which promoted scientific breeding methods, and the acclaimed Danish documentarist Theodor Christensen, who scripted and directed the MP film *All My Ships*, on the Danish shipbuilding industry. Christensen, who had been a communist in the 1930s but had left the party in 1937,[75] was a key figure in Danish documentary film and a passionate defender of the documentarist's right to complete freedom of expression.[76] The MFU pondered in a meeting whether it could be seen as problematic that most of the filmmakers had 'communist sympathies'. However, the fact that the film production was supervised by a three-man team, and that the head of the ECA film section, Lothar Wolff, had approved all scripts, was deemed sufficient to vouch for the films' political neutrality.[77] This assumption proved to be wrong.

In July 1950, the editor of the Danish newspaper *Sorø Amtstidende*, Hans Bagge, suggested in two editorials that communist filmmakers (such as Christensen) had undermined the documentary sector, and were now also taking over MP film production. Bagge's protest against 'Communists and Marshall films', as one of his headlines ran, was the offshoot of a dispute which had erupted a few weeks earlier, following an article by Theodor Christensen over the leadership of the Danish educational film organization *Dansk Kulturfilm*.[78] A couple of newspapers took up the story, either supporting Bagge's accusation or, in the case of the communist *Land og Folk*, stepping into the breach in defence of the filmmakers. The controversy over the MP films never went beyond a few spats. It was summer, and presumably the journalists were eager to fill the silly season with some hot news.

Nevertheless, the fact that communists and MP films were named in one breath caused considerable unease in the Danish ECA mission, whose staff had learnt of the political sympathies of the filmmakers and of the project's supervisor, Neergaard, after running a security check. It had decided to go through with the film production anyway 'to avoid embarrassing the Danish Government, as well as ourselves'. Now it found itself confronted with the allegation that the ECA had contracted Danish filmmakers who were 'distinct opponents of the Marshall aid and the ideology behind it'.[79] The ECA responded immediately and withdrew its representative from the supervisory team. It also revoked the financing agreement, insisting that the Danish government pay half of the production costs for the MP films.[80] The Danish education ministry grudgingly agreed to cover the rest of the costs, to avoid diplomatic tensions. However, it funded the films from the counterpart funds, which officially only the ECA was allowed to do; this decision would create another row further down the line.[81]

Before the ECA released the Danish MP films, it scrutinized them carefully for any element that might be interpreted as politically unsound. Christensen's film *All My Ships*, for example, showed a worker reading a newspaper in his garden (see figure 3.5). The headline on the newspaper's first page ran 'Americans advance in Korea'. The ECA representative and members of the supervisory team worried that this could be interpreted as covert communist propaganda, denouncing American imperialism, and demanded that the shot was cut. Christensen resisted, and so it was later mechanically altered so that the headline was no longer readable.[82]

Figure 3.5 The censored newspaper scene in *All My Ships* that sparked American concerns of communist propaganda.

Eventually, on 31 May 1951, *All My Ships* premiered in Denmark, together with *Caroline, the Cow*, which promoted modern dairy production, and a documentary on the Danish power station Kyndbyværket.[83] It met with a mixed critical response. This time, the Danish press made no mention of the political background of the filmmakers. *The Streamlined Pig* was completed later that same year and entered distribution abroad. It only premiered in Denmark in September 1952, to glowing reviews, which may have appeased the ECA information officers. The last two films, however, were never completed. Stuart Schulberg halted production, ostensibly on grounds of artistic quality. In a letter to the Danish information officer he objected to further productions in Denmark as long as 'Neergaard & Co', whom he described as 'undesirable characters', had such influence on the Danish film industry.[84]

The example illustrates how the tense atmosphere of the Cold War triggered a spell of Cold War hysteria. Even though these films did not address communism in any way, they were suspected to be subversive propaganda – for the communist cause. At its core, it was a conflict over influence and power in the Danish film industry. The Cold War did not create the dispute, but gave it an ideological dimension that presented the MP and the ECA in a negative light – something the film unit wanted to avoid at all costs.

The fear of negative reactions was probably the main reason why the ECA/MSA information offices did not promote defence or anti-communism more forcefully. One of the first information policy papers that the new MSA Information Division in Washington sent to its offices in Europe in January 1952 tackled the question of how to promote defence under the new Mutual Security programme. Andrew Berding, previously chief of the Italian information office and now head of the Washington Information Division, wrote the paper. Berding conceded that the delivery of armaments had not aroused the same enthusiasm as Marshall Aid deliveries. Since the 'Europeans only become depressed by military preparations', he believed it was 'not wise to exploit a "weapons" program', especially as prices and unemployment were rising due to the costs of rearmament. Berding's statement is significant, as it explicitly advised the information officers against addressing the issues of rearmament or the military. Instead, he suggested approaching the topic indirectly. One possibility was to highlight the need for defence by demonstrating 'the true nature of the Russian threat'; another was to present an increase in productivity as an essential means to build strength and sustain European living standards; a third approach was to underline the importance of economic integration. Berding's policy guidelines described productivity as being the best 'handle' in France, Italy, Austria and West Germany. Regarding Belgium, where labour unions were strongly opposed to productivity reforms, he deemed it more promising to convince the people that they were in real danger 'of being over-run and enslaved', and so needed to invest heavily in defence. In general, however, he recommended focusing on productivity, since it was a positive, rewarding subject that held the 'promise of a better life for all'.[85]

US Policy into Film: Productivity

The Marshall Plan, as the previous chapter illustrated, was not just a means to revive the European economy to strengthen the global liberal market order, and, along with it, bolster the economic vigour of the United States. It was also a political project, designed to secure influence and strategic alliances with Western Europe to curb the power of the ideological enemy. Productivity, one of the MP's key policies, served both aims.

In autumn 1949, the ECA intensified its efforts to increase the productivity of Europe's economies. The push for productivity was a result of Europe's continuing high trade deficit with the dollar area. Although one year into the MP many Western European economies were recovering strongly, ECA economists were alarmed about Europe's rapidly growing trade imbalance. Such a development threatened the achievement of the ERP's goal to 'create stable international economic relationships' and to make European economies 'independent of extraordinary outside assistance'.[1] Europe needed to either drastically reduce its dollar imports or increase its output and exports to balance its payment deficit.

The outbreak of the Korean War, which provoked a massive rearmament boom in the United States and the MP countries, gave further impetus to the ECA's policy of stimulating productivity. The ECA policymakers feared that the effects of the arms build-up could derail the economic progress achieved so far and produce social instability, thereby actually weakening the defence effort.[2] Under pressure to strengthen their military defences, most European governments delayed necessary economic reforms and cut social budgets, investing instead in building up their military security. The growing demand for raw materials, which were needed for rearmament, resulted in a drastic hike in prices, which further strained the European budgets and dollar reserves.[3] As a result, inflation grew rapidly and costs of living soared while wages remained on the same level, fuelling popular discontent.[4] While the West German economy, overall, profited from the increased demand for steel and machinery, other European countries suffered.[5] In the Netherlands, for example, exports had doubled from 1949 to

1950 to about $100 million. This increase was, however, not sufficient to close the country's trade imbalance with the dollar area, nor was it enough to finance the additional costs for defence. Since inflation and the rising prices of essential raw materials made imports more expensive, the ECA economists believed that the Netherlands needed to increase its exports by $300 million to $400 million in 1951 to enable it to purchase the same volume of imports it had procured in 1950. The ECA urged the Netherlands and other European countries to boost their output and exports by making more effective use of their available materials and manpower and by liberalizing intra-European trade.[6] Productivity was thus awarded the highest priority.

But what did productivity mean? And what was the aim of the ERP productivity drive? The four-minute French animation film *Productivité* (Productivity) offers the answers.[7] The animated short was directed by Jacques Asseo and produced by André Sarrut for the French ECA country mission in 1951.[8] Asseo had already directed the widely distributed *Story of a Rescue* (1949), which explained the birth of the MP. Like *Story of a Rescue*, *Productivité* uses a very simple format to describe the principles of productivity. The film opens with the off-screen narrator asking: 'Qu'est-ce que la productivité?' The following sequences, structured by a dialogue between two voices, set out to provide the answer. One voice represents the average man confused about productivity, the other the knowledgeable expert who explains how productivity works and how it benefits all. The film, though also distributed in other European countries, was primarily made to popularize productivity in France, where opposition against – perceived or real – American influence was particularly strong, as we have seen.[9] One of the most vocal critics of productivity was the communist-controlled French confederation of trade unions, the *Confédération générale du travail* (CGT). The ECA feared its influence on the French workers, whose cooperation was crucial to make the productivity programme a success.

The CGT denounced productivity as tool to exploit the workers.[10] The film *Productivité* takes up this allegation in an animated scene that depicts an industrial worker whose back is continuously pierced by bright lightning bolts that force him to work faster until he breaks down (see figure 4.1). The next scene addresses the popular criticism that productivity might achieve a higher quantity of output, but at the cost of quality. It shows an evidently happy cyclist selecting a shiny bike from a vast array of identical new bikes, jumping on his bike and riding off, only to crash a few metres further on as his front wheel buckles. After highlighting the absurdity of each allegation, each scene concludes with two white brushstrokes that wipe out the image on the screen, and so from the minds of the spectator.

Figure 4.1 *Productivité* illustrates the benefits of productivity.

Having rebutted the accusations, the expert's voice goes on to explain the principles of productivity by comparing two neighbouring countries. The people in the two countries may appear very similar, but they work very differently, as the animation now illustrates: in one country, five workers produce five bicycles in eight hours in a dark workshop, visibly straining themselves. In the other country, the same number of workers, this time standing smiling at a conveyor belt in a bright, modern factory, produce five bikes in half the time. The illustrations that accompany these scenes are largely self-explanatory: drawings of scales that measure the hourly output of two factories; or an animated scene that depicts how a large stone can be lifted, either with great human effort or easily with a simple lever. These images claim that standardization, mechanization and the utilization of industrial techniques result in an increase of output while facilitating the work process. The expert's voice merely supplements the imagery by pointing to the national dimension of the productivity drive. If a country modernizes its working facilities (visualized here by a de-cluttering of a workbench), the commentary explains, each worker can produce more, in less time, with less effort.

The narrator's counterpart then voices concern that rationalization may have a negative effect on the national economy. The film dispels these fears by highlighting the benefits to the consumer: modern production means an increase in quantity and a decrease in prices. From a factory, bicycles roll out in quick succession off the conveyer belt into the bike shop across the street. Window-shoppers excitedly watch as the shopkeeper replaces the original price tag with one showing half the price, and they storm the shop to purchase a bike (see figure 4.1). The camera follows one of the contented customers as he proudly cycles down the road. As he passes a row of newly built houses where people sit at plentifully laden dinner tables, the cyclist addresses the audience to explain that productivity also means better food and better housing. The fact that the narrator's voice switches from an off-screen location to the cyclist expresses a shift in meaning. The voice is no longer owned by the benevolent expert, but by a witness who can testify to the benefits of productivity. Although the figure that speaks to the audience is abstract, it invites identification, as it seems to represent the interests of the ordinary man. The cyclist cheerfully summarizes the benefits of productivity by pointing to a crowd of people entering the factory: productivity means a rise in salary (visualized by a stuffed worker's wallet), reduction of working hours and more time to enjoy the new comforts the worker can afford. The criticism that machines replace skilled workers is only addressed indirectly by the narrator's claim that productivity means 'a better life for everyone!' With these words, the cyclist bids farewell and cycles towards an idyllic village that is flanked by a large, modern factory building. This final frame wraps up the argument smoothly by providing visual reassurance that modern industry and traditional life will continue to exist in harmony.

Productivity as key element of the ERP

Productivity, as the first part of the animated short *Productivité* illustrates, does not just mean an increase in output; it encompasses the most efficient use of materials and labour to produce more in a shorter time and more cheaply. According to the official historian of the MP, Harry Price, productivity comprises 'multiple ingredients': standardization, simplification and specialization of production through mechanization; the application of scientific and technical research; technical training; new management techniques to increase efficiency; improvement of labour–management relations and financial incentives, such as pay rises or tax breaks to encourage workers and industrialists to increase production; and the expansion of markets and the dismantling of trade barriers to enable free trade, which stimulate competition.[11] Productivity was thus fundamental to the MP or, as Brian McKenzie put it, its leitmotif.[12]

Origins of productivity

The experiences of the First World War and the economic and political crises of the interwar period also decisively shaped US foreign policy after the Second World War. Already during the war, liberal economic experts and government officials from the United States and Great Britain had come together to develop the structures that would prevent another world economic crisis and the kind of economic nationalism that had undermined international stability. At the Bretton Woods Conference of July 1944, delegates from forty-four nations agreed to set up the International Monetary Fund and the World Bank to facilitate and foster international trade through stable exchange rates and the convertibility of currencies. As mentioned in the beginning of this book, their conclusions were rooted in traditional liberal ideology that believed in free trade as the basis for security and freedom. However, as Sheri Berman points out, the representatives at Bretton Woods also conceded that capitalism could have negative effects and therefore accepted that national governments exerted a certain level of control over their economies to ensure social stability.[13] The lessons the US decision-makers drew from the economic and political turmoil of the interwar years crystallized into two aims: to re-establish an open world market and to encourage the creation of democratic parliamentary systems. Competition in the political marketplace and economic competition were, as Volker Berghahn suggests, seen as two sides of the same coin; in the eyes of the liberal policymakers, a lack of 'economic democracy' fostered authoritarian politics and vice versa.[14] Their goal was to reorganize Western European economies along the lines of a liberal-capitalist economy to generate growth and revive the multilateral trading system. This would curb the influence of authoritarian, especially communist, regimes while enhancing American's security and power.

The productivity drive the US government launched through the ERP followed the principle that productivity could check inflation, reduce trade deficits and increase wages and living standards, and thereby curb the appeal of communism.[15] The American faith in productivity as a solution to almost any economic and social problem was, as Charles S. Maier argues, born from the boom the US economy experienced during the Second World. Interpreted as result of the switch to a planned war economy, the economic upswing also created broader acceptance for Roosevelt's interventionist New Deal economic policies, which comprised government planning and large-scale investment, ordinarily anathema to capitalists. It gave emphasis to the liberal credo that in a society where everybody prospered, class conflict and struggles for political power took a back seat.[16] The concept of productivity thus also appealed to capitalists, as it made superfluous the radical change to the existing socio-economic order that the communists demanded.

Maier explains its high appeal across the political spectrum also with the fact that it was perceived as an apolitical instrument that turned the transition to a prosperous, peaceful society into a 'problem of engineering, not of politics'.[17] This might explain why the ECA information officers found productivity an easier subject to promote than the politically more sensitive concept of European integration. Few could, Andrew Berding insisted in an address to his information officers in January 1952, resist the 'promise of a better life for all' that the productivity programme carried. The problem was that the United States was not the only nation convinced that it had found the solution to end all destitution. Berding, who had just been promoted to the director of the new MSA Information Division in Washington, conceded that 'the central appeal of Marxism is its promise that it can accomplish the same thing'. And it employed at least partly similar means to do so: increasing output through mechanization, standardization, technological innovation and governmental planning. It was the job of the US propagandists and European filmmakers to demonstrate that the US concept of productivity 'offers a desirable alternative to Communism or to an archaic capitalism'.[18] Productivity did not mean the unleashing of capitalist forces, the experts insisted. It described the rational and most efficient use of technology, manpower and raw materials to generate growth for the benefit of the workers, the industrialists and the national economy. As it involved government planning and required cooperation between labour and industry, productivity could be reconciled with the welfare state that emerged across Western Europe after the Second World War.

Implementing the productivity drive

The ECA/MSA mobilized in force to implement the productivity drive. The Productivity and Technical Assistance Program, organized by the ECA's Productivity and Technical Assistance Division, in the beginning largely underfunded, became the centrepiece of the productivity programme. It was designed to support economic modernization in Europe through training and special development projects, as well as through the exchange of technical knowledge and innovations between the US and the European MP countries.[19] The programme brought European workers, union representatives, government officials and journalists to the United States to study the newest production methods and to impress them with the high living standards of American workers.[20] American economic and agricultural experts and technicians were sent to Europe to provide training, give lectures and carry out development projects. Though initially designed as exchange programmes, it was exchange in name only; in reality the ECA sought to transfer American technical and scientific knowledge to Western Europe in order to speed up its economic modernization. The often week-long study visits to US plants and farms were primarily aimed at European opinion-makers who, after observing the modern production techniques and democratic labour–management relations, would act as catalysts of change in their home countries.[21]

The ECA Labor Division also played its part in the MP's productivity drive. It had been set up to curb the influence of radical labour groups by strengthening non-communist trade unions in order to win more European workers for industrial modernization.[22] Like the Information Division, the Labor Division produced and distributed information and educational material, including films, to trade unions and workers, chiefly on the issues of industrial relations or productivity.[23]

To ensure that the productivity drive continued beyond the termination of the ERP, the ECA worked towards a 'nationalization' of the productivity effort. Britain had already in 1948, on the initiative of the British Head of the Treasury Stafford Cribbs, set up the Anglo-American Productivity Council as a non-governmental committee of industry representatives with a remit to organize study visits between the two countries.[24] The ECA and the OEEC Council encouraged other European governments to create their own National Productivity Centres (NPCs), and financed them through counterpart funds during their first years. Austria,[25] France,[26] the Netherlands[27] and West Germany established NPCs in 1950;[28] by 1952, eleven NPCs had been created.[29] Some of these centres are still in existence today, united in the European Association of National Productivity Centres.

The aim of these NPCs was to commit the productive part of society to the productivity effort by bringing together representatives from industry, labour and government. The centres thus did not merely provide training and information, but were set up to establish a consensus between industry and workers over the need to expand production. However, the ECA economists also felt that Europeans needed to work together to remove any obstacles that hindered the productivity drive, and so pushed for the creation of a transnational agency. In many European countries the basic building blocks for increasing agricultural and industrial productivity were missing: technology, industrial structures and organization methods were lagging far behind modern, US-style production standards across

Europe. In 1953 the OEEC therefore established the European Productivity Agency to serve and coordinate the different national productivity centres.

European resistance to productivity

The ECA's efforts to implement productivity met with a mixed response. In general, the West European governments were keenly interested in importing American technology, novel production techniques and know-how, which would generate economic growth and also help them to implement their visions of a new society.[30] Britain, through its Labour government's social and economic modernization project, became a forerunner in the productivity programme. Already in 1948 it established, as mentioned, the Anglo-American Productivity Council to facilitate the exchange of technical know-how between Britain and the United States. Also many European manufacturers and industries, keen to increase their profits, welcomed the technical assistance programme as an opportunity to learn new methods from the most successful economy in the world.

At the same time, the American productivity drive encountered widespread opposition from different sectors of European society, and for several different reasons. Though principally in favour of productivity, some European governments, like those in Italy and France, rejected measures that contradicted with their own plans, citing as a reason the threat of political and social destabilization.[31] Indeed, the productivity reforms faced opposition from both the Left and the Right.[32] On the Left, many workers and union members, especially those organized in communist trade unions, objected to the productivity drive as a covert means to increase the profits of capitalists, leaving the workers to pay the price. A popular argument put forward was that the relentless drive for productivity drove workers to physical exhaustion, or resulted in lay-offs as a result of industrial restructuring. A publicity campaign against productivity launched by the French communist press went: 'I have lost five kilos of weight since my factory began to demand increased productivity.'[33] The workers' opposition also expressed a more principal 'dislike' for capitalism 'from which they feel they reap little or no benefits', a US State Department report concluded.[34]

But the ECA's productivity drive was also met with scepticism or outright rejection on the right of the political spectrum. Many industrialists, business owners and managers of traditional businesses rejected the American call to modernize. Fearing for their privileges and power, they also complained that modernization and standardization threatened their craft and expertise.

In France, industrialists were reluctant to abandon their traditional ways of leadership, and regarded modern American human relation techniques as nonsense.[35] In Italy, the monopolistic structure of industry, along with nepotism and conservative management practices, stood starkly opposed to the politics of productivity. Some private Italian industries, especially the car industry, embraced and profited from the technology and expertise provided through the technical assistance programme. However, the ECA administrators were forced to acknowledge that, overall, Italian industry and government remained negative towards the productivity programme.[36]

This 'uneven' response of European businesses and governments to productivity as a model of economic (and political) reform gave confirmation to Hoffman's assertion that 'technical assistance cannot be exported; it can only be imported'.[37] Opposition even came from parts of society that were not directly involved in the programme, which illustrates that the idea of productivity fuelled broader concerns about modernization and rapid social change.[38] The US efforts to modernize European industries fuelled anxieties of American domination and loss of national sovereignty.[39] Across Europe, conservative intellectual elites and the Catholic Church were among the most outspoken critics of the perceived Americanization of Europe – a convenient shorthand to describe the fast cultural and economic changes that were actually taking place irrespective of whether or not they were initiated by the United States. These critics accused America of forcing onto Europeans its 'soulless consumerism' and the 'fast and furious pace' of American society.[40] They lamented the loss of individuality and cultural traditions through the mechanization of everyday life and voiced suspicions about the free market and mass production that threatened to eradicate local traditions and skills.[41]

Realizing that much of the criticism launched against productivity was driven by these more fundamental anti-American feelings, the ECA aimed to downplay its own role. Its decision to 'nationalize' the productivity drive was thus also informed by the wish to increase popular support for the measures. At the same time, the ECA saw the need to expand its propaganda effort. Thus, on 7 September 1951 the ECA headquarters ordered all ECA information officers to take steps 'to correct the misapprehensions arising from the original stories'.[42] In a separate telegram, sent on the same day, the ECA asked the country missions to intensify their efforts to outsource the information work on productivity. The information offices should 'stimulate and assist' outside agencies, such as national productivity centres, non-communist labour unions and trade organizations, to produce their own material and spread information.[43]

Film propaganda for productivity

Productivity was essentially about an increase in production through mechanization and scientific innovation. And, since film could not only tell, but actually 'show', it was the ideal medium to explain the functioning of new machinery or illustrate how a change of work patterns could speed up production. The Information Division held the opinion that film was the most suitable medium to reach industrial workers, farmers and, not least, female consumers. The industrialists and small business owners were best targeted through brochures and leaflets, which the ECA offices produced in abundance.[44] This group, it was felt, would be more receptive to the persuasive power of numbers and graphs, which were printed on paper and could be carefully studied. The information officers' strategic thinking expressed, of course, a class (and gender) bias: the 'uneducated masses' of industrial and agricultural workers, as well as women, were more powerfully affected by moving images; in contrast, even though the educated male middle classes could be favourably influenced by film, it was thought that they needed printed evidence to really spur them into action.

The MP films that rallied the Europeans in support of the politics of productivity were different from those produced by the ECA Labor Division (and later also the national productivity centres). The Labor Division produced technical training films – often rather prosaic, factual films that provided instructions on how to operate a machine, for example. These educational films were tailored to the interests of specific professions; they were screened in factories or union halls, or to trainees in vocational schools – sometimes alone, but frequently in combination with other MP or USIS films.[45] The MP films that focused specifically on the question of productivity, on the other hand, were produced with a broader audience in mind, even if they addressed subjects that were of specific interest to farmers or industrial workers. In fact, the idea of productivity was so central to the ERP that most MP films promoted the idea of productivity in one way or the other. Take, for instance, MP documentaries depicting the economic reconstruction of Europe: they showed that the ERP did not just help to rebuild infrastructure and industry, but also modernized it. Film series such as *The Marshall Plan at Work* (ECA 1950), *ERP in Action* (ECA 1950), *The Changing Face of Europe* (ECA 1951) or *1-2-3. A Monthly Review from Europe* (MSA 1953–1954) presented as a self-evident 'truth' that economic modernization, mechanization and mass production automatically resulted in economic growth and rising living standards. The MP films thus fed into the powerful discourse of American modernity and progress.

To illustrate progress through productivity was one thing; quite another was to persuade the viewers to support the productivity drive actively by convincing them that the proposed methods were sound. The problem was that productivity, in the view of Thomas Wilson, a strategist at the Information Division's Special Media Section, was a 'pretty cold subject'.[46] Productivity had to be made interesting; therefore, the information officers agreed, it was necessary 'to get out of the rut of talking statistics, mechanics, and organisation of the program'. The films should care less about the technical details, but instead focus on the meaning of productivity for the individual.[47] Simply persuading the audience of the benefits of productivity did not suffice either; MP propaganda had to aim higher and 'induce individual human beings to take specific action'.[48] More than two years later, Berding's first inaugural address as newly appointed Director of Information at MSA Washington repeated the same message. Berding argued that 'to sell the productivity idea is perhaps the most challenging task of attitude changing that we have ever faced'. The challenge was not just to win passive acceptance, but to 'influence behaviour'. MP propaganda had to convert Western Europeans to the idea of productivity and spur them into 'vigorous action' to implement its principles. Berding made a reference to the appeal of Marxism to remind his information officers that they, too, were part of a revolution, tasked with 'inducing a revolutionary change in European attitudes'.[49]

How did the propagandists approach this brief? The body of MP films that have productivity as their main theme can be roughly divided into four categories: films that seek to explain what productivity means, films promoting agricultural modernization, films that highlight the benefits to the (female) consumer and films promoting modern labour–management relations. With the exception of the last category, aimed at industrial workers, these films addressed a general public. They thus had to present the topic in a simple, clear form that was both persuasive and interesting to ensure that the young and people with limited education could also understand it.

Films explaining productivity

The MP propagandists believed that much of the resistance to the politics of productivity stemmed from a lack of knowledge. If the Europeans could only understand what productivity really meant and what results it could achieve, they reasoned, then their resistance would melt away. The ECA thus commissioned several film productions that explained the concept and how it benefited the worker, the manufacturer and the consumer. These films also sought to allay popular fears that productivity would result in a loss of jobs or a decline in craftsmanship.

The films *Productivité* (discussed earlier) and *The Shoemaker and the Hatter* (ECA UK 1950) were animation films that sought to do this in a light-hearted manner. Animation was a particularly useful means to illustrate complex processes of production; it also had the advantage that it crossed cultural and linguistic barriers easily. *The Shoemaker and the Hatter*, produced for the Paris film unit by the British animation studio Halas and Batchelor, addresses the link between productivity and free trade and thus also makes a case for European integration. It forwards the argument that the economy can only thrive if trade barriers and tariffs are dismantled. The animation film juxtaposes two characters who represent two opposing ways of economic thinking: an open-minded, entrepreneurial shoemaker, who is looking for ways to solve the economic crisis he and his country faces, and his neighbour, a misanthropic hatter, who anxiously protects his privileges and calls for protective measures against imports.

The film begins by illustrating how public discontent is brewing because the people cannot afford to buy shoes or hats. They march past the hatter's shop in pouring rain, using pans and pots to protect their heads and clenching their fists in anger in full view of the overpriced bowler hat sitting in the shop window. The visual message is clear: a revolution is fomenting, and something needs to be done. While the hatter ignores their plight, the shoemaker travels from Britain to Europe to buy raw materials and machines for mass production, to produce more shoes at a cheaper price. As he travels, he discovers that other countries are confronted with similar problems: an abundance of one product in one country is sorely lacking in another, as national trade barriers hinder exchange. Although his efforts to get these barriers removed are continuously undermined by the disgruntled hatter, he succeeds in the end, and trade and production thrive. *The Shoemaker* illustrates the intertwining of productivity and free trade and thereby shows how everybody profits from modern mass production and closer economic cooperation: consumers, manufacturers and national economies across Europe (see figure 4.2). Only the hatter falls victim to the shoemaker's industrial expansion: he now works 'in the growing transport industry' driving a coach. The film gives only a slight nod to the popular criticism that productivity means a loss of jobs, and even then makes light of the problem: the hatter deserves his lot because he is unwilling to change.

Figure 4.2 Removal of trade barriers brings prosperity to everyone (*The Shoemaker and the Hatter*).

Light-hearted is also the tone of the French-British co-production *Machines at Work* (MSA 1952), which demonstrates how mankind has profited from the invention of the machine. Again, comedy is used to ease anxieties over machines taking over the lives – and jobs – of humans; the filmmaker inserts comic scenes to illustrate how impractical a return to the old ways of handmade production would be. The film argues that a life without machines is unimaginable, and that increased mechanization is not merely inevitable, but attractive.

The information officers realized that rational arguments in support of productivity were not enough to sway the minds of the public. Statistical evidence or scientific proof could not quell anxieties about modernization and concerns over the destruction of professions and traditional modes of production. To reassure the audiences that modernization would not undermine tradition or craftsmanship, some films argued that old and new production methods could exist side by side. Romolo Marcellini's *Handicraft Town* (ECA Italy 1949), for example, documents the long tradition of knife-making in the north Italian town of Maniago. Knives are still welded on small furnaces in dark, family-run workshops, as in the old days. But modern factories have opened that allow the town to expand its production and to begin exporting. The film claims that all producers, big and small, thrive because they are united in the effort to make the best knives.

The Italian documentary *Silkmakers of Como*, filmed around 1952, similarly promises that industrial mass production does not replace traditional crafts. Directed by Ubaldo Magnaghi and shot in glorious Technicolor, *Silkmakers of Como* attempts to relieve the tension between the old and the new by demonstrating how traditional silk-weaving practices coexist with modern, mechanized mass production. One of the first scenes shows a young woman eating her meal in a large room, while two old people dressed in black are working quietly at a spinning wheel, with a large wooden handloom in the background. This Italian family still manufactures silk through the traditional cottage industry system. The young generation, as the film goes on to show, has found work in the modern factories producing silk 'at the latest, most modern machines' (see figure 4.3). By following the girl from her home to the factory, the camera draws a direct connection between the two places, thus substantiating the commentary's argument that the local tradition, handed down over generations, informs modern production. However, the mode of narration leaves little doubt in which direction the future lies: in modern mass production. A cut to a large group of energetic and laughing young people cycling to work in the factory illustrates the appeal of modern production. As the camera enters the factory, the pace of the previously playful music suddenly quickens and turns into a jazz-like staccato that emulates the rhythmic spinning of the hundreds of colourful bobbins, signifying the arrival of modernity. The clean and bright work environment and the industrialist's interest in using the workers' traditional skills attest to the positive development of mechanization.

Figure 4.3 *Silkmakers of Como*: Easing the tension between the old and the new.

The old, who pursue their traditional working methods at home, are out of sight; yet their craftsmanship, the film argues, influences modern silk-making and thus fuels economic growth.

Promoting agricultural productivity

A second category of film promoted agricultural reform. An increase in agricultural output was an important goal of the ERP and was supported by schemes that brought experts to European farms and equipped the farmers with modern machinery. The agricultural productivity drive was intended to make European countries less dependent on food imports, especially from the dollar zone, where four-fifths of all wheat the Europeans consumed came from.[50] These imports presented a huge strain on the national budgets and thus contributed significantly to the trade imbalance of European countries. Raising agricultural productivity in countries with a large agricultural sector, such as Turkey or Denmark, should, it was thought, help to fill the European demand for grains and other produce while enabling the producing countries to reduce their trade deficit and bear the growing defence costs.

In the beginning, the measures put in place to expand agricultural production consisted mainly of the imports of fertilizers and seeds. Soon, however, the programmes were expanded: the ECA sent American experts to Europe to offer advice and implement agricultural reforms in close cooperation with national governmental agencies. Soil reclamation projects to irrigate dry land and drain the marshes in Italy, Greece and France (and its colonies) produced new arable land. The control of plant diseases and the introduction of scientifically based farming and breeding practices improved both the quantity and quality of output. To speed up and simplify work processes, the ECA introduced schemes that provided European farmers with American farm animals, iron ploughs and tractors, or helped to electrify farms.[51]

These agricultural projects formed the subject of many information films. Documentaries such as *Island of Faith* (ECA Netherlands 1950), *Victory at Thermopylae* (ECA Greece 1950) and *Rice and Bulls* and *Provence* (both ECA France 1950) depict Marshall Aid-sponsored land reclamation projects undertaken by the national governments. The Greek *Victory at Thermopylae* shows how American farmers helped de-salt marshes in central Greece so that the Greeks could now plant and harvest rice for their own and their country's benefit. The film's title celebrates the productivity drive as a victory of human innovation over nature, and thus underlines the revolutionary aspect of the programme. The French documentaries *Rice and Bulls* and *Provence* also depict desalination projects, this time turning the marshes of the Provence region into fertile ground for rice cultivation (see figure 4.4).

In southern Italy, drought presented a serious problem. It limited agricultural output and kept large parts of the population locked in poverty. In 1950, the Italian government implemented a land reform that redistributed land to the landless, and launched irrigation projects, sponsored by Marshall Aid, to produce arable land.[52] The Italian MP films *Rural Sardinia* and *Land Redeemed* (1950), as well as *Emilia* and *Land of Apulia* (1951), highlight how these projects benefit the poor rural population. The films claim that these reclamation projects achieve much more than an increase in agricultural yield; since the reforms require the building of dams and digging of wells, they also create jobs for the many unemployed men. Productivity thus creates opportunity and gives hope for the future.[53]

Mechanization of farming was another popular topic of MP films: *The Story of Mahmoud* and *Renaissance agricole* (both ECA France 1950), *The Village Tractor* (ECA Turkey 1951) and *Bull's Eye for Farmer Pietersen* (ECA

Figure 4.4 Turning unproductive land into fertile soil in *Land Redeemed, Rice and Bulls, The Village Tractor* and *Bull's Eye for Farmer Pietersen.*

Netherlands 1950) promote a MP scheme that enabled European farmers to purchase American ploughs, tractors and harvesters at low prices, and provided technical training (see figure 4.4). The central argument these films make is that mechanization of farming produces higher yields with less effort. Modernization does not stop at the mountainous Austrian villages, as the MP films *The Invisible Link* (ECA Austria 1950) and *A Farm in Four Countries* (MSA 1953) and an episode of *1-2-3. A Monthly Review from Europe* show. The Alpine farmer's problems, though, were different from those of his Greek or Italian counterpart. On the steep mountain slopes, oxen or horses cannot be used to tow the plough. Instead, as *The Invisible Link* illustrates, a group of six men and women have to drag it up (see figure 4.5). An ERP electrification project brings relief: now, a cord attached to a machine pulls up the plough, thereby facilitating the task and freeing up manpower. By using a rather archaic method of mountain farming as a means of contrast, the film prods the audience to conclude that, surely, the six adults pulling the plough could be more productively employed elsewhere.

Figure 4.5 Electricity frees up manpower in *The Invisible Link.*

The MP films promoting agricultural productivity thus had several goals: to convince the farmers that the adoption of new methods does pay, to educate them by showing how such reforms might be implemented and finally to prompt them to take action. The films were designed to mobilize the population, encouraging the people to make use of the opportunities the programmes offered. The documentaries often praise and reward individual entrepreneurship through the figure of a boy or a young man who pushes for reform and overcomes obstacles and traditional prejudices to finally succeed in his plan (see figure 4.6). They promote a version of the American dream that insists that success lies in the hands of the individual. Yet these protagonists do not pursue change for selfish reasons, but to improve the lives of their families, or their community, as the example of the young Dutch farmer Pietersen in *Bull's Eye for Farmer Pietersen* illustrates.

Pietersen convinces his neighbours to form a cooperative to purchase a tractor to speed up farm work and thus increase output. All agree but one; he argues that his forefathers have managed without such machines. Pietersen demonstrates his solidarity with his stubborn neighbour by saving his harvest from the approaching storm and thereby converts him to mechanized farming. Similarly, Yusef in *Yusef and His Plough* and Koula in *The Story of Koula* do not push for participation in ERP schemes for personal gain, but to help others.

These youths, unencumbered by old habits and eager to learn, symbolize the future and are presented as the driving force of change. This marks a difference from the MP films promoting cooperation and international understanding, which choose girls as their main protagonists (*As the Young Ones Sing, Let's Be Childish*). Productivity – especially in the realm of agriculture – remains a male domain. Hansl in *Hansl and His 200,000 Chicks* (ECA Austria 1952) allows his sister to assist him in implementing a new science-based method of chicken breeding. But he remains in charge, and reaps the benefits of his successful productivity drive – a new bike. In *Project for Tomorrow* (ECA Austria), the limelight belongs to the farmer's son Franzl, who takes second place in a cattle breeding competition, and not to his sister who applauds from the sidelines.

Figure 4.6 *Yusef and His Plough*: Young Yusef's entrepreneurial spirit serves his community well.

These MP narratives often address the traditional conservatism of farmers, whose reluctance to change impedes modernization. The older farmers are either directly opposed to it, as in *Bull's Eye for Farmer Petersen*, *Rice and Bulls* or *Concerning Dairy Production*, or they exhibit indifference, as in *Yusef and His Plough* or *The Story of Koula*. The filmmakers liked to use popular stereotypes of the farmer as stubborn and a creature of habit, which helped to foster identification either in those viewers who shared these conservative views or in those who pinned their hopes on the reformer (see also Chapter 1).

However, the actual experiences of the projectionists and educators who came into contact with the people give us reason to question the assertion that the farmers were really so resistant to change as the films claim. The farmers were largely informed about the productivity drive through radio, newspapers and the films themselves, which reached the rural population through mobile film units that travelled the countryside. These film screenings in village inns or schools were usually complemented with a discussion led by an expert or the projectionist. The above-mentioned Austrian MP film *A Project for Tomorrow* depicts such a film show in a local inn where the whole village, from small children to old men, gather to chat, drink beer and play before the screening starts.

In France, a large, rural country, a special agency, the *cinémathèque centrale agricole*, was created to bring information and educational films to the farming population. Jacques Colin, who toured the French countryside as an 'instituteure rurale' – an educator who screened the films and moderated the discussion – recalled that the French farmers showed great interest in the ECA's agricultural reform plans. Although many of them had strong communist sympathies, the French Communist Party's rejection of productivity did not impress them. They were pragmatists; Colin explained their mindset: 'On a été agriculteur avant tous, et communiste on l'occasion (one was first of all a farmer, and occasionally a communist).' Business interests overrode any communist affinities. According to Colin, the farmers' attitude was: 'One believes what one sees. The communists stood for ideology, the tractors were reality.'[54] While many French farmers might have believed the communist charge that the MP was a covert instrument of imperialism to meddle in French affairs, they happily embraced those elements of the ERP that profited them – a clear case of selective appropriation.[55] The Austrian Georg Tressler, a young filmmaker who also toured Austria with a mobile film unit, had similar experiences. He confirmed that the Austrian farmers were more open towards propositions to modernize production than is often assumed. In the first years, his film screenings mostly comprised American information films, as MP films were still scarce. Even so, though the Austrian farmers were much impressed by what they saw, they expressed no intention of embracing any of the methods depicted, as the large American farms bore no resemblance to their own small mountain farms. Tressler thus decided to make documentaries that tackled the particular problems the local farmers grappled with, and which spoke to them more intimately.[56] Tressler used the local vernacular to great effect, and also had a keen eye for comic situations.

Many documentary filmmakers felt that modern mass production called for a modern visual form, an opinion that was shared by the film officers and the educated elites in Western Europe. The documentary *Caroline, the Cow* (ECA Denmark 1951), directed by the Danish filmmaker Søren Nelson, thus received only 'meek and brittle applause' from the officials and diplomats invited to the first screening, and a lukewarm response from the Danish audience.[57] Nelson had used a cow as the main protagonist in this story about modern dairy farming in Denmark. However, he did so rather unimaginatively by alternating between scenes of cheese-making and cow-grazing, adding a voice-over that recited factual information. 'Dry' was the adjective the Danish critics most frequently used in describing the film. The conservative daily *Nationaltidene* described the film as extremely tiring, giving the scathing verdict: 'Too many machines, too little humour, no life.'[58]

Figure 4.7 Happy pigs thanks to scientific farming (*The Streamlined Pig*).

The Streamlined Pig (ECA Denmark 1951), a film on modern, science-based pig-breeding methods, was much more successful. Danish ham was a key export, and investment in the ham industry one of the priorities of the Danish government.[59] The documentary depicts the raising of Danish pigs in modern piggeries, which, according to the film, provides the animals with excellent living conditions and produces ham of the highest quality. The film's director, Jørgen Roos, made effective use of animated scenes, fast-forward techniques and a breezy swing tune to give the film momentum. Footage of evidently happy pigs did the rest to please the audience (see figure 4.7). The humorous marketing of Danish accomplishments in the rearing and handling of livestock on a scientific basis received a very favourable reception in Denmark. The film met with rave reviews in the Danish press, and earned first prize (The Golden Spike) at the Agricultural Film Festival in Rome 1953.[60] Although the British critics took a more detached view, describing it as 'a light-hearted treatment, which will interest if not particularly enlighten any British breeder or pig-raiser',[61] the ECA information officers were immensely pleased with the result.

A textbook example of how to make a technical topic accessible to a broad audience was *The Extraordinary Adventures of One Quart Milk* (ECA France 1951). Even the discerning British film distribution magazine *Film User* was delighted about the 'highly entertaining account, with a beautiful delivered commentary'.[62] The fourteen-minute-long documentary about the first European powder milk factory covers both agricultural and industrial modernization. It traces the journey of the milk from a dairy farm in the French Ardennes to the factory in the Bourgogne where it is processed. Pierre Grimblat, who wrote the script for the film, recalled that he had the idea of narrating the production process through the 'eyes' of a drop of milk.[63] The idea of using the milk as first-person narrator, combined with a witty voice-over, was the film's strong selling point. The French original version in particular, in which the talented comedian Jean Rigaux adopted an intimate, chatty tone and emulated various sounds to dramatize the story, encourages the spectator to suspend disbelief and listen attentively to the milk describing its exciting journey through various tanks, pipelines and machines. Starting with the 'birth' of the milk and its leave-taking from its mother the cow, the audience follows the milk through every step of production, from pasteurization and transportation to the processing into milk powder (see figure 4.8). Through a careful montage of sequences which show the different appliances and machines in motion, the film comprehensively visualizes the whole production process. Swift camera tilts and pans imitate the movement of the milk inside the apparatus and add momentum. The film does not rely on the commentary to tell the story; instead, the commentary interacts with the moving images, complementing the 'subjective view' of the milk inside the various vessels with the objective view of the camera. The clean, shiny machines and the white milk take centre stage. The camera moves among steel tanks and pipes and zooms in on gauges and thermometers to illustrate the mathematical precision that informs the process. The fact that humans are sidelined gives the production process a sterile appearance, which was of course intended to underline the purity and safety of the powdered milk.

Figure 4.8 The milk's journey from cow into milk powder in *The Extraordinary Adventures of One Quart Milk*.

Productivity benefiting the female consumer

Productivity films promised that the mechanization, simplification and standardization of production benefited the producer as much as the worker, whose workload eased while his salary rose. As the productivity drive accelerated, the MP strategists discovered a new target group: the female consumer.

The birth of the female consumer as a result of the socio-economic gender backlash in Western societies in the 1950s has been the subject of fascinating studies.[64] After women experienced a brief period of liberalization during the war and in the immediate post-war period, the elites and the media started to revive traditional values and extol the ideal of the middle-class family, with the man as the male breadwinner and the woman as housewife and mother. MP propaganda, as Chapter 1 illustrated, contributed to this discourse, presenting men as productive forces and decision-makers and relegating women to the margins. As the ECA intensified its efforts to win over European industry to the idea of rationalizing and standardizing production to increase output, women became more important – not professional women, but women as housewives and consumers. This is because in the 1950s female consumers came to be seen as a powerful group whose demands would put pressure on local industries to create more consumer goods, which in turn would speed up productivity. At least in Western and Northern Europe, women were often in charge of the household budget and did the daily shopping. 'Any real attempt to develop a mass market', a memo written by a female staff member of ECA Washington explained, has to 'raise expectations and desire for goods' among women.[65] The hope was to create a demand for industrially produced mass products among female consumers, forcing the industry to modernize its production methods to meet demand.

The British documentary *Productivity – Key to Progress* (ECA UK, 1951) presents women as the main beneficiaries of modernization.[66] The film claims that the introduction of the machine has changed the lives of the people, spurring economic growth, higher wages and higher living standards. The machine is, as the film title indicates, 'the key to progress'. In support of this argument, the film contrasts the ways of living of 'primitive' people with the modern Western lifestyle, in this case a British household. The camera follows a woman through her daily routines as she prepares a meal in a modern kitchen, changes her clothes, turns off the radio and picks up the letters delivered to her doorstep, before taking the bus into town to go to the library. Mechanization and mass production, the film claims, free up time, because machines make housework more efficient and render superfluous such time-consuming jobs as the sewing of clothes. It thus contributes to the discourse of the domestic revolution that calls for a more efficient use of time also in the realm of the private home. The timesaving machines allow the women to pursue other tasks, such as home decoration, bookkeeping, their children's education or a part-time job.[67] In *Productivity – Key to Progress*, the female protagonist uses the time won back in this way for more enjoyable things, such as listening to the radio, reading or taking a trip into town. The argument the film makes implicitly is that productivity, both in the realm of the private home and in industry, makes housework easier, and valorizes the work of the housewife.[68]

Another angle is adopted by the films *Expert Services* and *Marketing* (both MSA 1953), which emphasize the material benefits to the female consumer by countering the popular criticism that mass-produced goods were of lower quality.[69] As we have seen, European opposition to the standardization and simplification of production was often rooted in concerns about the loss of craftsmanship and culture. Critics of industrially produced products described them as uniform and soulless, since they carried no trace of the care and skill of the individual craftsman that went into handcrafted goods. The products of European craftsmen and industries were considered more durable and of higher quality because they were the product of centuries of expertise and handed-down skills. The Danish documentary *Expert Services* outlines how modern market research and advertising techniques benefit the customer, as they allow the industry to better identify and meet the needs of the consumer. The film claims that standardization replaces the need for tailor-made clothing, as standardized sizes fit most women. Moreover, it has the distinct advantage of making products more affordable, allowing the manufacturer to produce more at cheaper costs.

The French-British co-production *Marketing* points out another advantage of standardized production, namely its ability to save the consumer's time and nerves. The stylishly dressed French housewife no longer has to scour shops for the right button for her husband's shirt, as standardization reduces the number of different types of buttons. The film's main argument is that variety is troublesome: standardization reduces choice but guarantees functional products of high quality – an interesting argument for a free-market economy. To illustrate its point, the film shows people struggling in their daily lives with disparate and badly designed coat hangers, slippery doorknobs and wobbly pots (see figure 4.9). While industries and businesses have modernized, so the argument goes, the living standards of the people have been neglected. Consumers are forced to put up with faulty or impractical equipment, when their lives could be made easier and more comfortable through market research and product testing. *Marketing*, like *Productivity – Key to Progress*, highlights the liberalizing effect industrial modernization has on the female consumer, giving her the time and comfort she deserves.

The growing focus on consumption turned women – at least nominally – into important target audiences. It is worthwhile to note that their voice carried

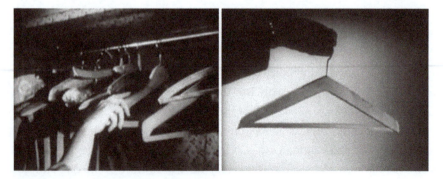

Figure 4.9 Variety is troublesome: *Marketing*.

little weight inside the ECA itself. The above-mentioned outline written by the ECA staffer Jane Joyce on why and how women should be targeted was brushed aside.[70] The memo's addressee, Director of Information in Washington Robert Mullen, forwarded Joyce's suggestions to the Deputy Director of European Information Division with a short note saying: 'This is obviously a good-hearted try on the part of one of our gals. Could you spare a moment to write a note of appreciation?'[71] Mullen's comment illustrates an attitude that was typical of the macho newsroom atmosphere of the ECA information offices. Women were not considered as producers, but only as recipients, of propaganda.

Promising the workers a fair profit share and protection of rights

The fourth category of films specifically targeted industrial workers and non-communist trade unions. Their acceptance of, and contribution to, the productivity programme was crucial, especially since it required the implementation of unpopular reforms that were likely to result in an increased workload and possibly in a loss of jobs. Victoria de Grazia explains the difficulties of persuading industrial workers to relinquish their resistance with the fact that they had experienced earlier efforts to speed up production, but had not profited from an increase in output in the past.[72] To win the workers' acceptance of the reforms, MP propaganda tried to dispel the suspicions that the MP was looking to implement a ruthless capitalist system that safeguarded the privileges of the elites. Instead, as Ellwood points out, it sought to convince the European worker that the ERP aimed to reconstruct society to produce material security and freedom, which the communists could not provide.[73]

Especially in the realm of productivity, the ECA/MSA was in direct competition with the communists. The communists, too, promised European workers prosperity and freedom, and so denounced the American productivity drive as a covert scheme of exploitation that failed to deliver on its promises. This charge was bolstered by the fact that even in the third year of the MP, the wages of Italian and French workers remained below pre-war levels, and living standards were poor. And the communists in Italy and France demonstrated that they were not merely rhetorically powerful; they actively obstructed the implementation of economic measures by calling strikes or by encouraging workers to other forms of resistance.[74]

To succeed in the productivity drive, the US government needed to isolate the communists and establish 'a broad middle-ground consensus' in Europe.[75] It did so by forming alliances with conservative and Social Democratic governments. In return, the United States had to accept that the Western European governments' had turned away from traditional capitalism. In the 'new order' that emerged in Western Europe after the war, the state pursued an active role in the economy and exerted a degree of control over the market for the greater good of society. The post-war European welfare state built on liberal-capitalist principles, but sought to minimize the negative effects of economic liberalism through a variety of interventionist policies and by providing a social safety net for its citizens.[76]

Apart from forging strategic alliances with centrist forces, the US government also supported trade unions 'with different ideological objectives' in order to break the power of the communist trade unions.[77] By strengthening the negotiating power of these 'free' trade unions, the ECA hoped to divorce more workers from the communist unions' 'political mobilisation'.[78] This would also benefit the productivity drive. The ECA needed the non-communist unions as mediators and links to the workers; they should cushion workers' frustration over soaring unemployment as a result of rationalization measures and explain why productivity benefited them – if not in the short term, then in the long term.[79] The ECA/MSA thus organized union member visits to the United States to influence their attitudes towards productivity and industrial relations.[80] It also produced films intended to convince workers that non-communist trade unions would secure a better deal for the workers because they were not fighting for political goals, but for economic improvement only. The underlying aim of the French fiction film *Jour de Peine* (A Tough Day), for example, was to illustrate that the modern liberal economy was in favour of trade unions and supported the workers' demand for an equal share in the profits they produced.[81] *Jour de Peine* was presumably contracted by the ECA Labor Division in 1951, but distributed as a regular MP film.[82]

In *Jour de Peine*, director Victor Vicas chose a neo-realist film language to show how a workers' strike at a French steel mill brings the community to breaking point. The sudden silence that replaces the noise of the shrill factory whistle, the pounding machines and screeching wheels, foreshadows what is to come: the whole community suffers under the deprivations of the prolonged strike, resulting in violent clashes between those who are desperate to return to work and those who continue the strike. The crisis is overcome only when a few conciliatory men win the workers' approval to reopen negotiations. A young union member who has attended courses on the economy and productivity manages to convince the factory management and his comrades that the economic problems can be solved if both sides compromise and take steps to rationalize production.

To ensure that the audience draws the correct conclusions, the film uses two workers who narrate the events from their point of view. Assigned the function of 'eyewitnesses', these protagonists convey the film's two main arguments: that the free trade union – unlike the communist union – respects the workers' right to decide themselves what actions they want to take; and that the success of negotiations between workers and employers depends on mutual respect, compromise and the willingness to look at the problem from both sides. *Jour de Peine* insists that the workers have a legitimate claim for a share of profits, and that a modern employer will accept this claim in exchange for the workers' commitment to increase production. The harmonization of the interests of the employer and the workers is visually expressed by a change of tone and clothes: the combative atmosphere of the first meetings between them gives way to a factual discussion where the unionists have exchanged their rough work clothes for suits and ties and debate with the management at eye level. Although the film's sympathies are with the workers, it also puts more demands on them to adapt to economic challenges. In the end, it is an enlightened worker who resolves the conflict by accepting the premise that the industry can increase the workers' salaries only if they produce more efficiently.

The ECA's efforts to strengthen non-communist organized labour were linked to the goal of bringing the industry and workers at the negotiation table. Improving the relations between industry and workers was also a central part of the socio-economic policies of the centrist post-war European governments, which sought to promote social cohesion and reduce the disruptive effects of capitalism by 'managing' the economy.[83] The ECA, on the other hand, was primarily interested in boosting productivity, which required the commitment of both industry and workers. The workers had to accept that they had to produce more, and not just demand higher wages. The manufacturers and industrialists had to modernize their factories to increase output and give the workers a fair share of their profits. To reach this goal, the ERP encouraged collective bargaining, through which both sides should reach an agreement over how productivity was to be implemented and profits shared. However, the system of collective bargaining did not work in all national contexts: in Italy, for instance, high unemployment diminished the workers' bargaining power; the non-communist trade unions in Italy and in France were too weak to exert pressure on the industries, whereas the powerful communist unions preferred militant action to push through their demands. What is more, in both countries industrialists rejected the very principle that workers should get an equal share of profits.[84]

Still, the ECA tried to convince the European workers of the benefits of productivity by demonstrating that the US model of a capitalist economy was in favour of collective bargaining and supported the workers' goals. The film *With these Hands* (1950) sought to challenge the popular stereotype that workers in the United States were exploited by ruthless capitalists. *With these Hands* was originally made for the International Ladies Garment Workers Union, and was purchased by the Information Division for European-wide distribution.[85] The main reason for distributing a US-produced film as a MP film was that the Information Division did not have enough films to counter left-wing criticism of productivity. The film was predominantly screened in countries with influential communist unions and was apparently quite popular. *With these Hands* tells the history of the successful struggle of the garment workers' union for better salaries and working conditions in the United States. It thereby demonstrates American support for free trade unions and their efforts to resolve conflicts peacefully.

This type of productivity films did not just counter 'misperceptions' about the American capitalist system, but also pursued a concrete political agenda. They were meant to bolster the combined efforts of the State Department and the US organized labour to encourage discord in, and even split, the European trade unions with the twin aims of altering the existing system of industrial relations and of weakening communist influence.[86] The same motivation informs the ECA's own production *European Labor Day* (ECA 1951), which presents the United States as protector of the workers' rights and freedoms. This openly anti-communist compilation documentary contrasts Labour Day celebrations in Western Europe with those in the Soviet Union. It presents the Western non-communist unions as liberal and democratic, while pointing out the lack of freedom and the violation of human rights in communist Eastern Europe.

While the films above promise higher wages and job security in exchange for the workers' commitment to industrial modernization, another set of films showed that close cooperation between industry and labour also improves working conditions. The British documentary *Over to You* (ECA UK 1951) reports on the popular US study visits for union members, workers and managers that the ECA organized through its Technical Assistance Program.[87] The film accompanies 'a most representative cross-section' of the British hosiery industry on a long tour through the United States. Visiting different textile factories and talking to American workers and managers, the British team, consisting of workers, unionists and members of management, is won over by the modern and highly efficient production standards in the United States. The voice-over emphasizes how hard the American workers work; in return, they earn high salaries and enjoy high standards of living, which is illustrated by the fact that even ordinary factory workers own a big car. While the filmic travelogue eulogizes the ingenuity of American machinery and efficiency, the images also promote another aspect of American business: flat hierarchies and an egalitarian spirit that seems to rub off on the visiting team. Upon returning to Britain, the team members immediately start implementing what they have seen overseas, transferring the knowledge and experience to their own workplace.

The importance of the workers' commitment to productivity is also underlined in another British production, the documentary *Ideas at Work* (ECA UK, 1950). The commentary argues that even in factories that have not yet modernized their equipment, productivity can be increased by simple methods that save human effort, time and money. For this, however, the experience and contribution of the workers is needed. The narration uses the mode of contrast to exemplify how a single operation can either be laborious and time-consuming or be quick and easy. *Ideas at Work* uses as a case study a British factory that has achieved a better workflow and higher level of efficiency by inviting its workers to submit ideas on how to improve their work. The film seeks to dispel concerns that workers might eliminate their own jobs if they propose ways to do a task faster. The narrator insists that a worker's skill and expertise are invaluable, and that rationalization produces more jobs as the factory profits from the economic upswing.

Making production more efficient was, however, not enough to secure lasting economic growth. Productivity was built on the principles of open markets and free trade for stimulating production and competition. The MP's productivity drive was thus intrinsically connected to the ECA's other policy goal: European integration. In the eyes of the US policymakers there existed thus no alternative to an economically and – ideally – politically united Europe. The strength and security of Europe, and with it, of the 'free' capitalist world, rested on closer cooperation between the European nations and the elimination of trade barriers. If Europe failed to unify, Hoffman was convinced, it would bring 'disaster for nations and poverty for peoples'.[88]

US Policy into Film:
European Integration

'It is further declared to be the policy of the United States to encourage the unification of Europe'[1] proclaimed the Amendments to the Economic Cooperation Act passed by US Congress in October 1949. Although the original Economic Cooperation Act had already stipulated as a goal 'the development of economic cooperation', the amendment spelt it out more clearly. The MP economists considered integration a prerequisite for Europe's long-term economic stability. A single European market that eliminated trade barriers, allowing the free movement of goods and people, would not only boost the Western European economies, but also be of financial benefit to the United States, and revive the international trading system. And there was another important motivation for the creation of a united Europe: the 'double containment' of German and Soviet power.[2] For the US government, an integrated Europe presented the solution to the 'problem' of Germany, whose growing economic power was causing considerable unease among its neighbours, in particular France. Because of its strong industry and coal reserves, Germany was considered the 'engine of growth' for Europe, and its contribution essential to the revival of the European economy; but this very strength was also perceived as dangerous.[3] By tying Germany into a Western European framework, its power could be utilized and controlled, thus preventing her from waging another disastrous war, either on its own or together with the Soviet Union. European integration could serve a dual purpose: forestall a possible Soviet-German alliance and strengthen the West against the Soviet enemy.[4] Furthermore, since this new Europe would be a part of a wider Atlantic framework with the United States at the helm, it would also bolster the position of the United States as a global power.[5]

European integration as key policy goal

In the first year of the ERP, the issue of European integration had received little attention, as the focus was on recovery and reconstruction. This changed in summer 1949. In July that year, Paul Hoffman, head of the ECA, addressed his employees in a speech titled 'What Each of Us Can Do to Make the ERP a Success.' Discussing 'the wider aspects of the recovery problem', Hoffman argued that lasting European recovery and the checking of communist expansion required more than economic measures alone. The ECA also had to spread new hope by fostering trust in freedom and democracy and by encouraging the creation of an economically and politically united Europe. Only this, Hoffman believed, could 'arouse Europeans to a much greater productivity effort' and thus secure their well-being in the future.[6]

A month later, Hoffman addressed the Council of the Organisation for European Economic Co-operation (OEEC), which the European governments had established a year earlier to coordinate the efforts to implement the measures of the ERP. He urged the European governments to put more effort into reducing intra-European trade restrictions, and cooperate more closely to reduce trade imbalances.[7] After his tour through Europe, Hoffman reiterated his message in Washington in September 1949. He called on his agency to produce more 'dramatic evidence' that Europe was taking steps towards closer cooperation.[8] Otherwise, he warned, US Congress and the American people might withhold the necessary funds to continue the ERP, and thus endanger the whole project.[9]

Hoffman's push towards European unification was mainly informed by two factors: first, the Americans' growing dissatisfaction with the MP's apparent lack of economic progress, fuelled by worrying reports about the situation in Great Britain, which was on the verge of economic collapse in summer 1949,[10] and second, the realization that, despite the satisfactory recovery in levels of production, the European trade deficit with the dollar area continued to grow. If Europe's economy was to be largely self-supporting by the time the MP ended in 1952, it needed to reduce this 'dollar gap', as the trade imbalance with the dollar area was called. This could be achieved by increasing exports to the dollar market or by replacing imports from the dollar area with imports from other European countries. Europeans thus needed to dismantle intra-European trade barriers and reduce tariffs, boosting inter-European trade and so increasing productivity.[11] Even though the ECA economists had addressed the problem earlier in 1949, concerns over Germany, in particular the ongoing Soviet blockade of Berlin and the European government's reluctance to work towards European integration, had delayed the implementation of decisive measures to solve these lingering problems.[12]

Hoffman's urgent call to take more decisive steps towards integration, which culminated in the proclamation of the 'second phase' of the ERP,[13] was also intended to placate the domestic critics of the MP. Hardach suggests that the ECA's prioritization of integration in autumn 1948 might have been a strategic device to regain support for the MP inside the United States, as many Americans looked favourably upon the idea of a united Europe.[14] By intensifying the efforts to win European support for unification and higher productivity, the ECA hoped to reassure the growing number of Americans who felt that the US taxpayers' money was simply being frizzled away in Europe without achieving visible improvements.[15] US Congress, which authorized the annual MP budget, expressed its frustration about the lack of progress by reducing funds for the fiscal year 1950. Furthermore, it demanded to see a rapid increase in production volume and exports, a reduction of the national debts and clear evidence that the MP had actually helped to contain communism.[16] Hoffman's announcement of the 'second phase', which marked a reorientation towards the MP's 'cardinal goals', has to be seen in the light of this criticism. From now on, productivity and European integration were to become 'the prime and overall theme' of MP propaganda.[17]

The meaning of European integration

What did US policymakers actually mean when they spoke of 'European integration'? And how did the Americans envision this new, integrated Europe? The truth is that most Americans had only a vague concept of the united Europe they wished for.[18] Even those in charge of selling the European idea to the Europeans were not quite sure what it meant. Frank Norall, the head of the Special Media Section, asked Hoffman for clarification; Hoffman explained that integration meant the same as unification. But unification was 'an embarrassing word in the United States', as it conjured up memories of the failure to unify the Armed Forces.[19] The State Department itself preferred the term 'integration', which sounded less 'specific'.[20] Hoffman, as head of the ECA, wished, as many Americans did, for political unification; his idea was of a united Europe shaped after the template of the United States, with its own supranational bodies, which would be politically and economically strong enough to contain both Germany and the Soviet Union.[21]

Hoffman's expressed desire to work for a politically unified Europe never found its way into the Information Division's newly formulated information targets.[22] The main reasons were disagreements within the US government over which form of unification was desirable and what methods should be taken to achieve it. While the ECA aimed initially for a politically united Europe, as did Jean Monnet, the French architect of the Schuman Plan, the US State Department adopted a more sceptical stance in 1949.[23] Although it accepted political unification of Europe as its final goal, it disagreed with the ECA on 'the pace of integration and the degree of European or American initiative involved'.[24] Hardach describes the State Department's stance under Secretary of State Dean Acheson as even more ambivalent. While it agreed that close European cooperation was necessary to increase Europe's fiscal and monetary stability, as well as to tie in and thereby control West Germany, some experts at the department expressed doubts that a unified Europe would resolve the problems of the dollar gap.[25]

The State Department did not think it wise to push openly for European unification, nor even to give any clear indications of what form of integration the US government preferred. Any efforts towards European unification should be given the 'appearance of European initiative'.[26] The State Department's concern was that if the US government committed itself publicly to the ECA's integration policies, any failure to achieve European unification could be interpreted as a failure of US foreign policy. This would not only damage the government's standing domestically, it reasoned, but also endanger the financing of the ERP.[27] Acheson's request to the French Foreign minister Robert Schuman to propose a framework to integrate West Germany into Western Europe has to be seen as an effort to downplay the involvement of the United States. The so-called Schuman Plan, designed by French economist and government advisor Jean Monnet to put the French and German coal and steel industry under the control of a High Authority, which formed the basis for the establishment of the European Coal and Steel Community in 1951, was a European initiative, albeit one to which the Americans contributed significantly.[28]

A matter 'of great difficulty':
Promoting the idea of a united Europe

The idea of an economically united Europe was by no means new; Europeans had already taken various initiatives to create customs unions that allowed free trade between its members. The idea of political union also had enthusiastic European advocates, not least in the person of Monnet, who envisaged a federal Europe modelled after the template of the United States.[29] But encouraging Europeans to work more closely together proved a matter 'of great difficulty', as Elmer Graper concluded in his assessment of US foreign policy in 1951.[30] Impediments to integration came from familiar avenues: national pride and anxiety over relinquishing national sovereignty, animosities fuelled by the previous wars and fear of a German military threat all presented major stumbling blocks towards closer cooperation and the creation of a common market. Matters were further complicated by the fact that Americans and Europeans had very different understandings of integration. The head of the Information Division, Al Friendly, warned the European head of the ECA, Averell Harriman, in November 1948 that the Europeans looked less favourably on the idea of a politically unified Europe than the Americans; they could, however, Friendly believed, be won over to the idea of economic integration.[31] The fact that many Europeans were also sceptical of America's 'true motives' did not help to further the cause. Even in countries such as the Netherlands, where 86 per cent approved of the MP, more than a third suspected that the United States used the ERP to gain influence on the country's politics and economy.[32] The Information Division thus shared the State Department's reluctance to push for political unification. It feared that any steps in that direction might confirm the people's suspicions that the United States merely wanted to enhance its strategic position in Europe against the Soviets.[33]

Friendly's concerns were echoed in an important information officers' conference that took place in Paris in October 1949. It brought together the information officers from the different country missions to discuss the implications of Hoffman's announcement of the 'second phase', which prioritized integration and productivity. Having no specific policy guidance, the conference participants decided to interpret Hoffman's call for integration in economic terms. They feared that advertising political unification could damage the reputation of the MP as a whole and jeopardize the achievement of the other goals. Moreover, as Friendly's successor Roscoe Drummond reasoned, pushing for political union could deter those Europeans who might otherwise be won to the idea of economic union. Thus, Roscoe argued: 'Let us not create resistance to the first vital step of economic unification by taking on ourselves that resistance which comes from formally identifying our objectives with political federation.'[34] The conference concluded that it was best to concentrate on economic integration and circumvent the question of political unification, yet without ruling it out explicitly – a conclusion that also illustrates the considerable elbowroom the information officers had in formulating their policies.[35]

The goal of MP propaganda was, at its heart, to persuade the Europeans that a united Europe was desirable and beneficial in that it guaranteed economic growth, prosperity and peace. The strategy was to 'create a public atmosphere of acceptance' of unification so that the people would push their governments to work towards that goal. Propaganda promoting European integration needed to touch the hearts of the people, argued Thomas Wilson of the Special Media Section, who described unification as a 'fundamentally abstract, political and emotional theme' that needed 'dramatic and inspirational treatment'.[36] To win the Europeans over to the idea of a united Europe, MP propaganda had to explain how closer cooperation would benefit each individual. Evaluating the results of opinion polls, the chief of the Research and Analysis Section, Thomas Hodges, suggested capitalizing on people's strong desire for security, understood as 'jobs, peace and liberty, not necessarily better roads or more goods'. He also urged the information officers to present the case in 'simple, human terms': 'You cannot talk about a vague concept of removing trade barriers, but you can talk about a feeling of security to Italians because their border can be crossed with goods.'[37] Drummond seconded Hodges, and advised telling the story of European integration 'in terms of more jobs, more security, less rationing, fewer black markets and lower prices'. The information officers' conference formulated the following guideline: to translate the abstract concept of integration into concrete benefits, and to link the issue of integration to the concept of productivity, since both were intertwined.[38]

The boundaries of Europe

To make a case for European unification, the MP films first had to explain what they meant by Europe. And they had to demarcate it. Fernand Braudel famously stipulated that 'the question of boundaries is the first to be encountered; from it all others flow. To draw a boundary around anything is to define, analyse and reconstruct it'.[39] Where were the borders of Europe? And was the Europe the MP films promoted a continent, a concept or both?

In 1950, the film unit in Paris commissioned a film series titled *The Marshall Plan at Work* to promote the ERP's recovery efforts and to foster an understanding of how European states were interconnected. Each of the twelve episodes depicts the modernization process in one ERP country; each begins with the same topographic map of Europe over which the opening titles run. Filmic maps of this type are filled with political meaning, as they express and produce collective identities.[40] In *The Marshall Plan at Work*, the monochrome map depicts the European continent up to the Ural Mountains (see figure 5.1), and thus references a traditional geographic demarcation of Europe that emerged in the eighteenth century. In order to capture the full geographical expanse of Europe, the frame also includes parts of Iran, as well as the northern stretches of Morocco and Algeria, but omits the northern tip of Scandinavia, as well as Iceland. While the opening thus offers a broad, geographic definition of Europe, the filmic narratives operate with a narrow, political understanding of Europe. The countries under communist rule are excluded from the European project by omission, while the positions of Spain and Finland remain vague. In this way, the films reinscribe the map with new meaning, as the narratives equate 'Europe' with those countries that participate in the MP.

A map of similar size and scope is used in the opening sequence of *The Changing Face of Europe* (1951) produced by Wessex Films for the film unit. As the series is filmed in Technicolor, colour and lighting add meaning to the map: Europe is painted in reddish colours (the tone varies from a coral red to a brownish red) and is surrounded by blue sea – which suggests that Europe is a natural entity, largely confined by water.[41] The map does not show national boundaries and does not differentiate between Eastern and Western Europe (although the films themselves do). Instead, a key light illuminates the area of central and northern Europe, leaving the southern regions of Europe darker (and hardly recognizable in most film copies). The eye is drawn to northern and central Europe, as the opening titles in large, white capital letters are positioned in the upper two-thirds of the screen. Bonifazio argues that this representation expresses the series' (and other MP films') tendency to reinscribe the North–

Figure 5.1 The mapping of Europe in *The Marshall Plan at Work* and *The Changing Face of Europe* series.

South divide, presenting Southern Europe as backward and impoverished, and Northern Europe as modern and economically thriving.[42] The series' mode of narration and storyline certainly give strength to this argument, although the film unit was most likely not involved in the production of the opening titles, since the Technicolor series was edited and finished in the United States.[43]

Both series invoke the notion of Europe as a continent in their opening sequence, but then revoke it, replacing it with a political definition of Europe that comprises only those countries that adopt the ideology set forth by the MP. An explanation for the filmic exclusion of Eastern Europe was provided by the Information Division's deputy Waldemar Nielsen, who ordered his film officers to 'strike out all references to Eastern European countries' from the original script of *The Changing Face of Europe*. Nielsen argued that 'we must be careful not to create any impression that these Eastern European countries are sincerely engaged in cooperative recovery and economic development activities with the countries of Western Europe'.[44] Nielsen's argument reveals a concern that European audiences might take the films' argument for European unification too literally and extend it to mean cooperation with communist countries: unimaginable for Americans, but not so for Europeans.

Significantly, the political and ideological categories are not identified as such, but disguised as cultural categories. Western culture is presented as sophisticated and civilized, whereas by omission or allusion, Eastern Europe is defined as uncultured, uncivilized and backward. This strategy of framing the political in cultural terms is also used in *The Hour of Choice* (1951), written and directed by Stuart Legg for the British ECA mission. The compilation documentary seeks to convince the viewer that Europe's future lies in unification because Europeans are linked by a shared heritage and culture.

Figure 5.2 Is Europe Christian or Muslim – or both? (*The Hour of Choice*).

Largely compiled of footage from existing MP films, the documentary begins with the image and sound of a tolling bell, which gives way to a rousing orchestral score and a montage of scenes showing various European landscapes and cities. The narrator invites the audience to interpret the meaning of these images by describing the scene: 'The land of the setting sun; the world beyond the West. That's how the Ancient Assyrians described this complex continent; this infinite variety of scene and setting. This continent we know as Europe.' A shot of the Ortaköy Mosque in Istanbul (see figure 5.2), with the Bosphorus river in the distance, prompts the viewer to ask: Does the Bosphorus represent the geographic border of Europe? Do Turkey and Islam belong to Europe? The rest of the film remains vague about this issue: it shows scenes of Christian, Jewish and Greek Orthodox worship, but no Muslim prayers, thereby suggesting that Europe's roots lie in Christianity (as the bell at the very beginning insinuates) and Judaism, but not in Islam.

The Hour of Choice defines the boundaries of Europe first and foremost as cultural. Europeans are bound to together by values that 'every Western European shares today' (see figure 5.3). Freedom of speech is presented as such a value, and scenes from

Figure 5.3 *The Hour of Choice* presents the Europeans as diverse, but tied together by the same values.

the Speakers' Corner in London illustrate the point. Here, the narrator subtly demarcates Western Europe from Eastern Europe by arguing that Western Europeans have succeeded in their struggle for freedom. The Europe which the narrator formulates does include 'our European kith and kin' in Eastern Europe, but only theoretically, since 'towards the East looms a giant totalitarian state' that has enforced its 'rigid unity' on these countries. The alternative idea of unity that the film envisages is one that allows diversity, illustrated by bustling street scenes and idyllic landscapes as emblems of democratic Western Europe. The unity the communist fights for is 'rigid' and suppresses the freedom of the people, as footage showing a military parade with orderly rows of tanks and marching soldiers starkly illustrates. *The Hour of Choice* makes the argument that Europe is defined by its adherence to liberal values, which makes membership of Europe a matter of ideological choice.

But how European are the values that demarcate Europe from the rest of the world? The French compilation documentary *Liberté* (Liberty, 1950) is interesting in this respect. It seeks to promote transatlantic relations, and was presumably made to counter the strong anti-Americanism sentiment in France – or at least to dispel American concerns about it. The documentary depicts the conversion of the German ocean liner *Europa* into the French passenger ship *Liberté*, which now carries passengers across the Atlantic. The German ship had been confiscated by the Americans and was later donated to the French; it therefore symbolizes the close ties between France and the United States.[45] The new name is highly symbolic: '*Liberté*' is, the French narrator argues, 'typiquement français', an argument that implicitly contests the US claim to be the nation of freedom. But the replacement of the old name, *Europa*, with *Liberté*, is also significant, and to an extent ambiguous, since it implies that Europe is an old, German-dominated concept, whereas the future lies in close transatlantic relations. This ambiguity reveals that the ECA's rhetorical strategies were not always coherent, since it had to adapt to national sensibilities: here, to convince the French it had to undercut its own idea of a unified Europe. In any case, the ECA mission in France was deeply unhappy with the film, though it restricted its criticism to the droning music and bad camera work.[46]

Arguments for European integration

The film unit in Paris initiated most films on the subject of European integration. However, their number is relatively small; apart from those already mentioned they comprise only *The Shoemaker and the Hatter* (ECA 1950), *The Council of Europe, E comme Europe* (all MSA 1952), *River Without Frontiers* (ECA West Germany 1950) and *Without Fear* (ECA UK 1951). Although they do not speak of Europe specifically, *Let's Be Childish* (ECA France 1950) and *As the Young Ones Sing* (MSA Austria 1954) can be included, as they advocate integration by promoting mutual understanding and international cooperation.

These films highlight the economic benefits of European integration, and sometimes add promises of security and peace. They claim that closer cooperation and exchange between European states will produce growth, job security and rising living standards. Yet as long as national barriers and trade restrictions are in place, the promise cannot be fulfilled. Images of customs officers, closing boom gates and stop signs visualize these national barriers and connote them as negative. Films by other sponsors on the subject of European unification use the same icons of borders. Frontiers and border controls hem people in, hindering the movement of goods and thus stemming the flow of the economy. They are artificial and outdated and need to be removed.[47]

The call to dismantle national barriers was also supported by cultural arguments. The film *The Hour of Choice* claims that national frontiers in Western Europe are in fact opposed to the very nature of Europeans, who share a 'freedom of spirit'. Images of statues of great artists, cathedrals and castles illustrate the genius of Europeans. They are used to bolster the narrator's argument that Europeans have, throughout the ages, sought to 'leap across' or 'soar above' these frontiers. A cut to a Catholic Church service indicates that, so far, the efforts to overcome these frontiers have been only spiritual. Now, the narration implies, the time has come to act, and to dismantle the borders and keep apart what actually belongs together.[48] The French film *E comme Europe* (MSA 1952) also insists that national borders are unnatural and keep apart what 'naturally' belongs together. Removing these borders is only logical, the film claims, since they give no protection or security. An animated map that shows how often national frontier lines have changed in Europe over the last centuries highlights the volatility of borders in order to convince the viewer that they are instable and cannot be trusted.[49]

Similar to *E comme Europe*, the two MP film series *The Marshall Plan at Work* (ECA 1950) and *The Changing Face of Europe* (ECA 1951) highlight the 'natural' connections between European nations. Although they do not speak directly of European cooperation, they imply connection through their mode of narration. Each episode of *The Changing Face* takes up a problem that is presented as relevant to the whole of Europe: energy, food, housing, industry, transport and health. The films juxtapose the efforts that are being made in different European countries to solve each problem, and show how the countries help each other by offering expertise or goods. The episode *Somewhere to Live*, for example, by comparing the housing problems in Northern France and Greece, points out similarities, and thereby suggests a connection. The same episode shows how Finland expresses its solidarity with Greece by delivering prefabricated houses to ameliorate the housing situation. Yet, while the series illustrates the interdependence of (Western) Europe, it also reaffirms the image of Southern Europe as poor and Northern Europe as rich: it is the North that delivers its knowledge and products. Greece and Italy are presented as the cradles of European civilization. Europe, as the narrator in the episode *The Good Life* explains, returns its thanks 'in kind'.[50] The *Marshall Plan at Work* series adopts a similar strategy. Although each episode focuses on a single country, the mode of narration emphasizes how the national is linked to the European. The episode titled *The Marshall Plan at Work in the Netherlands*, for instance, lauds the British efforts to liberate the Netherlands from Nazi occupation in a scene that depicts a Dutch memorial for killed British soldiers.

These films claim that Europe shares a 'common legacy' (*The Hour of Choice*) and common interests, thereby arguing that unification is a 'natural', and therefore desirable, development. Here, the primary motivation for demanding the removal of national borders and trade barriers is not a thriving economy, but lasting peace, which can be achieved only through mutual understanding and cooperation. These narratives point to the impact of war, visualized through

Figure 5.4 In *E comme Europe*, young Europeans meet at the river Rhine to celebrate the European idea.

destroyed buildings, explosions or hungry children in rags, to illustrate the horrible effects of nationalist thinking. Europe is thus framed as a peace project, a striving for a community of values that bridges outward differences. The youths of Europe, in particular, represent the hope and future of Europe. In *E comme Europe*, young people travel from all over Europe to meet at a youth camp at the French–German border above the Rhine, a frontier that has seen many wars (see figure 5.4). It is not only the location where they meet that is symbolic, but the efforts they undertake to come together. The young men and women walk, cycle and take the train from remote locations to reach this camp to build up a new, united Europe.

Let's Be Childish, directed by Russian émigré George Freedland, tells a similar story. Unlike in *E comme Europe*, where the youths work towards the realization of a still abstract united Europe, the children in Freedland's film are more practically inclined, and together build a castle in the snow. But the initial harmony between the children from different parts of Europe soon shows cracks when an outsider asks to be admitted to the community. The message the film conveys is that before the children can achieve peaceful cooperation they too must overcome differences, and learn that violence does not solve problems.

Let's Be Childish starts with the arrival of a girl named Toni at a winter holiday resort in the French Alps, where she finds herself amid children from different nations who are playing in the snow. The camera follows Toni's timid – and unsuccessful – attempts to make contact with the other children. In this way the film introduces the individual children, who betray stereotypical nationalistic behaviour: the Italian children fight loudly, the British boy is polite but snobbish and a German boy decorates his orderly snow house.[51] As a result of a mild dispute, the children's peaceful play erupts into a snowball fight, during which the girl suffers a head wound (see figure 5.5). Shocked by the outcome, the children show remorse, pool their pocket money for a present and visit Toni in hospital. The final sequence shows the children's participation in a competition to build the most beautiful figure out of snow. Much to the surprise (and disappointment) of their parents, who are keen to show off their children's unique talents, the children cooperate, and subsequently win the prize as a group: a huge box of chocolates. The film uses irony and humour to make this parable of European cooperation more effective.[52] Mostly filmed at the children's eye level, and thus showing only the adults' legs or lower bodies, the film offers an interesting perspective that also carries symbolic meaning: it separates the children from the adults, and creates a world in which the children implement the lessons they have learnt – that by working together everybody gets a piece of the chocolate.

Figure 5.5 Children learn the benefits of peaceful collaboration in *Let's Be Childish*.

Indirect propaganda for a united Europe

Considering that European integration was a key policy goal of the MP, whose importance was further underlined by Hoffman's announcement of the 'second phase', the overall number of films promoting the subject appears small. However, by scrutinizing the films more closely we find that many more promote the European idea, albeit indirectly, and often under cover of another theme. Many MP films implicitly make a case for European unification by illustrating how Europeans are connected to each other. In view of the widespread scepticism towards European unification, the MP propagandists were obviously anxious not to arouse misgivings by forcing the issue. The strategy was to spur the viewers into concluding that European unity logically evolves from an already existing community and is not something abstract and artificial. They hoped that films that only addressed the issue of Europe in passing would influence audiences on a subconscious level, encouraging them to be more open to the idea of closer cooperation with their former enemies.

The motif of the ship

Filmmakers often resorted to symbols and visual metaphors to illustrate European interdependence. Two of the most popular motifs were the ship and the stream. In the first half of the ERP, the ECA gave priority to the production of energy and the expansion of transport networks to revive production and trade.[53] It is therefore not surprising that a considerable number of MP films depict activities in shipyards and harbours, with the ship as medium of transport taking central place. Yet the symbol of the ship also appears in documentaries that do not deal directly with fishing, sea trade or shipbuilding. The unloading of a ship is a staple theme in many MP films, in which machinery and crates carrying the conspicuous ERP logo are loaded onto the European quays, from where they travel to the needy. The ship as carrier of Marshall Aid symbolizes the strong link between the United States and Europe. It functions not merely as a mobile bridge between the United States and Europe, but, even more importantly, reconnects European nations forcefully separated by the war. Saved, like the nations, from destruction, the newly built ships now carry goods and people – through the Mediterranean and across the Atlantic, as in *Liquid Sunshine* (ECA Italy 1949), on the Rhine, as in *Henry's Story* (ECA France 1950) and *River without Frontiers* (ECA West Germany 1950), or through the Corinth Canal, as in the documentary *Corinth Canal* (ECA Greece 1950). The ship is assigned a double function: it serves as a link and a promise of the revival of intra-European trade and economic growth (see figure 5.6).

The ship brings goods to those in need, but also information and entertainment, as the Greek compilation film *Island Odyssey* (ECA Greece 1950) illustrates. In *Island Odyssey*, the camera accompanies a sailing boat carrying an ECA exhibition and a mobile film unit to remote Greek islands, to inform the inhabitants about the MP. A long shot captures the white ship with the ERP logo on her bow as it ploughs through the waves. The scene conveys a sense of optimism; it carries good news to the islanders and brings them closer together, uniting them in the goal of reviving Europe.

Figure 5.6 The ship as promise of revival in *Henry's Story* and *Provence*.

The ship and her crew know no borders, as Hermann van der Horst's documentary *Shoot the Nets!* (ECA Netherlands 1951) seeks to demonstrate. Van der Horst relied on the strength of the visual language to promote the message, using only a sparse commentary to fill in information. The British *Monthly Film Bulletin* described this prizewinning Dutch documentary on herring fishing as 'an efficient, orthodox piece of film-making' and lauded it for its 'adherence to the most respectable of documentary schools'.[54] Indeed, *Shoot the Nets!* with its slow pace and detailed recording of the fishermen's work on board, is very reminiscent of Grierson's herring fishing documentary *Drifters* (1929).[55] *Shoot the Nets!* accompanies a fleet of Dutch fishing vessels on their yearly journey up the North Sea to Dogger Bank, the summer territory of the herring shoals (see figure 5.7). Ships from eight different European countries gather on these fishing grounds to make a catch. The off-screen commentary argues that in this 'world where frontiers and barriers are unknown' the idea of a united Europe has been realized, as the fishermen 'set day to day an example of peace and tolerance'. The narrator claims that the fishermen themselves have laid down the laws that apply to all, even though they speak different languages, as the continuous crackling of different voices through the radio sets illustrates. The common purpose brings them together, and they rely on each other in the rough conditions of the North Sea, where the mountain-high waves and heavy gales toss their little boats around. Each crew carries home a big catch. The images of nets filled to the brim with fish suggest that the big haul is the result of transnational cooperation, when, in fact, the real reason behind the plentiful fish stocks was that the Second World War prevented commercial fishing in the North Sea. The fishermen who defy both the rough conditions and nationalistic sentiments are presented as a model of European cooperation – and as trailblazers for a modern Europe.

The ship is a messenger of a brighter future. In the documentary *Free City* (ECA Trieste 1951), produced and directed by the Italian Romolo Marcellini, the ship launch signifies the start of a new era and – implicitly – the birth of a new Europe. It marks the successful recovery of a city that was damaged by the war and reassures the audience, both through the programmatic title and through the story it tells, that Trieste and its population are safe under the protection of the West. The documentary depicts a day in the life of an Italian worker, illustrating Trieste's economic recovery, which comes as a result of US assistance – and protection. The city of Trieste was, after the Second World War, located in the internationally controlled Free Territory of Trieste, which had been set up by UN Security Council Resolution 16. Trieste was of high strategic importance to the West because of its proximity to communist Yugoslavia. And even though

Figure 5.7 Fishermen in the North Sea – trailblazers for a united Europe in *Shoot the Nets!*

Trieste was under no immediate threat of communist expansion after Tito's split from Stalin in 1949, which turned Yugoslavia into a recipient of American aid, the city remained of symbolic significance. The scene of the launching of a new steamer conveys optimism for Trieste's and, implicitly, Europe's future. Even so, the head of the film unit, Lothar Wolff, who had written the script, came to doubt that the imagery was strong enough to sell the message of a free, united Europe. He had initially planned a film without a commentary, but after seeing the final version he concluded that 'too many things need explanation'. A sparse narration, written by the head of the Rome film unit, John Secondari, was added.[56] The central scene, which shows the newly built steamer gliding into the sea to the applause of a large crowd, is thus commented by the narrator who interprets the event as 'assurance that Trieste will be alright'.

The complicated and lengthy process of building this new Europe is tackled in the visually striking documentary *A Ship Is Born* (ECA Italy 1951), directed by the Italian Ubaldo Magnaghi. Magnaghi had already made a documentary on a similar topic for the Italian mission in 1948, *Two Counts*, which captures the reconstruction of the Italian mercantile fleets at Genoa, Monfalcone and Naples. The two documentaries display strong stylistic similarities, especially with regard to cinematography and montage (Magnaghi used the same editor), although *A Ship Is Born*, filmed in Technicolor at the shipyard of Genoa and accompanied by a monumental symphonic musical score, is more grandiose. Through visual analogy it draws attention to the similarities between the building of a ship and the building of Europe; both require careful planning and the skills of many different (male) talents who toil on the enormous ship's body. Having shown in detail the different work processes that shipbuilding involves, the sense of achievement is almost tangible, as we see the new vessels lying in the harbour, ready to start their journey into the wide world. The hulls gleam in golden yellow, hinting at future prosperity. The film closes with a scene that leaves the camera briefly lingering on the reflection of a ship's bow on the water (see figure 5.8); the camera then moves slowly and almost caressingly upwards to emphasize the scale of the achievement, until finally the top of the bow comes into view. Frank Gervasi, head of the Rome information unit, delivers the English commentary with a pathos that underlines the symbolic significance of the newly built ships: 'Behind each ship lies a country. A country left in ruins by the war, rebuilt now, strong and capable of contributing to its own – and the free world's – strength.' As in *Free City*, the ship serves as a symbol of recovery and signals the start of a new era. It brings Europeans and the world closer together and holds the promise of a prosperous and peaceful future.

Figure 5.8 'Behind each ship lies a country' – the ship as a symbol of recovery in *A Ship Is Born*.

It also serves, as for example in *Village without Words*, as a metaphor for the realization of a dream. *Village without Words* was produced for the Italian country mission in 1950 by the American filmmaker David Kurland, who had established himself as a producer in Rome and made several MP films for the country missions in Italy and Greece (see Chapter 2).[57] As the title indicates, the documentary dispenses with a voice-over. Instead, the message is conveyed entirely visually and through Alberico Vitalini's musical score, which structures the narration. *Village without Words* shows a desolate Italian town, badly in need of repair and employment (see figure 5.9). The factory is closed, the streets are deserted and the shop windows are empty. The camera zooms in on a boy who is sitting alone at a fountain in the deserted town square, playing silently with a miniature model war ship, a visual hint at the war that caused the present desolate situation. The measured musical score in minor keys underlines the depressive mood that has fallen upon this town. A few harp chords underscoring the boy's play at the fountain suddenly lift into a rousing orchestral tune heralding a change, as an establishing shot captures a steamer that glides into the town's harbour. The camera approaches the ship step by step, finally climbing on deck to show in close-up the faces of smiling men who prepare to land and offload the cargo. The rhythmic musical score emulates the movements of the crew and expresses the mood change the ship's arrival has brought about. Goods carrying the ERP logo – the only direct reference to the MP – are offloaded and put on carts and train carriages. The last sequence shows people streaming back to work and into the shops as the factory reopens, thus constructing a logical link between the delivery of Marshall Aid and the town's revival. It concludes with a scene of children playing happily on the carousel that lay rusting at the beginning of the film; the world is moving again.

Figure 5.9 The ship as a symbol of hope in *Village without Words*.

The examples presented here illustrate that the ship's symbolic meaning is closely linked to its context. The coding of the ship in the MP films is different from that in popular cinema or literary text where, as Roland Barthes argues, 'a ship is a habitat before being a means of transport'.[58] Through the imagery of ship construction, the arrival of a steamer or the loading and unloading of cargo in the harbour, the MP films highlight the connective element of the ship. Here, the symbol of the ship does not signify a closed universe. Nor does it function as an 'emblem of closure', but highlights the exchange between the ship and the mainland. The ship in the MP films aggregates different symbolic meanings and serves simultaneously as a beacon of hope, an intermediary and an envoy of prosperity.

The motif of the stream

Another popular motif that appears, sometimes in connection with the ship, is the stream. The stream in the MP films takes various forms: an actual river or waterway, a stream of traffic on railways and roads, a flow of electricity or the steady flow of goods and machines on assembly lines. Through its ability to cross borders, both artificial and natural, the stream functions as a metaphor for cooperation, for the breaking down of barriers, and for overcoming differences. The narrator in Géza von Rádvanyi's documentary *E comme Europe* (MSA 1952), for instance, explains that the stream is oblivious to the national borders it crosses during its journey to the sea, as it naturally connects people and countries that are separated by artificial borders. The location of the international youth camp on the shores of the river Rhine in *E comme Europe* is therefore highly symbolic. The Rhine, once a fiercely contested boundary, now serves as symbol of unity between the former enemies Germany and France, bringing together young people from different parts of Europe to celebrate their shared values in constant view of the unifying river.

Whereas Rádvanyi uses the stream as a symbol of unity, the Swedish filmmaker Arne Sucksdorff employs it to visualize Europe's interdependency. His documentary *The Living Stream* (ECA Sweden, Denmark, Norway 1950) shows how people in Scandinavia rely on each other. The cyclical narration describes how the brooks and rivers in Norway generate the electricity that is needed to produce fertilizer, which is exported to Denmark to boost growth in the Danish wheat fields; Danish farm produce is then exported to Sweden to feed the steel workers who produce the ships the Norwegians need for their trade and fishing. Cutting between the flow of sparks of a blowpipe in a Swedish steel factory and the rapids of a Norwegian river, the imagery reinforces the message of the narrator, who underlines the interdependency not only of the Scandinavian people, but also of the Scandinavians and the wider world: 'Only when people understand that they depend on each other, only when they learn to create from this interdependence a living and fruitful relationship, only then can man achieve security for today and for tomorrow.' Again and again Sucksdorff returns to the water, inserting scenes of a gushing river or a still sea at sunset to underline the connecting power of water. *The Living Stream* replicates the metaphor of the stream in the continuous flow of crates loaded at a Swedish dockyard, the repetitive turn of the reaper cutting down the golden wheat on a Danish field, the baby suckling at his mother's breast.

Some critics felt that the symbolically rich language distracted from the message. Ned Nordness, information officer at the ECA mission in Norway, which co-produced the film with Denmark and Sweden, had warned earlier that Sucksdorff's script was 'so lyrical as to weaken its purpose and impact'.[59] When the film was released, others expressed similar scepticism. The British film magazine *The Film User* criticized the film by stating that – the beautiful visuals notwithstanding – the 'preoccupation with pictorial symbolism has been carried too far for the film to succeed in its purpose'.[60] The Danish press, though full of praise for the Swedish filmmaker and lauding the poetic tone of the film, also concluded that the argument for the interrelations between the Europeans appeared too contrived and flimsy to be convincing.[61]

The motif of the stream appears very often in films about electric power, such as in *Treasure of the Rhone* and *Liquid Force* (both ECA France 1950), *Breakthrough* (ECA Norway 1950), *The Invisible Link* (ECA Austria 1950) and in several episodes of *1-2-3: A Monthly Review from Europe* (MSA 1952–1953). *Power for All*, part of *The Changing Face of Europe* series, promotes the expansion of the hydroelectric power network that spans the Alps. The camera emulates the movement of a stream by accompanying a group of men who carry metal parts up the slopes of a mountain. It shows the men erecting a pylon high in the Italian Alps, eventually mounting the pylon itself to open up the view of the valleys below. Matching breathtaking long shots over the mountains with close-ups of men working in the iron framework, the camera then turns direction and follows the water pipeline down into the valley, even moving underground where engineers are setting up the power station. The voice-over underlines the European dimension of this project by explaining that the electricity generated here will be exported to Switzerland, Germany and France. By contrasting vertical movements with horizontal sweeps, the camera emphasizes the spatiality of Europe, but also produces a balance: the vigour of the wild brook gushing down the mountains is calmed by the slow pan over the slowly flowing, mighty River Rhone. From a bird's eye view the camera follows the bends of the Rhone

and lingers on dams and power stations built to harness the force of the river –
for the benefit of all Europeans.

The message that runs through all these narratives is that the stream, whether
in the shape of water, electricity or goods, ties Europe together. It is, as the title
of one documentary indicates, 'the invisible link' that joins Europeans, who are
dependent on each other. Simultaneously, the symbol of the stream promotes a
key argument of productivity, namely that movement is positive, while standing
still is negative. Only the uninterrupted flow of information, goods and people
can guarantee a prosperous and secure Europe. The blocking of the Corinth
Canal by the Germans during the Second World War, which John Ferno's
documentary *Corinth Canal* (ECA Greece 1950) takes up, is therefore presented
as an anti-European act. The documentary begins with a scene that illustrates
the cooperative efforts of Greek and US personnel to clear the canal from debris
to make it again passable for traffic.

The film's key scene (see figure 5.10) depicts the journey of a ship through the
newly reopened canal. It shows the waterway busy with boats that transport goods and
people from one sea to the other. Positioned on the deck of a sailing ship, the camera

Figure 5.10 The MP clears the blocked waterway and connects what belongs
together in *Corinth Canal*.

glides through the canal and, using tilts and zooms, examines closely the steep white cliffs that rise up on each side. The camera conveys a sense of achievement by emulating the gaze of the men on the ship, who look with interest at the man-hewn cliffs. The framing of the shots combined with the splashing noises of pieces of rubble that fall from the cliffs into the water produce an almost cathedral-like atmosphere, which prompted the head of the film unit, Stuart Schulberg, to pronounce the film as 'breathtakingly beautiful'.[62] The voice-over, which is factual and unobtrusive, does not distract from the powerful imagery. Running over a subdued musical score, it explains the significance of the waterway: water, and with it goods and people, flow unrestrictedly through the Corinth Canal, and bring prosperity – and peace. As the sun sets in the harbour of Corinth, the lighthouse keeper turns on the electric lights that guide the ships into the open sea, an act that signals the dawn of a new age. The closing image of an ancient temple in the foreground, emblem of Europe's cultural heritage, and a white ship passing slowly in the far background towards the West, provides reassurance about the future, while promising the endurance of the old.

The (national) past and Europe's future

The above scene exemplifies how filmmakers used the past to make the Europeans more receptive to the idea of a united Europe. By referencing, for example, traditional representations of Europe as civilized and cultured, the films sought to instil a sense of communality.[63] Ancient Greek or Roman sites were popular motifs to support the claim of a shared European heritage (see *Corinth Canal*). The British documentary *I Went Back* (ECA UK 1950) also uses shots of historical buildings to reassure the audience that 'Europe is alright'. The travelogue follows the famous British actor and war veteran Leo Genn, whom the ECA has dispatched to continental Europe to assess the developments that had taken place over the last five years.[64] The film produces an interesting contrast between Glenn's use of every means of modern transport – plane, car and train – and his particular interest in the state of the heritage sites he visits. Genn, as an envoy of the new world, visits the 'old world' and is able to report back that the countries he has visited have made an impressive recovery. His optimistic verdict must have held considerable weight, since Genn was not only a well-known actor who received an Oscar nomination for his role in *Quo Vadis* (1951) but had also served as an officer in the Royal Artillery and acted as an assistant prosecutor in the Belsen trial. Though in the film Genn finds that the traces of the war are still evident, he also discovers that building and production are going strong everywhere. Most importantly, the documentary provides visual evidence that the historical sites of Vienna, Rome and Athens are still intact, confirming Europe's steadfastness.

While these films reference a positive ancient past, others seek to redefine the trauma of the Second World War into a foundation for a new, better Europe. Although some MP films point to nationalism and nationalist hatred as reasons for the Second World War, they largely refrain from laying blame on any one side in particular. The war is presented as an inevitable event that presented the Europeans with a cathartic experience. Out of the ashes, so the argument goes, a new Europe will rise, welded together by the shared experience of suffering, and united in purpose to overcome its problems through collective action.[65] The third episode of the *Changing Face of Europe* series, titled *Somewhere to Live*, begins with a scene that shows a young couple searching for a place to live in the war-damaged French city of Caen. The musical score – the famous Harry Lime theme from the British noir film *The Third Man* (1949) – conjures up memories of war-torn Vienna. For many contemporaries the tune epitomized the bleak post-war years, and the narrator refers to it as 'theme song of the weary continent'. To the sounds of the zither, the camera follows a one-legged man walking on crutches through the ruins, another iconic image of the war (see figure 5.11). Stills of bombed-out cities and scenes of children playing in the rubble document that 'from one end of Europe to the other' people are in dire need of housing. A montage of visually similar scenes suggests that the war has affected all Europeans in the same way, regardless on which side they stood. *Somewhere to Live* does not pose the question of guilt, or differentiate between the victor and the defeated.[66] Instead, the imagery constructs a collective of suffering that is presented as a foundation for the new, reborn Europe.

Figure 5.11 The experience of war has tied the Europeans together (*Somewhere to Live*).

The interpretation of war as a bonding, rather than divisive, factor, is also forwarded in the *1-2-3: A Monthly Review from Europe* series. Episode number six, for example, depicts a village in French Provence in which the villagers live harmoniously with former German POWs. The film does not inform the viewer why the Germans chose to stay on. Instead, it offers evidence of the reconciliation of the two nations by pointing to the local war memorial that was built by a German sculptor, and by showing the baptism of child with a French mother and a German father. A more persuasive argument for the war as a unifying bond is presented in the eleventh episode of the same series. Here in the Dutch town of Breda live former Polish soldiers who helped to liberate the town from German occupation. The film presents the Poles as fully integrated and – as the narrative emphasizes – productive members of the community, working as shop owners, businessmen or hairdressers. The war brought the Dutch and the Poles together in solidarity and gratitude, creating a bond that is further strengthened by the Cold War that split the continent into communist Eastern and 'free' Western Europe. The commentary draws parallels between the Second World War and the Cold War, suggesting that the 'free' world will always prevail: 'The Poles gave Breda its freedom, now Breda gives the Poles who chose not to live in Poland their freedom.'

As we have seen, European scepticism towards European integration was also the result of fears about the loss of tradition and national culture. Filmmakers sought to ameliorate these fears by establishing a link between the old and the new, between the (national) past and a (European) future. The Norwegian documentary *Breakthrough* (ECA Norway 1950), on the expansion of hydroelectric power in Norway, integrates the past into the present. Directed by the Norwegian filmmaker Lauritz Falk, the documentary tells the story of the hydroelectric power station Aura through the eyes of a man who witnessed the start of the project as a young boy at the beginning of the twentieth century. By linking the history of the hydroelectric station with that of a worker, the narration gives the story a personal touch. The story is told in one long flashback, starting with the arrival of the young boy in the fjord where his father has found work laying the foundations for the power station. Following in the footsteps of his father, the son also starts working for Aura, digging tunnels into the mountains, until the world economic crisis brings closure and mass unemployment (see figure 5.12). The young narrator strolls aimlessly through the empty building site that no longer provides him with a livelihood. The scene indicates how the national is connected to the global. The depression years are, however, not described in terms of poverty, but rather in terms of limitations and lack of opportunity that hinder (personal and national) development.

Figure 5.12 *Breakthrough*: Men return to work at Aura thanks to the ERP.

This interpretation makes the injection of Marshall Aid into the Aura project after the war even more momentous: it brings men back into work and accelerates progress through mechanization, thus opening up opportunities that could previously be found only by emigrating to the United States. The last sequence implies that, thanks to the MP, Norwegians can now live the American Dream in their home country; the tempo accelerates as the workers arrive in buses and are swiftly transported up the mountain slopes by cable car and cog railways (see figure 5.12). There is a noticeable spring in the step of these men and a smile on their faces as they operate the mechanic drills in the mines where their fathers had to work with chisels and hammers. The narrator comments that 'work is hard at Aura', but 'that is what we wanted. That is what we have been wanting for over close to 40 years,' suggesting that Aura is more than paid work: it is a lifelong mission. If Aura thrives, so do the workers and the country. The efforts and suffering that went into the development of the hydroelectric power station are presented as the foundation for the future. The achievement revives Norway's economy and brings it closer to Europe: 'We will send the electricity over the mountains to found new towns and industries. We will send it to other countries. Norway delivers electricity for the peaceful reconstruction of Europe!'

The past is coloured slightly differently in the two versions of *Breakthrough*. In the longer, eighteen-minute original version the past is given more space. Though this version depicts an idyllic life in a small, poor village community, it also describes the past as the 'black days'.[67] The worker's struggle for more rights before the First World War, which resulted in the formation of a union, the impact of the Spanish Flu, and the Nazi occupation that lands the narrator in jail for sabotage are addressed in the original version, but are missing from the shorter twelve-minute version that was, for example, distributed in Germany. The historical past in the longer version appears more burdensome, but produces a different sense of achievement, as the first-person narrator succeeds in his struggle through difficult times. Both versions, however, describe the trajectory from a past marked by deprivation to the industrialized present as evolutionary movement. The filmic narrative of *Breakthrough* thus builds on the dominant Western notion of continuous progress in history to illustrate how industrial modernization has benefited the Norwegians. It does not separate the present from the past, but presents it as an integral and important part of modern Norway and Europe.

Other MP films rhetorically dissociate Europe from its past.[68] In particular films with European integration as their main theme often suggest that the past needs to be left behind in order to build a new Europe. Tradition and national thinking are claimed to be a hindrance to progress and to Europe's economic and political development. The 'old' Europe is described as divided, bureaucratic, narrow-minded and unproductive. 'Charming enough they were, our little separate histories,' comments the narrator in *The Hour of Choice* slightly mockingly over a scene that shows Dutch women in traditional dress sitting idly on a porch, chatting and knitting. His argument that the past has no place in modern Europe – for 'we cannot live in history now' – is emphasized by a pan to a pair of girls in clunky wooden shoes; with this footwear, the image suggests, there can be no speedy progress.

The cobwebs in the shoemaker's workshop in *The Shoemaker and the Hatter* point to a past that must be brushed away to make room for something new. The shoemaker's verve to clean does not stop at the cobwebs, but extends to the traditional monopolies and high tariffs which he seeks to sweep away to allow progress. *Somewhere to Live* similarly expresses no nostalgia for the past; it decries the unhealthy, crammed living quarters of European cities before the war and presents the destruction of housing that the war caused as an opportunity to build modern housing fit for Europeans.[69] The argument that the past does not fit into a modern Europe is exemplified by the MP film *Life and Death of a Cave City* (ECA Italy, 1950), which depicts the southern Italian town of Materna, where people live in caves. Though the dwellings are clean and furnished, they are presented as an anomaly. A governmental housing project provides the cave dwellers with modern flats, whose rectangular frames mark a clean cut with the past. Whereas the film presents the move from the caves to the modern flats as an improvement, in reality the people found it hard to adapt to modernity, and eventually returned to their cave homes.[70]

These examples show that the filmic discourse on the place of the past in modern Europe was ambiguous. The films employed a variety of visual and narrative strategies to rally support for European unification, promoting arguments that sometimes contradicted each other. Since the propagandists struggled with finding the right tone to promote European integration, the issue was often addressed only indirectly. Many films thus spoke of Europe in general terms, highlighting the need for economic cooperation and exchange, but shying away from offering concrete concepts or prescribing specific steps towards unification. Europe is presented as a homogenous entity, but also as a diverse cluster of nations, both modern and traditionalist, thriving and poor. The films sometimes describe Europe as a geographical continent and sometimes as a cultural and political concept, defined first and foremost by its demarcation from communism and communist-ruled Eastern Europe.

One reason why the concepts of Europe the MP films projected were so vague was the broad resistance to the idea of political unification in Europe. In view of the Europeans' negative stance towards a united Europe, the US policymakers and strategists decided to work towards economic integration, postponing political unification to an indefinite point in the future. The film unit felt it was best not to push the issue too aggressively, fearing that this might fuel anti-American sentiments and thus undermine the other ERP goals. Moreover, neither the film officers nor the US policymakers at the top had a very clear concept of the Europe they wanted. They left it to the filmmakers to come up with ideas on how to visualize this Europe, providing them with the simple brief to produce films that 'will show and interpret the life of Western Europe, and will be based on the fundamental ideas of democracy, European unity, and progress towards a better standard of living'.[71] This, of course, raises the question of whose vision the MP films actually promoted – those of the filmmakers? Or those of the information officers and US policymakers?

6

Filmmakers and Information Officers as Cultural Transmitters

On 24 September 1950, the renowned British documentary filmmaker Humphrey Jennings (1907–1950) fell to his death from a cliff on the Greek island of Poros while on reconnaissance for a MP documentary. He died a few hours later in hospital and was buried in a cemetery in Athens.[1] His last films were for Wessex Films, set up by the former key producer of the Crown Film Unit and Jennings' friend Ian Dalrymple. The film he was working on when he died was to promote the European exchange of medical services and knowledge in an effort to eradicate tuberculosis, malaria and other diseases. It was intended as part of the *Changing Face of Europe* series, which Dalrymple produced for the ECA film unit in Paris. Jennings' assistant Graham Wallace finished the film. It entered European-wide commercial distribution in 1951 as the sixth and final episode of the series under the title *The Good Life* – paraphrasing a statement of ancient Greek physicians that a good life rests on good health.

Jennings was only forty-three years old when he died in the accident. He had been a key figure in the British documentary movement. A Cambridge graduate in English Literature, he had worked as a painter and costume designer before he moved into filmmaking by joining the General Post Office (GPO) Film Unit in 1934. His later documentary films were greatly influenced by the Mass Observation project he founded together with two friends in 1937. Informed by socialist-reformist thinking, this ambitious project studied the lives, habits and thinking of ordinary people, especially the working class, through close observation and interviews.[2] Jennings came into his own as a filmmaker during the war, when the Ministry of Information replaced the GPO with the Crown Film Unit in 1940.[3] During the war he made some of his finest documentaries, in support of the British war effort: *Listen to Britain* (1942), *Fires Were Started* (1943) and *A Diary of Timothy* (1945). Jennings continued to make documentaries 'designed to help cheer up a nation that seemed to be settling into a spiritual as well as economic depression' after the war.[4]

Jennings was one of a number of European filmmakers who made MP films. In crisis-ridden post-war Europe, the ECA offered a welcome source of income to many documentary filmmakers, who relied on public sponsorship to finance their films. Stuart Schulberg, the second head of the ECA film unit, believed that its practice of commissioning only European filmmakers was 'a regular documentary Marshall Plan, for ECA contracts sent many good filmmakers back to work.'[5] However, the ECA and its successor, the MSA, never made a concerted effort to build up a (documentary) film industry, although they did set up structures that facilitated the non-commercial distribution of films. The aim of the ECA's hiring policy was to produce more effective propaganda films, not to revive European (documentary) film.

Still, the ECA provided many European filmmakers with funding for their film projects, and younger, inexperienced documentarists with the opportunity to develop their style. What did it mean for European filmmakers to be making films for an agency of the US government, promoting US policies to the European public? How much influence did they have on the films they created, and on the messages the films promoted? The ECA film unit prided itself on its *laissez-faire* attitude towards the filmmakers,[6] but it was able to exert considerable control, and thus shape the form and content of the MP films. To understand the connection between MP films and their makers, we have to investigate the film production process and examine the relations between the filmmakers and the US information or film officers who commissioned and oversaw film production. We also need to understand the background and the interests of both of these parties. As this chapter shows, there existed a general harmony of interests between the European filmmakers and the US information officers. They had a common interest in promoting social change through economic modernization; they also had similar professional and cultural backgrounds. The US information officers, who were often first- or second-generation emigrants, were ideally suited to be cultural transmitters because they were situated in between cultures and had a cosmopolitan outlook – as, in fact, did many filmmakers.[7]

The European filmmakers

The filmmakers who produced MP films were a diverse group, at least with regard to their nationality, experience and age. Yet they were (almost) all men, and they were all white and middle class.[8] On the ECA/MSA's payroll were renowned filmmakers who had already left their mark in documentary cinema, such as the above-named Humphrey Jennings (1907–1950) and Stuart Legg (1910–1988), both key figures of the British Documentary Movement. Legg directed the documentary *The Hour of Choice* (1951), promoting European unification, for the ECA. The Swedish documentarist Arne Sucksdorff (1917–2001), who achieved international acclaim with his nature films, and who won an Oscar for his documentary on the lives of people in Stockholm in *Symphony of a City* (Människor i stad, 1947), produced and directed the MP film *A Living Stream* (1950) for the Scandinavian country missions.[9] Romolo Marcellini (1910–1999), though hardly known outside Italy's borders, had already under Mussolini been a successful producer of documentaries, mostly on colonial subjects. He also produced feature films, most importantly *Sentinels of Bronze* (Sentinelle di bronzo, 1937), a propagandistic war film set in East Africa he himself referred to as the first neo-realist film. Marcellini made at least six MP films for the country missions in Italy and Trieste, among them *Free City* (1950), *Handicraft Town* (1950) and *Life and Death of Cave City* (1950).[10] Also the Dutch documentarist John Ferno/Johannes Fernhout (1913–1987), discussed in detail further below, whose international career spanned several continents, directed and produced several MP films.

Not all filmmakers came from the documentary field. The Hungarian film director Géza von Radványi (1907–1986), brother of the famous writer Sándor Márai, temporarily switched from fiction to non-fiction to make the MP film *E comme Europe* (1952), a celebration of the European idea. From Hungary, where he had started his career, Radványi moved on to become a successful director in West German popular cinema in the 1950s. The ECA also contracted Halas & Batchelor, Britain's most influential animation studio, for *The Shoemaker and the Hatter* (1950). Founded by the English animation designer Joy Batchelor and her Hungarian husband John Halas in 1940, the studio produced a large number of humorous information and educational films for British governmental agencies during and after the war. It is perhaps most famous for the feature-length animation *Animal Farm* (1954), based on the novel by George Orwell, which was secretly financed by the CIA and scripted by former film officer Lothar Wolff.[11]

For other artists, working for the ECA/MSA represented an important stepping stone in their career. The Dutch filmmaker Herman van der Horst (1910–1976) started out as a filmmaker during the war with small nature documentaries. After the war he became involved in a few documentary shorts on reconstruction efforts in the Netherlands, commissioned by the Dutch Ministry of Public Works. However, it was the MP documentary *Shoot the Nets!*

(1951) which brought his international breakthrough and earned him the award for the best documentary short at the Cannes film festival in 1952. The next year, he won the same price with a poetic documentary on the revival of the city of Rotterdam, titled *Houen Zo!* (Steady, 1952), also sponsored by the Dutch country mission. Russian-born Jewish émigré Victor Vicas (1918–1985) was also on his way to becoming a successful film director when he was contracted by the ECA in 1950. Having managed to escape France to the United States in 1942, the trained cameraman joined the US Army and made training and information films for the soldiers. Returning to Europe after the war, Vicas directed several documentaries for public organizations in Europe and the newly created state of Israel, and was also involved in Louis de Rochement's documentary series *The Earth and Its Peoples* (1947–1948).[12] There he met de Rochement's executive producer Lothar Wolff, who in 1949 became the first head of the ECA film unit.[13]

Finally, there were those young talents for whom the ECA/MSA represented a chance to enter the filmmaking world; this was the case with the young Austrian Georg Tressler (1917–2007). After a public screening of one of his first documentary shorts in Vienna, an ECA information officer approached him. He was hired as a projectionist to tour rural Austria with a mobile film unit, but was also commissioned to make films, mostly on agricultural themes. Tressler, who made seven MP films and became a celebrated film director in West Germany in the late 1950s, described in an interview the important role MP films played in his career: 'I was trying to be a film director, and you didn't necessarily, in Austria at that time, have the money to *do* films. ... And I took these films also to build up my career in the film industry.'[14]

Working in the tradition of public sponsorship

Many of the filmmakers the film unit hired had worked for governmental agencies before. Since documentary or animation was, unlike fiction, commercially not viable, the filmmakers usually depended on public (and partly business) sponsorship to finance their work. In the interwar period, governments had begun to recognize the usefulness of film and other media to 'manufacture consent' (Walter Lippmann). Authoritarian and democratic governments alike began to use film to inform, educate and influence their citizens in order to garner support for their policies. The film artists themselves played a crucial role in this development, most notably the legendary Scottish documentary filmmaker John Grierson, founder of the British documentary movement and advocate of documentary film as a means of social reform. He was instrumental in the creation of the GPO film unit in Britain, and later the National Film Board of Canada. In the United States, Pare Lorentz's work convinced President Franklin Roosevelt to set up the US Film Service in 1938.[15] Some large private enterprises, most importantly the Shell Petroleum group in 1934, also created film units that produced documentaries. The films made by the Shell Film Unit did not advertise the company's products, but aimed to show how humans and modern technology could, in the company's own words, 'overcome challenges in health, food and transport'.[16]

The Second World War provided further stimulus to documentary film, as governments sought to rally their nations to support the war effort and explain '*Why We Fight*', as the title of Hollywood director Frank Capra's famous war documentary series went. A number of European filmmakers who would later make films for the ECA/MSA worked for governmental information agencies during the war. The Canadian National Film Board provided a temporary workplace for the English filmmaker Stuart Legg and the Dutch documentarist John Ferno. Legg also made documentaries for the Canadian Department of Labour, and moved back to Britain in 1948 to join the government's Crown Film Unit. Joy Batchelor and John Halas produced a number of cartoons for the British Ministry of Information, promoting recycling and wartime production.[17] Victor Vicas worked as a film editor for the US Office of War Information and then joined the US Army Signal Corps, where he produced information and training films for the US Army. Romolo Marcellini made documentaries for Mussolini's powerful propaganda institute Istituto Luce (LUCE), and continued his career seamlessly after the war with films for the Italian government and the Catholic Centre of Cinematography.[18]

These careers also shed light on ECA's hiring practices which are scarcely documented. Networks played a crucial role. Most filmmakers who landed contracts with the ECA were either personally known to the film officers or were recommended to them. We must not forget that the film officers who hired the filmmakers came from the same field. The film unit's first head, the German-born Lothar Wolff, had for many years been an executive producer of de Rochement's *The March of Time* film magazine.[19] Wolff's successor, Stuart Schulberg, was the son of B.P. Schulberg, the powerful head of Paramount studios. Schulberg also headed the documentary film unit of the US military government in Germany before joining the ECA. Cases where ECA information officers actively scouted for new talent, as with the Austrian filmmaker Tressler, were thus relatively rare. The records show that filmmakers who offered their services unsolicited to the ECA/MSA had little chance of being hired.[20]

Cultural background of European filmmakers

Being reliant on public sponsorship, documentary filmmakers were by necessity very mobile. They worked not only for various public and private sponsors, but often in different national settings. Some, like John Ferno, were true cosmopolitans.

John Ferno

John Ferno (1913–1987) was one of the most prolific producers of MP films. By 1950, he had already completed three MP films: *Corinth Canal* and *Return from the Valley* for the Greek country mission and *Island of Faith* for the Dutch mission. He produced another three MP documentaries, *Doctor for Ardaknos* (1951, never released), *A Farm in Four Countries* (1953, directed by his collaborator Nelo Risi) and *The Miner's Window* (1954), in addition to several episodes for the MSA film series *1-2-3: A Monthly Review from Europe* (1952–1953). The film unit also proposed him to the French foreign ministry for two MP films on North Africa, although these were never realized.[21] Ferno was thus a regular contributor to the ECA's propaganda work.

Ferno was born Johannes Fernhout in North Holland in 1913. He started off shooting street photography in socially deprived areas in the early 1930s, when his mentor, the Dutch filmmaker and communist Joris Ivens, introduced him to filming.[22] Through Ivens, Ferno came into contact with the Belgian filmmaker Henri Storck. Ferno accompanied him to South America, where he made his first documentary, about Easter Island (1934). Back in Europe, Ferno worked as a cameraman on Iven's famous Spanish Civil War documentary *Spanish Earth* (1937), written by Ernest Hemingway, and on a documentary about the Japanese invasion of China titled *The 400 Million* (1939). Like his mentors, Ferno was a political filmmaker who made films that addressed pressing social issues. When the American documentarist Lorentz invited Ivens to the United States in 1939, Ferno followed him and changed his name to John Ferno. During the war years, he made films for a number of public agencies, such as the documentary *And So They Live* (1940) for the Educational Film Institute of New York University, which depicts the life of poor farmer communities in the Appalachian Mountains. He also worked for Grierson's National Film Board of Canada.

In 1944, Ferno returned to Europe as a war correspondent of the US Forces to film the liberation of his home country. He turned the footage into two documentaries, *Broken Dykes* and *The Last Shot*, both financed by the British Ministry of Information (MOI).[23] The films were widely shown in cinemas across Western Europe and the United States in 1945, and cemented Ferno's reputation as one of the most talented documentary filmmakers of his time. The British magazine *The Spectator* lauded *Broken Dykes* for its 'artistry and feeling' and attested that Ferno had, as in the film *Spanish Earth*, 'succeeded in investing his interior groupings and individual heads with the qualities of a whole people'.[24] Ferno's MP film *Island of Faith* can be seen as a sequel to *Broken Dykes* in that it documents the rebuilding of the dykes and desalting of farming land in the Dutch province of Walcheren, which had been destroyed to aid the Western Allies' war effort.

The above illustrates that Ferno was already an established and very well connected filmmaker when the head of the ECA film unit, Lothar Wolff, first approached him in 1949. Wolff knew Ferno personally through his job as executive producer of de Rochement's documentary series *The Earth and Its Peoples* (1947–1948), for which Ferno directed seven films in Europe and Morocco.[25] Ferno was a true cosmopolitan. He was constantly travelling for his work and lived in many countries for a prolonged length of time. After his return from the United States, Ferno settled in Paris and set up his production company John Ferno Productions. In 1957 he moved to London, and then in 1960 back to his home country of the Netherlands, where he filmed his documentary *Sky over Holland*, which won the Golden Palm in Cannes in 1967. From the 1960s, Ferno commuted between his homes in the Netherlands, Italy and Israel; the latter became the focus of his professional interest in his later career. With his son, he made three documentaries on Israel and the struggle of the Jewish diaspora.[26] He died in 1987 and was buried in Jerusalem.

Throughout his life, Ferno moved easily between different cultures. His concern for humanity is also reflected in the style and themes of his MP films, which focus on human efforts to return to a life of peace: Dutch farmers rebuild dykes and reclaim their lost land in *Islands of Faith*, Greek refugees return to their destroyed homes after the end of the civil war in *Return from the Valley* and in *Corinth Canal*, Greek and American men join forces to clear the canal of Corinth which had been blocked by the retreating German army. Obviously influenced by his own life history, the loss of home and the need to build a new life are major themes in Ferno's MP films; in his last MP film, titled *The Miner's Window* (1954), he returned to his roots as a documentarist of working-class culture by filming the lives of Scottish, Italian and German men working in the Belgian coal mines.

Victor Vicas

Equally cosmopolitan was Victor Vicas (1918–1985). Unlike Ferno, who was a global traveller in pursuit of his vocation, it was political circumstances that uprooted the young Vicas. Born Victor Katz in Moscow, he emigrated with his family to Berlin in 1925. As Jews and stateless Russians they then had to flee from Nazi persecution in 1933; they resettled in France, where Vicas trained and worked as a cameraman. He joined the French Army in 1939, and was briefly imprisoned by the Germans in June 1940, but escaped. In 1942 he managed to emigrate to the United States and became a US citizen, changing his last name to Vicas. During the war, he made training and information films for the US Army. The transition to peacetime proved less difficult for Vicas than for other young documentary filmmakers. Vicas signed film contracts with United Nations Relief and Rehabilitation Administration (UNRRA) and de Rochement.[27] He also made six films for Jewish agencies in the newly created state of Israel, all of which depict the building up of the state of Israel.

For the ECA film unit, Vicas made four films, two of them for the Austrian country mission: *The Invisible Link* (1950) documents the expansion of hydroelectric power production in Austria and the dangerous work of the builders of the massive Kaprun dam. *Project for Tomorrow* (1950) is also set in the Alps, and shows the implementation of an American '4-H-Club' educational programme that teaches children the practices of modern farming, husbandry and household management. His other two films emphasize the spirit of cooperation: the *Council of Europe* (1952), which explains the function and aims of this nascent supranational organization, demonstrates that mutual understanding is possible despite the variety of languages spoken in Europe. The fiction film *Jour de Peine* (1952) promotes dialogue between industry and labour. Though clearly anti-communist in its message, the film, directed primarily at French labour, takes pains not to disparage communist workers, but outlines the advantages of 'free' non-communist labour unions.

The conflict between communism and Western liberalism remained the theme of his first feature film titled *No Way Back* (Weg ohne Umkehr, Germany 1953), which tells the story of a Soviet engineer who, disillusioned by the communist system, tries to escape to West Berlin. *No Way Back* won the Golden Globe for the best foreign film in 1955, and laid the ground for an impressive international career as a film and TV director. The fact that Schulberg, the second head of the ECA film unit, produced the film (as well as Vicas's next feature film), illustrates the close networks in which all these filmmakers operated.

George Freedland

George Freedland (1910–1993) had a similar, though less illustrious, career. Born Georg Friedland in St. Petersburg in 1910. Like Vicas, Freedland moved to Berlin, where he worked as an assistant director, cutter and critic. Also driven out of Germany by the Nazis, he lived and worked in France before he emigrated to the United States in 1940. He continued to work as a writer and cutter, mainly in the field of information and educational films. After the war, he returned to Europe, again directing educational films for both public and commercial sponsors and cultural institutions.[28] He produced and directed the only Irish MP film, *The Promise of Barty O'Brien* (1952), a short fiction film that promoted Ireland's electrification programme through a father–son conflict. His cheerful *Let's be Childish* (1950), produced for the French country mission, used children as protagonists to promote cultural understanding and closer international cooperation.[29]

Mobility and exchange

These three filmmakers lived and worked in various national settings. This experience not only gave them unique insights into different cultures and filmmaking practices, but also made them a part of a transnational professional network that proved advantageous to their careers. While other European filmmakers were more strongly rooted in their own specific national contexts, there existed a considerable degree of exchange within the documentary field. The difficult funding situation encouraged mobility, as did the fact that many documentary film projects required a great deal of travelling; documentary from its inception had been concerned with exploring and cataloguing foreign cultures. Moreover, documentary was, unlike commercial cinema, a relatively small field, and filmmakers had to look for inspiration beyond their borders. Figures like the 'father of Danish documentary', Theodor Christensen (1914–1967), who produced the MP film *All My Ships* (1951) for the Danish country mission, cited the British documentary school and Robert Flaherty as his key inspirations.[30] Through his work as a film theorist, filmmaker and teacher (he taught film at the Cuban Film Institute from 1963), Christensen exerted considerable influence on other filmmakers, in both Denmark and abroad, either through direct cooperation or through his writings and films.[31]

The field of animation film was also highly mobile. The German country mission contracted the Dutch animation studio of Marten Toonder to produce the cartoon series *Hugo* (1952). Toonder assigned the direction of the project to the British animator Harald Mack, and hired as illustrators the Danish animators Bjørn Ring and Bjørn Frank Jensen, who were unable to make a living in Denmark.[32] The Paris film unit engaged the two largest British animation studios for the projects *The Shoemaker and the Hatter* and *Without Fear*. Both studios were greatly influenced by Central European émigrés. The animators John Halas, a Hungarian, and the German Peter Sachs, both Jews, came to London in the 1930s, which would go on to become the centre of animation.

Halas moved to London in 1936 because he was finding it hard to earn a living as an animator in Hungary. There he met his future wife, Joy Batchelor, a designer and illustrator. They married in 1940 and set up the animation studio Halas and Batchelor, which would become one of the largest studios in Europe. They started making cartoons for commercial advertising, but were soon contracted by the British Ministry of Information to produce informational cartoons that encouraged the British to contribute to the war effort. After the war, they continued making informational films, this time for the Labour government, as well as experimental films. Sachs, who directed the anti-communist *Without Fear*, was a German Jew who fled from Nazi persecution to Great Britain. First interned as an enemy alien on the Isle of Man, he was then hired by the Ministry of Information, which was looking for animators.[33] Sachs started to work for Larkins Studio, and became its main creative force. Like Halas, Sachs was greatly influenced by the Bauhaus movement, and was known for his enthusiasm for experimenting with new styles and modern art.[34]

Although both Sachs and Halas became British citizens, their art and outlook were decisively shaped by their culture of origin. To his co-workers, Sachs was 'almost the animation version of the continental film director' with his professional zeal and heavy German accent ('Zis schwill happen!').[35] Their influence was not merely felt on the aesthetic level; they shaped the way the British animation industry was run, as the cultural historian Robert Hewison points out: 'They'd been used to running things in their own countries, a kind of entrepreneurialism which meant that suddenly the British animation industry was forced to get its act together, cause here were people who weren't just good animators, they were also good businessmen.'[36] The ECA's contracting of Halas and Sachs also has to be seen in this context. They were transcultural entrepreneurs who perfectly embodied the liberal-capitalist values the MP administration wanted to sell. Moreover, their personal experience of authoritarian regimes made them ideal promoters of anti-totalitarian messages.

All these filmmakers were hired for their expertise and, in many cases, because they were well connected. Yet the most important reason was that they were Europeans. As has been discussed in Chapter 1, the ECA's practice of commissioning European filmmakers was based on the hope that 'programs conducted with, through, and whenever possible, by nationals of a country ... were at once more acceptable and less productive of negative reactions'.[37] The ECA, anxious of anti-American sentiments, sought to downplay the American presence in its films. Their information officers were convinced that European filmmakers knew their audiences better than they did, and that consequently they could produce more effective propaganda films. The ECA was, it seems, dependent on the filmmakers' familiarity with their own culture to reach European audiences.

The US information officers

The decision-makers and strategists within the ECA Information Division and its information offices were all American. They were not, however, entirely ignorant of Europe when they took up their jobs as information officers. Harry Price's assertion that 'a large part' of the ECA information personnel 'had never worked outside the United States before', and thus faced 'formidable barriers of language and culture', requires some qualification.[38] A number of information officers, especially those in decision-making positions, had lived and worked in Europe before.

Helen Kirkpatrick, for example, the only woman in a high position, and the first director of information at the French country mission, had covered the European theatre of war as a foreign correspondent of the *Chicago Daily News* throughout the war.[39] Frank Shea, journalist for *TIME* magazine and chief of the Field Branch at the Information Division in Paris in 1949, had accompanied the British Naval Forces as a war correspondent in 1944, covering the liberation of Greece. Before he took up his job at the ECA, he had reported on the communist takeovers in Hungary, Bulgaria and Rumania for *TIME*; he had also headed the US propaganda office on the Greek Military and Economic Aid Mission.[40] Walter Ridder, first head of the information office of the West German country mission and from September 1950 Chief of Operations at the European Information Division, was the grandson of the German immigrant Herman Ridder, founder of the second-largest newspaper publisher Knight-Ridder. Ridder had also served as a war correspondent in Europe during the Second World War and covered the liberation of the Dachau concentration camp in 1945.[41] Particularly closely connected to their country of operation were the information staff of the Italian country mission. Its first director, Andrew Berding, who later became head of the ECA/MSA Information Division in Washington, had been the chief of the Rome bureau of the Associated Press for four years in the 1930s. During the war, he had served as the chief of counterintelligence for the American wartime intelligence agency Office of Strategic Services (OSS) in Italy and Germany.[42] Berding's successor as the director of information at the Italian country mission was the Italian-American Frank Gervasi, who since 1934 had lived as a foreign correspondent in Europe, mostly in Rome.[43] His colleague John Secondari, who headed the Italian film unit, was actually born in Rome in 1920. His parents later emigrated to the United States, where Secondari studied journalism. Secondari joined the army in 1941, served in Europe and stayed in Italy after the war. He first worked as a reporter for the *Rome Daily American* and then as a foreign correspondent for the CBS before starting as a film officer at the newly set up ECA information office in Rome in 1948.[44]

The ECA film officers were a particularly cosmopolitan group. Like Secondari, they were often first-generation emigrants. Moving between different cultures, they acquired the cultural 'savviness' – and networks – which served them well in their line of work. Lothar Wolff, the first head of the film unit in Paris, was a German Jew who fled Nazi Germany in 1936. He emigrated to New York in January 1936 and started as a cutter at de Rochemont's *The March of Time* film magazine. He continued there as a film editor and executive producer until 1949, when he was headhunted by Al Friendly, the head of the ECA Information Division.[45] His successor as the head of the film unit was Stuart Schulberg, the son of famous Hollywood producer B. P. Schulberg. Although not an emigrant, Stuart Schulberg had been in schooled in Switzerland and spoke French and German fluently. He played a leading role in the 're-education' efforts of the US Military Government (OMGUS) in Germany as the head of the documentary film unit. Friendly successfully persuaded OMGUS to permit the transfer of Schulberg to the ECA, insisting that none of his other candidates had 'the special kind of European, documentary, governmental experience that is essential'.[46] Schulberg was succeeded as the head of the ECA film unit by Nils Nilson, son of a German mother and a Swedish father, who had worked with Schulberg at the OMGUS information office. Nilson quit after the MSA was replaced by the US Information Agency in summer 1953. The last head of the film unit, who took over from Nilson, was Albert 'Al' Hemsing, who was born in Germany but attended school and university in the United States.

What these biographies illustrate is that the ECA information officers, though American, shared an international outlook. Many of them had lived in Europe before or had close relations to Europe, and consequently some understanding of the national sensibilities of Europeans and the impact of war. Situated between cultures, they were, it seems, ideally suited to act as cultural transmitters between the United States and Europe. They also had the professional skills to do so. Most ECA information staff had backgrounds in the media or film. Wolff had worked as a film editor and director's assistant for a number of directors in Germany, France, Hungary and Austria before he emigrated to the United States, where he carved out his career as a film editor and executive producer.[47] Al Friendly wooed him away with the help of the British information officer Thomas Wilson, who pleaded with de Rochemont to relinquish Wolff as 'western civilisation and everything dear to the hearts of free man would come crashing down within six months if he did not come through'.[48] Wolff's successor, Schulberg, came from a film-producing family and began his own filmmaking career at the OMGUS documentary film unit. Here he produced a number of documentaries, among them the noted documentary on the Nuremberg trials *Nuremberg* (Nürnberg und seine Lehre, 1948), which he also directed.[49] Schulberg, as indicated above, worked as a film producer after he left the ECA and then moved into television. Nilson had also learnt his trade at OMGUS, and continued as a film producer in West Germany after he left the ECA film unit, mostly working for television. One of his last productions was a feature film on the Auschwitz commandant Rudolf Höss, *Death is My Trade* (1977).[50] Hemsing, who joined the film unit in 1951, had worked for the film division of the Office of War Information during the war. After the war, he produced a film for the Textile Workers Union which brought him to the attention of the ECA film unit.[51] A keen interest in film production was also shown by the information officers of the Italian mission, Gervasi and Secondari. During their time at the ECA in Rome they built up useful connections with the Italian film industry, which served them well in their later careers. Gervasi wrote the film scripts for the Italian adventure film *Rommel's Treasure* (1955) and the comedy *Beautiful but Dangerous* (1955), the latter featuring the Italian superstar Gina Lollobrigida.[52] Also the head of the Italian film unit Secondari wrote novels and film scripts after having left his job as a film officer in 1951, among them the script for the Oscar-winning romantic comedy *Three Coins in a Fountain* (1954). He later moved on to produce documentary films for ABC television.[53] Their professional background and interest illustrates that the film officers understood the craft and artistic ambitions of these filmmakers. They were therefore in a good position to harmonize their visions with the policy demands of the ECA/MSA.

The job of an ECA information officer

Waldemar Nielsen, who was first the deputy and later the head of the European Information Division, rather admiringly described his information officers as people whose indifference to red tape and whose professional drive produced momentum and furthered imaginative projects. But he also saw that this occasionally created unnecessary frictions with other agencies, in particular with USIS. Nielsen painted an interesting picture of his colleagues, characterizing them as people who displayed 'bureaucratic naiveté, high morale and great enthusiasm, superior competence in their respective professional fields, interest in but lack of knowledge about the people and cultures they were dealing with'.[54] Nielsen's characterization is striking, particularly in view of the international background that many, although certainly not all, ECA information officers had. Or was Nielsen suggesting that the information personnel lacked cultural understanding *despite* their international background? Were they, as suggested in Chapter 2, perhaps familiar with one or two European cultures, but knew little about the rest of Europe?

The ECA information officers' role very much resembled that of their counterparts in the State Department's overseas information offices, USIS. Unlike most of the State Department's information personnel, however, they had, by and large, no experience in international relations, and were not conversant with US foreign policy. They came from the field of public relations or from the media. There were other differences between USIS, which conducted more traditional cultural diplomacy, and the ECA. The ECA was a newly created agency unconstrained by traditions or rigid structures. In embarking on a propaganda campaign on an unprecedented scale, the ECA information officers entered unchartered territory. They were granted considerable freedom to experiment as well as a generous budget.[55] Roscoe Drummond, who headed the Information Division in autumn 1949, assured his information officers that the ECA allowed them 'the largest latitude' in promoting the agreed information objectives in a manner they felt most suitable.[56] This was not a hollow promise; Lawrence Hall, who had worked as an information officer at the ECA Information Division until October 1950, recalled having experienced little interference – or policy guidance – from above: 'It [i.e. the policy] was completely derivative. We made it up as we went along, by interpreting public speeches or by contact with the operating divisions.'[57]

The minutes of meetings and the correspondences between the information officers suggest that the work atmosphere was convivial. Criticism of policies and propaganda strategies was voiced freely and even encouraged by the leadership. Drummond remarked jokily that his fellow information officers 'will waste no time being tactful' when commenting on the ECA's policies and plans – or those of their competitors in the field, the Foreign Service and USIS offices.[58] There seems to have been a bustling, energetic, laddish newsroom atmosphere at the European Information Division that did not respond well to bureaucratic hurdles or interference from above. The liberal climate, along with the fact that the ECA paid higher wages than the Department of State and offered a higher per diem rate for travel expenses, made the ECA a highly attractive employer, especially since ECA staff received the same diplomatic privileges and rank as members of the Foreign Service. By August 1948, the ECA had received 50,000 applications.[59] At the end of 1948, 20 Americans were working for the European Information Division in Paris and 35 as information officers in the different country missions.[60] Three years later, the number had risen to 224 Americans and 782 Europeans.[61] The film unit in Paris alone listed 6 Americans and 40 Europeans on its payroll in summer 1951.[62]

The ECA predominantly recruited personnel through networks and recommendations. Unsolicited applications for positions in the information offices seldom resulted in a job offer, except for menial or secretarial jobs. The archival records show that many people who joined the ECA information unit knew some of their colleagues from earlier employments. The reliance on personal and professional networks also guaranteed a certain homogeneity within the group. The ECA information personnel were mostly male, white, middle-class, Christian and educated. Women were seldom given a leading role, but worked as secretaries or archivists. The former war correspondent Helen Kirkpatrick, who was chief of information at the French country mission from 1949 to 1951, was clearly an exception.[63] The American ECA personnel were also very similar in terms of social background, values and outlook, although the ECA administration aimed to illustrate its bipartisanship by hiring people from both political camps – the head of the ECA, Hoffman, was a Republican, and his representative in Europe, Harriman, a Democrat.[64]

Just as important as networks and the right educational background for landing a job with the ECA were 'clean' political credentials. Every prospective employee had to be cleared by security before being offered a contract. If the candidate had in the past come into contact with organizations or groups deemed to be communist, he or she was automatically disregarded. This happened, for instance, to the writer and journalist Blake Ehrlich, whom Al Friendly and Waldemar Nielsen wanted to employ. Blake had attended several meetings at the Washington Bookshop, a left-leaning cooperative, which made it 'impossible for the Administrator to certify him as loyal'.[65]

The ECA information officers were, then, a politically and socially quite homogenous group whose professional and often cultural make-up was similar to those of the filmmakers they worked with. The information officers acted as both allies and supervisors of the filmmakers. On the one hand, they had to grant the filmmaker sufficient artistic licence to ensure good cooperation, as well as to avoid any accusation of censorship or undue interference. On the other hand, they had to make sure that MP policies were presented correctly and given adequate publicity. Positioned at the intersection between different interests and cultures, they were not just US envoys, but also mediators between the United States and the European filmmakers and, not least, the audiences.

The information officers' role in film production

The European Information Division's prescribed functions was to assist the information work of the country missions, to develop strategies and set policy goals, and to assist the head of the European headquarters of the ECA.[66] The decision-makers of the Information Division were, according to Price, regularly included in top-level policy conferences.[67] Although obliged to consult the ECA and the State Department on questions of policy, the Information Division and its subunits were, as mentioned earlier, largely free to interpret policies and tailor the information programme to local conditions and needs.[68] The film unit in Paris was in charge of overseeing the production and distribution of MP films across Europe. It also dealt with administrative issues, such as finalizing contracts with filmmakers or commercial distributors and organizing necessary visa and permits. The information officers in the country missions organized the dissemination of films, proposed film projects and assisted filmmakers by providing local currency, transport, interpreters and sometimes film stock.[69]

The production process of an MP film started when the heads of the ECA Special Media Section decided that 'the object of the film is desirable'.[70] Their decision was taken on the basis of an outline describing the topic, scope and form of the film, usually submitted by a country mission or a filmmaker. Occasionally, filmmakers were initially contracted to scout locations and shoot some scenes to develop an outline; some films never went beyond this initial stage, either because the film unit felt that the topic did not warrant closer attention or because it was no longer politically expedient.[71] The film unit then commissioned a filmmaker, usually, as mentioned, on the basis of personal contact or recommendation. The contract was then concluded between the government of the United States of America, represented by the supervising film officer, and the film producer as contractor. The producer, if he did not also direct the film, entered into separate subcontracts with the director, as well as with the cinematographer, writers, editors and composers.[72] The ECA retained the right to make changes to the general specifications of the contract during the production (against compensation), allowing for changes in policy and strategy.[73] Sometimes, it also reserved the contractual right to examine the work 'at any reasonable time' and to 'reject or require the correction of any item' in accordance with the stipulations of the contract.[74] Before the actual shooting could start, the production outline and a shooting and commentary script had to be approved by the supervising film officer. Occasionally, the script was sent to other departments for fact-checking and input before it was handed over to the director.[75]

It was not unusual for the film officers themselves to produce the outline or the commentary script, as Ian Dalrymple, the producer of *The Changing Face of Europe* series, remembered: 'We had to accept a rather literal and straight commentary from the man who commissioned it ... and do our best in the shooting to make it not quite a magic-lantern picture.'[76] Dalrymple's recollection also points to a tension and potential conflict between the vision of the information personnel and that of the filmmaker. The film officers in Paris wrote the script for John Ferno's *Corinth Canal* and *Doctor for Ardaknos*, David Kurland's *Mill Town*, Romollo Marcellini's *Free City* and Vittorio Gallo's *The Story of Koula*.[77] The powerful Italian information office also exerted its influence: John Secondari wrote the commentary to *Free City* and the script for another of Marcellini's films, *Life and Death of a Cave City* (1950). Secondari is even mentioned in the opening titles, which was highly unusual, as the ECA film unit liked to keep a low profile.[78] Secondari was also involved in Gallo's *The Story of Koula*, which was paid for by the Greek country mission but produced by an Italian team. However, the film unit in Paris was anxious to have its version of the script realized, and reminded the information officer in Greece to instruct Gallo accordingly: 'Will you make it clear to Gallo that this (with your emendations) is the final draft and supersedes any script he may have brought from Rome?'[79] The case of *The Story of Koula* illustrates that conflicts of interest did not occur just between filmmakers and information officers, but also between the information officers themselves, who fought to have their ideas brought to the screen.

Levels of editorial control

As a rule, those supervising did not get involved in the actual filming. It was only at the stage of the rough cut that the supervising officer asked for 'the changes, additions or corrections he desires'.[80] A typical scenario would be for the film director, the supervising officer and the information officer from the country mission that financed the film to watch the rough cut together and then discuss alterations. In the case of the Kurland documentary *Mill Town*, produced for the Greek country mission, agreement was reached that the film needed 'more crowd activity' and that Kurland should return to Greece to shoot additional scenes. Soon, however, it was discovered that the textile factory on which the film focuses had not even started production. Since the Greek information officer Clark did not want to put the project on ice until the machines that had been imported from the United States were finally installed, he suggested adapting the script.[81]

Georg Tressler's last MP film on the subject of cooperation and international understanding also drew criticism, this time from the supervising officer Al Hemsing. The documentary *As the Young Ones Sing* (1954) tells the story of a young, white Viennese girl during her first days at an international French school in Vienna, where she becomes friends with a black boy. The two befriended each other in real life. Tressler, always with a good eye for the moment, noticed the two children clowning about during a bus ride and filmed them through the rear-view mirror (see figure 6.1). Hemsing, however, was not happy with this playful scene. He voiced concern that for supporters of racial segregation in the United States the film showed 'too [much] fraternization' and asked Tressler to cut the scene. Tressler recalled that he protested: 'Well, the film *is* for fraternization!' But he gave in: 'If you want to, but I find it ridiculous! But we did shorten it a little bit,

Figure 6.1 The limits of international understanding. This scene from *As the Young Ones Sing* gave the film officer reason for concern.

so he was satisfied.'[82] Hemsing's intervention did not change the character of the film – the bus scene is still in the film. But the example illustrates the degree of control the supervising officer was able to exert.

Not all filmmakers accepted the ECA's interference, as Chapter 3 illustrated. The Danish documentarist Theodor Christensen refused the Danish information officer's request to cut a scene from his documentary *All My Ships*, which the officer had made on the grounds that it might be interpreted as covert criticism of American imperialism. In this case, the film unit in Paris agreed with the director that the 'shot is a necessary visual link between two important sequences'.[83] Also, in a controversy between the film unit in Paris and the British Larkins Studio, the film unit was able to compel Larkins only to record a new commentary, not to edit scenes or change the style of its animations.

Such intrusions into the actual film material were, however, fairly rare. Much more frequent were changes to the commentary. As has been discussed in Chapter 1, the voice-over could alter the meaning and mood of a film substantially. By writing or rewriting the commentary (the head of the Italian information office Frank Gervasi even narrated the English version of several MP films himself), the information officers were thus able to exert considerable control. Al Hemsing's portrayal of the film unit as a liberal organization which 'did not dictate their [the filmmakers'] approach to the subject assigned, nor the message of the narration' thus needs to be taken with a pinch of salt.[84] But the records do suggest that the ECA/MSA did not exert a greater degree of control on the filmmakers than other, comparable, sponsoring bodies, and possibly even less. The film officers' understanding of the filmmaking profession, as well as their general trust in, and sometimes even admiration for, the talent of the European filmmakers, gave the filmmakers elbow room for realizing their visions.

However, it is important to point out that the extent of control varied from filmmaker to filmmaker, as well as from country to country. German and Austrian filmmakers, for example, were much more closely supervised than filmmakers from other countries. The Paris film unit believed that the German film industry's collaboration with the Nazi regime, and years of Nazi indoctrination, had made German film artists unfit to work for the ECA. Schulberg argued that German filmmakers lacked the skills and mindset to produce MP films because of their 'long-isolation and … their unfamiliarity with the basic idea that we are trying to put across, not to mention the spirit and technique'. Schulberg, who knew the German situation intimately because of his role in the OMGUS re-education programme, justified closer control because the filmmakers 'need more help and guidance than in any other country'.[85]

Interestingly, the ECA was much more lenient with the Italian filmmakers who had collaborated closely with the Fascist regime. Andrew Berding and his film officer Secondari had no qualms about hiring known collaborators such as Marcellini or Gallo. Marcellini had since the late 1920s worked for LUCE, the *L'Unione Cinematografica Educativa*, set up in 1924 by Mussolini to produce documentaries and newsreels to rally the support of the Italians for the Fascist cause. His colleague Gallo had been the head of LUCE during the Fascist era, and remained in this position after the war. Both men produced a number of films for the ECA: Marcellini at least six, Gallo at least eight. Hence, the same men who had promoted an image of Fascist Italy were, as Longo criticized, now put in charge of 'representing post-Fascist Italy to an international audience through documentary'.[86] Charles Edmundson, who briefly headed the Italian information office, was seemingly the only one who questioned the Italian mission's lax attitude: 'It is easy to shrug and say, "well, everybody was a Fascist or a Fascist sympathizer in those days", and this is said around our building a great deal'.[87] But the information officers at the Italian country mission pursued their own ambitions in the film business and were thus keen to cultivate good relations with the Italian film industry.

The degree of interference depended also on the status of the filmmaker. Renowned filmmakers were given more freedom than lesser knowns; they presumably also found it easier to reject intrusions. A case in point is the Dutch documentarist Herman van der Horst, who produced two films for the Dutch country mission, *Shoot the Nets!* (1951) and *Houen Zo* (1952). The fact that van der Horst retained the commercial rights over his films is indicative of his status. However, the Dutch filmmaker was obviously not in the habit of keeping a tight line of communication with the contracting body. When Nils Nilson, then head of film unit, heard that a French version of *Shoot the Nets!* had entered commercial distribution in Belgium before final approval by Paris, he was slightly piqued. In a letter to van der Horst he expressed his indignation that Horst had allowed the poorly synchronized film to enter distribution, not knowing that the filmmaker had produced a newly dubbed French version. A dispute erupted between the Dutch filmmaker, who felt unfairly judged since he held the rights for commercial distribution, and the Paris film unit, which felt that van der Horst had simply ignored the terms of his contract. The Dutch country mission, situated in the middle, implored Nilson to straighten out the matter, as 'the ill-feeling which it may generate can have an adverse effect upon us'. For *Shoot the Nets!* had in the meantime won the Grand Prix for the best short film at the 1952 Cannes Film Festival. The prize also reflected positively on the ECA and its film officers, who felt acknowledged as producers of documentaries of high artistic quality in the best tradition of government sponsorship. The honours bestowed upon van der Horst, together with the glowing press reviews, also generated considerable public interest in the film, and thus gave the MP greater publicity.[88] The Dutch information officer was therefore anxious to retain good relations with the filmmaker. Nilson wrote an apologetic letter to van der Horst, explaining the roots of the misunderstanding while gently reminding the filmmaker that 'a telephone call or a little postcard would have obviated this problem'.[89] To ensure that van der Horst continued with his work on the second MP film, *Houen Zo*, Nilson gave the order 'to handle Van der Horst with kid gloves'.[90]

Motives for making MP films

The reasons why the ECA wanted to hire European filmmakers for their propaganda campaign have been explored earlier. But why did the European filmmakers want to make films for a US agency? Financial considerations were, as suggested above, certainly a key factor. In post-war Europe, funding resources for documentary filmmaking were scarce, as national economies struggled. Governmental offices and war departments, which had kept many documentary filmmakers and animation designers in bread during the war, had closed down or substantially reduced their personnel and budgets. The lack of public or business sponsorship, as well as the reduced opportunities to distribute documentaries, brought non-fiction film to a 'low point'.[91] So, when it became known that a new American sponsor equipped with a generous budget was financing information films, the ECA could count on considerable interest. Nonetheless, while for some filmmakers making a MP film was just another job that paid expenses and a decent fee, financial considerations were not the only factor behind filmmakers' decisions to work for the ECA.

Noël van Rens argues that the Dutch documentarist Ferno accepted the offer to work for the ECA because he identified with the goals of the MP and wanted to contribute to their implementation.[92] Ferno was, at this point in his career, not dependent on accepting any contract; he had rejected an earlier offer by the US War Department to make films for OMGUS because he was engaged elsewhere. But as a humanist and leftist filmmaker who documented the devastations he witnessed as he advanced with the US Army, he had a keen sense for the Europeans' plight. Having lived in the United States for several years, he appreciated America's willingness to provide assistance to Europe.

In this, he was not alone: influenced by John Grierson, Pare Lorentz and Joris Ivens, who saw in documentary a medium for social change, and regarded it as a filmmaker's duty to promote social and economic reform, many European filmmakers were willing to lend their skills in support of the ECA, which was working to improve the economic situation.[93] This explains why the filmmakers easily identified with the ECA's liberal-democratic principles and the MP's broadly formulated policy goals: reviving the European economy; promoting economic modernization to produce jobs, higher living standards and peace; and encouraging closer cooperation and free movement.

The Austrian filmmaker Tressler described his work for the ECA/MSA as 'worthwhile' because he appreciated the provision of Marshall Aid to Austria: 'I was very much for it! I think it was very generous ... for the Americans to spend big money, [and to] say, "Come on, get up again and forget this Hitler business"'.[94] Julian Spiro, who directed an episode of the *Changing Face of Europe* series, approved of the 'whole Marshall Plan ethic'.[95] The left-wing sympathies of many documentary filmmakers did not conflict with the decidedly anti-communist stance of the American sponsors. In fact, many filmmakers were themselves opposed to communism. And those few who did not reject communism completely could still work for the ECA without compromising their conscience, since the MP was framed as an economic aid programme that aimed to improve the lives of the ordinary people. There were, of course, those filmmakers who adapted easily to regime changes and attuned their skills to whatever purpose was needed; the Italian filmmakers Marcellini or Gallo are a case in point. But in many cases there seems to have existed a genuine harmony of interest between the filmmakers and the ECA.

The fact that documentary filmmakers had come to rely on public funding is important here. Far from regarding governmental funding as a necessary evil to express one's artistic visions, the documentary filmmakers expected the state to support documentary filmmaking for the benefit of society. Yet public sponsorship, whether by governmental agency, state-owned enterprise or a transnational organization such as the UN, inevitably imposed limits on artistic expression. The degree to which sponsors exerted control over the films varied. Even under the most liberal sponsorship, however, filmmakers were constricted by contractual obligations. The films they produced were not merely works of art; they had to carry the sponsor's message, and serve a propagandistic or educational purpose.

How did the filmmakers reconcile their own aims with those of the sponsor? Grierson, though instrumental in persuading Western democratic governments to utilize documentary film to improve relations between the state and the public, never engaged critically with the implications of government sponsorship. As a strong advocate of governmental sponsorship and the use of documentary 'in all fields of public instruction and enlightenment',[96] he advised the filmmaker to be pragmatic: the filmmaker should 'take the situation for what it is and do his utmost within the limitations set', rather than refuse to enter governmental service.[97] The tradition of public sponsorship, and the purpose of documentary to enlighten and educate, meant that documentary filmmakers were used to extending the sponsor's remit if they were to fulfil their artistic aspirations.[98] Filmmaking was, after all, also a business, as Tressler, the young Austrian filmmaker, admitted. Tressler saw no problems in working for a governmental sponsor and explained that he always tried 'to enter the mind-set of the people who awarded me a contract. That was part of the business.'[99]

Many film scholars approach the work of filmmakers as an expression of the director's artistic vision; this goes particularly for the field of documentary, regardless of whether the films were produced for a government sponsor or not. Historians of propaganda, on the other hand, regard the very same films as illustrations of a government's policy aims. The films are, of course, always both: they express an artistic vision and 'visualize' a policy or message. It is impossible to identify exactly how much each person involved in a given film influenced its production. However, as this chapter has shown, it is possible to dissect the process to determine different levels of influence.

The MP films were a result of sometimes diverging, and sometimes similar and overlapping interests. Although the filmmakers were in most cases free to realize their visions on a visual level, the information officers structured and shaped these ideas by exerting control over the commentary, and sometimes also over the script. Since these elements were crucial to the meaning of the film, the degree of control was greater than the ECA and its staff admitted.[100] The supervising information officers, tasked with implementing US policy, thus decisively influenced the films and the messages they conveyed. But, except for a few documented cases of conflict over how a policy should be translated into imagery, the filmmakers and information officers more or less agreed over their final form. This had to do with the tradition of public sponsorship in which the filmmakers were working, but it was also the result of a consensus over the principles of the MP. There was, of course, a third party that exerted influence on the MP films: the audiences. Their role is explored in the next chapter.

Audience Reception

Having analysed the policy making and film production, the translation of ERP policies into films and the role of filmmakers and information officers, it is time to direct our attention to those at the receiving end of the propaganda effort: the European audiences. The field of reception represents perhaps the biggest lacuna in film history and propaganda studies. Who were the audiences, and how did they respond to the MP films? Did the films manage to captivate European viewers, as the title of this book asks? While some MP films had a very broad appeal and were well received by audiences across Europe, others did less well. The question then arises: How can we measure 'appeal'? What do we know about the audiences themselves? And what did the information officers working for the ECA/MSA and USIS, the agencies involved in the distribution of MP films, know about them? How did these agencies gauge people's opinions and preferences, and in what way did this knowledge feed back into the MP film campaign?

I sought to find answers to these vital questions by exploring the large arsenal of US records. media impact studies and audience surveys conducted by independent agencies, activity reports of the country missions, attendance figures, screening and audience statistics, film print and dubbing orders, correspondences between local information offices and the ECA headquarters in Paris, policy guidelines and conference protocols. What can we learn about the views and reactions of audiences from these documents? And what are the limitations of these sources? In the following I analyse these materials to establish which films or film types attracted and engaged people's interest, and how audience tastes varied across Europe. I examine how and what kind of information the propagandists gathered about the audiences, and discuss the ways in which this information influenced MP film policy and strategies.

Audiences of Marshall Plan Films

The Italian MP film *Talking to the Italians* (1950), directed by Romolo Marcellini, offers us a rare glimpse of the audience. The compilation documentary illustrates the propaganda efforts of the Italian country mission, and was primarily aimed at an American audience, intended to demonstrate the effectiveness of the information programme in Italy.[1] One sequence depicts an open-air film screening in an Italian town. It shows the arrival of the bus with the projector on board; a screen is then set up in the town square, attracting a growing number of curious people, and eventually the projectionist starts the show at nightfall.

The camera wanders over the tightly packed town square, showing elderly men sitting at the front and boys and younger men standing behind them, all looking with intense interest at the screen (see figure 7.1). The camera captures the mostly male spectators, zooming in on individuals to illustrate their reactions. The camera crosscuts between this seemingly spellbound audience and the film on the screen, which seems to be *Handicraft Town*, a MP film also made by Marcellini, the same director as *Talking to the Italians*; he may even have inserted scenes from *Handicraft Town* into *Talking to the Italians* to showcase his own work. The whole sequence gives a realistic impression of what such film screenings may have looked like: These outdoor film shows were informal gatherings of people of different ages and backgrounds. The people in the film are not dressed up, but wear their ordinary work clothes; they talk, gesture or lean on each other while watching the film. One can imagine that there was a certain level of noise as well, with people coming and going, as the screenings would have taken place in a public square with hardly any seating.

Figure 7.1 *Talking to the Italians* offers a glimpse of the audience at an open-air MP film show.

MP films were, as the next chapter illustrates in detail, shown in two different contexts: either in commercial cinemas, as part of the regular film programme, or, usually for free, in schools, town halls, libraries, trade unions, club houses – and, in the warmer seasons, outdoors. The ECA/MSA organized these non-commercial film screenings often jointly with USIS, which also operated mobile film units that toured the country. In addition, the ECA distributed MP films through national or regional organizations and non-governmental agencies. By combining commercial with non-commercial distribution, the ECA gained access to a vast and diverse audience. The ECA's claim that (in the second year of the ERP) 'every week an estimated average of 30,000,000 Europeans see Marshall Plan newsreels or documentary films' may sound like a massive exaggeration.[2] Yet, considering that in 1950 around 12,000,000 Italians and 26,000,000 British visited the cinema per week, the estimate, which comprised commercial and non-commercial screenings in seventeen European nation states, is quite plausible.

Audience numbers

The US information offices kept meticulous count of the number of people who attended non-commercial screenings of MP and USIS films.[3] Although fewer people were reached through non-commercial than through commercial screenings, the non-theatrical circuit was of particular importance as many people did not go, or had no access to cinemas. In Greece, the non-theatrical film shows organized jointly by USIS and the ECA counted 3 million spectators between October 1948 and August 1949.[4] In West Germany, almost 13 million Germans attended a combined total of 137,274 non-commercial screenings between April 1949 and March 1950.[5] In the small Free Territory of Trieste, 7,010 people attended a total of 24 non-commercial film screenings in July 1949, which amounts to an attendance of almost 300 people per show.[6] The Italian country mission calculated that from summer 1948 to December 1950 – a span of two-and-a half years – a total of 58,283,380 spectators had seen a MP film in Italy, which had a population of around 47 million in 1950.[7]

And the audience numbers kept rising. In France, the ECA/MSA distributed its films through a number of channels. In 1951 it set up the distribution company Mondial Film, whose shows attracted about 240,000 people per month in the second quarter of 1952. An additional monthly audience of 400,000 was reached through the Cinema Service of the French Armed Forces.[8] In Austria, 2.23 million people reportedly saw a MP film in a non-commercial setting in the first quarter of 1953. The figure seems very high considering that Austria's population was less than seven million; possibly, the statistics counted the spectators for each separate film, rather than whole film programmes, which customarily consisted of several films.[9]

Estimating how many people saw a MP film in commercial cinemas is much more difficult. The country missions in Austria and West Germany were, to my knowledge, the only ones that started to record attendance figures for commercial MP film screenings from 1952 onwards.[10] We therefore know that 2.5 million people saw the German MP documentary *We and the Others* (1951) in West German cinemas between July and September 1952, while 537,819 saw the Greek *Corinth Canal* (1950) during the same period. In Austria, 21 MP films were screened in cinemas in the second quarter of 1953, reaching a total of 531,215 spectators. Among the most seen MP documentaries in Austria around this time were the Dutch film *Shoot the Nets* (1951), with 54,172 spectators, and the British cartoon *The Shoemaker and the Hatter*, which was seen by 46,210 cinema-goers. However, as mentioned above, more than four times as many Austrians saw a MP film in a non-theatrical setting in the first quarter of 1953.[11]

No commercial attendance figures are available for other European countries. It would, of course, be possible to calculate attendance figures of commercial MP film screenings on the basis of ticket sales of individual cinemas, programme listings or audience statistics, which the film industry or statistical offices compiled for a number of European countries. Yet such a laborious task would be of limited informational value for the purpose of this study. Box-office takings can serve as a measure of the popularity of the main feature, but not of the information film that accompanied it.[12]

Studying reception

So, what do we know about the audiences and the reception of the films – a notoriously difficult subject of study? The interest in audiences is almost as old as cinema itself. In the early twentieth century, scholars began to investigate the attitudes and effects of films on audiences, often motivated by concerns about the harmful effects of cinema. A milestone in audience research was the empirical study published in 1914 by the German sociologist Emilie Altenloh on cinema-goers and their attitudes towards film in the German town of Mannheim.[13] Audience studies are interested in the audience as a collective and in the social function of cinema – this is different from spectator theory, which seeks to grasp analytically what happens to the spectator during the viewing of a film.[14] The question of who goes to the cinema and what pleasure people derive from doing so is central to audience studies. Film historians who research audiences often aim to identify national, regional or class-specific audience tastes and cinema-going practices by analysing the location and audience of specific cinemas, as well as cinema-booking patterns.[15] Some scholars adopt an ethnographic approach, and use oral history interviews to explore the social function of cinema and people's memory of going to the cinema.[16] Others examine the film industry's exhibition and distribution data or popularity charts to establish regionally specific distribution and popularity patterns or audience preferences.[17]

Unfortunately, we have no oral or written testimonies of spectators who remember MP film screenings. Neither do we have detailed records on how often a particular MP film was shown in a specific country or town. However, we do have records on the distribution practices and audiences of MP films, although the available documentation is patchy. While the situation in countries, such as West Germany and Greece, is comparatively well documented, few, if any, records exist for other countries.

The ECA and the State Department regularly commissioned audience surveys and media impact studies that give some insights into the social composition of the audiences, their media preferences and their attitudes towards the United States, the MP and its policies. Obviously, these studies need to be treated with the necessary critical distance; although independent research institutes conducted them, they were informed by the aim to show the effectiveness of US propaganda. Nevertheless, they contain valuable information about the audiences and their views, while at the same time giving insights into the strategies of the US authorities that commissioned them.

In addition to these more general surveys, the US authorities also conducted a number of reaction studies in West Germany and Italy. Only a few of them concerned MP films. One such study investigated the reaction of a general German cinema audience to the anti-communist MP film *Without Fear* (1951, analysed in detail in Chapter 3);[18] another polled the opinions of Hessian civil servants on the MP film *The Hour of Choice* (1951), which promoted European unification;[19] and a third investigated how German workers responded to a selection of productivity films, among them the MP films *Ideas at Work* and *Key to Progress* (1950 and 1951).[20] However, for our purposes these reaction studies are of limited use, as they say little about the popularity of the films.

Highly valuable sources for gauging the likes and dislikes of the European audiences are the reports and memoranda from the ECA country missions and USIS information offices operating in the different European countries. It was part of their job to record attendance figures, handle letters of complaint or praise, document how the national press reported the MP and the United States, discuss the films with government representatives and learn from their projectionists and drivers who toured the country how audiences responded to the films. The local information offices were also in charge of organizing the non-theatrical film distribution of MP films, which involved selecting films and ordering the film prints needed. The number of ordered prints for a film indicates how widely a film was distributed, and thus allows us to draw some conclusions about its popularity. Of course, the decision to give wide coverage to a film could be based on a number of factors, especially strategic considerations or directives from above that called for an extra effort to promote specific subjects. If a country mission repeatedly asked for more prints of the same film, however, we can assume that it was well received by audiences.

Popularity of MP films

The records indicate that the MP film screenings overall met with considerable interest, especially in areas where there were few opportunities for entertainment, and cinema was still rare. Children and youths, in particular, made up a large part of the audience of non-commercial film screenings.[21] A report from Greece from December 1949 noted with satisfaction that 'film showings in Peloponnesus are so effective that there is quick response from young members as soon as the red jeep appears'.[22] Research for Iceland has shown that people came with tractors and horses to attend USIS film screenings. They presented a welcome change from the monotonous life in secluded areas, providing entertainment and education as well as an opportunity to get together with distant neighbours.[23]

What films did audiences like? While the records available are not sufficient to map in detail the reception of MP films in the different European regions, they can still give us some insights. According to an audience survey conducted in Greece around 1950, Greeks showed a keen interest in documentaries, especially on general educational topics. Though the older generations, especially in rural areas, still considered cinema immoral, they appreciated documentaries as educational and informative.[24] The head of the USIS information office in Greece reported in 1952 that 'action pictures' (*ERP in Action* series) and films on Greek subjects appealed the most: 'Regardless how many times we have shown the Refugee [*Return from the Valley*], the Mule [*The Story of Koula*], Korea [*The Lesson of Korea*, produced by the film unit for ECA Washington in 1951],

Thermopylae [*Victory at Thermopylae*], Defence of Peace [presumably *Alliance of Peace*, a NATO film] and few other similar pictures, they still want to see them.'[25] Some of the non-Greek MP films were shown in the original versions with subtitles,[26] which did not seem to spoil the effect of these films. The power of visuals was obviously strong enough to make an impression on the partly illiterate Greek audience.

The Italians liked short and entertaining films. The fact that seating facilities were scarce for outdoor screenings explains why an evaluation study warned against films 'of undue length and tedious treatment', as the audience was standing. To keep the Italian spectators from simply walking away, the study advised tailoring the MP films to the preferences of the average Italian cinema-goer. Italians were particularly keen on adventure and 'emotional dramatic movies', followed by musicals and sentimental comedies. But even documentaries of considerable length, such as the 48-minute *With these Hands* (1950), could work with Italian audiences if they told a good story. The documentary on the history of a non-communist US labour union for female garment workers was 'still one of our top attractions' in Italy in May 1952.[27]

In West Germany, the US information officers found that 'political, economic and MSA European integration films are being received favourably'. The Germans liked so-called *Kulturfilme* – documentary reports on foreign countries, sports events, or scientific and technological developments. The genre had a long tradition in Germany, and had enjoyed great popularity in the Third Reich as a form of apolitical entertainment.[28] The MP films that were most widely distributed in 1952 reflected this interest in foreign countries. Based on the number of prints in circulation, John Ferno's Greek documentary *Corinth Canal* had the widest coverage, with 250 prints. Almost as popular were *Island of Faith*, made by Ferno for the Dutch country mission, the French colonial documentary *The Jungle that Was*, the British *Adventure in Sardinia* and the Dutch documentary on agricultural modernization, *Bull's Eye for Farmer Pietersen*.[29] Similar were the interests of Austrian audiences: *Corinth Canal*, *Island of Faith* and *Bull's Eye for Farmer Pietersen* were among those with the highest numbers of bookings and audiences in the second quarter of 1953. Also popular were documentaries on hydroelectric power, such as *Breakthrough* and *The Invisible Link*, the Dutch fishing documentary *Shoot the Nets!*, the British animation film *The Shoemaker and the Hatter* and the technical information film *Care and Maintenance of Farm Machinery*.[30] Both hydroelectric power and farming were important subjects in mountainous Austria, but the audiences obviously also liked films that transported them to more exotic places.

The topics of the films most widely distributed in Norway suggest that the Norwegians were particularly interested in fishing and modern production techniques. *Shoot the Nets!* had the highest number of prints in circulation in the first quarter of 1953. Also popular were *Corinth Canal*, the French *Let's Be Childish*, promoting the virtues of cooperation, the productivity films *Productivity – Key to Progress*, *Ideas at Work* and *The Streamlined Pig*, as well as the Scandinavian *The Living Stream*.[31]

Levels of commercial distribution can, with some reservations, serve as measures of popularity,[32] since commercial distributors usually included in their film programmes only those information films they deemed to be of broad popular interest. While many MP films entered commercial distribution in their country of origin, it was more difficult to win a commercial distribution contract for a foreign-produced MP film due to import regulations, but also for reasons of audience preferences. It is for this reason that we can presume that MP films screened in cinemas across Europe must have had a particularly broad appeal. Among these can be found the Greek MP documentaries *The Story of Koula* and *Corinth Canal*, the Dutch *Island of Faith* and *Shoot the Nets!*, the French colonial documentary *The Jungle that Was*, the British productions *Adventure in Sardinia* and *The Shoemaker and the Hatter,* or the Italian *Village without Water*.[33] Most of these films can be classified as 'story-type' movies – narrative documentaries that tell the story from the angle of an individual or focus on a specific place. Except for the animation film *The Shoemaker*, they all show people interacting with their rural environment. The settings are exotic, at least for Western audiences: the documentaries depict the struggle of people in rural Greece and southern Italy, modernization projects in the French colonial territories in West Africa, the building of dykes on a Dutch island and the fight of fishermen against the forces of nature in the North Sea.

Some films were rejected by audiences – or rather by the local information offices, which tailored the film programmes to the interests and preferences of local audiences. The Norwegian information officer sent back the compilation documentary *Island Odyssey*, which follows the journey of a ship carrying a MP travelling exhibit to the Greek islands, explaining that it 'was found to be without any interest to Norway at all'.[34] In thinly populated Iceland, where the United States had caused a controversy by establishing a military base in 1951, the ECA country mission refused to dub or distribute the anti-communist *Without Fear* (UK 1951). Presumably it did not want to upset the equilibrium between those who were pro-American and the considerable number of communists and socialists in the country.[35] In Turkey, many films were never distributed as 'many of the themes which we are stressing in such Western countries as Britain, the Netherlands, and Scandinavia ... make almost no sense in Turkey.'[36] The information officer organizing the dissemination of MP films in Greece was also highly selective. Many MP films sent to him never entered distribution on the grounds that these documentaries 'intended for more sophisticated Western European audiences' were 'unusable' in Greece. He explained that the Greeks did not like to see films on European integration since the subject was 'beyond the interest range of many Greeks'. He also feared that films promoting economic progress in other European countries 'could create more animosity in Greece than goodwill' unless they were paired with domestically produced films that illustrated similar modernization projects in Greece.[37]

The above illustrates how information officers working on the ground tailored each film programme to the tastes and interests of their local audiences. Although they sometimes based their decisions merely on assumptions about their audiences, very often they had a keen sense of what films would work on the basis of reports from their projectionists or the demand for a particular film. The information officers working in the ECA country missions were the link between the national audiences and the headquarters in Paris: they informed Paris about audience reactions and moderated the information flow from the centre to the local level. The local information staff held considerable power because they decided what audiences got to see: they refused to distribute certain films, withdrew films that failed to attract sufficient interest, demanded re-edits or ordered only a few prints to satisfy the wishes of Paris. Like commercial distributors, they had to vie for the audiences' attention, as the MP films could serve their purpose only if they attracted and engaged the spectators' interest. The local information offices were not always in agreement with the Paris film unit (or, in fact, with each other) over which policies should be pushed, nor how this should be done. Yet the analysis of the records shows two significant results: first, the power of the local information officers to adapt the film programmes to the national or regional context, and second, the power of audiences to influence the US propaganda strategies.

Learning about the audience

The ECA policymakers were fully aware that knowing the audience was a crucial prerequisite for a successful propaganda campaign. As mentioned earlier, the head of the ECA, Paul Hoffman, had likened the ERP to a business whose services and achievements had to be advertised using modern marketing techniques and consumer research.[38] Since the United States was the birthplace of modern public relations and marketing, it comes as no surprise that the ECA propagandists were familiar with the literature on public relations, propaganda and marketing. At the request of the Information Division, the Research and Analysis Section compiled a list of literature that contained fifteen items, among them classic texts by Bernays and Lippmann, but also newer studies, such as Carroll's *Persuade or Perish* and Doob's *Public Opinion and Propaganda*, both published in 1948.[39] The ECA and the State Department also hired independent research institutes and polling companies to study European audiences and gauge their opinions on a number of matters related to the ERP. The first surveys aimed at establishing their media preferences and level of knowledge about the MP. Later, the focus shifted towards measuring the impact of MP propaganda. The studies took a variety of forms, and ranged from sociologically informed, statistical market research, to simple feedback questionnaires handed out to cinema-goers and in-depth, interview-based studies conducted over a prolonged period of time.

At the ECA, the Research and Analysis Section, a subunit of the Information Division, was in charge of administering the opinion studies, analysing the results and formulating recommendations. One of the ECA's chief contractors was a polling company called the Public Opinion Research Organization. It was created and run by Eric Stern, a former member of the market research centre of Elmo Roper, one of the pioneers in international opinion research.[40] Stern occupied offices in New York and Zurich and had come into contact with the ECA via Franklin Roosevelt Jr, who introduced Stern to Ambrose Chambers, at the time special assistant to the European head of ECA Harriman. The Information Division hired Stern in summer 1949 to survey the 'attitudes, understanding and approval of the Marshall Plan' in Norway, the Netherlands and France. The countries were selected on the basis of 'the presence of ample counterpart funds' to finance the surveys.[41] In August 1949, Stern's contract was extended to include Austria and Denmark. His reports were obviously found to be so satisfactory that he was immediately commissioned for another survey of public opinion, in Germany, France, Italy, the Netherlands and Norway, this time on the issue of European unification.[42] The US authorities remained keenly interested in gathering data about European attitudes. After the MSA replaced the ECA and started to merge with USIS in 1952, it was the State Department that commissioned studies evaluating US propaganda activities and European attitudes towards the MP. The State Department's chief contractor was the

Bureau of Social Science Research in Washington DC, a non-profit research agency set up in 1950 to conduct sociological studies.

Attitudes and media preferences of Europeans

The first surveys evaluated 'the relative effectiveness of the informational media' by comparing Europeans' media preferences with their knowledge of the MP.[43] The aim was to find out which media formats were most useful for promoting the MP in the different European countries. On the basis of the finding that 80 per cent of Norwegians and 72 per cent of Dutch people read a newspaper at least once a day, the study concluded that northern Europeans were best reached by print media. In thinly populated Norway, where 90 per cent owned a radio set, the radio was considered another important medium for disseminating propaganda. Film, on the other hand, seemed of limited usefulness, also in the Netherlands, where a striking 60 per cent never went to the movies, and only 26 per cent went to the cinema at least once a month.[44]

Quite different was the picture in Italy: only 23 per cent of the Italian population never went to the movies, while 37 per cent professed to going to the cinema at least once, or more than once, a week. Even in rural areas, 19 per cent of Italians went to the movies once a week.[45] The broad popularity of cinema in Italy, combined with cheap ticket prices and a relatively high rate of illiteracy, made film the key medium of propaganda. In France, cinema attendance was traditionally much lower than in Italy or Britain (see Chapter 8), though not as low as in the Netherlands. Almost half of the French interviewed never went to the movies, while 43 per cent went at least once a month (though not every week).[46]

These surveys also aimed to assess Europeans' knowledge of and attitude towards the MP so that the propaganda effort could be concentrated on those regions where people were most sceptical. The first surveys conducted from July to October 1949 showed a relatively high level of support for and knowledge about the MP. The Dutch and the Norwegians were found to be quite well informed which, in the terms of the survey, meant that they had some basic knowledge of how the MP worked and who was behind it. Also, the approval rate for the MP was high: among the Dutch, 82 per cent agreed that the MP was 'a good thing', while 67 per cent of Norwegians held the same opinion.[47] The survey confirmed an earlier assessment by the noted historian Arthur Schlesinger Jr, who inspected the Norwegian ECA mission as Harriman's assistant in September 1948. Schlesinger credited Norwegians with strong anti-communist convictions and 'the highest degree of natural enthusiasm about

ERP' of all Scandinavian countries.[48] Much lower was the rate of approval in the Austrian provinces (though not in Austria's capital), with 41 per cent. Even worse was the situation in France, where only 38 per cent viewed the MP as positive. This widespread scepticism towards the MP in France coincided with an equally low level of detailed knowledge about the MP.[49] The negative findings alarmed the ECA policymakers, especially as approval rates in France had fallen from 52 per cent in 1948 to 38 per cent in 1949.[50] What was wrong with France?

The French problem

In September 1949, an independent committee of members of the US Congress travelled to Europe to evaluate the impact of the MP. Its findings were very similar to those of Stern's survey. The report of this watchdog committee painted a bleak picture of the situation in France. It pointed out that the French showed the firmest opposition to the MP in Europe, and that opposition was particularly pronounced in Paris and among the organized industrial workers.[51] When the report leaked in October 1949, the French Foreign Ministry responded indignantly to its conclusions that the French 'seraient à la fois les plus hostiles et les plus ignorants':[52] they were not only the most hostile towards the MP in Europe, but also knew least about the MP's aims and how it worked – with the exception of the readers of the communist press, who proved to be very well informed.[53]

Trying to make sense of the low approval rates in France, Stern explained that it would be 'too easy and too cheap a way-out to explain this away with generalizations about national character'. He suggested that the widespread negative attitude towards the MP in France was probably down to ineffective promotion and administration. He ascribed the poor reception to a lack of 'truthful' information about the MP, as well as the people's distrust of mainstream media, and to economic dissatisfaction across France. Since the disappointing results were rooted in ignorance rather than prejudice, Stern called on the French government 'and any other organization interested in the revival of the country to present the facts and future aims of reconstruction and to find ways and means to raise more enthusiasm and cooperation'.[54]

However, in a letter to the director of the Information Division a few months later, Stern offered a different interpretation. It was not the ECA's propaganda strategies that were to blame for the low approval rates, he suggested, but 'the much more sceptical attitude of French people in general and towards everything'.[55] Interestingly, Stern shifted the blame for the disappointing results from the contracting body, the ECA, onto the subjects of the study. Was this an opportunistic move or a re-evaluation based on new findings? And why were the French really so overwhelmingly negative towards the MP? An ill-informed populace or a poorly implemented propaganda campaign might be conducive to opposition to the MP, but could hardly be the sole reason. Widespread anti-American sentiment, which found expression in the almost hyperbolic responses of the French to the import of Coca Cola, for example, certainly also played a part in the mistrust against the MP in France.[56] The 'coherent and sustained campaign' of the French communist press against the United States, as well as the conservative, elitist disdain for American culture and economics, further fuelled the anti-American discourse into which the MP was drawn.[57] This discourse was informed by popular French concerns over what many saw as a threat to France's culture and its hegemony as a nation state.[58]

Henry S. Reuss, deputy general counsel for ECA Paris, and later a Democratic congressman, offered another interpretation of why the ECA's propaganda efforts seemingly failed to convince the French and the Italians of the advantages of the MP. In a confidential memo to Al Friendly in February 1949, Reuss voiced the opinion that MP propagandists had misunderstood the needs of the audiences. He argued that the French and Italian workers, who were among the most critical voices, were not primarily interested in the political goals of the MP – namely combatting communism – nor even in their country's economic viability at the end of the MP. Rather, they were interested in concrete benefits, such as the ability to buy a new suit, go to the cinema, afford a bigger flat or receive an old-age pension. The positive effects that MP propaganda promised had so far not trickled down to the lower social classes, and this had dampened people's enthusiasm. The European worker, Reuss suggested, 'listens listlessly while we tell him we are saving Europe, unconvinced that it is *his* [emphasis Reuss] Europe we are saving'.[59]

Measuring the effects of mass media

The case above also illustrates the ECA's shift of interest towards evaluating the impact of MP propaganda. Whereas in the first two years of the information campaign the ECA had worked to reach as many people as possible, by expanding film production as well as increasing the number of distribution facilities, this approach gradually came under greater scrutiny. Confronted with the disheartening results from opinion polls, the strategists at the ECA Information Division started to grapple with the question of what the people actually 'saw' when they watched a MP film. What did they remember? Did the MP films actually trigger a thinking process that resulted in a change of behaviour?

This shift of interest from acquiring knowledge about the audiences to measuring the impact of propaganda was the outcome of two main developments. First, there was the realization that many Europeans still knew surprisingly little about the MP and its aims. In the eyes of the policymakers, this led to misconceptions about the ERP or about the aims of the US government. Second, there was growing domestic pressure on the ECA to prove that the money allocated to the MP (and MP propaganda) was well spent. The media impact studies thus served a double purpose: they provided guidance on how to improve propaganda techniques, and they helped to justify the existence of the ECA Information Division and the MP information programme. This is not to suggest that the research agencies which conducted the studies were biased, or sought to influence the results. But they were motivated by the fundamental conviction that the media had a powerful impact on the viewer or the reader. These audience and impact studies thus inevitably confirmed the core belief that film, radio and the press were the most suitable mediums to exert influence over audiences, even though they could not provide conclusive evidence that a positive attitude towards the MP was the result of this propaganda effort.

Still, the results of the impact studies were often chastening, particularly for the film unit. Research conducted in West Germany in September 1950, for instance, showed that only 39 per cent of those interviewed remembered 'having seen in the movies any pictures about the MP'. This result seems surprising, considering that 15 per cent of them went to the movies at least once a week, and 34 per cent one to three times a month. Considering the extent of the US propaganda activities in West Germany, it is unlikely that those interviewed never saw at least one of the many newsreel reports about the MP or a MP film; it is more likely that they did, but then did not recognize it as film about the MP, since the film unit drove a strategy of subtle propaganda.[60] A second study, conducted in November 1950, delivered more positive results. It established that among avid German moviegoers 40 per cent were 'well informed' about the MP, although it did not define what 'well informed' meant. The film unit could interpret this result optimistically as evidence that the MP films were effective in explaining the MP to the people. Viewed more critically, however, the results fail to confirm that film was a particularly effective tool of propaganda, as 40 per cent of those who read a magazine regularly and 41 per cent of those who listened to the radio 'quite a bit' were just as well informed as the regular cinema-goers.[61]

The problem of reaching audiences, as well as the question of which method was best suited to reaching the 'right' audience, was intensely debated in the offices of the Information Division. What did the information officers make of the results of the impact studies or of the feedback from the country missions? How did the responses and preferences of European audiences shape the ECA's film policy and propaganda strategies?

Finding the right tone

Although the findings were carefully discussed, and also informed the decisions of the film and information officers, at least to some extent, the ECA propagandists were not slave to them. Cases in point were the surveys that suggested that film was not more effective than other media in communicating knowledge or exerting influence. These findings did little to shake the information officers' belief in its usefulness. That film was *the* most influential medium in their view was confirmed by external experts such as Siegfried Kracauer, noted film theorist and sociologist at the time, who in May 1952 conducted a study on the use of media in southeast Europe and the Middle East for the State Department. Kracauer spoke very favourably of the mobile film units, which he described as 'mental tractors conquering virgin territory', helping to vanquish 'ingrained prejudices'. Having found that even conservative Turkish villagers seemed to appreciate documentary film shows, he concluded that it 'would hardly be justified to leave the immense propaganda value of film unexplored'. Kracauer had already expounded his theory of the power of moving images in his key work, *From Caligari to Hitler: A Psychological History of the German Film*, published in 1947. In his study for the State Department, he reasserted his theory of the manipulative power of film by insisting that images 'affect the spectator's unconscious and thus subtly sensitize him to the championed cause'.[62]

Kracauer's views were widely shared by his contemporaries. The head of the Motion Picture Unit of HICOG in Germany, for example, explained that film had a unique advantage over other media: 'Audiences can turn off radios ... but an audience in a movie is a captive audience.'[63] His reasoning was that people would go to the cinema to be entertained, and therefore were not guarded against propaganda: 'They will absorb virtually everything and anything through their emotions if it is wrapped up in a story or interesting presentation.' Effective propaganda films therefore had to touch the viewer on an emotional rather than intellectual level, because 'people don't want to think, especially not when seeing a film'. HICOG's film unit chief perceived the audience as an unthinking mass that could easily be manipulated, suggesting that spectators 'will express the ideas they absorbed through the film without realising where they got them'.[64]

What appears today as a rather simplistic understanding of the complex workings of film reception was widely accepted at the time. The ECA film and information officers also believed strongly in the influence and manipulative power of film, even though they were only too well aware of how difficult it was to sway people's minds. The Information Division thus looked to experts for help. Advice on how to increase the effectiveness of MP propaganda – both solicited and unsolicited – was plentiful. How did these external consultants and (self-styled) experts view European audiences? What problems did they identify, and what solutions did they propose?

The outsider's view on the MP film campaign and its audiences

One of the experts that was invited to give advice on the American propaganda strategies overseas was the sociologist Kracauer. In his study on media preferences in Greece, Turkey and the Middle East he suggested that the audiences in these regions were largely peasants who were 'not conditioned to grasp information about remote or abstract subjects'. Kracauer also pointed out that, because of a lack of cinematic culture in these regions, most people were unaccustomed to cinematic language and would therefore easily be confused by flashbacks, close-ups and transitions. Information films should thus employ a concrete, simple language and address local topics to which the people could relate. He also suggested that filmmakers make special efforts to communicate the message on the visual rather than the verbal level, as the audiences were so captivated by the imagery that they paid little attention to the commentary.[65]

Although Kracauer's report sounds slightly dismissive of the audiences' intellectual abilities, he raised an important issue, namely that the cultural background of the audiences and their familiarity with cinematic language (or the lack thereof) influenced what they saw when they watched a MP film.[66] His advice came too late to have any impact on the MP film production, which had been scaled down by the time he submitted his study. But the mission reports that came from Greece echoed Kracauer's observations insofar as the Greek audiences apparently showed little interest in films that promoted subjects that seemed irrelevant to their own lives, such as European unification.

Earlier, the ECA had commissioned the marketing specialist Vergil D. Reed to evaluate the information programme. Reed did not study the audiences directly, but analysed mission reports, previous audience surveys and interviews with ECA information personnel.[67] Unsurprisingly, none of the points Reed raised were novel, which suggests that the study was chiefly commissioned to underline the need for propaganda and so endorse the strategic goals of the Information Division. Reed's report urged the ECA to make a greater effort to arouse public interest in the MP, as enthusiasm was lacking 'to a disturbing degree in all countries and to a critical degree in France'. Reed recommended intensifying the overall propaganda effort, and particularly expanding the commercial distribution of films. However, special efforts should be made to reach the industrial, agricultural and white-collar workers as 'the most critical group in all countries'.[68] Reed advised the ECA not to respond to Soviet criticism, and thus confirmed the line of the film unit. MP propaganda, he suggested, should strive to be 'consistent, simple, undeviating, credible and at relatively low pressure, even seeming to ignore the Russian attacks'.[69]

The ECA also received plenty of unsolicited advice from outsiders, which was much less welcomed, especially if it came from women. One such impromptu advisor was Mary Hoyt Wiborg, the famous New York socialite and playwright, who lived in France for a while; she offered her thoughts to the ECA mission chief on how to increase the French people's interest in the MP. Wiborg pointed out that spending money on posters or circulation letters was useless in France, as nobody bothered to read them. In her view, the ordinary Frenchman wanted to be shown and to be entertained – desires that the French communists readily exploited.[70] If the ECA wanted to be heard, Wiborg insisted, it had to step up its film production. It should also organize more free film screenings at local cinemas, which French men preferred to their 'dreary lodgings with a complaining wife and half-hungry children'. Her suggestions, though sound and confirmed by the media preference studies, fell on deaf ears, and were discussed no further. The Information Division's new director, Roscoe Drummond, expressed 'certain reservations' about her suggestions; the fact that she was a woman certainly did not help in the masculine world of the Information Division.[71]

Another, highly illuminative report was prepared by Peter Rathvon, president of RKO Pictures between 1942 and 1949 and later an independent film producer. In early 1951, the State Department sent Rathvon and his wife Helen on a two-month inspection tour of France, Italy, Austria and Germany. Rathvon's brief was to study USIS and ECA operations and provide concrete recommendations for future film production and distribution policy. Later in 1951 Rathvon signed a contract with the State Department to produce and commercially distribute several information films through his French company, among them one documentary on the United Nations and one on the Schuman Plan.[72] This fact seems important, as it illustrates that Rathvon did not act as an entirely disinterested observer. Rathvon's assessment was also strongly coloured by the US government's recent policy shift towards rearmament and the visit of NATO's new Supreme Commander, Eisenhower, to Europe, in whose footsteps Rathvon travelled. This might explain why he found pessimism and cynicism to be so widespread in all the countries he visited.

Particularly negative was his view on the French. Like previous American visitors, he found a lack of understanding of US aims and widespread antipathy towards the United States, which he ascribed to a 'bad inferiority complex' of the French. Rathvon sympathized with the information officers trying to promote the MP in France, as 'every effort, effective or not, will be criticized and ridiculed'. Rathvon suggested using 'subtlety and satire' in documentaries to make them more palatable to the French. He also advised producing more films locally, 'spiced with Gallic touches', to strengthen French pride and morale – and took it upon himself to produce them.

Concerning Italy, Rathvon felt that the problem lay not, as in France, with the people. Neither was MP propaganda to blame for the fact that 'the remarkable accomplishments of the Marshall Plan have met with so little popular understanding and enthusiasm'. The Italian information office had no shortage of production facilities and Italian talent and made, as the output of MP films illustrated, good use of it. The problem was, Rathvon believed, with MP policy. Rathvon blamed the ECA's approach of investing Marshall Aid in free enterprise for the high levels of support for the Italian communists, as the distribution of funds left many Italian workers and farm labourers empty-handed and locked in poverty. For Rathvon, the main challenge was to convince the Italian worker that US-style capitalism, and not communism, could really improve his life, because for the Italian 'all hope of betterment lies in some form of socialism'. He also believed that US propaganda would find more acceptance if it acknowledged the dominance of socialist thinking in European governments and thus presented other, 'benign' forms of socialism as alternatives to communism.

In the case of West Germany, the main challenge was, in Rathvon's eyes, to counter Germans' desire for national unity and their strong neutralist tendencies. The communists were not in themselves a serious threat, but they exploited these tendencies by calling for a unified, neutral Germany. Rathvon realized that it would be difficult to implement a policy shift from economic reconstruction to defence, given that the Allies had made such an effort to demilitarize Germany and the Germans. These efforts had obviously been successful, since convincing the Germans of the need to invest in rearmament was now much harder than promoting productivity and European integration. Rathvon suggested capitalizing instead on Germans' fear of war, and presenting West Germany's integration into the Western alliance as the only guarantee of lasting peace and prosperity.

In Austria, as in West Germany, communism posed no threat. The Austrians, Rathvon found, 'do not need films to persuade them to anti-communism', not least because the Austrian communist party was doing such a bad propaganda job. The problem with the Austrians was that they showed a lack of enthusiasm for the future: 'They are apparently resigned to the idea of being a small and threatened country. Like the French, they cherish memories of past glories.' Although Rathvon described the MP film production of the Austrian country mission as satisfactory, he recommended that future films reassure the Austrians that their nation could play an important part in the European community, not least through her culture.

Rathvon's report called for more dramatic feature films to supplement the documentaries. He also identified a major weakness of the regular information film, namely the lengthy production time. Newsreels were much quicker to make, and could therefore more easily adapt to policy shifts than documentary films. Rathvon's views chimed with the experiences of the film and information officers, and gave weight to the argument that film propaganda was needed more than ever. In face of the looming budget cuts, such testimony was crucial to legitimizing the propaganda effort.[73]

Strategies for reaching the audience

It is important to remember that the Information Division had no template on how to conduct an information programme on such an immense scale. The MP film campaign did not follow a carefully developed plan, but was largely a process of trial and error. During the operation, the propagandists encountered a number of problems, some of which they had expected, whereas others came as a surprise. A key problem was the question of how to reach the audience; here, the film policymakers struggled with three main issues. First, there was the problem of how to conduct a pan-European campaign while speaking to national or local preferences. Second, there was the question of whether to adopt a subtle or more hard-hitting approach. Third, there was the issue of whether it was better to disseminate the material as broadly as possible or to focus on specific target audiences.

The European versus the national

Perhaps least expected was the problem of national preferences. It only gradually dawned on the film policymakers how difficult it was to produce information films that could attract people's interest *across* Europe. Rob Kroes, referring to an observation made by Henry James, argues that the Americans approached Europe 'as one cultural canvas of a scale commensurate with that of America – as one large continental culture'.[74] This also holds, at least partly, true for the ECA. When the head of the film unit, Stuart Schulberg, discussed the film production problems in West Germany, he identified the vastness of the operation as the root of the problem: 'As usual, it was a geographical fault. We could not be in fourteen countries at once'.[75] But the problem was not merely spatial distance, making it difficult to supervise production closely; it was also cultural.

The previous chapter has illustrated that many of the people who held key positions at the ECA information offices were familiar with certain aspects of European culture. However, although they brought with them an intimate knowledge of Germany, Italy or Great Britain, they knew just as little about Greece or Belgium as their colleagues who had never been to Europe. Even within the same country, mentalities, mindsets or tastes could diverge considerably. The film policymakers had to come to grips with the fact that Europe was culturally much more diverse than they had initially envisaged. They were confronted with a problem they never managed to resolve satisfactorily: on the one hand, they realized that in order to get the message across, the films had to be tailored to the interests of national audiences, but on the other hand, the films needed to be distributed as widely as possible – both for reasons of efficiency and of fostering a sense of a shared cultural identity. The films were supposed to serve two, possibly mutually exclusive, functions: they needed to fuel national pride in order to make the viewers more receptive to their message, while at the same time open them up to the idea of European unification.

In view of these problems it is perhaps not surprising that the information officers were less concerned with whether film was a good medium to convey information than in finding the right tone. How could they deal with audiences who were not just culturally but also socially, intellectually and politically so diverse? How to reconcile the fact that a clerk in Copenhagen might find a film interesting that bored a Sicilian farmer, and vice versa? This was about finding the right approach, but it was also a matter of weighing the benefits of a direct versus a subtle approach.

Subtle versus hard-hitting approach

Some European audiences, especially those who had been exposed to the elaborate Nazi or Fascist propaganda machinery for years, reacted especially sensitively to films that smacked of political propaganda. In order to be considered trustworthy, then, films had to adopt a measured tone and appear factual and objective. The danger was that if the tone was too neutral then the film might fail to get the message across.

We have seen in the previous chapters that the ECA film unit preferred a subtle approach to film propaganda. The films downplayed the involvement of the ECA and foregrounded European contribution. Moreover, they refrained from discussing the communist enemy and from making statements that could be interpreted politically, a strategy that lasted at least until the ripple effects of the Korean War induced a shift in direction. The film unit's propaganda strategy was considerably influenced by its second head, Stuart Schulberg. As a result of his first-hand experience with sceptical audiences from his prior involvement in the re-education efforts of the US military government in West Germany, he consistently advised against 'the use of the "holzhammer" [sledgehammer] method'.[76]

A memo from the Belgian mission in 1950 shows that not all ECA information offices agreed with Schulberg's approach. While the film unit was anxious not to put off audiences with films that appeared overtly propagandist, the country missions were keen to have their work and goals publicized. Henry McNulty from the Belgian mission pointed to the conflicting interests in his letter to Schulberg: 'For commercial purposes you want it to have as little Marshall Plan propaganda as possible; from the point of view of the Mission, too little propaganda will make the film worthless.'[77]

The majority of information officers acknowledged the advantages of the film unit's tactics. The USIS information offices in Italy, obviously responding to domestic criticism that film showings of 'innocuous' information and fiction films were useless and a waste of money, defended the use of subtler propaganda. They explained that by screening 'technical training or other non-propaganda films' to the predominantly communist communities, USIS could build up trust, allowing it to introduce political propaganda films at a later stage. The Italian information officers described the seemingly neutral films as 'entry wedges', and argued that even entertainment films could influence the audience through their 'covert messages'. 'Too blunt or sustained' film propaganda, on the other hand, was useless 'to attract and hold the attention of extremist Left-Wingers'.[78] For their part, the Dutch country mission argued that a good MP film needed a visually interesting story and a way of conveying the message that was 'not too conspicuous' in its propaganda; it therefore considered the humorous *The Shoemaker and the Hatter* and the dramatic *With these Hands*, which showed the struggle of workers for more rights, as the 'best' MP films.[79]

Of course, the question of what constitutes subtle, non-political propaganda has to be considered in its historical context. Although most MP films would not be seen as either today, their tone of persuasion was decisively more measured than, for example, the more aggressive US war propaganda films. However, when the outbreak of the Korean War escalated the conflict with the Soviet Union, the voices that demanded a more forceful approach grew stronger. The above-mentioned American producer Rathvon, who principally favoured a moderate tone in information films, changed his view in the light of his government's recent policy shift. He argued that 'it appears to be time to attack Russian propaganda directly in films. It is time to show that the Soviet is a ruthless power state and that what it stands for is a negation of all the values of Western civilisation'.[80] The fact that the film unit began to produce information films, albeit few, with a direct anti-communist message suggests that these voices became too influential to be completely ignored. However, as an evaluation report of the propaganda operations in Italy from May 1952 shows, the information offices did not abandon their original course of action. The report made the criticism that many of the MSA and USIS documentaries shown in Italian cinemas 'are so toned down in order to appear non-propagandistic that they lose all impact'.[81]

Broad versus targeted approach

The question was not only about *how* to reach the audiences, but also about *which* audiences should be reached. Since the start of the film campaign in summer 1948, the Information Division had been able to report a continuous expansion of its activities: the number of produced films grew, more areas were covered and more and more people attended the film screenings. Nevertheless, in spite of the ECA's intensifying propaganda efforts, opinion polls conducted in the second half of 1949 found that many Europeans were still ignorant of or sceptical towards the MP. This caused a stir in the US Congress and was grist to the mill of the critics, who felt that the ERP had failed to curb communism or push European governments to do more for recovery. The ECA responded to the criticism by stepping up its propaganda effort through the expansion of film production and distribution. Later opinion polls, which measured a rise in attendance figures and a growing 'understanding of the nature and scope of American aid', were considered proof that the MP film campaign was working.[82]

The MP information programme came under scrutiny again after the outbreak of the Korean War. Approval rates for the MP fell sharply as European governments had to shoulder the heavy defence costs, which resulted in high inflation and a rapid increase in prices and unemployment. The Information Division once again had to demonstrate to the US Congress and the American taxpayer that its strategies were effective in winning over the Europeans to the US policy goals and curbing support for communism. But the Information Division was also coming under pressure from within the organization to revise its information strategies. The fact that some sectors of the European population remained doggedly resistant to the concept of productivity and/or European integration endangered the implementation of the MP reforms.

While re-examining their strategies on the basis of expert advice and feedback from the country missions it gradually dawned on the propagandists that those who were outright opposed to the MP could not be converted. The propaganda effort therefore ought to focus on the uninterested and the sceptical, they believed. But wasn't showing the films through USIS cultural centres or to trade unions and various associations preaching to the converted? How could those who did not attend these film screenings be won over? As the question of impact grew more important, the original aim to reach as many people as possible was gradually abandoned in favour of a more focused approach.

The Information Division and film unit began to focus their efforts on selected groups whose support was deemed crucial to realize the necessary economic reforms. In Italy, for instance, industrial and agricultural workers, housewives and managers were identified as the main targets; after the outbreak of the Korean War, schoolteachers and students – as opinion-makers in the often semi-literate families – were included into the target groups. Convincing Italian workers and managers to accept the ideas of the MP was essential, both to ensure that economic reforms could be implemented and to curb the influence of the communist party. Winning the support of the housewives and students was deemed important because 'the housewife is a voter and the student is the voter of tomorrow'.[83] With the passing of the Mutual Security Act in 1951, certain sections of society that were particularly resistant to defence and rearmament were singled out for special attention: organized labour, women and youths

– in particular young men of military age (18–25 years old). Not just in the Netherlands did women 'present the most difficult psychological problem'; also in other European countries were women among those who were most opposed to rearmament.[84] The fact that the communists sought to capitalize on their fear by depicting women and children as the victims of a US-instigated nuclear war made women an important target group.

Even though the policy and strategy discussions reveal a shift of emphasis towards a more targeted approach, distribution practices were still oriented towards reaching as many people as possible. The target groups were so broadly defined that they comprised most sections of the population: only a minority was not covered by one of the categories that covered schoolchildren and youths, agricultural and industrial workers, management, students, the military and women. Moreover, the commercial distribution of MP films expanded just as the film unit decided to adopt a more targeted approach in the non-commercial sector. The reason for the expansion was that high attendance figures remained, after all, key evidence of a successful propaganda effort.

The above illustrates the pressures under which the Information Division and its units operated: they had to persuade Europeans to accept the promises of the ERP in order to facilitate the implementation of the necessary reforms; they had to placate their domestic critics by convincing them that the information programme fostered support for the MP and US intervention and thus stopped the advance of communism; and they had to tailor the films to the interests and tastes of national audiences in order to make them receptive to the messages. The propagandists were much more pragmatic than their official rhetoric suggests. They registered which films or types of films worked with the audiences, and tried to adapt their methods, messages and even policy aims in order to reach them. The ECA's pragmatism was reflected in the MP films themselves, which did not promote all ERP policy goals with equal zeal. Policies unpopular with audiences were either avoided, as in the case of rearmament, or promoted only indirectly, as in the case of European integration. This pragmatism was also reflected in film distribution and programming, which allowed for considerable flexibility. The degree of audience interest, as well as the consideration of local political dynamics and cultural codes, determined which MP films were distributed, as the next chapter shows. Thus the Europeans unwittingly played their part in the transfer of US policies, ideals and values. Pleasing the European audiences was not the first priority of the ECA film unit, and policy aims or strategic interests occasionally took precedence over audience interest. Even so, as this and also the next chapter illustrate, the film unit and the local information officers sought to promote ERP policies in ways that were palatable to their audiences.

8

Distribution and Exhibition

Bringing the message to the people

Producing MP films was, according to Al Hemsing, the last head of the ECA/
MSA film unit, 'only half the battle'.[1] The other half was bringing the message to
the people. How did the propagandists realize their plan to send MP films to the
remotest corners of Europe?

The distribution of films in seventeen European states, each with its own
cultural and geopolitical make-up, presented the information officers with
numerous challenges. The ECA built up or expanded existing distribution and
screening facilities in each European country and collaborated closely with
governmental, non-governmental and commercial agencies. The following
examines the channels the ECA used to disseminate its films and explores
how sociopolitical conditions, cultural traditions and infrastructures shaped,
facilitated or complicated the propaganda effort.

Non-commercial distribution and exhibition

The ECA/MSA distributed the MP films commercially as well as non-
commercially. Both circuits were important to the propaganda effort, as they
gave access to different audiences.

Non-commercial or non-theatrical exhibition refers to the non-profit-
orientated distribution and screening of films. It was the traditional route for
the dissemination of documentary films. John Grierson held the opinion that
documentary film was not – and should not be – commercially orientated,
and had pushed for the expansion of non-theatrical venues in the 1930s. He
also believed that documentaries screened to non-theatrical audiences had a
higher impact, because such spectators wanted to see this type of film, whereas

traditional cinema audiences were primarily interested in the main feature films, and not the documentary shorts that preceded them.[2] The non-theatrical circuit was also for the ECA the most important route of film distribution in many European countries. The MP films were shown in schools, town halls, local inns, factories or outdoors, usually free of charge.

In the field of non-commercial distribution, the ECA/MSA cooperated very closely with USIS, whose local offices had mobile film units, projectors and a film lending service at their disposal. In fact, the ECA was not only allowed, but legally obliged to use USIS facilities. In 1948, the Department of State and the ECA had signed a formal agreement in which the Secretary of State guaranteed to 'extend to ECA all facilities possible overseas, including facilities of U.S. information offices and libraries, for the widest for the widest possible dissemination of ECA information abroad'. In return, the ECA agreed to make use of USIS facilities and furnish USIS with the information materials (including films) it produced.[3]

While the agreement was meant to prevent a duplication of services, neither side complied fully with it. Also USIS produced films that promoted the MP, while the ECA/MSA continued to distribute its films independently of USIS. Several ECA missions operated their own mobile film units or rented facilities to screen MP film programmes; the French mission even set up its own non-commercial distribution company to give MP films the broadest coverage.[4] What is more, the USIS distribution channels were often inadequate, which is why both the ECA and USIS continuously sought to expand their local distribution networks.

Cooperation with national agencies was thus of key importance. The ECA and USIS were keen to build up a strong, non-commercial distribution sector, with the aim of 'nationalizing' the propaganda effort after the ECA/MSA ceased operating. They helped to set up the necessary infrastructure for the distribution of information and educational films, and expanded and modernized existing structures. The local country missions were primarily in charge of establishing distribution networks through national and local organizations that used film for educational or informational purposes or operated lending services. They provided national educational boards, trade unions, productivity centres, farmers' associations and church and youth organizations with film prints, along with technical training and equipment such as projectors or film trucks. In Norway, the country mission purchased, for instance, eighteen sound projectors for the Norwegian technical training schools, and loaned another thirteen projectors to the Norwegian Ministry of Agriculture to be used by agricultural schools and societies.[5]

One of the key advantages of non-commercial exhibition was that it required only a basic infrastructure: all that was needed was a projector, some 16 mm film prints, a screen onto which the films could be projected and some seating facilities. A white wall or a sheet could serve as a screen. The 16 mm projectors were relatively cheap and small, and thus easier to transport than the ordinary 35 mm cinema projectors; moreover, operating the projector was relatively easy to learn. Since only a minimum of equipment was needed, films could be shown to audiences who had no access to regular cinemas.

The settings in which the MP films were exhibited were as diverse as the audiences. Rural areas were served by mobile film units; these were small lorries or buses equipped with a projector, and sometimes a generator, a collection of film prints, some brochures and a projectionist who often doubled as moderator. Following a fixed schedule, they stopped at villages to screen film programmes, often several in one day for different groups. Schools and training schools, youth groups, trade unions, farmers' groups, societies and associations of various kinds were encouraged to arrange their own film programmes, and were provided with free film prints, information leaflets and projectors if needed. In Iceland, even private persons hosted film shows in their living rooms; one neighbour, for example, showed US information films, and another one Soviet films provided by MIR, the Soviet counterpart of USIS.[6]

USIS operated libraries and cultural centres that could be found in cities across Europe offering rich cultural programmes, including regular film screenings. MP films were also shown at industrial fairs that advertised American products and production methods, and were part of the travelling exhibitions promoting the MP. The MP films were usually screened as film packages comprising several different information films, forming a film programme that would last at least an hour or longer. Sometimes, these film programmes consisted only of MP films. More often, they combined MP films with other, mostly American produced, documentaries and newsreels. The reason for these 'mixed' programmes was that the ECA, especially in the first years, had only a very limited number of MP films at hand. Moreover, USIS, which was the main distributor of MP films, was interested in publicizing its own productions. The effect of combining films from different sponsors was, of course, that the audience often did not – and could not – distinguish MP films from other information films.

A way to make the non-commercial film shows more attractive was to pair information films with cartoons or a feature film. Andrew Berding, the head of the Italian information office, for example, asked the Information Division to provide him with 'old Mickey Mouse films or other American cartoon films' for the mobile film trucks that were touring the Italian countryside. To break up the factual MP documentaries with something more diverting had proved successful, and Berding insisted that 'it is a very good idea to utilize something of an amusing or entertaining nature to intersperse in our series of ERP documentaries'.[7] Thus, by mimicking a regular cinema programme, the organizers were able to attract more spectators, and also tempt those who might not usually attend cultural or educational film programmes. MP film screenings that targeted specific professional groups, such as farmers, workers or apprentices, often included so-called technical training films – fairly prosaic educational films that explained the use of new tools, or illustrated a production process. They were usually followed by a discussion, with the projectionist typically doubling as discussion leader, answering questions and providing additional information.[8]

Although the number of people reached through non-theatrical distribution was generally lower than those reached through commercial cinemas, it was, overall, the more important of the two circuits. Non-theatrical exhibition was essential to achieve wide coverage and to reach people who could not – or would not – go to the cinema. Mobile film units brought films to remote corners of the country, while open-air screenings in cities attracted passers-by who would never go to the cinema or attend a screening of information films. The non-theatrical sector played a particularly important role in countries with few cinemas outside urban centres, such as Greece or Turkey, or in countries with a rich tradition of non-theatrical film shows, such as Britain. It was also important because the opportunities for distributing MP documentaries commercially were limited, as the commercial circuit was very competitive; in addition, governments often imposed national quotas to limit the import of foreign films. Another advantage was that MP films remained longer in the non-commercial circuit than in the short-lived commercial sector. Thanks to the network of governmental and non-governmental agencies the ECA had set up, MP films continued to circulate several years after the MP itself had ended.[9]

One of the disadvantages of non-theatrical exhibition was that people needed to be encouraged to attend the screenings, whereas commercial exhibition 'guaranteed' an audience. Another was that fewer people were reached through non-theatrical than through theatrical exhibition. Although the free film screenings attracted many curious spectators in the early years of the MP when cinema and film screenings were still a rare treat in many European regions, this rapid growth in non-theatrical audience numbers began to stagnate from the early 1950s. The ECA/MSA responded to this trend with a twofold approach: first, by producing more dramatic and entertaining films, and second, by pursuing a more targeted approach that concentrated on specific groups, with documentaries tailored to their interests.

Commercial distribution and exhibition

In post-war Europe, it was customary that in commercial cinemas a mixed programme consisting of trailers, a cartoon or documentary short and a newsreel preceded the main feature film. Because of the enormous popularity of cinema in the 1940s and the 1950s, a theatrical release of a MP film granted access to a vast audience. Yet it was not only quantity that spoke in favour of commercial distribution; by including a MP film in the regular cinema programme, propaganda reached people who would not ordinarily attend a non-commercial film showing. Advocates of the commercial distribution of MP films argued that the regular cinema audience members were less guarded, since they went to the cinema to be entertained; others suggested that spectators who paid to see a film were more appreciative of the films they got to see.[10] Although these theories were never substantiated by hard evidence, the film unit strove to secure theatrical release for as many MP films as possible, in order to achieve widest publicity.

However, getting a MP film onto the big screen was not easy. Many European states had introduced import quotas or other regulations to protect national film production from foreign competition. Since the ECA/MSA produced the MP films in different European countries, national protective measures could restrict or even preclude entirely the distribution of MP films outside their country of origin.[11] In Italy, for example, only nationally produced documentaries and informational films could be shown in regular cinemas. This explains why the Italian country mission became such a prolific producer of MP films, and even produced films for the country missions in Trieste and Greece, as these could enter the commercial circuit in Italy.

The biggest problem, however, was how to find a commercial distributor willing to include a MP film in his programme. Commercial distribution has always been profit based. Thus, commercial distributors selected documentary shorts on the basis of their probable appeal to prospective audiences – or because they granted tax incentives. However, the competition to win theatrical release for documentary films was fierce, as the number of documentary shorts on offer far exceeded the distributors' demand. The film officer in charge of organizing distribution for Belgium, for example, found that neither Metro-

Goldwyn-Mayer nor RKO Films was interested in including MP films in their programmes, 'because they have a big surplus of shorts already'.[12]

As a rule, the ECA as film sponsor had the commercial and non-commercial distribution rights for all MP films, and was therefore also in charge of concluding contracts with commercial distributors. The film unit in Paris normally negotiated contracts with commercial distributors for several countries. Commercial distribution on the national level was organized by the local information office or by the filmmaker himself, who sometimes retained national distribution rights (and thus earned the profits).[13] Among the most sought-after commercial distributors were the big Hollywood studios, which also operated their own cinema chains in many European countries, guaranteeing wide coverage to MP films. The Hollywood studios were fastidious, however, and usually demanded considerable concessions.

Some MP films, such as documentaries filmed in colour or animation films, were much easier to sell than others. The six-part series *The Changing Face of Europe* (ECA 1951), filmed in Technicolor, found a ready buyer in Twentieth Century Fox. The studio acquired the commercial distribution rights for most European countries, including the French and Portuguese colonies, as well as for Israel, Egypt, Iran and Iraq.[14] In 1950, the film unit entered into a contract with the Hollywood company Warner Bros. to distribute the three French MP documentaries *The Story of a Rescue*, *Henry's Story* and *Rice and Bulls*, as well as the British *Adventure in Sardinia* in France, the French colonies, Belgium and Switzerland.[15] Warner Bros. also attached the German MP films *City out of Darkness* and *Hides for Tomorrow* (both 1950) to its feature films in West Germany.[16] The New York-based All Star Productions Corporation, which had set up an office in Munich to financially exploit old Laurel and Hardy slapstick comedies in the European market,[17] distributed the Dutch MP documentary *Island of Faith* in West Germany and Austria. British Pathé, which had produced *Adventure of Sardinia* for the ECA mission in Britain, arranged for this documentary to be distributed in Britain through the British ABC cinema chain.[18] As 1952 drew to a close, negotiations were underway with United Artists for the commercial distribution of *The Living Stream* and *Shoot the Nets!*[19]

The MP films were distributed in a package with specific feature films. An activities report of the Paris film unit in 1950 shows that Warner Bros. paired the French MP film *Henry's Story* with the Western movie *Montana* (1950), starring Errol Flynn as the male outsider who clashes with the local cattle ranchers over the use of land. *Henry's Story* depicts the rebuilding of the French barge fleet on the Rhine River, and promotes the ERP as a creator of jobs. The French animation film *Story of a Rescue* (1948), which had already been commercially distributed in France and Belgium in 1949, was rereleased in France, Switzerland and Belgium in the second half of 1950 through Warner Bros. This film was distributed together with the Warner Bros.' movie *The Hasty Heart* (1949), starring Ronald Reagan in a drama about the friendship of a group of Allied soldiers in a military hospital in Burma at the end of the war.[20] In each case there was no thematic link between the main feature and the MP film that preceded it. It was usually the commercial distributors who decided on the pairing, and they based their decision – presumably – on the estimated popularity of the main feature film. The success of the feature could thus either strengthen or weaken the propaganda message. In the event, neither *Montana* nor *The Hasty Heart* became box-office hits. In a similar case, the experts who studied the audience reactions of a regular cinema-going audience in a West German town made a clever move by screening the aggressively anti-communist MP film *Without Fear* after the popular Italian comedy *Don Camillo and Peppone*. The humorous battles between the communist mayor and its true hero, the feisty Catholic priest, muted the confrontational tone of the MP film but confirmed its main premise, namely that there exists an insurmountable difference between communism and capitalism.[21]

Disseminating MP films in Europe – Local influences and strategies

Even though the propagandists utilized both theatrical and non-theatrical channels of distribution, the strategies themselves varied from country to country, and were greatly influenced by local conditions. A number of factors could either hamper or facilitate the distribution of MP films, such as the level of cooperation with other agencies, national regulations on film production and distribution, the existence or lack of cinematic infrastructure, the impact of local culture and traditions, and the prevailing political climate.

In some countries, such as Britain, Italy or West Germany, the ECA information offices were able to make use of existing facilities for the distribution of educational and information films, which greatly facilitated the dissemination of MP films. In other countries, such as Greece or Turkey, the non-commercial distribution sector was virtually non-existent, and had to be built up from scratch. The level of cooperation with governmental and non-governmental organizations also varied considerably. Finally, national cultural traditions and cinema-going practices affected the distribution practices, as the following illustrates.

Distribution and exhibition in northern and western Europe

Overall, the ECA encountered fewer difficulties in distributing MP films in northern and western Europe than in Mediterranean countries. Scandinavian countries posed relatively few challenges. Keen to increase national productivity, the governments in Denmark and Norway had a vested interest in promoting the goals of the ERP. Films that highlighted the benefits of economic modernization and educated the populace about measures designed to achieve higher output in particular, were welcomed. In Denmark, the local ECA mission entered into a profitable cooperation with the film centre of the Danish Ministry of Education, the *Statens Filmcentral*, which was in charge of distributing documentary and cultural films, both commercially and non-commercially. It agreed to distribute and print MP films in 35 mm and 16 mm formats at no cost to the ECA (except for the dubbing expenses), on the condition that the ECA did 'not offer any propaganda material'. The fact that the ECA country mission also distributed the ERP funds certainly facilitated the conclusion of this deal since the Danish government wanted to demonstrate its cooperative spirit. The agreement was also advantageous for the ECA, which gained access to over 400 Danish cinemas and was able to distribute its films to Danish schools and a number of professional and political organizations, which regularly borrowed films from the film centre.[22] In Norway, the governmental departments, local authorities and private industries proved similarly cooperative.[23] Because of the country's large size and widely dispersed population, the ECA country mission relied on these organizations' support to disseminate the MP films to Norwegian schools, labour and farmer groups, and the military.[24] In return, it provided them with film prints for educational and informative purposes, as well as projectors.[25]

In Great Britain, the conditions were particularly favourable to the ECA's propaganda effort, first because the British government itself was conducting an extensive information programme that covered the role and goals of the ERP,[26] and second because Britain had efficient channels of commercial and non-commercial distribution. The British loved going to the cinema. Around 4,600 cinemas were in operation at the end of the 1940s. Although attendance figures started to shrink after their peak in 1946, admission numbers were at a still impressive 1,365 million (out of a population of about 50 million) in 1951.[27] Also, the non-commercial distribution circuit was, not least due to the influence of the British documentary movement, well developed in Britain. The tradition of non-theatrical film screenings at labour organizations, women's groups, schools and film societies continued after the war. Mobile film vans toured both Britain and the Empire's colonies, the latter to educate imperial subjects about their motherland and to generate support for the British.[28] The Second World War had boosted the popularity of the documentary, which became a regular feature in commercial cinemas, encouraging more documentary filmmakers to aim for theatrical release.[29] This widespread acceptance of the genre benefited the ECA's film campaign on the one hand, but on the other hand, it also generated considerable competition for the MP films, as a large number of public and business-sponsored documentaries competed with the MP films for the viewer's attention.

Unlike in Britain, going to the cinema was not a particularly popular pastime in the Netherlands. Even so, the ECA country mission succeeded in creating public interest by hiring some of the Netherland's most noted documentary filmmakers. Herman van der Horst, Bert Haanstra and the Dutch-born John Ferno were also internationally successful. The Dutch mission capitalized on the fact that van der Horst's *Shoot the Nets!* (1951) was awarded the prize for the best short at the Cannes Film Festival in May 1952. The film was distributed by the Dutch distributor *Nederland Film*, together with Ferno's *Island of Faith* and Horst's second MP documentary, *Houen Zo*, which won him his second prize at Cannes in 1953. The British J. Arthur Rank company, which owned 142 cinemas in the Netherlands, distributed Ferno's *Corinth Canal*.[30] Although Rank included in its programme three MP films that were not produced by Dutch filmmakers, the majority of imported MP films were only screened non-theatrically. In 1952, 32 different MP films, with a total of 900 prints, entered the non-theatrical circuit, reaching 123,000 Dutch spectators in the first quarter of the year. The Dutch country mission distributed the MP films exclusively through its intermediaries. It furnished various Dutch governmental departments, trade unions and cultural centres, such as the British Council, with free film prints, and – if needed – projectors, and utilized commercial companies that lent 16 mm documentaries to film and youth clubs.[31]

In West Germany, the ECA's main partner in the distribution of MP films was the Information Service Division of HICOG, the civil administration that replaced the US military government in September 1949. HICOG was in charge of the State Department's information programmes in Germany.[32] The propaganda activities of the two agencies were greatly facilitated by the fact that they were able to use the networks and facilities the Western Allies had set up as occupying forces.[33] The MP films were distributed through an intricate network of federal and state educational film agencies (Land und Kreisbildstellen), regional film committees and a chain of US information centres and reading rooms called America Houses (*Amerikahäuser*). HICOG's plan was to create a non-commercial film distribution network that could function independently from US assistance. For this purpose it initially employed 300 German full-time projectionists, each of whom was in charge of organizing film programmes and debates especially targeted at youth organizations and schools in a district.[34] HICOG also fostered the formation of regional film committees that consisted of educators, experts, civic officials and representatives of various organizations. These committees were required to preview the films and schedule film screenings for the groups they represented. In January 1952, around 500 film committees existed across West Germany. Many of the committees operated a mobile film unit and employed one or several full-time projectionists, whereas others worked with volunteer projectionists. HICOG and the ECA provided the films and the projectors. In 1954, the film committees were conducting up to 1,000 film screenings a day for audiences of 90,000 to 100,000. A large percentage of these screenings were held in classrooms and formed part of the school curricula: school children made up the largest share of the target audience with 43 per cent.[35]

In addition, the 27 America Houses and their 135 reading rooms spread across West Germany organized regular film programmes.[36] The large numbers of visitors were attracted by the varied cultural programmes of lectures, concerts and film screenings, but also by the modern interiors and heated reading rooms.[37] HICOG estimated that in 1950 a total of over 17.5 million Germans had attended a non-theatrical film screening.[38] By 1954 this number had risen to an annual estimate of 25–30 million.[39] It is, however, important to note that most of these film programmes combined USIS with MP films. Only 8,393 of these film shows, attracting an audience of 660,364 people in the last quarter of 1952, were 'pure' MP film programmes.[40]

The ECA and HICOG also made considerable efforts to enter the commercial sector, which consisted of approximately 4,000 cinemas.[41] Cinema boomed in West Germany, and attendance figures kept rising until 1956, when they eventually reached their limit with 800 million visitors. Crucially, West Germany had, unlike Italy or France, no import quotas or regulations to hinder the commercial distribution of foreign-produced documentaries, thanks to the enormous influence of the United States as the occupying power (see next chapter). Even so, as in other countries, commercial distributors and cinema owners had a limited interest in documentary shorts unless they gave tax reductions or promised broad audience interest. The ECA country mission tried to stimulate interest in MP films by offering generous funding to HICOG 'for extremely vigorous promotional campaigns' in trade papers or in the regular press 'to attract really a lot of attention and get a lot of interest in these films'.[42] HICOG, which operated its own distribution agency, also employed other means to get the information films into the cinemas. One was its popular newsreel *Welt im Film*, which cinema owners were eager to purchase. HICOG committed cinema owners who wanted to show the newsreel to screening a certain number of information films per month as well. By obtaining tax reductions for its information films in Hamburg, it was also able to secure a contract with 95 out of 101 cinemas.[43] Through these measures, the two agencies managed to get a considerable number of MP films into regular cinemas: in the last quarter of 1952, 20 MP films were either in or awaiting commercial distribution.[44]

Distribution and exhibition in southern Europe

Reaching audiences in economically less well-developed countries, such as Greece, Turkey or Portugal, was considerably more difficult. The lack of basic infrastructure, access to electricity, seating facilities or poor or non-existent roads presented major obstacles to distribution and exhibition in these regions. Added to this came, in the case of Turkey, strong religious prejudices against cinema, as well as a lack of cinematic traditions – and film theatres. Even though a cinema-going culture slowly emerged in the urban centres of Istanbul and Ankara, as the increase in the number of cinemas from 130 in 1939 to 275 in 1952 illustrates, the vast majority of the Turkish population had never seen a film.[45] Confronted with these 'exceedingly primitive' channels of communication, and Turkey's military and strategic, rather than economic, importance, the ECA Information Division was inclined to leave the dissemination of MP propaganda largely in the hands of USIS and its six mobile film units.[46] Also Portugal was of limited interest to the ECA. Greece, on the other hand, was a key target of MP propaganda, as were the two other Mediterranean countries, France and Italy.

Italy – The battle for the viewer's attention

In many ways, Italy presented ideal conditions for the ECA propagandists. They were able to take advantage of the structures that had been established under Mussolini's dictatorship. Mussolini, like Hitler, had considered film the ideal vehicle of fascist propaganda, and had disseminated his ideas through cinemas and mobile film units that toured the country.[47] No less conducive to the ECA's film campaign was the fact that Italy had a thriving film industry, and that Italians were avid cinema-goers.

Commercial exhibition in Italy

In Italy, the theatrical circuit was of crucial importance. It gave access to a broad spectrum of Italian society: cinema was popular and tickets were cheap enough that even the poor could afford to go to the movies.[48] Unlike in many other European countries, where cinemas were often confined to larger towns and cities, Italy had a plethora of cinemas in rural areas as well. A US study on mass media calculated that the seating capacity for spectators across Italy was roughly 4 million in 1950. An estimated 8,000 commercial cinemas served a population of 47 million Italians; in addition, there existed 1,250 open-air cinemas, which operated in the warmer seasons, and 2,500 club cinemas. Communist organizations as well as the Catholic Church operated theatres that vied for the attention of the Italians.[49] Estimated cinema attendance rose from 600 million in 1949 to 630 million in 1950 and again to 700 million in 1951, reaching its peak in 1956 with over 800 million visitors.[50]

However, the benefit of having access to a cinephile population was counteracted by the protective measures the Italian government had implemented to boost the production and distribution of Italian films. While the high taxes on foreign imports and incentives to further Italian documentary filmmaking did not prevent Hollywood's quick advance into the Italian market, they did present serious obstacles to the ECA/MSA.[51] Measures that privileged domestic productions combined with an oversupply of documentaries made it increasingly difficult to win commercial distribution for MP films. The Italian government introduced a subsidy in the form of a '3 per cent prize' for Italian-produced documentaries of high artistic standard. Documentaries that were awarded the prize earned 3 per cent of the gross intake of the feature film to which they were attached. The result was a 'flooding [of] the market with films of dubious quality'. The number of Italian documentaries climbed from 310 in 1949 to 500 in 1950, as producers and filmmakers sought to cash in on the prize. Yet it was the Italian distributors who really profited from this 'inflationary production of documentary': the sale prices for documentaries dropped, and the distributors were able to push for a higher share of the profits, as many film producers fought to get their films into the cinema.[52]

According to a report from the Italian country mission, the prize became the 'sine qua non for distribution' in Italy, as it partly covered the distribution costs.[53] Since it was only awarded to domestic productions, this measure made it effectively impossible to win theatrical release for MP films produced outside of Italy. This explains why the Italian country mission became such a prolific film producer. And it was successful: all except two of its MP documentaries were awarded the 3 per cent prize and entered commercial distribution; four of its documentaries received a special 5 per cent prize.[54] The Italian mission also succeeded in winning theatrical release for two other MP films that had not been filmed in Italy: *Mill Town* (1950) and *Victory at Thermopylae* (1950) were both sponsored by the ECA mission in Greece, but produced by Italian filmmakers.[55]

Non-theatrical exhibition in Italy

As the high levels of competition and the severe protectionist measures reduced the possibilities for commercial exhibition, the Italian information office sought to expand the non-commercial distribution of MP films, even though it attracted a proportionally much smaller audience. But more, and a greater variety, of information films could be distributed non-commercially, including those MP films that had not been produced in Italy. In a memorandum to the US Congress, the Italian information office estimated that approximately 10 million Italians per year saw a MP film distributed through the ECA/MSA, whereas another 8 million people a year were reached through USIS channels.[56]

The ECA and USIS information offices distributed MP films in two main ways: by operating a loan service that provided national and local educational bodies, associations, unions and groups with film prints (and occasionally projectors), and by using mobile film units. In 1950, the ECA operated 12 film trucks, expanding to 26 in 1951.[57] The primary targets for the mobile film units were the 7 million Italians who lived in areas with no cinemas.[58] The main function – and advantage – of mobile film units was, according to an evaluation report from 1953, that they 'actively seek out audiences ordinarily inaccessible because of location and attitudes'. Mobile units could reach not only isolated rural communities with high illiteracy, but also 'hostile communist audiences' in urban areas that were otherwise inaccessible to US propaganda. The outdoor screenings were meant to attract the curious passers-by who would neither go to the cinema nor attend a non-theatrical film programme that primarily served 'friendly groups'.[59] Complying with the regulations of the Italian authorities that forbade the public screening of political propaganda, these film shows screened seemingly apolitical information and entertainment films.

A USIS report from the time describes these film shows. In the Italian province of Emilia, a region with strong communist support, the USIS office in Bologna organized film shows in different towns, each running over several days. The film screenings attracted an increasing number of spectators who were drawn by word of mouth. The report noted with satisfaction that the USIS staff even succeeded in enlisting the help of local communist authorities: communist mayors who were suspicious about the films shows would become 'positively cordial and cooperative' in the end, and even allow street lights to be turned off. In the small towns of the region, 'persons known to be communists' would help the projectionist crews to carry and install equipment.[60] The self-congratulatory tone of the report implies that the communists were brought round through the shrewd tactics of USIS or through the quality of the film programmes. However, a study conducted on behalf of the State Department to evaluate the propaganda situation in Italy provided another, more convincing explanation for the high attendance figures and the cooperative spirit of the communist mayors: in a 'non-totalitarian context' like Italy, when people heard of these film shows through the grapevine, they pressured their officials to allow them to be shown in their town.[61] It is important to remember that the film programmes first and foremost provided entertainment. Hence, the local authorities could not withhold the film screenings from the people if they did not want to risk losing their votes in the next election.

Yet, in spite of the apolitical nature of film shows, and the often cordial relations with the local authorities, the operators of the USIS and ECA mobile film units occasionally encountered opposition, especially in the cities. According to the reports from various Italian USIS branches, communist officials prevented USIS film screenings in Bologna, Florence, Livorno and Sienna on Labour Day in 1950. In many towns, communist mayors left the streetlights on to disturb the projections, although some turned them off later, perhaps under pressure from audiences. Elsewhere, US agencies and local communists arranged public film screenings at the same time, playing an almost comical tit-for-tat game to disturb each other's shows. For example, in the town of Barberino di Mugello, the local communist party responded to an advertisement announcing a USIS event by setting up a screening of a *Sovexport* film. The US report noted with glee (and probably exaggeration) that 250 Italians came to see the film programme organized by the Americans, whereas only 15 went to the Soviet film. In another town, Genazzone in the province of Rome, USIS set up an open-air screening on 8 May to divert people from a communist rally in the neighbouring square that was presumably held to commemorate the end of the Second World War. The Americans started their show with a newsreel played at the highest possible volume, which encouraged people to leave the rally and go to the USIS screening instead.[62] These examples, and the manner in which they were reported, illustrate vividly how the cultural Cold War was fought out as a proxy war in the streets and squares of Italian towns. The two ideological antagonists competed over access to public spaces and influence over audiences. People made their choices not on the basis of a film's ideological merits; instead, the side that offered the more interesting or entertaining product emerged victorious from the battle. In a context where the spectator could simply join in or walk away, it was vital to present films that would hold their attention, if only to prevent them moving into the opponent's clutches.

France – The struggle with bureaucracy

France traditionally had a much lower level of cinema attendance than its large European neighbours Italy, Britain and Germany. At around 400 million visits per year in the 1950s, audience numbers were half the size of the Italian or German audiences.[63] In 1953 France counted 4,874 commercial cinemas, as well as 560 non-commercial cinemas, which were operated by the Catholic Church and other organizations. Unlike in Italy, many rural communities in France were without a cinema. They sometimes had 16 mm screening facilities, which showed films on a commercial basis on selected days, often at weekends; or they were served by mobile film units.[64]

The commercial distribution of MP films in France was also complicated by numerous regulations, which the government had introduced to protect the domestic cinema industry. The stipulation that a foreign documentary short needed to be coupled to a foreign film reduced the possibilities for commercial distribution, as foreign films fell under strict quota regulations.[65] Moreover, the eight major Hollywood companies, which as main distributors of foreign films were the logical partners for the ECA, typically preferred to couple their main features with their own shorts. Even winning theatrical release for MP films that had been produced in France was not easy. Commercial distribution in France was not concentrated in one place, but operated by around 350 small licenced distributors who could choose from a 'superabundance of films competing for desirable distribution'. Thus, to give the films wide coverage, the ECA had to secure contracts with a number of distribution companies.[66] In spite of these problems, most French MP films entered the commercial circuit in France. The film unit also managed to win theatrical release for some MP films that had been produced outside France, mostly through US companies, which in 1951 distributed the British-produced *Adventure in Sardinia* (1950) and *The Shoemaker and the Hatter* (1950), as well as the German *River Without Borders* (1950).[67]

Because the opportunities for commercial distribution were 'decidedly limited by market conditions', the ECA information office in France focused on the non-theatrical circuit to disseminate MP films.[68] As in other countries, it cooperated closely with the local USIS branches. In 1950, each provincial USIS centre in France was equipped with three projectors, three screens and a mobile unit. USIS organized a total of 26,000 stationary and mobile film screenings in 1950, showing a combination of USIS and MP films that attracted approximately 4 million spectators.[69] A report by the French ECA mission from 1951 gives a more precise breakdown, and states that 32 MP films were shown through USIS across 8,820 screenings, reaching an audience of about a million people. As a direct result of the Korean War, and in an attempt to strengthen Europe's defence efforts, the ECA and its successor, the MSA, began to furnish the Cinema Service of the French Army with MP films. Seventeen MP films were shown to about 1.5 million French army recruits in 1951.[70]

The ECA also built up cooperations with national educational bodies, such as the *cinéma éducateurs*, a network of regional offices in charge of distributing audio-visual materials to state-run schools.[71] These *offices du cinémas éducateurs* had been established in the 1920s to promote media education in French schools. For the ECA, they were invaluable partners in the effort to reach French school children, who were one of the key target groups for MP propaganda.[72] In addition, the ECA set up its own distribution company in 1951. Mondial Films Documentaire, not to be confused with the commercial French distributor Mondial Films, screened 26 MP films in a total of 8,855 showings, and thereby reached an audience of around one million. By June 1952, Mondial had already recorded around 1,600 monthly film showings across France, reaching an audience of approximately 240,000 people per month.[73] The country mission's aim had been to turn Mondial into a permanent, self-supporting, non-profit distribution agency to match the network of *cinéclubs* operated by the French communists. However, its plans were repeatedly frustrated. While the French mission considered Mondial a vital partner in influencing the French people, the new US Information Agency (USIA), which replaced the MSA in summer 1953, was reluctant to renew the contract.[74]

Chapter 2 illustrated how the intricacy of French bureaucracy, the reluctance of the French government to support the ECA's propaganda effort and the (real and imagined) power of the communist party, all hampered the production of MP films. The same was true for the field of distribution. In no other country that participated in the ERP was the opposition to the MP so vocal than in France. The communist-led French trade union confederation and the French Communist Party, which was the strongest party in the Fourth Republic, repeatedly organized demonstrations or instigated actions against the MP, as Bossuat has documented meticulously.[75] The climate was apparently so hostile that the ECA information office preferred not to show MP films in some Paris neighbourhoods at all, out of fear of attacks from local communists. The power of the communist labour movement, which wielded influence over a large number of French workers, is illustrated by an incident in Le Havre, where French dockworkers would not unload MP goods, and by the refusal of the French rail company SNCF to affix posters that advertised the MP.[76] What added to the problem was the reluctance of the French governments to support the ECA's propaganda efforts.[77] Although Georges Bidault's new cabinet launched a rather ambitious promotional campaign for the MP in December 1949, it never realized the plans, not least because his government proved to be as short-lived as the others before it.[78] Despite these difficulties, the ECA country mission eventually managed to gain a foothold. It was able to substantially expand the non-commercial distribution of MP films, but, unlike the missions in West Germany or Britain, did not succeed in 'nationalizing' the propaganda effort.

Greece – Reliance on local dignitaries

The ECA country mission in Greece started its operation in summer 1948 in an impoverished country that was deeply politically split and still in a state of civil war. Substantial parts of the population were internal refugees, and the Greek economy was only kept afloat through outside assistance. Although Greece was of the highest strategic importance to the US government, the information offices of the ECA and USIS struggled to reach the people in the more remote areas. Even as the economy and infrastructure gradually improved, the information situation in the 'small and relatively isolated country' of Greece, where 'the average Greek peasant rarely raises his sights beyond his small village', remained very different from that of more industrialized MP countries.[79]

Since many Greeks were still (semi)-illiterate, film was the key medium for propaganda.[80] Commercial distribution, however, played only a minor role. The

Greek film industry had collapsed in the mid-1930s as a result of deep political and economic crisis, and only gradually recovered after the civil war.[81] Cinema-going remained a largely urban phenomenon until the mid-1950s, but Athens and its suburbs still counted only around sixty winter cinemas in the early 1950s.[82] What is more, because of the economic crisis and the drafting of large numbers of men to fight in the civil war, cinema attendance in the metropolises of Athens and Salonika had dropped considerably since 1948.[83]

It was thus the non-theatrical circuit on which the ECA and USIS concentrated their efforts. The ECA distributed MP films through two main channels: through USIS and the local ECA Labor Division. USIS had (in March 1953) thirteen mobile film units at its disposal. In addition, it operated eight information centres, and had built up ten Community Information Councils (CICs). These CICs, which were presided over by the local priest, the mayor and union and school representatives, would eventually take over the distribution of education films. The ECA Labor information office undertook similar activities as the ECA information office. However, it specifically targeted workers and organized labour groups, aiming to increase productivity and curtail communist influence by improving working conditions and strengthening non-communist trade unions. In 1953 it operated sixty-four labour centres across Greece, which served as educational and information facilities for organized and unorganized workers, hosting talks and film shows.[84] In 1952, the Labor information office also received a film truck 'devoted entirely to MSA Information purposes'.[85] This mobile film unit toured the country to visit the various labour centres, presenting exhibits and film screenings of technical training and MP films.[86]

The distribution of MP films, however, got off to a slow start, for reasons indicated above. The geographical remoteness, the dispersed islands and the lack of basic infrastructure presented major stumbling blocks. The operators of the USIS mobile film units struggled with a lack of seating facilities, intermittent or no electric current, and with poor roads that made remote Greek villages inaccessible in winter; in the early phase of the operation, when the civil war was still ongoing, they also feared guerrilla attacks on their open-air shows.[87] Unlike in other countries, where many schools were in possession of a projector, the Greek Ministry of Education had only 30 silent 16 mm projectors for the whole of Greece at its disposal.[88]

During the first years of the ERP, the MP film campaign concentrated largely on the densely populated Athens-Piraeus area. In 1951, the ECA country mission intensified the propaganda effort as a result of the Korean War and Greece's planned joining of NATO. Priority was given to the hitherto neglected industrialized regions northwest of Thessaloniki, close to the Albanian and Yugoslav border, and the Thessaly region northeast of Athens, because of their 'war-shattered industry, impoverished economic conditions and Communist voting strength'. Here, the primary targets were the Greek workers, which also explains why the ECA information office cooperated closely with the Labor information office.[89]

In preparation for the film shows, the ECA information office sent out local staff to scout the villages in the area for schools, churches or coffee houses that could accommodate (though not necessarily seat) around 100–200 people for the screenings.[90] Apart from cataloguing the facilities and enlisting the help of volunteers, they had to establish good connections with those who yielded power: the local union heads, the mayor or the Greek Orthodox clergy which one report described as 'our best associate'.[91]

In the beginning, the ECA encountered some local resistance to film screenings, as the reports by Basil Glossotis from the ECA Labor information office illustrate. In October 1951, Glossotis tried twice to establish contact with the labour officials of the Greek town of Verria, but with no success. Their representative, the general secretary of the labour centre, was 'not eager to give a solution', either. Although the town had a large theatre, the secretary informed Glossotis that there was no hall available, but promised to forward Glossotis's request. After waiting in vain for a response, Glossotis eventually bypassed the labour officials and went straight to the director of the local school, who agreed to let him use a large classroom under the condition that the education supervisor gave his consent.[92] Glossotis encountered similar problems in Trikkala, a town with a population of 23,000 people. In this case, it was the education supervisor and the local prefect who refused to let the ECA use the school hall, citing the habit of the workers of leaving written slogans on the walls as the reason for denying access to the newly renovated building.[93] In most places, however, the film unit operators were well received, both by local officials and by audiences. Attendance was overall good, ranging from 150 to 3,000 spectators per screening.[94]

However, when the ECA/MSA Labor Division started operating its own mobile film unit in 1953, it soon ran into troubles, both with local officials and with USIS. In Volos, a Greek town with 80,000 inhabitants, the operator of the film unit had failed to inform the president of the labour centre about the upcoming film screening. Indignant, the president refused to advertise the event to the workers at short notice. The screening started therefore in an empty hall, with only the president and his office staff present. They soon left, claiming tiredness. The operator explained away the labour centre president's reaction with the fact that he was a communist, but the real reason seems to have been the operator's failure to pay the president due respect.[95]

This was also the opinion of USIS, which in June 1953 accused the ECA Labor information office of upsetting the carefully groomed relations with town officials and clergy. It also demanded that the Labor Division temporarily suspend its film showings on account of a number of violations of protocol.[96] The minor fiasco in the Greek town of Volos illustrated the importance of following the proper channels, which required cultural sensitivity and familiarity with the complex hierarchy of town and union officials. Ideological differences, as the case of Italy illustrated, were of secondary importance when it came to the screening of MP films. Audiences wanted to be entertained; local dignitaries wanted to be treated respectfully.

The question of effectiveness

The above illustrates how the patterns and strategies of film distribution varied from country to country. Which strategies the ECA pursued to bring the message to the people, and how many people it reached, depended on a number of factors: the local infrastructure, the degree of cooperation with governmental and non-governmental organizations and commercial distributors, the sociopolitical climate in each country, cultural traditions and cinema-going habits. National regulatory frameworks, such as import quotas, also determined the selection of the distribution channels. In Italy, commercial distribution remained the most important route in the first three years of the MP film campaign, thanks to the large number of cinemas and Italy's traditionally high cinema attendance. The commercial sector, however, lost importance when the Italian country mission ceased producing MP films in 1951, as strict government regulations made it virtually impossible to win theatrical release for non-Italian MP films. In countries like Greece, Iceland or Turkey, on the other hand, the scarcity of cinemas outside urban centres made non-theatrical exhibition the only available avenue of film distribution. In many other European countries, the commercial sector gained in importance as production increased and more MP films became available from 1951 onwards. But the non-theatrical exhibition sector presented also here the most opportunities for bringing the message to the people. By distributing films non-commercially, the ECA was able to reach people who lived in areas with no cinematic infrastructure, as well as specific groups, such as school children or factory workers. Moreover, non-theatrical, especially open-air, film screenings of seemingly apolitical entertainment films managed to lure onlookers who were sceptical of or outright opposed to the United States.

These non-theatrical film shows attracted considerable interest, especially in rural areas. Attendance figures rose rapidly during the first half of the MP film campaign, and the shortage of MP films was the biggest problem.[97] The country missions were in need of a steady flow of new films to keep the subject alive. For a couple of years, demand for MP films by far exceeded supply. Although output increased sharply in 1950, it still took a considerable amount of time for the films to reach audiences in the various countries, as they had to be dubbed and printed.

However, as the ECA expanded the production and distribution of MP films, it was confronted with new problems. One was the realization that, despite the impressive growth of attendance figures, the films obviously were not managing to sway European minds to the extent the ECA had hoped. Opinion polls in Italy or France still registered widespread and persistent scepticism of American motives, a lack of trust in the promises of the ERP and obstinate resistance to the MP policies of productivity and European integration. These disappointing findings alarmed the US Congress, which wanted to see compelling and immediate evidence that the MP 'worked'. The ECA and its Information Division responded to the pressure by reconsidering its tactics. Following expert advice, the film unit decided to pay more attention to target groups, whose consent became even more important as US foreign policy shifted towards defence with the outbreak of the Korean War. Thus, at the same time as ECA was expanding the commercial distribution of MP films, it was also intensifying its propaganda efforts in schools, farmers' and workers' organizations and the military, with film programmes tailored to the interests of these groups.

Another problem that arose was that the continuous expansion of distribution networks and film screenings did not translate into an equally rapid growth in the number of spectators: in fact, audience numbers started to stagnate – largely as a result of growing competition from other agencies. The commercial sector was a very competitive market for documentary film, as the number of documentary shorts now by far outstripped demand. At the same time, also in the non-commercial sector competition was growing increasingly fierce. The ECA/MSA vied with a growing number of other agencies for the attention of the viewer. Governmental bodies, trade unions, churches and various interest groups were organizing their own film screenings, often indirectly helped by the ECA or by USIS, which had provided them with projectors or other forms of assistance. Not least represented USIS film screenings direct competition for the ECA unless the programmes included MP films.

A survey conducted on behalf of the State Department in 1951 established that the overall attendance for US film programmes in Europe was not growing as much as it had done during the previous years. The survey assessed the performance of the US government's International Motion Picture Service (IMS) and identified four different types of non-commercial film programmes: film screenings in USIS centres using IMS projectors; film shows through mobile USIS film units; film screenings by cooperating US Agencies (ECA); and screenings by cooperating local government and commercial agencies. The survey revealed that the number of film screenings had risen massively across the world, especially in Europe. However, overall attendance figures had not kept up with this expansion.[98] Instead, the audience numbers in Europe had steadily dropped from an average of 250 people per screening in summer 1950 to 195 in summer 1951. The report concluded that it took 'more than 3 times the effort … to reach the same number of people in Europe as it does in the Far East'. The analysts largely blamed the 'greater competition from other forms of commercial leisure-time activity' for this negative development.[99] The free film screenings were no longer as attractive as they had been in the past, when entertainment opportunities had been scarce and a film show a rare treat.

The survey seems to indicate that the US film propaganda efforts reached their saturation point in Western Europe around 1951. But this was not the whole picture: there were enormous differences between the different European regions, as well as substantial variations between different types of film programmes. While overall attendance stagnated, the numbers of pure MP film shows continued to rise. Although the ECA organized only 7 per cent of all US film programmes in Europe between summer 1950 and the end of 1951, it attracted 25 per cent of the total audience.[100] It is difficult to establish whether the higher attendance of MP film screenings was due to the films themselves, to better advertising or to the choice of locations. What the figures certainly illustrate is the enormous efforts the ECA made to bring the films to as many Europeans as possible.

Even though the stagnation of audience numbers was perhaps not as serious a problem for the ECA/MSA as it was for USIS, given that the MP films continued to reach large audiences, it still gave cause for concern. Combined with the sobering results from opinion polls, the stagnating attendance figures drew attention to the question of effectiveness. The previous chapter has shown how the issue of impact became increasingly important, as the Information Division was under pressure to justify the costs of propaganda – and its own existence. How effective was the MP film campaign, really? If the rise in audience figures attested to the success of MP propaganda, did the decrease in audience numbers mean that the propagandists failed? What indicators were used to measure 'effectiveness'?

The information officers debated the question of the 'effectiveness' of MP film propaganda often in connection with distribution: audience figures and numbers of screenings served as indicators of how effective the propaganda campaign was. Hence, the Italian country mission expressed satisfaction about the 'effectiveness' of its information activities by stating that between 1948 and 1950 'more workers, farmers, housewives and children were reached through several media ... than ever before'. This mission report defined 'effectiveness' chiefly in terms of numbers, and assigned only secondary importance to the 'perceptible improvement' of the peoples' understanding of 'the nature and scope of American aid'.[101]

The term 'effectiveness', as it was used by the ECA and USIS, could mean both the size of the audiences reached and the proof that a given film had an impact on spectators.[102] A published booklet promoting the achievements of the ECA Overseas Information Program in the second year of the ERP begins by highlighting the magnitude of the operation, which it illustrates by giving the number of people reached via each medium. It continues on a more critical note, pointing out that 'magnitude is at best a crude measure of the information program's effectiveness. The real test is what the people toward whom the information is directed think about the Marshall Plan.'[103]

The question of impact was a crucial one. It decided whether the MP film campaign was judged a success or a failure. However, the question of impact or 'efficiency' remains a very tricky one to answer. Did and could the MP films change European attitudes towards the MP and its policy goals in the short and/ or long term? And how can impact be measured, if at all?

Conclusion

In the 1980s, Alan Milward sparked a scholarly controversy on the impact of the MP by questioning the received wisdom that the programme had helped to save Europe from economic collapse.[1] The issue of impact is of course also pertinent to the MP film campaign. What were the films meant to achieve? We remember that Al Hemsing, the last head of the ECA film unit, described the purpose of the MP films as 'to give Europeans the facts and figures on Marshall Aid, to stimulate industrial and agricultural productivity, and to promote the idea of a European community'.[2] Hemsing makes no mention of the films' political aim, but it is clear that the goals he cites are imbued with political meaning.

There exists now widespread consensus that the US government launched the MP not merely out of concern for the precarious state of European economies and its destabilizing effect on the world economy, but also to *restructure* Western Europe economically and politically. Scholars agree that the MP served concrete political and strategic interests. In the Cold War battle for spheres of influence, the MP helped to secure power for the United States, which sought to build up a Western alliance against the Soviet Union – with the United States at its helm. However, it is still a matter of contention as to what degree the ERP was the outcome of well-founded fears of an economic collapse, and what role it actually played in the European economic recovery. In the scholarly debate on the motivations behind the MP, the focus has been laid on its economic aspects: the fears of an economic collapse and its repercussions for the world economy; the ambitions to shape the European economy according to US economic principles in order to stimulate growth; and the desire to revive the multilateral trade system. As discussed in this book, these economic motivations cannot be separated from the US government's political interests, since they are rooted in the same ideology. The idea of producing security by strengthening liberal economy was central to the MP. Milward, who saw in the MP a political project, underlined the US government's intent to influence the political developments in Western Europe through the MP.[3] Other historians, such as Ellwood or Saunders, have also shown how the US government used Marshall Aid strategically by secretly funding non-communist trade unions, and by sponsoring the conservative candidate in the Italian elections to strengthen its allies.[4]

The policy discussions inside the ECA and the State Department reflect the policymakers' immense concern about communism and communist propaganda, and about the Soviets' (alleged) power to undermine the implementation of the ERP and weaken the United States. However, as this book has illustrated, containing communism was, except in the cases of France and Italy, not high on the agenda of most US information officers. Their main struggle lay with the mindset of the Europeans, who rejected the American proposals for reform and appeared unwilling to abandon their ways of thinking and working. The information officers attributed the Europeans' resistance to the films' promises to communist agitation; to ignorance that could be remedied with more propaganda; or they interpreted it as an expression of cultural backwardness. There were other voices that called attention to the more complicated reasons for the scepticism shown by a segment of the European population towards the MP. Still, the tenor was that Europeans had much to learn from the United States and needed to adopt US-style liberal-capitalist practices and values. The main aim of the MP propaganda campaign was thus to produce a change in attitude. In this regard, the findings support Milward's argument that the MP's purpose was to 'develop a bloc of states which would share similar political, social, economic and cultural values to those which the United States itself publicly valued and claimed to uphold'.[5] But this endeavour did not just spring from the desire to strengthen America's power or to undermine support for communism. It was also informed by the will to revive the multilateral trade system as a basis for global security. A successful transfer of American liberal values and ideals to Europe would also substantially reduce opposition to economic modernization and the liberalization of trade. The hope was that the European electorate, once converted, might even press their national governments to modernize.

So, how effective was the MP information campaign? If we consider effectiveness not in terms of audience figures, but in terms of changes in attitude and possibly behaviour, what was its impact? The Averoff prison project attempted to find an answer to this question. From September 1952 until February 1953, the USIS office in Greece conducted an impact study in a prison in northern Athens to evaluate the effectiveness of its propaganda strategies. The majority of the approximately 1,000 inmates at the Averoff prison were communists being held on political grounds. For the study they were divided into three sections: male communists; male criminals and 'repentants' who had rejected communism and were therefore promised earlier release; and female communists and repentants. Each section was provided with pulp magazines and information brochures promoting American life and industry. In addition, the inmates attended a weekly film show of MP and USIS films combined with some newsreels, cartoons and slapstick comedies. The aim was to find out whether the steady flow of propaganda would encourage reflection and change the prisoners' stance towards the United States, the capitalist system and the MP. The experiment encountered numerous difficulties, which compromised the validity of the study. Still, the final report makes for some interesting reading. It relies partly on the observations of the projectionist, who was tasked with presenting the films and encouraging discussion. He reported that the political prisoners' usual reserve during the compulsory screenings was only sometimes punctuated by sarcastic remarks or outbursts of protest to what they saw on screen. Quite different was the response of the repentants and criminals. They apparently were 'so excited and restless it was difficult to get them quieted down to begin the showings'. However, over time all three groups began to 'show some signs of boredom' with the film programme composed almost entirely of documentary films. Asked what kinds of films they would like to see more of, the criminals requested more 'sports films, pretty girls and comedies'. The communists, true to the party line, demanded to see Soviet-produced films, or movies that showed the United States in a less flattering light, such as John Ford's *Grapes of Wrath* (1940), which depicts the misery of impoverished American farmers in the Great Depression. As regards the question of impact – the study could not confirm that the prisoners who rejected communism during their imprisonment did so because of the films they had seen.[6]

The rather crude experiment highlights two important issues: the US policymakers' desire to change European attitudes and their concern over the failure to do so. How important the question of impact was to them is reflected in the large number of audience surveys and opinion polls commissioned, the numerous statistical reports of screenings and audience figures compiled to document the continuous expansion of the propaganda campaign, and, not least, in the practice of hiring European filmmakers to increase the films' appeal. Yet, despite the enormous effort undertaken to reach people even in the far-flung corners of Europe, success seemed elusive.

The opinion polls conducted to measure public opinion towards the MP and the United States brought mixed results; even in northern Europe, where attitudes towards the MP were predominantly positive, many people suspected that the US government had political motives for extending a helping hand to

Europe. American calls to modernize production and lift trade barriers met with considerable resistance among parts of the European population. Fears over loss of jobs and tradition, national pride and growing frustration over the lack of visible improvement fuelled European opposition or at least scepticism to the ERP and the reforms it demanded. Approval rates further sank as the outbreak of the Korean War and subsequent rearmament boom sparked fears of another world war and frustration over rapidly rising inflation and skyrocketing prices. The US propagandists were successful insofar as they reached an impressive number of Europeans with their films. Yet persuading the audiences to embrace the US principles of free trade, rationalized production or modern management proved much more difficult. They had to acknowledge that widespread anti-communism did not automatically translate into pro-Americanism.

To overcome popular resistance against economic reform and to win the audiences for the MP's underlying ideals, the ECA film policy planners continuously worked to boost the appeal of their films. As the previous chapters have shown, they increased the number of story-type movies and produced more films in Technicolor. They encouraged the filmmakers to experiment with drama or humour, and tried to keep information about technical details to a minimum. Anxious of alienating audiences, the film officers minimized direct references to the United States and skirted issues that might be interpreted as political. In addition, the country missions sought to adapt the film programmes to the preferences of local audiences, and encouraged attendance by pairing MP films with entertaining cartoons or fiction films.

Whether these efforts eventually paid off is difficult to say, since many MP films reached the audiences only after long delays. A synchronization report by the High Commissioner of Germany (HICOG), which oversaw the distribution of information films in West Germany, illustrates how the time-consuming process of translating, dubbing and printing of films hampered the campaign's effectiveness. Compiled in November 1952, the report noted that the dubbing of the French MP film *The Story of Mahmoud* (1950) was finally completed and the film was ready to enter distribution in Germany – two-and-a-half years after it had been completed. The German synchronization of the Danish film *The Streamlined Pig*, produced in summer 1951, was only just being recorded and would be ready for distribution in 1953. The German version of the series *The Marshall Plan at Work*, also produced in 1950, had just been released on 16 mm and awaited printing on 35 mm for commercial exhibition. Only the recently completed first episodes of the twelve-part series *1-2-3: A Monthly Review from Europe* were fast-tracked.[7] As a consequence, many of the MP films that were produced in 1950 and 1951 (the output of films before that was marginal and limited to Italy) did not reach European audiences before 1952 or 1953, or sometimes later. By this time, the ECA had been replaced with the MSA, and the MP was nearing its end or had already been concluded. The length of time that passed between a film's first release in one country and its distribution in another country had, of course, implications. It meant that some MP policies received only limited publicity, and that the audience surveys never captured the full impact of the MP films. In any case, the polls built on the implicit assumption that film, or propaganda in general, could change people's opinions in a relatively short space of time. The Averoff prison project mentioned in the beginning suggests that this was unlikely. We therefore have to consider whether the MP film campaign possibly shaped European attitudes and behaviour if not in the short term, then in the long term. The difficulty is, of course, determining whether any changes in attitude can be linked to the consumption of (MP) films.

The Americanization of Europe

If we look at the development of Western European societies after the Second World War, it seems that the American efforts to transfer their values and ideas were successful. The way Europeans worked, produced, consumed, lived and spent their free time changed fundamentally after 1945. The United States played a crucial, possibly the most important role in this development. Continental Europe had suffered years of wartime deprivation and cultural isolation until they were freed by the Allies. Apart from providing badly needed economic aid and investments, the victorious Americans also brought with them new consumer products and mass culture in the form of movies, musical records, comics and fashion. They also introduced Europeans to a different set of social norms, behaviours and ways of thinking.[8] The MP, but also the MP films, played their part in this transfer. They familiarized Europeans with American production and management methods, socio-economic standards and new attitudes to work and consumption. Though outwardly documenting the reconstruction efforts across Europe and introducing the viewer to new modes of production, they made a case for liberalism, democracy, free trade and free movement, competition, entrepreneurship and productivity. The films sought to persuade the Europeans to embrace these economic and sociopolitical values as key to lasting growth, security and peace, and as guarantor of the rights and the freedom of the individual.

This influx of US culture, products and norms in Europe after the Second World War has often been likened to a wave or flood that swept over European societies – images that evoke a sense of drowning and helplessness. But the image of a flood does not adequately describe the complex process of change that ensued. Many Europeans eagerly embraced the American mass culture and consumer goods they first encountered through Hollywood films or US soldiers. Yet there existed also considerable unease about, and resistance to, what many Europeans perceived as American dominance. The politically conservative classes and the churches, ever fearful of the masses, reacted strongly against the American 'obsession' with consumption. They also condemned the permissiveness of American popular culture. Their criticism was not dissimilar to that from the Left, which warned against the ruthlessness of American capitalism and the influence of consumerism; they also decried America's apparent lack of culture. Europe's cultural elites from both the Left and the Right united to voice concern about European national cultures and traditions, which they saw threatened by the influx – and broad popularity – of American mass culture.[9]

Already in the 1920s intellectual elites had used the term 'Americanization' to describe the influence of American ideas, values or forms of production on Europe. But Americanization is also a scholarly concept that aims to illuminate the relation between America's power and the swift economic, social and cultural changes that occurred in Europe, particularly after the Second World War.[10] Americanization has often been likened to colonialism or cultural imperialism. On the basis of an understanding of culture as something pure and static, it has been conceived as the attempt of one nation to impress its culture and ideology on another, weaker nation, mostly through the use of indirect force.[11] However, in historical scholarship, this understanding has given way to a more nuanced view that accentuates the permeability of culture. The concept of Americanization operates with the assumption that culture cannot be imposed or simply transplanted from one cultural context; rather, culture or ideas are transferred through a process of negotiation that involves the active participation of the 'recipients'.[12] The head of the ECA Paul Hoffman acknowledged the difficulties of exporting US socio-economic norms and industrial practices by pointing out that 'technical assistance cannot be exported; it can only be imported'.[13] Transfers are, moreover, seldom unidirectional: the 'American' mass culture, products or techniques that entered Western Europe in the aftermath of the Second World War were themselves the result of earlier exchanges between the two continents and beyond.[14] In fact the term 'American' itself is imprecise, assuming a homogeneity that does not exist.

Philipp Gassert coined the term 'Americanisms' to define those products, values, manners or symbols that the recipients identify as American, regardless whether they actually originate in the United States or are just perceived to be American.[15] Gassert's definition is very useful, not least because it points to the often simultaneous presence of positive and negative feelings that 'America' has evoked. In post-war Western Europe, 'America' represented modernity, dynamism, efficiency, individual freedom and optimism; but it also stood for ruthless capitalist exploitation, selfishness, materialism, violence, rootlessness and lack of 'real' culture; depending on the stance of the individual, America meant one or the other, and often both.[16]

Whether we describe the rapid economic, cultural and political changes Europe experienced in the twentieth century, particularly after 1945, as modernization, Westernization or Americanization,[17] it is undeniable that the United States played an influential role in this process, both through active intervention and through indirect promotion. The specific economic and political conditions after the Second World War – the exhaustion of Europe and the Soviet Union, the fear of growing communist power – allowed the United States to expand its influence and cement its hegemonic role in the Western world. Several US governmental agencies were engaged in advertising 'America' abroad: apart from the ECA/MSA, the overseas US Information Service of the State Department, the military governments in Germany and Austria OMGUS and their successor HICOG, and the CIA. They employed a mixture of coercion and persuasion to win acceptance for American liberal values and socio-economic norms. Also American business shaped European production and consumption through advertising, exports, investments and trade deals. Looking to regain access to the European market after the war, it extended its influence often through concerted actions with the US government.

Hollywood played a particularly strong role in the transformation of Western Europe. It was both a powerful industry and an influential promoter of American goods and the American way of life, and thus an indispensable ally for American business and government alike. After the end of the Second World War, Hollywood moved with incredible speed – and remarkable shrewdness – to reconquer Europe. A showcase of American innovation and consumer products, Hollywood cinema instilled in the European spectators a desire for American fashion, beauty products, kitchen appliances or cars, along with the lifestyle they represented. Hollywood movies also familiarized foreign audiences with what the Americans believed to be their superior way of life: high standards of living, progressive gender roles, modern work and management practices, and democratic small-town communities.[18] The Hollywood industry was therefore, as Wagnleitner has emphasized, an agent of immense cultural, economic and – especially in times of hot and cold wars – political influence.[19]

Hollywood's influence rested on its dominant position on the European and other overseas markets, which it had acquired during the interwar years.[20] Hollywood's advance in Europe had been stopped by the rise of authoritarian regimes and their strict protectionist policies; by 1940, Hollywood had lost access to most European markets, which had come under the occupation of Nazi Germany and its allies.[21] During the war, Hollywood supported the US war effort with the production of entertainment and instructional films, free film copies for the US Army, movie-star performances for overseas troops and the purchase of war bonds.[22] With the war over, it enlisted the help of the US government to regain access to the European market.[23] The US government, seeking to promote America abroad, had a vested interest in securing the widest distribution of Hollywood movies. Many European governments had introduced protectionist measures since the war to reassert their national power and protect their domestic industries against the sudden influx of Hollywood movies.[24] Brandishing the liberal values of free trade and open markets, the Truman Administration pressured the European states to revoke barriers against Hollywood imports.

The US government's influence was particularly strong in West Germany and Austria, where the United States as occupant held supreme power. Hollywood and the US government relied on each other in their attempt to expand their respective spheres of influence. The US military government OMGUS needed Hollywood to distract the starving German population with apolitical entertainment films and to support its re-education efforts.[25] Hollywood, represented by the newly formed export cartel, the Motion Picture Exchange Association (MPEA), complied;[26] it distributed American newsreels and propaganda through its channels, and later also some MP films. Thanks to the partial overlap of interests, but also close personnel connections between the MPEA and OMGUS, Hollywood gained unrestricted access to the West German and Austrian markets.[27]

But relations between the two main exporters of American culture were not as smooth as they appear at first glance. Although the interests of Hollywood and the US government overlapped, their aims were not the same. Whereas the US government wanted to project a positive image of America in order to win acceptance for its foreign policies and proposed reforms, Hollywood pursued purely economic interests.[28] Hollywood, taking advantage of the Europeans' hunger for entertainment, flooded the continental market with a backlog of films that had accumulated while it had been barred from the continent. The American films that entered European cinemas after the war were predominantly mediocre, second- and third-class movies, often gangster and horror films.[29] They depicted an American society immersed in crime, corruption and promiscuity – an image of America that was the exact opposite of what the US State Department wanted to convey.

In Germany and Austria, the US military government had the power to refuse screening permission for films that conflicted with its re-education policies. It banned not only Nazi films, but also Hollywood films on the grounds that they glorified violence, ridiculed US institutions or laws, depicted the United States in an unflattering light or illustrated social inequality or racial prejudices in the United States. Films such as *Key Largo*, *Grapes of Wrath*, *Ghost of Frankenstein*, *Casablanca* and *The Hunchback of Notre Dame* were barred from German and Austrian cinemas 'on grounds of immorality, irrelevance or misinterpretation'. OMGUS also refused permission to screen the *Tarzan* movies as it found them 'totally irrelevant to reorientation'.[30] The State Department made similar attempts in other European countries, but failed, as Hollywood's power proved to be stronger.[31]

Thus, the cooperation between the US governmental agencies and Hollywood worked well only as long as both parties profited. Counting on Hollywood's ability to promote the 'myth of America' to the Europeans, the Truman Administration helped Hollywood's entry into the European markets, using the threat of withholding financial assistance as leverage to influence national regulations. Hollywood, in turn, actively assisted US propaganda efforts by distributing American newsreels and information films through their cinema chains. However, its cooperative spirit slackened as soon as it had secured free access to the Western European market.[32] By the early 1950s, Hollywood movies had acquired the largest market share in many Western European countries.[33] As Hollywood was no longer in need of the helping hand of the US government, the ECA struggled to persuade Hollywood companies to distribute MP films.

The cultural and economic dominance of Hollywood in post-war Europe should, however, not be equated with the obliteration of European and national cultures. Cinema was a contested space where national identities and cultural boundaries were formulated and asserted – also against Hollywood.[34] Pierre Sorlin's claim that Hollywood productions, though plentiful, were generally 'less successful than their European rivals', has been substantiated by a number of empirical studies. Whether in Britain, France, Italy or West Germany, national film productions regularly topped the lists of popularity and were usually exhibited over a much longer period than Hollywood movies.[35] A US Foreign Office survey of German and Austrian cinema audiences concluded in May 1946 that 'an imported film must be outstandingly good to attract anything like the audiences of the more popular German films'.[36] Of course, we must not think of 'national cinema' (or Hollywood cinema, for that matter) as a homogenous, closed-off entity, but as permeable. Still, national cinema, or rather strands of it, embraced national or local cultural traditions and thus spoke to audiences more directly.[37] Well aware of the Europeans' penchant for domestically produced films, the ECA sought to exploit this preference by hiring European filmmakers for their MP film production.

While Europeans may have preferred national film productions, they also flocked to the cinemas to see Hollywood movies, as the box-office takings illustrate. Hollywood's glamour and stars appealed particularly, but not exclusively, to the young, urban, working-class audiences who were inspired by the fashion, hairstyles and mannerisms of the American stars on screen.[38] But the influence of Hollywood cinema, as we have seen, was much broader. Hollywood conveyed the promise of opportunity and a good life. Its images attested to the high living standards that ordinary Americans enjoyed; it glamourized consumption, popularized American social, gender and moral norms, marketed modern work environments and work ethics, and created a desire for American products and the American way of life more generally.

The MP films were something different entirely. Although the confidence and bravado of Hollywood movies often eclipsed the more factual MP films, the latter, too, were watched by a considerable number of Europeans. The MP films' focus, however, was on Europe. The narratives and imagery spoke of European recovery, European modernization, European effort – and very little of the United States. Yet implicitly the United States was always present. It was the template by which the progress of Western Europe – and communist Eastern Europe – was measured. In showing how, for example, the import of modern American tractors increased yield on European farms, the films explained and popularized US-style economic principles and practices. In outlining the interdependency of the Europeans and the benefits of cooperation, they sought to foster acceptance for the liberal principle of free trade. In hinting at America's thriving economy and prosperous society, the films substantiated the claim that prosperity and security could be achieved only by following the US liberal-capitalist model.

Ellwood has pointed out that, though outwardly different, the functions of Hollywood and MP film propaganda overlapped. Hollywood worked on the demand side, creating a desire for American living standards, culture and consumer products, while the MP films showed how these could be achieved.[39] The impact of the projections of MP film propaganda can therefore not be separated from that of Hollywood cinema, or from the films of other US governmental or commercial agencies. Nor can the possible influence of the MP film campaign be isolated from the influx of American mass culture, consumer products, machinery, techniques or expert knowledge that the United States exported to Europe. MP films were part of a wider transfer of American culture, values and practices, and were thus subject to a complex process of negotiation.

The propagandists at the ECA, well aware of the Europeans' ambiguous feelings towards America, sought to downplay the role of the United States. The ECA policy of hiring European filmmakers was part of this effort to engage European audiences and spur them into action. These European filmmakers, like the US information officers, were situated between the European audiences and the American sponsors. They were tasked with translating US policy into effective imagery and transmitting US ideals, culture and socio-economic norms to the European context. The filmmakers were, as this study has shown, by no means mere puppets who produced propaganda following the stipulations of the US policymakers. They pursued their own interests and artistic aspirations – aspirations that were, however, often similar to those of the ECA's information officers. European filmmakers and American information officers shared a cosmopolitan outlook, believed in documentary film as a means of social change and supported the overt aims of the MP. This created a harmony of interests, which is also tangible in the films themselves. Although the ECA Information Division and its film unit had considerable power over the filmmaking process and occasionally made use of it, there was, overall, little conflict with the filmmakers over the films' form or messages. The information officers, for their part, experienced little interference from above, but enjoyed extensive freedom in the formulation of policies and strategies. The main pressure thus did not come from the higher echelons of the ECA/MSA or the State Department. It came from the European audiences. It was to their interests and preferences that the US information officers had to tailor the films and messages. Selling the US government's economic and political policy goals to the Europeans thus often resulted in their adaption to local contexts.

How Europeans have rejected, adopted or adapted American practices, values or products has been subject to illuminating studies. In the case of the MP film campaign, it is most often the rejection – of the films or the messages they carried – that has left traces in the records: the Greek audiences, for example, who did not like films on European integration, or the Austrian farmers who dismissed films about mechanized farming on US farms as irrelevant. What practices or ideas the audiences actually adopted is much more difficult to establish, at least if we do not accept at face value the self-congratulatory claims of the US strategists that MP propaganda was very effective. As the case of the French farmers in Chapter 4 illustrated, the European responses were often contradictory – and highly selective; they accepted the arguments of communist propaganda, but also welcomed the tractors the Americans provided, because one was, above all, a farmer, interested in increasing one's profit.

The fact that Western European societies changed rapidly and profoundly in the decades after the Second World War was the result of a wider modernization process, in which the United States played a leading – and an active – role. The MP and MP films demonstrate America's efforts to reshape Western Europe economically, culturally and politically. The played their part in a wider cultural transfer, although it is impossible to isolate their impact on European production and consumption practices from other American influences. The results of the ECA's efforts to sway the minds of the Europeans were mixed, and did not always turn out as intended. One thing, however, is certain. In Europe and in the wider world, the MP is remembered in very positive terms, which might, to some extent, be also a result of the propaganda campaign. The fact that politicians still call for a 'new Marshall Plan' whenever they are confronted with an unsolvable crisis, suggests that MP propaganda at least succeeded in its goal of convincing Europeans that the MP was necessary for the successful recovery of the European economy.

Filmography

About the filmography

The filmography contains the production data of the 167 MP films I analyzed for this study. The production details are taken from the film credits, various film catalogues and the detailed Marshall Plan Filmography Linda Christenson has compiled. She also provides summaries of the films, and I advise anybody who is interested in the topic to consult it: http://www.marshallfilms.org. Please be aware that the information details I give here are not complete. Also, in some cases the same film was distributed in different lengths and/or under different titles. I give the English production title with the original title (if known) in brackets, except for those few MP films where the ECA usually used the original title.

Copies of many of these films are held at the National Archives at College Park, Maryland, and are accessible for everyone. More and more film archives provide online access to their holdings, which is why a growing number of MP films can also be found on YouTube and other online platforms. The German Historical Museum provides online access to more than 40 MP films, many in the English version http://www.dhm. de/filmarchiv/die-filme/ . Also the French Institut national de l'audiovisuel: (http://www.ina.fr/recherche) and the Italian Archivio Audiovisivo del Movimento Operaio e Democratico (https://www.youtube.com/user/AAMODAAMOD) have published many MP films online.

Abbreviations: Dir: director; Prod: producer; Specs: (technical) specifications

Adventure in Sardinia. Produced for ECA UK 1950 by Associated Pathé Ltd, London, in association with Nucleus Film Unit. Dir: Jack Chambers, Arthur Elton. Prod: Peter Baylis. Camera: Wolfgang Suschitzky. Music: Thomas Henderson. Specs: b/w, 20 min.

Air of Freedom (Berliner Luft). Produced for ECA W-Germany & HICOG 1951 by Zeit im Film. Specs: b/w, 20 min.

All My Ships (Alle mine skibe). Produced for ECA Denmark 1951 by Minerva Film. Dir: Theodor Christensen. Camera: Rolf Rønne. Script: Theodor Christensen. Music: Niels Viggo Bentzon. Specs: b/w, 13 min.

Appian Way, The (Via Appia). Produced for ECA Italy 1950 by Telefilm. Dir: Vittorio Gallo. Camera: Francesco Vitrotti. Music: Mario Tamanini. Specs: b/w, 10 min.

Aquila (Aquila). Produced for ECA Italy 1949. Dir, Prod & Script: Jacopo Erbi. Camera: Franco & Gianni Vitrotti. Music: Mario Bugamelli. Specs: b/w, 21 min.

As the Young Ones Sing (Wie die Jungen sungen). Produced for MSA/USIS Austria 1954. Dir: Georg Tressler. Prod: Carlheinz Langbein. Camera: Sepp Riff. Script: Georg & Beatrice Tressler. Music: Hanns Elin. Specs: b/w, 26 min.

Assignment for Europe. Produced for MSA 1952 by Film Unit, Paris. Specs: b/w, 27 min.

Belgium – A Year of Progress. Produced for ECA 1950 by Fox Movietone News. Specs: b/w, 10 min.

Bigger Potato Crops (Ertragreicher Kartoffelanbau). Produced for ECA Austria 1950. Dir & Prod: Georg Tressler. Camera: Paul Bruck. Specs: b/w, 20 min.

Breakthrough (Aura). Produced for ECA Norway 1950 by Norsk Dokumentarfilm. Dir: Lauritz Falk. Prod: Per Borgerson. Camera: Per Johnson. Script: Per Borgerson. Music: Gunnar Soenstevold, E.F. Brein. Specs: b/w, 18 min.

Bull's Eye for Farmer Pietersen (Boer Pietersen schoot in de roos). Produced for ECA Netherlands 1950 by Cinetone. Dir & Prod: Ytsen Brusse. Camera: Bert Haanstra. Script: John Amand D'Heynneaux. Music: Hugo de Groot. Specs: b/w, 20 min.

Calabria. Produced for ECA Italy 1950. Dir: Vittorio Gallo. Prod: Silvio Gigli. Camera: R. Fillipini. Music: Carlo Innocenzi. Specs: b/w, 12 min.

Care of Tractors (Traktör Bakımı). Produced for ECA Turkey 1951 by Clarke and Hornby Productions.

Caroline, the Cow (Fabrikken Caroline). Produced for ECA Denmark 1951 by Nordisk Film. Dir: Søren Melson. Camera: Jørgen Skov. Script: Susanne Palsbo. Music: H.C. Lumbye. Specs: b/w, 12 min.

Changing Face of Europe, no. 1: Power for All. Produced for ECA 1951 by Wessex Productions. Dir: Graham Wallace, Anthony Squire. Prod: Ian Dalrymple. Camera: Cedric Williams, Peter Newbrook, John Corbett. Music: Peter Seabourne. Specs: colour, 20 min.

Changing Face of Europe, no. 2: 300.000.000 Mouths. Produced for ECA 1951 by Wessex Productions. Dir: Julian Spiro. Prod: Ian Dalrymple. Camera: Bob Ziller, Sydney Samuelson, Michael Reed. Specs: colour, 16 min.

Changing Face of Europe, no. 3: Somewhere to Live. Produced for ECA 1951 by Wessex Productions. Dir: Jacques Brunius. Prod: Ian Dalrymple. Camera: Ernest Palmer, Harold Britten. Specs: colour, 16 min.

Changing Face of Europe, no. 4: Men and Machines. Produced for ECA 1951 by Wessex Productions. Dir: Diana Pine. Prod: Ian Dalrymple. Camera: Ian Wooldridge, Denis Fox. Specs: colour, 18 min.

Changing Face of Europe, no. 5: Clearing the Lines. Produced for ECA 1951 by Wessex Productions. Dir: Kay Mander. Prod: Ian Dalrymple. Camera: Jonah Jones, Len Harris, Gerry Fisher. Specs: colour, 19 min.

Changing Face of Europe, no. 6: The Good Life. Produced for ECA 1951 by Wessex Productions. Dir & Script: Humphrey Jennings (†), Graham Wallace, Anthony Squire. Prod: Ian Dalrymple. Camera: Freddie Gamage, Eddie Harris. Specs: colour, 20 min.

Ciampino aeroporto d'Europa. Produced for MSA 1953 by Gallo Produzione Cinematografica, Rome. Dir & Prod: Vittorio Gallo. Camera: Francesco Vitrotti. Specs: b/w, 10 min.

City out of Darkness (Es wurde Licht). Produced for ECA W-Germany 1950 by Merkurius Film. Dir: Max Diekhout. Camera: Karl F. Wagner. Music: Hans Ebert. Specs: b/w, 9 min.

Concerning Dairy Production (Rund um die Milchwirtschaft). Produced for ECA Austria 1954 by Cosmopol Film. Dir: Georg Tressler. Camera: Sepp Riff. Script: Philipp von Zeska, Georg Tressler. Music: Carl de Groof. Specs: b/w, 25 min.

Control of Water (Suyun Kontrolü). Produced for ECA Turkey 1951 by Clarke and Hornby Productions, London.

Corinth Canal. Produced for ECA Greece 1950 by Ferno Productions, Paris. Dir: John Ferno. Prod: John Ferno, Nelo Risi. Camera: Jacques Letellier. Script: ECA Film Unit. Music: Maurice Thiriet. Specs: b/w, 11 min.

Cotton (Cotone). Produced for ECA Italy 1950 by Phoenix Films. Dir & Prod: Ubaldo Magnaghi. Camera: Renato Sistri. Music: Ennio Porrino. Specs: b/w, 11 min.

Council of Europe, The. Produced for MSA 1952. Dir: Victor Vicas. Camera: Edmond Sechan. Script: Norman Borisoff. Music: Louis Hochet. Specs: b/w, 27 min.

Doctor for Ardaknos, A. Produced for ECA Greece 1951 by John Ferno Productions, Paris. Dir & Prod: John Ferno. Script: ECA Film Unit. Specs: b/w, 14 min.

Dunkirk to Dunkerque / A Tale of Two Cities (Et c'est arrivé ainsi). Produced for ECA France 1951 by Boris Morros Productions. Dir: Z.A. Touroff. Prod: Roger Rosen. Camera: Marcel Weiss. Script: Henry Altimus. Music: Alexandre Tansman. Specs: b/w, 11 min.

E comme Europe (no English title). Produced for MSA 1952 by DOC Films, Paris. Dir: Géza von Radványi. Camera: Roger Fellows. Script: Rene Barjavel, Geza Rádvanyi. Music: Alain Romans. Specs: b/w, 35 min.

Emilia. Produced for ECA Italy 1951 by Vittorio Gallo Films. Dir & Prod: Vittorio Gallo. Camera: Francesco Vitrotti. Script: James Wellard. Music: Ennio Porrino. Specs: b/w, 22 min.

ERP in Action no. 1–12. Produced for ECA 1950 by Fox Movietone News. Specs: b/w, 11 min.

Europe Looks Ahead. Produced for ECA 1950 by March of the Time. Specs: b/w, 19 min.

European Labor Day. Produced for ECA 1951 by ECA Film Unit, Paris. Specs: b/w, 9 min.

Expert Services. Produced for MSA Denmark 1952 by Nordisk Film & Film Centre Ltd. London. Dir: Søren Melson. Camera: Henning Kristiansen. Script: Ove Sevel. Music: Svend Erik Tarp. Specs: b/w, 17 min.

Extraordinary Adventures of one Quart Milk, The (Les aventures extraordinaires d'un litre de lait). Produced for ECA France 1951 by Tele-Radio-Cine Productions. Dir: Alain Pol. Camera: Rollan Paillas. Script: Pierre Grimblat. Music: Jacques Metehen. Specs: b/w, 14 min.

Farm in Four Countries, A (Terre d'Europe). Produced for MSA 1953 by Ferno Productions, Paris. Dir: Nelo Risi. Prod: John Ferno. Camera: Jacques Manier, Franco de Paolis. Script: Ian Stuart Black. Music: Maurice Thiriet. Specs: b/w, 31 min / 16 min (Italian).

Free City. Produced for ECA Trieste 1950 by Telefilm. Dir & Prod: Romolo Marcellini. Camera: Rino Fillipini. Script: Lothar Wolff (ECA Film Unit), John Secondari (Information Division Italy). Music: Alberico Vitalini. Specs: b/w, 10 min.

Handicraft Town (Ritratto di un paese). Produced for ECA Italy 1949 by Marcellini Films. Dir: Romolo Marcellini. Prod: Alain Pol. Camera: Mario Bonicatti. Music: Vittorio Chiti. Specs: b/w, 10 min.

Hansl and the 200,000 Chicks (Hansl und die 200,000 Kücken). Produced for ECA Austria & BM für Land- und Forstwirtschaft 1952. Dir & Script: Georg Tressler. Prod & Camera: Julius Jonak. Music: Frank Silten. Specs: b/w, 15 min.

Henry's Story (Une histoire d'Henri). Produced for ECA France 1950 by Tele-Radio-Cine. Camera: A. Militon. Script: W. Massee. Commentary script: Jaqueline d'Arcole. Music: Paul Baron. Specs: b/w, 16 min.

Hidden Power (Larderello). Produced for ECA Italy 1950 by Phoenix Films. Dir & Prod: Vittorio Gallo. Camera: Francesco Vitrotti. Music: Mario Tamanini. Specs: b/w, 10 min.

Hidden Treasures (Tesori nacosti). Produced for ECA Italy 1948–49 by Phoenix Films. Dir & Prod: Vittorio Gallo. Camera: Antonio Schiavinotto. Music: Mario Tamanini. Specs: b/w, 11 min.

Hides for Tomorrow (Häute für Morgen). Produced for ECA W-Germany 1950 by Ikaros Film. Dir & Prod: Wolfgang Kiepenheuer. Specs: b/w, 11 min.

Home We Love, The (Lou Mas Aimat). Produced for ECA France 1950 by Tele-Radio-Cine Productions. Dir: Alain Pol. Camera: R. Pailles. Script: M. O'Hara. Music: Paul Baron. Specs: b/w, 15 min.

Houen Zo (Steady). Produced for ECA Netherlands 1951 by Cinetone. Dir, Prod & Script: Herman van der Horst. Specs: b/w, 21 min.

Hour of Choice, The. Produced for ECA UK 1951 by Gaumont British Picture Corporation. Dir & Script: Stuart Legg. Music: Jack Beaver. Specs: b/w, 21 min.

Hugo and the Harp (Hugo macht Musik). Produced for ECA W-Germany 1952 by Marten Toonder Film, Netherlands. Dir: Mack Harold. Animation: Bjørn Ring, Bjørn Frank Jensen. Script: Philip Stapp. Music: Gijs Reyns. Specs: Animation, colour, 4 min.

Hugo and the House of Europe (Hugo baut auf). Produced for ECA W-Germany 1952 by Marten Toonder Film, Netherlands. Dir: Mack Harold. Animation: Bjørn Ring, Bjørn Frank Jensen. Script: Philip Stapp. Music: Lex van Delden. Specs: Animation, colour, 4 min.

Hugo in the Circus (Hugo am Trapez). Produced for ECA W-Germany 1952 by Marten Toonder Film, Netherlands. Dir: Mack Harold. Animation: Bjørn Ring, Bjørn Frank Jensen. Script: Philip Stapp. Music: Gijs Reyns. Specs: Animation, colour, 4 min.

I Went Back. Produced for ECA UK 1950 by Associated British Pathe Ltd, London. Prod: Terry Ashwood. Camera: George Stevens, Bernard Till. Script: W. Richardson. Music: Walter Goehr. Specs: b/w, 17 min.

Ideas at Work. Produced for ECA UK & Economic Information Unit of the British Treasury 1950 by Crown Film Unit. Specs: b/w, 14 min.

Independent People, An. Produced for ECA 1950. Specs: b/w, 16 min.

Invisible Link, The (Strom der Berge). Produced for ECA Austria 1950 by Victor Vicas Films. Dir & Prod: Victor Vicas. Camera: Helmuth Ashley. Script: Edith Knoll. Music: Claude Arrieu. Specs: b/w, 13 min.

Island Odyssey. Produced for ECA Greece 1950. Specs: b/w, 9 min.

Island of Faith (Walcheren). Produced for ECA Netherlands 1950 by Ferno Productions, Paris. Dir & Prod: John Ferno, Nelo Risi. Camera: Jacques Letellier. Music: Joseph Kosma. Specs: b/w, 20 min.

Italy Today (Italia d'oggi). Produced for MSA Italy 1953 by Europa Telefilm. Dir: Romolo Marcellini. Prod: Pietro Notarianni. Camera: Rino Filippini, Vittorio del Monte. Music: Paolo Girlando. Specs: b/w, 11 min.

Jour de Peine (Tough Day, A). Produced for MSA (Labor Division) 1952 by Victor Vicas Productions, Paris. Dir & Prod: Victor Vicas. Camera: Jean Leherissey. Script: Michael Elkins. Music: Claude Arrieu. Specs: b/w, 30/48 min.

Kyndbyværket (no English title). Produced for ECA Denmark 1951 by Nordisk Film. Dir & Script: Ove Sevel. Camera: Poul Pedersen. Music: Hans Schreiber. Specs: b/w, 20 min.

Land of Apulia. Produced for ECA Italy 1951 by Panorama Films. Dir: Francesco de Feo. Camera: Francesco Attenni. Script: Sandro de Feo. Music: Franco Mannino. Specs: b/w, 11 min.

Land Redeemed (Bonifiche). Produced for ECA Italy 1950 by Telefilm. Dir: Vittorio Gallo. Camera: Francesco Vitrotti. Music: Mario Tamanini. Specs: b/w, 10 min.

Let's Be Childish (Enfantillages). Produced for ECA France 1950 by George Freedland Productions. Dir, Prod & Script: George Freedland. Camera: J. Mercanton. Music: Van Hoorebeke. Specs: b/w, 19 min.

Liberty (Liberté). Produced for ECA France 1950 by Tadie-Cinema Productions. Dir: Jean Mitry. Camera: Roger Caron, André Tadié, Gaston Tadié. Script: Emmanuel Renard. Music: Marcel Despard. Specs: b/w, 13 min.

Life and Death of a Cave City (Matera). Produced for ECA Italy 1950 by Documento Film. Dir: Romolo Marcellini. Prod: Pino Giomini. Camera: Cyril Knowles. Script: John Secondari (ECA Italy). Music: Franco Mannino, played by Symphonic Orchestra of St. Cecilia. Specs: colour, 11 min.

Liquid Force (Force Liquide). Produced for ECA France 1950 by Tele-Radio-Cine Productions. Dir: Pierre Chevalier. Camera: Julien Manier, Alain Pol. Script: P. Ferenczi, P. Leaud. Music: Paul Baron. Specs: b/w, 13 min.

Liquid Sunshine (Agrumeti d'Italia). Produced for ECA Italy 1949 by Europeo Film. Dir: Primo Zeglio. Camera: Rino Fillipini. Script: Paliotta & G.A. Longo. Music: Virgino Chiti. Specs: b/w, 11 min.

Living Stream, The (Ett hörn i norr). Produced for ECA Sweden, Denmark, Norway 1950 by Svensk Filmindustri Stockholm. Dir, Prod & Camera: Arne Sucksdorff. Music: Hilding Rosenberg. Specs: b/w, 24/13 min.

Machines at Work. Produced for MSA 1952 by Société française Chronophotographie, Paris & Film Centre Ltd, London. Dir: William Novik. Prod: Henri Lorand. Camera: Roger Fellous. Music: Pierre Barbaud. Specs: b/w, 21 min.

Marketing. Produced for MSA 1953 by Pierre Long, Son et Lumière Films, Paris, & Film Centre Ltd, London. Dir & Prod: Pierre Long. Camera: Jacques Klein, Felix Forestier. Music: Michel Magne. Specs: b/w, 17 min.

Marshall Plan at Work in Austria, The. Produced for ECA 1950 by Editorial Film Productions Ltd, London. Dir: James Hill. Prod: Jim Mellor. Camera: Kenneth Talbot. Script: Arthur Calder Marshall. Specs: b/w, 11 min.

Marshall Plan at Work in Belgium (and Luxembourg), The. Produced for ECA 1950 by Editorial Film Productions Ltd, London. Dir & Camera: Guy Blanchard. Prod: Jim Mellor. Script: Arthur Calder Marshall. Specs: b/w, 11 min.

Marshall Plan at Work in Denmark, The. Produced for ECA 1950 by Editorial Film Productions Ltd, London. Dir: Guy Blanchard. Prod: Jim Mellor. Camera: Eric Lindeman. Script: Arthur Calder Marshall. Specs: b/w, 11 min.

Marshall Plan at Work in France, The. Produced for ECA 1950 by Editorial Film Productions Ltd, London. Dir: F. Conquet. Prod: Jim Mellor. Camera: F. Conquet. Script: Arthur Calder Marshall. Specs: b/w, 11 min.

Marshall Plan at Work in Great Britain, The. Produced for ECA 1950 by Editorial Film Productions Ltd, London. Dir: Robin Carruthers. Prod: Jim

Mellor. Camera: Brendan Stafford. Script: Arthur Calder Marshall. Specs: b/w, 11 min.

Marshall Plan at Work in Greece, The. Produced for ECA 1950 by Editorial Film Productions Ltd, London. Dir: James Hill. Prod: Jim Mellor. Camera: Kenneth Talbot. Script: Arthur Calder Marshall. Specs: b/w, 11 min.

Marshall Plan at Work in Holland, The. Produced for ECA 1950 by Editorial Film Productions Ltd, London. Dir & Camera: Guy Blanchard. Prod: Jim Mellor. Script: Arthur Calder Marshall. Specs: b/w, 11 min.

Marshall Plan at Work in Ireland, The. Produced for ECA 1950 by Editorial Film Productions Ltd, London. Dir & Camera: Brendan Stafford. Prod: Jim Mellor. Script: Arthur Calder Marshall. Specs: b/w, 11 min.

Marshall Plan at Work in Italy, The. Produced for ECA 1950 by Editorial Film Productions Ltd, London. Dir: James Hill. Prod: Jim Mellor. Camera: Kenneth Talbot. Script: Arthur Calder Marshall. Specs: b/w, 11 min.

Marshall Plan at Work in Norway, The. Produced for ECA 1950 by Editorial Film Productions Ltd, London. Dir & Camera: Guy Blanchard. Prod: Jim Mellor. Script: Arthur Calder Marshall. Specs: b/w, 11 min.

Marshall Plan at Work in Turkey, The. Produced for ECA 1950 by Editorial Film Productions Ltd, London. Dir: James Hill. Prod: Jim Mellor. Camera: Kenneth Talbot. Script: Arthur Calder Marshall. Specs: b/w, 11 min.

Marshall Plan at Work in Western Germany, The. Produced for ECA 1950 by Editorial Film Productions Ltd, London. Dir: James Hill. Prod: Jim Mellor. Camera: Kenneth Talbot. Script: Arthur Calder Marshall. Specs: b/w, 11 min.

Men at Work (Uomini al lavoro). Produced for ECA Italy 1948–49 by Europeo Film. Dir: Paolo Moffa. Camera: Giorgio Orsini. Script: Antonio Pietrucci. Music: G. Dangelo, G. Castorina. Specs: b/w, 11 min.

Mill Town. Produced for ECA Greece 1950 by David Kurland Productions, Rome. Dir & Prod: David Kurland. Camera: Dale Kurland. Script: ECA Film Unit. Music: Aldrico Vitalini. Specs: b/w, 10 min.

Miner's Window, The (Minatori d'Europa). Produced for MSA 1954 by John Ferno. Dir: John Ferno, Nelo Risi, Budge Cooper. Prod: John Ferno. Camera: Jacques Manier, Louis Mialle, Joe Jago, Geoffrey Williams. Script: Arthur Calder-Marshall. Music: Cedric Thorpe Davie. Specs: b/w, 38 min.

Miracle of Cassino, The (Il miracolo di Cassino). Produced for ECA Italy 1950 by Europeo Film. Camera: Angelo Jannarelli. Script: Antonio Jannotta. Music: Alberico Vitalini. Specs: b/w, 11 min.

My Trip Abroad. Produced for ECA 1951 by The March of the Time. Specs: b/w, 10 min.

North Sea Harbour (Strength for the Free World). Produced by MSA Film Unit, Paris, & Cinetone Studio for MSA Washington 1951. Dir: Peter Hopkinson. Prod: Philip Mackie. Camera: John Baxter Peters. Script: Edgar Pike. Specs: b/w, 16 min/23 min.

Norway, Nation on Skis. Produced for ECA Norway 1951 by Dick Durrance Films. Dir: Dick Durrance.

Oldest Enemy, The (De oude vijand). Produced for MSA 1953 by Cinetone Studios, Amsterdam. Dir & Script: Henry Sandoz. Specs: b/w, 10 min.

Our Drawings (Wir zeichnen). Produced for ECA Austria 1950 by Georg Tressler. Dir, Prod & Script: Georg Tressler. Camera: Walter Partsch. Music: Paul Kont. Specs: b/w, 11 min.

Over to You. Produced for ECA UK & the Economic Information Unit of the British Treasury 1951 by Crown Film Unit. Specs: b/w, 18 min.

Piece of Coal, A (Un pezzo di carbone). Produced for ECA Italy 1949 by Phoenix Films. Dir: Giuliano Tomei. Camera: Antonio Schiavinotto. Music: Carlo Innocenzi. Specs: b/w, 11 min.

Power for Peace (The North Atlantic Treaty). Produced for MSA & NATO 1952 by MSA Film Unit, Paris. Specs: b/w, 14 min.

Productivité (Productivity). Produced for ECA France 1951 by La Comete. Dir: Jacques Asseo. Prod: Andre Sarrut. Music: Gvan Parys. Specs: Animation, colour, 4 min.

Productivity – Key to Progress. Machines in the Service of Man. Produced for ECA UK & the Economic Information Unit of the British Treasury 1951 by Crown Film Unit. Specs: b/w, 13 min.

Project for Tomorrow (Bergbauern von Morgen). Produced for ECA Austria 1950 by Victor Vicas Films. Dir: Victor Vicas, George Vicas. Camera: Helmuth Ashley. Script: Edith Knoll. Music: Claude Arrieu. Specs: b/w, 21 min.

Promise of Barty O'Brien, The. Produced for MSA Ireland 1952 by Freedland Productions, Paris. Dir & Prod: George Freedland. Camera: Brendan Stafford. Script: Sean O'Fáolain, George Freedland. Music: Rudolf Goehr. Specs: b/w, 49 min.

Provence – terre de peuplement. Produced for ECA France 1950 by Jean Hubinet. Dir: Jean Hubinet, Fernand Pelatant. Camera: Jean Hubinet. Music: Darius Milhaud. Specs: b/w, 30 min.

Railroads (Rotaie). Produced for ECA Italy 1948–49 by Europeo Film. Dir: Francesco de Feo. Camera: Angelo Jannarelli. Script: Gino Palese. Music: Virgilio Chiti. Specs: b/w, 12 min.

Renaissance agricole. Produced for ECA France 1950 by Technifilm. Dir & Prod: Pierre Gout. Camera: Georges Delaunay. Specs: b/w, 19 min.

Report from Britain. Produced for ECA UK 1951 by Associated British Pathe, London. Specs: b/w, 15 min.

Return from the Valley. Produced for ECA Greece 1950 by Ferno Productions, Paris. Dir: Nelo Risi. Prod: John Ferno. Camera: Jacques Letellier. Script: Stephen L. James. Music: Maurice Thiriet. Specs: b/w, 15 min.

Rice and Bulls (Riz et taureaux). Produced for ECA France 1950 by Tele-Radio-Cine Productions. Dir & Prod: Wesley Ruggles. Camera: A. Militon. Script: W. Massee. Music: Paul Baron. Specs: b/w, 15 min.

River without Borders (Strom ohne Grenzen). Produced for ECA W-Germany 1950 by UNA Film. Dir & Script: Herbert Fredersdorf. Prod: Georg Mohr. Camera: Felix Forrestier. Music: Jacques Metehen. Specs: b/w, 24 min.

Ruhr, The (Die Ruhr). Produced for MSA 1952 by Cinetone Studios, Amsterdam. Dir & Camera: Peter Hopkinson. Prod: Philip Mackie. Script: Edgar Pike. Specs: b/w, 10 min.

Rural Sardinia (Sardegna agricola). Produced for ECA Italy 1950 by Documenta Film. Dir: Romolo Marcellini. Camera: Rino Filippini. Music: Paolo Girlando. Specs: b/w, 12 min.

School for Colonels. Produced for MSA & NATO 1953. Camera: France: Jacques Curtis; Britain: Sydney Samuelson; Norway: Aryld Nybakken; Netherlands: Ytzen Brusse, Herman van der Horst; Germany: Eric Ringelband. Music: Elisabeth Lutyens. Specs: b/w, 22 min.

Seed Is Sown, A. Produced for ECA 1950 by March of the Time. Specs: b/w, 14 min.

Ship Is Born, A (Nave in cantiere, Nascita di una nave). Produced for ECA Italy 1951 by Documento Film. Dir: Ubaldo Magnaghi. Prod: Enzo Muscianisi. Camera: Cyril Knowles. Music: G. Pomerant. Specs: colour, 10 min.

Shoemaker and the Hatter, The. Produced for ECA 1950 by John Halas and Joy Batchelor Ltd., London. Dir & Prod: John Halas. Animations: Stand Pearsall, Bob Privett, Wally Crook. Script: Joy Batchelor. Music: Matyas Seiber. Specs: Animation, colour, 16 min.

Shoot the Nets! (Het schot is te boord!). Produced for ECA Netherlands 1951 by Herman van der Horst. Dir & Script: Herman van der Horst. Specs: b/w, 19 min.

Silkmakers of Como. Produced for ECA Italy 1951 by Documento Film. Dir: Ubaldo Magnaghi. Prod: Enzo Muscianisi. Camera: Cyril Knowles, Angelo Jannarelli. Music: Paul Baron. Specs: colour, 10 min.

Simplification (Jo enklere, jo bedre). Produced for MSA 1952 by Nordisk Film & Film Centre Ltd, London. Dir: Søren Melson. Camera: Henning Christiansen. Script: Ove Sevel. Music: Svend Erik Tarp. Specs: b/w, 21 min.

Smiths and the Robinsons, The. Produced for MSA 1952 by Cinetone Studios, Amsterdam. Dir: Peter Hopkinson. Prod & Script: Philip Mackie. Camera: Peter Hopkinson, John Baxter Peters. Specs: b/w, 19 min.

Smoke (Blauer Dunst). Produced for ECA W-Germany 1950 by Diana Tonfilm. Dir: Herbert Lander. Camera: Herbert Lander, Emil Schünemann, Erich Grohmann. Script: Herbert Lander, Günter Neumann. Music: Günter Neumann. Specs: b/w, 17 min.

Storm over Italy. Produced for ECA Italy 1953. Specs: b/w, 12 min.

Story of a Rescue (Histoire d'un sauvetage). Produced for ECA 1949 by Les Gémeaux. Dir: Jaques Asseo. Animations: Maurice Henri. Script: Paul Guth, Pierre Watrin, Philippe Landrot. Music: George Parys. Specs: Animation, colour, 7 min.

Story of Koula, The. Produced for ECA Greece 1951 by Vittorio Gallo Films, Rome. Dir & Prod: Vittorio Gallo. Camera: Franco Vittroti. Script: Stephen L. James (ECA Film Unit). Music: Ennio Porrino. Specs: b/w, 21 min.

Story of Mahmoud, The (La fugue du Mahmoud). Produced for ECA France 1950 by Les Films du Compas. Dir: Pierre Levent. Prod: Roger Leenhardt. Camera: Marcel Devriez. Music: Guy Bernard,. Specs: b/w, 23/36 min.

Streamlined Pig, The (Den strømlinede gris). Produced for ECA Denmark 1951 by Teknisk Film. Dir & Script: Jørgen Roos. Camera: Jørgen Roos, Arne Jensen. Music: Bent Fabricius-Bjerre. Specs: b/w, 10 min.

Talking to the Italians. Produced for ECA Italy 1950 by Marcellini Films. Dir & Prod: Romolo Marcellini. Specs: b/w, 23 min.

The Jungle That Was (Le Niger). Produced for ECA France 1950 by Andre Gillet. Dir: Roger Verdier, Andre Gillet. Specs: b/w, 22 min.

Three Cities. Produced for MSA 1952. Specs: b/w, 27 min.

Tomorrow We Live (Dobbiamo vivere ancora). Produced for ECA Italy 1949 by Phoenix Films. Dir: Vittorio Gallo. Camera: Gabor Pogany. Music: Ennio Porrino. Specs: b/w, 14 min.

Transatlantic. Produced for MSA 1953 by Madeleine Films (Philip Stapp). Dir & Prod: André Sarrut, Jacques Asseo. Script: Philip Stapp. Music: Gail Kubik. Specs: Animation, colour, 10 min.

Traudl's New Kitchen Garden (Traudls neuer Gemüsegarten). Produced for MSA Austria 1952. Dir, Prod & Script: Georg Tressler. Camera: Sepp Riff. Music: Friedrich Witeschnik. Specs: b/w, 16 min.

Treasure of the Rhône (L'or du Rhône). Produced for ECA France 1950 by Les Films Caravelle. Dir: François Villiers. Prod: Claude Roger Clert. Camera: Pierre Dolley. Music: Tony Aubin. Specs: b/w, 20 min.

Trieste to Lampedusa. Produced for ECA Trieste 1951. Specs: b/w, 14/16 min.

Trip in Sicily (Viaggio in Sicilia). Produced for ECA Italy 1948–49 by Europeo Film. Dir: Antonio Jannotta. Camera: Rino Formica. Music: Nuccio Fiorda. Specs: b/w, 11 min.

Turkish Harvest. Produced for ECA Turkey 1952 by Clarke & Hornby Productions & Film Centre Ltd, London. Dir: Clifford Hornby. Camera: Ian Barrowman. Script: Sinclair Road. Music: Thomas Henderson. Specs: b/w, 22 min.

Twenty Hours a Day (Twintig uur per dag). Produced for MSA Netherlands 1952 by Cinetone. Prod & Camera: Albert Brosens. Music: Guus van Mannen. Specs: b/w, 15 min.

Two Counts (I due 'conti'). Produced for ECA Italy 1948–49 by Europeo Film. Dir: Ubaldo Magnaghi. Camera: Renato Sinistri. Script: Mario Pannunzio. Music: Virgilio Chiti. Specs: b/w, 11 min.

Victory at Thermopylae (Vittoria alle Termopili). Produced for ECA Greece 1950 by Kurland Productions, Rome. Dir & Prod: David Kurland. Camera: Dale Kurland. Music: Alberico Vitalini. Specs: b/w, 11 min.

Village That Wouldn't Die, The (Ce village ne voulait pas mourir). Produced for ECA France 1950 by Tele-Radio-Cine Productions. Dir & Camera: Alain Pol. Prod: Wesley Ruggles. Script: Eugene Lerner. Music: Paul Baron. Specs: b/w, 13 min.

Village Tractor, The (Köy Traktörü). Produced for ECA Turkey 1951 by Clarke and Hornby Productions, London. Dir: Clifford Hornby. Camera: Ian Barrowman. Script: Sinclair Road. Specs: b/w, 20 min.

Village without Water (Paese senz' aqua). Produced for ECA Italy 1949 by Phoenix Films. Dir: Giuliano Tomei. Camera: Antonio Schiavinotto. Script: Ercole Patti. Music: Alberico Vitalini. Specs: b/w, 13 min.

Village without Words (Vita nuova). Produced for ECA Italy 1950 by David Kurland Productions. Dir & Prod: David Kurland. Music: Alberico Vitalini. Specs: b/w, 12 min.

We and the Others (Wir und die Anderen). Produced for ECA W-Germany 1951 by Audax-Film Ernst Niederreither. Dir, Prod & Camera: Ernst Niederreither. Specs: b/w, 18 min.

Whitsun Holiday. Produced for MSA 1953 by CAPAC. Dir: Peter Baylis. Specs: b/w, 11/15 min (Italian version)

Without Fear. Produced for ECA 1951 by W.M. Larkins Studio, London. Dir: Peter Sachs. Prod: Philip Stapp. Animations: Denis Gilpin, Richard Taylor, Beryl Stevens. Script: Allan Mackinnon. Music: Francis Chagrin. Specs: Animation, colour, 15 min.

Work Flow. Produced for MSA 1952 by Interfilm and Dinkel Film, Düsseldorf, & Film Centre Ltd, London. Music: Richard Cornu. Specs: b/w, 17 min.

Years of Decision, The. Produced for ECA 1950 by The March of the Time. Specs: b/w, 21 min.

Yusef and His Plough (Yusuf ve Sabanı). Produced for ECA Turkey 1951 by Clarke & Hornby Film Productions Ltd, London. Dir: Clifford Hornby. Camera: Ian Barrowman. Script: Sinclair Road. Specs: b/w, 13 min.

Zinc Valley (La valle del zinco). Produced for ECA Italy 1948–49. Dir: Joe Falletta. Camera: Massimo Sallusti. Specs: b/w, 11 min.

1-2-3: A Monthly Review from Europe, no. 1–12. Produced for MSA 1952–54 by Cinetone Studios, Amsterdam. Dir: Victor Vicas, John Ferno, Jacques Letellier, Nelo Risi, Ove Sevel, Lauritz Falk, Jacques Curtis, R.H.B. Mason, Joe Fallets, Maruice Harley, Wim Huender, Harald Kubens, James McKechnie, Georges Regnier, Edmond Sechan, Julian Spiro, Franco Vitrotti, Alan Waple, Per Borgersen, Peter Brodjord, Ytzen Brusse, Prosper Dekeukdeire, Jonah Jones, Reidar Tund, Kurt Wahlgren, Jack Chambers, Arthur Elton. Prod: Peter Baylis, Philip Mackie, John Ferno. Camera: Jacques Letellier, Poul Pedersen, Raymond Cluny, Gunnar Syvertsen, Jacques Curtis, S. Beadle. Script: Peter Baylis. Music: Maurice Thiriet. Specs: b/w, 11–19 min.

Notes

Introduction

1   *The Cold War* (1998), [TV documentary series], Prod. Jeremy Isaacs, USA: CNN.

2   Robert A. Pollard, *Economic Security and the Origins of the Cold War, 1945–1950* (New York: Columbia University Press, 1985).

3   A.W. Purdue, 'The Transformative Impact of World War II', *European History Online (EGO)* (2016). Available online: http://www.ieg-ego.eu/purduea-2016-en (accessed 4 July 2017). The terms required, for example, that the participating nations laid open their economic records. See Walter LaFeber, *America, Russia, and the Cold War, 1945–2002.* 10th edn (New York: McGraw-Hill, 2003), 67; John Lewis Gaddis, *The Cold War. A New History* (New York: Penguin Press, 2005), 32, 98.

4   On the bilateral agreement with the German zones and its critics, see Werner Bührer, *Westdeutschland in der OEEC: Eingliederung, Krise, Bewährung 1947–1961* (München: Oldenbourg, 1997), 90–93.

5   For an overview of the developments prior to the passing of the MP, see Barry Machado, *In Search of a Usable Past. The Marshall Plan and Postwar Reconstruction Today* (Lexington, VA: George C. Marshall Foundation, 2007), 16–22.

6   Economic Cooperation Act of 1948, Public Law 472, 80th Congress, 2nd session.

7   Geir Lundestad, 'Empire by Invitation? The United States and Western Europe, 1945–1952', *Journal of Peace Research* 23, no. 3 (1986), 57; Charles S. Maier, 'Alliance and Autonomy: European Identity and U.S. Foreign Policy Objectives in the Truman Years', in *The Truman Presidency*, ed. Michael J. Lacey (Cambridge: Woodrow Wilson International Center for Scholars, 1989), 290; David Ellwood, 'Italian Modernisation and the Propaganda of the Marshall Plan', in *The Art of Persuasion. Political Communication in Italy from 1945 to the 1990s*, ed. Luciano Cheles and Lucio Spinoza (Manchester: Manchester University Press, 2001), 42; Chiarella Esposito, *America's Feeble Weapon. Funding the Marshall Plan in France and Italy, 1948–1950* (Westport, CT: Greenwood Press, 1994), 53–59.

8   Machado, *In Search of a Usable Past*, 21.

9   These assumptions are shared by modern scholarship. See Winfried Fluck, 'The Americanization of Modern Culture: A Cultural History of the Popular Media', in *Romance with America? Essays on Culture, Literature, and American Studies*, ed. Laura Bieger and Johannes Voelz (Heidelberg: Winter, 2009), 255.

10 Albert Hemsing, 'The Marshall Plan's European Film Unit, 1948–1955. A Memoir and Filmography', *Historical Journal of Film, Radio and Television* 14, no. 3 (1994).

11 David Ellwood, 'The 1948 Elections in Italy. A Cold War Propaganda Battle'. *Historical Journal of Film, Radio and Television* 13, no. 1 (1993); Ellwood, '"You too can be like us." Selling the Marshall Plan', *History Today* 48, no. 10 (1998); Ellwood, 'The Propaganda of the Marshall Plan in Italy in a Cold War Context', *Intelligence & National Security* 18, no. 2 (2003); Ellwood, 'Film and the Marshall Plan', in *Images of the Marshall Plan in Europe: Film, Photographs, Exhibits, Posters*, ed. Günter Bischof and Dieter Stiefel (Innsbruck: Studienverlag, 2009).

12 Regina M. Longo, 'Between Documentary and Neorealism: Marshall Plan Films in Italy (1948–1955)', *California Italian Studies* 3, no. 2 (2012). Available online: http://escholarship.org/uc/item/0dq0394d#page-1 (accessed 26 January 2017); Longo, 'Marshall Plan Films in Italy 1948–1955: Cinema as Soft Power' (PhD thesis, University of California, Santa Barbara, 2012); Paola Bonifazio, 'United We Drill: ENI, Films, and the Culture of Work', *Annali d'italianistica* 32 (2014); *Schooling in Modernity. The Politics of Sponsored Films in Postwar Italy* (Toronto, ON: University of Toronto Press, 2014).

13 Brian Angus McKenzie, *Remaking France: Americanization, Public Diplomacy, and the Marshall Plan* (New York: Berghahn, 2005).

14 Richard F. Kuisel, *Seducing the French. The Dilemma of Americanization* (Berkeley and Los Angeles: University of California Press, 1993); Richard F. Kuisel, 'The French Cinema and Hollywood. A Case Study of Americanization', in *Transactions, Transgressions, Transformations: American Culture in Western Europe and Japan*, ed. Heide Fehrenbach and Uta Poiger (Oxford, New York: Berghahn, 2000).

15 Frank Mehring, 'Propaganda für die Demokratie? Deutschland und das Neue Europa' in den Filmen des Marshallplans' (2005). Available online: http://www.dhm.de/filmarchiv/film-im-kontext/propaganda/ (accessed 26 January 2017); Mehring, 'The Promises of "Young Europe": Cultural Diplomacy, Cosmopolitanism, and Youth Culture in the Films of the Marshall Plan', *European Journal of American Studies* 7, no. 2 (2012). Available online: http://ejas.revues.org/9701 (accessed 26 January 2017); Hans-Jürgen Schröder, 'Marshall Plan Propaganda in Austria and Western Germany', in *The Marshall Plan in Austria*, ed. Günter Bischof, Anton Pelinka and Dieter Stiefel (New Brunswick, NJ; London: Transaction Publishers, 2000); Schröder, 'Informationskampagnen zum Marshall-Plan'. *Orientierungen zur Wirtschafts- und Gesellschaftspolitik*, no. 112 (2007); 'Visualizing the Marshall Plan in Western Germany: Films, Exhibits, Posters', in *Images of the Marshall Plan in Europe*, ed. Bischof and Stiefel.

16 Ramón Reichert, 'Film und Rationalisierung. Die Produktivitätsfilme des ÖPWZ während des European Recovery Program', *Blätter für Technikgeschichte* 62 (2000); Reichert, 'Marshallplan und Film: Intermedialität, narrative Strategien

und Geschlechterrepräsentation', in *Besetzte Bilder. Film, Kultur und Propaganda in Österreich 1945–1955*, ed. Karin Moser (Wien: Filmarchiv Austria, 2005); Reichert, 'Culture and Identity Politics: Narrative Strategies in Austrian Marshall Plan Movies', in *Images of the Marshall Plan in Europe*, ed. Bischof and Stiefel; Reinhold Wagnleitner, *Coca-Colonisation und Kalter Krieg. Die Kulturmission der USA in Österreich nach dem Zweiten Weltkrieg*, Österreichische Texte zur Gesellschaftskritik (Wien: Verlag für Gesellschaftskritik, 1991). English Translation: *Coca-Colonization and the Cold War: The Cultural Mission of the United States in Austria after the Second World War* (Chapel Hill: University of North Carolina Press, 1994).

17 Bernadette Whelan, 'Marshall Plan Publicity and Propaganda in Italy and Ireland, 1947–1951', *Historical Journal of Film, Radio and Television* 23, no. 4 (2003); Bischof and Stiefel, eds. *Images of the Marshall Plan in Europe*; Noël van Rens, 'Een Nederlander filmt voor Europe. TERUG NAAR HUIS van John Fernhout', in *Jaarboek Mediageschiedenis* 7 (Amsterdam, 1995); 'Les films du plan Marshall: 1948–1952. La naissance de l'Europe dans l'image', in *L'âge d'or du documentaire. Europe: Années cinquante. Grande-Bretagne, Belgique, Pays-Bas, Danemark, Norvège, Suède Europe*, ed. Roger Odin (Paris, Montréal: l'Harmattan, 1998); Marianne Thys, 'Idéologies. Les Films du Plan Marshall', in *Mémoires du Monde. Prologue de Jean-Louis Jean-Louis Comolli*, ed. Marianne Thys (Crisnée, Bruxelles: Cinémathèque de la Fédération Wallonie-Bruxelles, 2011).

18 Elizabeth Heffelfinger, 'Foreign Policy, Domestic Fiction: Government-Sponsored Documentaries and Network Television Promote the Marshall Plan at Home', *Historical Journal of Film, Radio and Television* 28, no. 1 (2008).

19 Gabriele Clemens, ed. *Werben für Europa. Die mediale Konstruktion europäischer Identität durch Europafilme* (Paderborn: Ferdinand Schöningh, 2016); see also Gabriele Clemens, 'Europa – nur ein gemeinsamer Markt? Die Öffentlichkeitsarbeit für den europäischen Integrationsprozess am Beispiel der Europafilme zwischen Marshallplan und Römischen Verträgen 1947–1957', in *Vom gemeinsamen Markt zur europäischen Unionsbildung. 50 Jahre Römische Verträge 1957–2007*, ed. Michael Gehler (Wien, Köln, Weimar: Böhlau, 2009).

20 Heide Fehrenbach and Uta G. Poiger, 'Americanization Reconsidered. Introduction', in *Transactions, Transgressions, Transformations*, ed. Fehrenbach and Poiger, xiv.

21 The same goes, of course, for other actors. See, for example, the efforts to influence European scientists in John Krige, *American Hegemony and the Postwar Reconstruction of Science in Europe* (Cambridge, MA; London: MIT, 2006).

22 See, for example, Philipp Gassert, 'Amerikanismus, Antiamerikanismus, Amerikanisierung', *Archiv für Sozialgeschichte* 39 (1999); Richard Kuisel, 'Commentary. Americanization for Historians', *Diplomatic History* 24, no. 3 (2000): 509; Fluck, 'The Americanization of Modern Culture', 262.

23 Jessica Gienow-Hecht, 'Shame on US? Academics, Cultural Transfer, and the Cold War: A Critical Review', *Diplomatic History* 24, no. 3 (2000); Rob Kroes, Robert W. Rydell and Doeko F.J. Bosscher, 'Introduction', in *Cultural Transmission and Receptions: American Mass Culture in Europe*, ed. Rob Kroes, Robert W. Rydell and Doeko F.J. Bosscher (Amsterdam: VU University Press, 1993).

24 Kuisel, 'Americanization for Historians', 510.

25 The term 'Marshall Plan film' is used in this book to define those films that were produced for the Information Division of the ECA/MSA for the purpose of promoting the MP and its goals to Europeans. This definition thus excludes technical training films produced by the ECA Labor Division, as well as the 24-part *Strength for the Free World*-series, which was produced for an American audience.

26 For more information on the films and the archival situation, see Chapter 1 and the Filmography.

27 For a discussion of the term and misconceptions about propaganda, see Kenneth A. Osgood, 'Propaganda', in *Encyclopedia of American Foreign Policy*, ed. Alexander DeConde et al. (New York: Charles Scribner's Sons, 2002), 239–40.

28 Ibid., 239.

29 Bruce Lannes Smith, 'Propaganda', *Encyclopædia Britannica*, https://global .britannica.com/topic/propaganda (accessed 22 January 2017).

30 Eckhardt Fuchs, Anne Bruch and Michael Annegarn-Gläß, 'Educational Films: A Historical Review of Media Innovation in Schools'. *Journal of Educational Media, Memory, and Society* 8, no. 1 (2016).

31 Mark Crispin Miller, 'Introduction', in Edward Bernays, *Propaganda*. 1928. (Brooklyn: IG Publishing, 2005); Osgood, 'Propaganda', 243–44.

32 Edward Bernays, *Propaganda*. With an Introduction by Mark Crispin Miller (1928; Brooklyn: IG Publishing, 2005), 57.

33 Walter Lippmann, *Public Opinion* (1922; New York, London: Free Press Paperbacks, 1997), 158.

34 Jack C. Ellis, *John Grierson. Life, Contributions, Influence* (Carbondale, IL: Southern Illinois University Press, 2000), 180.

35 Simona Tobia, *Advertising America. The United States Information Service in Italy (1945–1956)* (Milano: LED, 2008), 48–50. Tobia provides a detailed account of the creation of the US Information Services. See also Emily S. Rosenberg, *Spreading the American Dream: American Economic and Cultural Expansion, 1890–1945*. 1st edn (New York: Hill and Wang, 1982), 212–13, 216; Nicholas John Cull, '"The Man Who Invented Truth": The Tenure of Edward R. Murrow as Director of the United States Information Agency during the Kennedy Years', in *Across the Blocs. Cold War Cultural and Social History*, ed. Patrick Major and Rana Mitter (London, Portland, OR: Frank Cass, 2004). For West Germany, see Maritta Hein-Kremer, *Die amerikanische Kulturoffensive Gründung und Entwicklung der amerikanischen*

Information Centers in Westdeutschland und West-Berlin 1945–1955 (Köln: Böhlau, 1996).

36 Harry B. Price, *The Marshall Plan and Its Meaning* (Ithaca, NY: Cornell University Press, 1955), 245.

37 See Gienow-Hecht, 'Shame on US?', 467.

38 See, for example, Brigitte Hahn, *Umerziehung durch Dokumentarfilm? Ein Instrument amerikanischer Kulturpolitik im Nachkriegsdeutschland (1945–1953)* (Berlin: Lit Verlag, 1993); Hahn, 'Dokumentarfilm im Dienste der Umerziehung. Amerikanische Filmpolitik 1945–1953', in *Lernen Sie diskutieren! Re-education durch Film: Strategien der westlichen Alliierten nach 1945*, ed. Heiner Ross (Berlin: Cinegraph Babelsberg, Berlin-Brandenburgisches Centrum für Filmforschung, 2005); Gabriele Clemens, 'Umerziehung durch Film. Britische und Amerikanische Filmpolitik in Deutschland 1945–1949', in *Mediale Mobilmachung II: Hollywood, Exil, Nachkriegszeit*, ed. Harro Segeberg (München: Ferdinand Schöningh Verlag, 2004); Ulrike Weckel, *Beschämende Bilder. Deutsche Reaktionen auf alliierte Dokumentarfilme über befreite Konzentrationslager* (Stuttgart: Steiner, 2012).

39 See Hahn, 'Dokumentarfilm im Dienste der Umerziehung', 2005; Jeanpaul Goergen, 'Orientierung und Ausrichtung. Die amerikanische Dokumentarfilmproduktion "Zeit im Film 1949–1952"', in *Lernen Sie diskutieren!*, ed. Ross.

40 Weckel, *Beschämende Bilder*, 418–518; Ronny Loewy, 'Atrocity Pictures. Alliierte Filmaufnahmen aus den befreiten Konzentrations- und Vernichtungslagern', in *Lernen Sie diskutieren!*, ed. Ross; also Research Department of the Foreign Office, The Film Situation in all the Zones of Germany, 5 May 1946. OMGUS, RG 260, Entry 260 (A1), box 266.

41 Rhodri Jeffreys-Jones, 'Eternal Vigilance? 50 years of the CIA', in *Studies in Intelligence*, ed. Rhodri Jeffreys-Jones and Andrew Christopher (London, Portland: Cass, 1997), 23, 33.

42 See Frances Stonor Saunders, *The Cultural Cold War. The CIA and the World of Arts and Letters* (New York: The New Press, 2000), 63–66, 74–76, 130–32; Giles Scott-Smith, *The Politics of Apolitical Culture: The Congress for Cultural Freedom and the Political Economy of American Hegemony 1945–1955* (London, New York: Routledge, 2002); Ingeborg Philipsen, 'Out of Tune: The Congress for Cultural Freedom in Denmark 1953–1960', in *The Cultural Cold War in Western Europe, 1945–1960*, ed. Giles Scott-Smith and Hans Krabbendam (London: Frank Cass, 2003); Sallie Pisani, *The CIA and the Marshall Plan* (Edinburgh: Edinburgh University Press, 1991).

43 See Anthony Carew, 'The Politics of Productivity and the Politics of Anti-Communism: American and European Labour in the Cold War', in *The Cultural Cold War in Western Europe*, ed. Scott-Smith and Krabbendam, 85–86; Saunders, *The Cultural Cold War*, 68, 91.

44 Tobia, *Advertising America*, 48–50; Rosenberg, *Spreading the American Dream*, 212–13.

45 See Tobia, *Advertising America*, 48–49, 54–64.

46 Memorandum Secretary of State and the Economic Cooperation Administrator, 24 May 1948. NARA RG 469, entry 1029, box 2.

47 Several ECA personnel remembered these conflicts. See interviews with Lawrence Hall, ECA Information Division Paris and ECA Turkey, 1950–53. Interview conducted by Hans Tuch, 23 August 1988; James C. Warren, economic analyst at ECA Athens, 1950–1954. Interview conducted by Charles Stuart Kennedy, 22 March 2001. Foreign Affairs Oral History Collection, Association for Diplomatic Studies and Training, Arlington, VA. Available online: www.adst.org. See also Gerd Hardach, *Der Marshall-Plan. Auslandshilfe und Wiederaufbau in Westdeutschland 1948–1952* (München: dtv, 1994), 65.

48 W. Nielsen, ECA Information Division, to W. Stone, Department of State, 13 October 1949. NARA 469, entry 1029, box 7.

49 Alan S. Milward, *The Reconstruction of Western Europe, 1945–51* (Berkley, Los Angeles: University of California Press, 1984), 90–113; Alan S. Milward, 'Was the Marshall Plan Necessary?', *Diplomatic History* 13, no. 2 (1989): 237–38; Werner Abelshauser, *Wirtschaft in Westdeutschland 1945–1948: Rekonstruktion und Wachstumsbedingungen in der amerikanischen und britischen Zone* (Stuttgart: DVA, 1975), 63, 126–30.

50 Michael J. Hogan, *The Marshall Plan: America, Britain, and the Reconstruction of Western Europe 1947–1952* (Cambridge, UK; New York: Cambridge University Press, 1987), 22. Among others, Ellwood, Hardach and Maier put forward a similar argument. See David Ellwood, *Rebuilding Europe: Western Europe, America and Postwar Reconstruction* (London, New York: Longman, 1992); Hardach, *Der Marshall-Plan*; Charles S. Maier, 'The Politics of Productivity: Foundations of American International Economic Policy after World War II', *International Organization* 31, no. 4 (1977).

51 Pollard, *Economic Security*; also Maier, 'The Politics of Productivity', 619, 623.

52 Hogan, *The Marshall Plan*, 197; see also Maier, 'The Politics of Productivity', 622, 627; Hardach, *Der Marshall-Plan*, 11, 29.

53 Milward, 'Was the Marshall Plan Necessary?' 247; Milward, *The Reconstruction of Western Europe*, 90–113, 465–66.

54 Werner Abelshauser, 'Kriegswirtschaft und Wirtschaftswunder. Deutschlands wirtschaftliche Mobilisierung für den Zweiten Weltkrieg und die Folgen für die Nachkrieszeit', *Vierteljahreshefte für Zeitgeschichte* 47, no. 4 (1999): 529–33, 536–38.

55 Milward, 'Was the Marshall Plan Necessary?' 247; Milward, *The Reconstruction of Western Europe*, 90–113; The German historian Abelshauser goes further by arguing that the MP hardly made any difference to the recovery of the West

German economy, which Milward calls an 'exaggeration', outlining the considerable degree to which West Germany depended especially on food imports. See Werner Abelshauser, 'Der Kleine Marshallplan. Handelsintegration durch innereuropäische Wirtschaftshilfe 1948–1950', *Geschichte und Gesellschaft*. Sonderheft 10 (1984).

56 Purdue, 'The Transformative Impact of World War II', 4.

57 Machado speaks of the 'myth of belly communism'. Machado, *In Search of a Usable Past*, 53.

58 Milward, *The Reconstruction of Western Europe*, 60, 123.

59 See Carew, 'The Politics of Productivity and the Politics of Anti-Communism', 84.

60 Lundestad, 'Empire by Invitation?' 42–53.

Chapter 1

1 Cited by Price, *The Marshall Plan and Its Meaning*, 242.

2 Machado, *In Search of a Usable Past*, 18.

3 In numbers: 180 people. See ibid., 24.

4 Job Description, Assistant to Chief, Special Media Section (ca. 1948). NARA, RG 469, entry 1029, box 6.

5 ECA Information Overseas, Description of Functions, 5 June 1948. NARA, RG 469, entry 1029, box 7.

6 Memo Waldemar Nielsen, cited by Price, *The Marshall Plan and Its Meaning*, 246.

7 Marshall Plan Filmography, created by Linda Christenson for The George C. Marshall Foundation, 2002. Available online: http://www.marshallfilms.org.

8 Bruch, Clemens, Goergen and Tode, 'Werben für die Integration', in *Werben für Europa*, ed. Clemens, 195.

9 Hemsing, 'The Marshall Plan's European Film Unit', 275–76.

10 The majority of MP films are held at the National Archives in College Park, Maryland, USA (NARA). I am very grateful to Linda Christenson for providing me with copies of these films. I also received copies of other MP films through the French Institut national de l'audiovisuel, the Danish Det Danske filminstitut, the film archive of the German Bundesarchiv in Berlin and the Austrian Filmarchiv. The German Historical Museum has made more than 40 MP films available online on its website: http://www.dhm.de/ filmarchiv/die-filme/. Also the French ina: http://www.ina.fr/recherche and the Italian Archivio Audiovisivo del Movimento Operaio e Democratico have published many MP films online: https://www.youtube.com/user/ AAMODAAMOD.

11 Report of the Film Program of the Office of the US High Commissioner of Germany, 15 March 1951. NARA, RG 59, entry 5323, box 1.

12 A list of release dates compiled by the information office of the Norwegian mission in 1953 shows, for instance, that many MP films from 1950 entered distribution in 1952. Airgram MSA Oslo to State Department, 18 April 1953. NARA, RG 469, entry 947, box 33.

13 Statement R. Drummond, Minutes Information Officers Meeting Paris, 24–25 October 1949. NARA 469, entry 1029, box 4.

14 The majority of the information staff was transferred to the new agencies. See Tobia, *Advertising America*, 104–6.

15 The film unit cancelled its first film projects in October 1951 and the Italian Information Division suspended film production in November 1951. Schulberg to Vicas, 8 October 1951. DFI, Nachlass Victor Vicas; Review of Activities, Information Division Italy, June 1948 to December 1950 (no date, presumably 1951). NARA 469, entry 303, box 2.

16 A number of informal letters and memos give voice to the information officers' dissatisfaction, especially with the merger with USIS. See, for example, Carter to Berding, 28 May 1952. NARA, RG 469, entry 303, box 2.

17 Hemsing, 'The Marshall Plan's European Film Unit', 275.

18 Ibid., 269–70.

19 James Keogh, 'Dark Horse with Best Handlers', *Life Magazine*, 11 June 1956, 82.

20 Minutes, Regional Meeting of Information Officers, 3–4 January 1949. NARA, RG 469, entry 1029, box 4.

21 J. Carter, ECA Netherlands, to Walter Ridder, ECA Paris, 11 May 1951. NARA, RG 469, entry 1335, box 10.

22 Richard Dyer MacCann, 'Film and Foreign Policy: The USIA, 1962–67', *Cinema Journal* 9, no. 1 (1969): 23–42.

23 Stella Bruzzi, *New Documentary. A Critical Introduction*. 2nd edn (London, New York: Routledge, 2006), 7, 56; John Grierson, 'First Principles of Documentary (1932–1934)', in *Nonfiction Film: Theory and Criticism*, ed. Richard Barsam (New York: Dutton, 1976), 21.

24 John Grierson, 'Documentary: The Bright Example', in *Grierson on Documentary*, ed. Hardy Forsyth (1947; London: Faber and Faber, 1979), 188.

25 'They describe, and even expose, but, in any aesthetic sense, only rarely reveal.' Grierson, 'First Principles', 20.

26 Report Conference of Mission Information Officers, 23–24 May 1949. NARA, RG 469, entry 1029, box 4. In France, the film entered regular cinemas in spring 1949. Information Activities Report, ECA France, 1 March 1949. NARA, RG 469, entry 1029, box 7.

27 See also Bonifazio, *Schooling in Modernity*, 97.

28 Ibid., 124–28.

29 Anne Bruch and Gabriele Clemens, 'Die filmische (Re-)Konstruktion des Europäer', in *Werben für Europa*, ed. Clemens, 497.

30 Bruch et al., 'Werben für die Integration', 209.

31 Heffelfinger gives the number of 26 films, but does not provide a detailed list. See Heffelfinger, *Foreign Policy*, 13.

32 The films were shown on ABC Television and resulted in problems for the MSA Washington, for it was legally prohibited from engaging in propaganda on domestic territory. See Linda Christenson, 'Strength of the Free World', *Marshall Plan Filmography*. Available online: http://www.marshallfilms.org

33 Review of Activities, Information Division Italy, June 1948 to December 1950 (no date, presumably 1951). NARA 469, entry 303, box 2.

34 For the use of maps in MP films, see Anne Bruch, 'Die Visualisierung des europäischen Raumes', in *Werben für Europa*, ed. Clemens, 507–530.

35 For an illuminating analysis of *The Story of Koula*, see Victoria De Grazia, *Irresistible Empire: America's Advance through the Twentieth-Century Europe* (Cambridge, MA: Belknap Press of Harvard University Press, 2005), 348–49.

36 The documentary entered non-commercial distribution in Austria in November 1953. Information Activities in Second Quarter of 1953, High Commissioner for Austria. NARA, RG 469, entry 1203, box 6.

37 Review of Activities, Information Division Italy, June 1948 to December 1950 (no date, presumably 1951). NARA, RG 469, entry 303, box 2.

38 Hemsing, 'The Marshall Plan's European Film Unit', 273.

39 However, the tone of the information films produced for the purpose of German re-education also changed over time, as the Germans reacted negatively to the aggressive didactics of the early films. For a concise overview over the developments in the use education and information films in West Germany, see Hahn, 'Dokumentarfilm im Dienste der Umerziehung', and Loewy, 'Atrocity Pictures'. For the reception of the atrocity films, see Weckel, *Beschämende Bilder*.

40 Maier, 'The Politics of Productivity', 613–15.

41 See, for example, Bill Nichols, 'The Voice of Documentar', in *Movies and Methods. An Anthology*, ed. Bill Nichols (Berkeley, London: University of California Press, 1985), 259.

42 Bruzzi, *New Documentary*, 56.

43 Siegfried Kracauer, Appeals to the Near and the Middle East. Report, Bureau of Social Research, Columbia University May 1952. NARA, RG 306, entry 1007A, box 24.

44 Millar, ECA Norway, to Sussmann, Film Unit Paris, 20 July 1951. NARA, RG 469, entry 947, box 33.

45 Ørnbak, Scandinavian Information Center Copenhagen, to Schulberg, Film Unit Paris, 9 May 1951, ibid.

46 The Belgium information officer John Tobler had previously advised ECA Paris against producing the Dutch version in Belgium. Tobler to Norall, 19 April 1949; Shea to Tobler, 6 May 1949. NARA, RG 469, entry 1030, box 2.

47   English version accessed at NARA. Ina has made the French version available online: http://www.ina.fr/video/VDD09016137/village-sans-eau-video.html.

48   A copy of the commentary script was enclosed with the distributor's application for a screening permit. Les Films Dispa to Centre National de la Cinématographie, 13 July 1950. AN, F60ter 393.

49   Although the ECA/MSA film officers prided themselves on their *laissez-faire* attitude, they exerted considerable control over certain film projects, as Chapter 6 illustrates. Hemsing, 'The Marshall Plan's European Film Unit', 273.

50   OMGUS pursued a similar, yet different strategy in Germany: In 1948, it began to hand out licences for documentaries to German filmmakers – productions that were independent, yet closely watched. See Hahn, *Umerziehung durch Dokumentarfilm?*, 26–27.

51   Georg Tressler, Austrian filmmaker. Interview conducted by Linda and Eric Christenson, Berlin, 15 February 2004.

52   The MP film *Talking to the Italians* (ECA Italy 1950) openly discusses these strategies.

53   Lothar Wolff, 15 June 1951, cited by Hemsing, 'The Marshall Plan's European Film Unit', 273.

54   For a discussion of the concept of national cinema, see Andrew Higson, 'The Concept of National Cinema', in *The European Cinema Reader*, ed. Catherine Fowler (London: Routledge, 2002); Andrew Higson, 'The Limiting Imagination of National Cinema', in *Cinema and Nation*, ed. Mette Hjort and Scott MacKenzie (London, New York: Routledge, 2000); Tim Bergfelder, 'National, Transnational or Supranational cinema? Rethinking European Film Studies', *Media, Culture & Society* 27, no. 3 (2005).

55   For an insightful in-depth analysis of *Aquila* and the language of Neorealism, see Bonifazio, *Schooling in Modernity*, 34–40.

56   Ibid., 26; Ellis, *John Grierson*, 84; Steen Dalin, 'Dansk dokumentarfilms far', *filmmagasinet ekko* (2014). Available online: http://www.ekkofilm.dk/artikler/dansk-dokumentarfilms-far/ (accessed 26 January 2017).

57   See, for example, Bruch et al., 'Werben für die Integration'.

58   Friendly to Andrew Berding, 22 July 1949. NARA, RG 469, entry 1029, box 1.

59   Andrew Higson and Richard Maltby, '"Film Europe" and "Film America": An Introduction', in *'Film Europe' and 'Film America'. Cinema, Commerce and Cultural Exchange 1920–1939*, ed. Andrew Higson and Richard Maltby (Exeter: University of Exeter Press, 1999), 20–21; Joseph Garncarz, 'Hollywood in Germany. The Role of American Films in Germany, 1925–1990', in *Hollywood in Europe. Experiences of a Cultural Hegemony*, ed. David W. Ellwood and Rob Kroes (Amsterdam: VU University Press, 1994), 101–3.

Chapter 2

1 Higson and Maltby, 'Film Europe', 4; Thomas Guback, 'Hollywood's International Market', in *Film Theory. Critical Concepts in Media and Cultural Studies*, ed. K.J. Shepherdson, Philip Simpson and Andrew Utterson (London: Routledge, 2004), 297; Kristin Thompson, 'The End of the "Film Europe" Movement', in *History on/ and/in Film*, ed. Tom O'Regan and Brian Shoesmith (Perth: History and Film Association of Australia, 1987).

2 Higson and Maltby, 'Film Europe', 17–18.

3 Lothar Wolff, cited by Hemsing, 'The Marshall Plan's European Film Unit', 273.

4 Regional Information Officer Meeting, 3–4 January 1949. NARA, RG 469, entry 1029, box 4.

5 Emerson Waldman to Stuart Schulberg, 22 November 1949. NARA, RG 469, entry 1030, box 7.

6 Minutes, HICOG – ECA Motion Picture Conference, Paris, 30 November to 1 December 1950. NARA, RG 59, entry 5323, box 9.

7 Machado, *In Search of a Usable Past*, 87, Appendix D, 142.

8 Charles P. Kindleberger, *Marshall Plan Days* (1987; Abingdon: Routledge, 2010), 190–92; Hadley Arkes, *Bureaucracy, the Marshall Plan, and the National Interest* (Princeton, NJ: Princeton University Press, 1972), 253.

9 Memo Frank Norall to Waldemar Nielsen, 28 March 1950. NARA, RG 469, entry 1029, box 18.

10 Hardach, *Der Marshall-Plan*, 37, 43.

11 'The Marshall Plan. US Economic Assistance under the European Recovery Program. April 3, 1948–June 20, 1952.' Compiled by Statistics & Reports Division, Agency for International Development, 17 November 1975. Available online: http://pdf.usaid.gov/pdf_docs/Pdacs197.pdf (accessed 30 January 2017). See also Christoph Buchheim, *Die Wiedereingliederung Westdeutschlands in die Weltwirtschaft 1945–1958* (München: Oldenbourg, 1990), 70.

12 Bührer, *Westdeutschland in der OEEC*, 92–93.

13 Volker R. Berghahn, *American Big Business in Britain and Germany. A Comparative History of Two 'Special Relationships' in the 20th Century* (Princeton, NJ: Princeton University Press, 2014), 325.

14 Switzerland profited from the multilateral clearing agreements, which assigned the Swiss Bank for International Settlement (BIS) a central role as a platform of monetary exchange. See Hardach, *Der Marshall-Plan*, 56, 157–62; Kathleen Burk, 'The Marshall Plan: Filling in Some of the Blanks', *Contemporary European History* 10, no. 2 (2001): 272; Abelshauser, 'Der Kleine Marshallplan', 219.

15 'The Marshall Plan. US Economic Assistance under the European Recovery Program. April 3, 1948–June 20, 1952.' Compiled by Statistics & Reports Division,

Agency for International Development, 17 November 1975. Available online: http://pdf.usaid.gov/pdf_docs/Pdacs197.pdf (accessed 30 January 2017). Also Machado, *In Search of a Usable Past*, 87, Appendix D, 142.

16 See Burk, 'The Marshall Plan', 284–86; Palash Gosh, 'The Irish Nationalist And The Nazi: When Eamon De Valera Paid His Respects to Adolf Hitler', *The International Business Times*, 10 September 2013. Available online: http://www.ibtimes.com/irish-nationalist-nazi-when-eamon-de-valera-paid-his-respects-adolf-hitler-1403768 (accessed 30 January 2017).

17 Costs of distribution would usually be met by the Department of State if the ECA used USIS facilities. Memo Agreement between Secretary of State and ECA, 24 May 1948. NARA, RG 469, entry 1029, box 2.

18 Memo Kingman Brewster to James Fleming, Information Division, ECA Paris, 4 August 1948. NARA, RG 469, entry 1029, box 3.

19 See Saunders, *Cultural Cold War*, 68, 91.

20 Report Information Officers Meeting, 23–24 May 1949. NARA, RG 469, entry 1029, box 4.

21 Al Friendly to Colonel Gordon E. Textor, OMGUS, 20 April 1949. NARA, RG 469, entry 1029, box 7.

22 Hemsing, 'The Marshall Plan's European Film Unit', 274.

23 Tressler, Interview.

24 Emerson Waldman to Lothar Wolff, 8 December 1949. NARA, RG 469, entry 1030, box 7.

25 Emerson Waldman, ECA Norway, to Frank Dennis, Chief Special Media, 15 December 1949. NARA, RG 469, entry 1030, box 7.

26 Frank Gervasi to Lothar Wolff, 10 October 1950. NARA, RG 469, entry 1034, box 1.

27 Minutes, Regional Information and Labor Information Officers Conference, London, 4–6 April 1950. NARA, RG 469, entry 1029, box 14.

28 Frank R. Shea, Summary of Cooperative Activity in Information, 27 April 1949. NARA, RG 469, entry 1029, box 7.

29 Minutes, Regional Information and Labor Information Officers Conference, London, 4–6 April 1950. NARA, RG 469, entry 1029, box 14.

30 Thomas W. Wilson, Information Officer ECA UK. Interview conducted by Charles Stuart Kennedy, 30 October 1996. Foreign Affairs Oral History Collection, Association for Diplomatic Studies and Training, Arlington, VA. Available online: http://www.adst.org/OH%20TOCs/Wilson,%20Thomas%20W.toc.pdf (accessed 30 January 2017).

31 The original was called *The Sardinian Project*. For the re-edit, see handwritten note on memo from Lothar Wolff to Roscoe Drummond, 7 October 1949; Drummond to A. Wolcough, Shell, 10 October 1949. NARA, RG 469, entry 1029, box 10.

32 See Longo, 'Between Documentary and Neorealism', 28–31.

33 Tobia, *Advertising America*, 54–64.

34 Ellwood, 'The 1948 Elections in Italy'; see Tony Shaw, *Hollywood's Cold War* (Edinburgh: University of Edinburgh Press, 2007), 25–26.

35 Memo Nielsen to Colonel J. Tappin, 27 May 1949. NARA, RG 469, entry 1028, box 2.

36 On the information activities of the Italian country mission, see Ellwood, 'Italian Modernisation', 29–32.

37 Public Relations Monthly Report February, ECA Italy, 9 March 1949. NARA, RG 469, entry 1029, box 7.

38 Report Information Officers Meeting, 23–24 May 1949. NARA, RG 469, entry 1029, box 4.

39 Telegram from Gervasi to Drummond and Rachlis, 6 October 1950. NARA, RG 469, entry 1030, box 11.

40 These included the reclamation and irrigation of 2.4 million acres of land in Italy. See Price, *The Marshall Plan and Its Meaning*, 98.

41 In the second half of the 1950s, the Italian government and Italian industries started producing films on industrial productivity. See Bonifazio, 'United We Drill'; also Ellwood, 'Propaganda of the Marshall Plan', 231.

42 Svetozar Rajak, 'The Cold War in the Balkans, 1945–1956', in *The Cambridge History of the Cold War*, ed. Melvyn P. Leffler and Odd Arne Westad (Cambridge; New York: Cambridge University Press, 2010), 203–5.

43 Interview with Ben Franklin Dixon, Officer of Greek Affairs, US State Department. Interview conducted by Charles Stuart Kennedy, 31 October 1990. Foreign Affairs Oral History Collection, Association for Diplomatic Studies and Training, Arlington, VA. Available online: http://www.adst.org/OH%20TOCs/Dixon,%20Ben%20F.toc.pdf (accessed 30 January 2017). See also Price, *The Marshall Plan and Its Meaning*, 314.

44 Dixon, Interview.

45 Clark to Wolff, 22 September 1949. NARA, RG 469, entry 1030, box 5.

46 Wolff to Clark, 22 September 1949. NARA, RG 469, entry 1030, box 5.

47 Clark to Wolff, 30 September 1949. NARA, RG 469, entry 1030, box 5.

48 Vrasidas Karalis, *A History of Greek Cinema* (New York: Continuum, 2012), 50.

49 Clark to Wolff, 17 February 1950. NARA, RG 469, entry 1222, box 2. For the recovery of the Greek film industry, see Karalis, *A History of Greek Cinema*, 50–56.

50 The film unit intended John Ferno for the project, but Secondari persuaded the head of the Italian mission to suggest Gallo. Zellerbach to Wolff, ECA Paris, 29 April 1950. NARA, RG 469, entry 1030, box 11. See also Longo, 'Between Documentary and Neorealism', 28–29. However, I do not agree with Longo's interpretation over the wrangle of 'Mule Story': Corinth Canal and the 'Mule Story' were two different projects (both realized) and not one.

51 See Longo, 'Between Documentary and Neorealism', 28–29. For Secondari's ambitions as screenwriter, see his propositions to Roscoe Drummond. NARA, RG 469, entry 1030, box 11.

52 The Greek missions covered the expenses for preparation and production and ECA Italy agreed to pay editorial and salary expenses out of its counterpart funds. Lothar Wolff to Dowsley Clark, 22 September 1949. NARA, RG 469, entry 1030, box 5.

53 The film was deemed 'not suitable for distribution'. Patricia Sussmann, Chief Distribution Section, Report on film distribution in Greece, 13 March 1953. NARA, RG 469, entry 1223, box 3.

54 Dowsley Clark to Stephanos Rocanas, Under-Secretariat of State for Press and Information, Athens, 5 December 1949. NARA, RG 469, entry 1030, box 5.

55 Cark to Wolff, 22 May 1950. NARA, RG 469, entry 1222, box 2.

56 Clark to Wolff, 22 November 1949. NARA, RG 469, entry 1030, box 5.

57 William I. Hitchcock, 'The Marshall Plan and the Creation of the West', in *The Cambridge History of the Cold War*, ed. Leffler and Westad, 72–77; Frances M.B. Lynch, *France and the International Economy. From Vichy to the Treaty of Rome* (London; New York: Routledge, 1997), 52–56.

58 Susan Hayward, *French National Cinema* (London; New York: Routledge, 1993), 49–50.

59 Study of Theatrical Distribution in France, submitted to the State Department by the US embassy France, 18 May 1953. NARA, RG 84, entry 2462, box 13.

60 Helen Kirkpatrick, Head of Information Division, ECA France. Interview conducted by Ann Kasper, 4 April 1990, Session 2. Washington Press Club Foundation. Available online: http://beta.wpcf.org/oralhistory/kirk2.html (accessed 30 January 2017).

61 See Gérard Bossuat, *La France, l'aide américaine et la construction européenne, 1944–1954.* Vol.1 (Paris: Ministère de l'Économie et des Finances, 1997), 396, 401; McKenzie, *Remaking France*, 25, 179.

62 See chapters 2 & 3, Esposito, *America's Feeble Weapon*.

63 Ibid., 95–97, 102; McKenzie, *Remaking France*, 26–27, 41.

64 Secrétaire SGCI to Président du Conseil, 12 November 1948. AN France, F 60ter 381. 'Une campagne qui échapperait a son autorité risquerait, si elle ne tenait pas compte des légitimes susceptibilités de notre population, de heurter l'amour propre national …, et, en fin de compte, d'aller a l'encontre du but propose.' See also telegramme Ministère des Affaires Etrangères to SGCI and other ministries, 16 October 1949. AN France, F 60ter 381.

65 SGCI, Secret note pour le President du Conseil, no. 1455, 22 October 1949. AN France, F 60ter 357.

66   Esposito, *America's Feeble Weapon*, 95.

67   Bossuat, *La France, l'aide américaine*, 398–99, 401.

68   Rik Schreurs, 'A Marshall Plan for Africa? The Overseas Territories Committee and the Origins of European Co-Operation in Africa', in *Explorations in OEEC History*, ed. Richard T. Griffiths (Paris: Organisation for Economic Co-operation and Development, 1997), 88; also Price, *The Marshall Plan and Its Meaning*, 149–51, 384–85.

69   Stuart Schulberg to Henri Claudel, Ministère des Affaires Etrangères, 11 October 1950. NARA, RG 469, entry 1034, box 1.

70   For Wessex Films, see Philip C. Logan, *Humphrey Jennings and British Documentary Film: A Re-assessment* (Farnham: Ashgate, 2011), 309–36.

71   Henry Parkman, Head of ECA France, to Georges Elgozy, Secrétaire Général Adjoint Comité Inter-Ministériel, 6 September 1950; Compte-Rendu de la séance de travail du 21 September 1950, Ministère de l'Information. AN France, F 60ter 393.

72   Volker R. Berghahn, 'The Marshall Plan and the Recasting of Europe's Postwar Industrial Systems', in *The Marshall Plan. Lessons Learned for the 21st Century*, ed. Eliot Sorel and Pier Carlo Padoan (Paris: OECD, 2008), 33–34; Hardach, *Der Marshall-Plan*, 60.

73   Bührer, *Westdeutschland in der OEEC*, 105–07.

74   Thomas Schwartz, 'European Integration and the "Special Relationship". Implementing the Marshall Plan in the Federal Republic', in *The Marshall Plan and Germany. West German Development within the Framework of the European Recovery Program*, ed. Charles S. Maier and Günter Bischof (New York; Oxford: Berg, 1991), 173–78; on Clay's opposition to the OEEC, see Milward, *The Reconstruction of Western Europe*, 187–88.

75   Hahn, *Umerziehung durch Dokumentarfilm?*; Hahn, 'Dokumentarfilm im Dienste der Umerziehung'; Clemens, 'Umerziehung durch Film'; Axel Schildt and Detlef Siegfried, *Deutsche Kulturgeschichte: Die Bundesrepublik. 1945 bis zur Gegenwart* (München: Hanser, 2009), 45; Jessica C. E. Gienow-Hecht, *Transmission Impossible. American Journalism as Cultural Diplomacy in Postwar Germany, 1945–1955* (Baton Rouge: Louisiana State University Press, 1999).

76   Schildt and Siegfried, *Deutsche Kulturgeschichte*, 54.

77   See Hahn, *Umerziehung durch Dokumentarfilm?*, 27.

78   Al Friendly to Averell Harriman, 23 May 1949. NARA, RG 69, entry 1029, box 1.

79   Memo Friendly to Wally Nielsen, 29 June 1949. NARA, RG 469, entry 1028, box 1.

80   The ECA was initially strongly opposed to such a merger, fearing that this would undermine its position as an economic advisor and involve it in the High Commissioner's political and security issues. Secretary of State Acheson pushed for an integrated organization in order to guarantee that the authority of the High

Commissioner was not undermined by the presence of a powerful ECA mission chief, as had happened in other countries. The choice of leadership – McCloy was an internationalist and strong supporter of the MP – allegedly made the merger more acceptable to the ECA. See Schwartz, 'European Integration'.

81 Goergen, 'Orientierung und Ausrichtung', 36, 46–47.

82 'Bei aller Dankbarkeit', *Der Spiegel*, 13 August 1952, 21.

83 Jan Willem de Vries, 'When Amsterdam Went UPA: Dutch Modern Cartoons in the 1950s', 13 November 2013. Available online: http://www.cartoonbrew.com/cartoon-modern/when-amsterdam-went-upa-dutch-modern-cartoons-in-the-1950s-90904.html (accessed 24 January 2017).

84 Minutes HICOG – ECA Motion Picture Conference, Paris, 30 November to 1 December 1950. NARA, RG 59, entry 5323, box 9.

85 Helen and Peter Rathvon, Motion Picture Survey, conducted between 6 February and 26 March 1951, 29. NARA, RG 59, entry 5323, box 24.

86 Minutes HICOG – ECA Motion Picture Conference, Paris, 30 November to 1 December 1950. NARA, RG 59, entry 5323, box 9.

87 Helen and Peter Rathvon, Motion Picture Survey, conducted between 6 February and 26 March 1951, 29. NARA, RG 59, entry 5323, box 24.

88 On NATO films, see Linda Risso, '"Enlightening Public Opinion": A Study of NATO's Information Policies between 1949 and 1959 Based on Recently Declassified Documents', *Cold War History* 7, no. 1 (2007). The Federal Ministry for the Marshall Plan also produced films promoting the MP: *Nicht Vergessen* (1951) and *Ein Weg – Deutschland im ERP* (1951). See Thomas Tode, 'Die Grenze als zentrales Motiv der Europafilm-Rhetorik', in *Werben für Europa*, ed. Clemens, 460; Jeanpaul Goergen, 'Verbreitung der Europafilme in der Bundesrepublik', in *Werben für Europa*, ed. Clemens, 345.

89 Quarterly Report, MSA Information Office Western Germany, 1 October to 31 December 1952. NARA, RG 59, entry 5323, box 18.

90 For West German views on the US occupier and the ERP, see Hans Woller, 'Zur Demokratiebereitschaft in der Provinz des amerikanischen Besatzungsgebiets: aus den Stimmungsberichten des Ansbacher Oberbürgermeisters an die Militärregierung 1946–1949', *Vierteljahreshefte für Zeitgeschichte* 3, no. 2 (1983); Peter Wagner, *Mythos Marshall-Plan. Das europäische Weideraufbauprogramm in der deutschen öffentlichen Meinung 1947–1952* (Pfaffenweiler: Centaurus Verlagsgesellschaft, 1996), 106–7, 120.

91 Turkey had initially asked for a total of $615 million in Marshall Aid. See George S. Harris, *Troubled Alliance. Turkish-American Problems in Historical Perspective, 1945–1971* (Washington, DC: American Enterprise Institute for Public Policy Research, Hoover Institution on War, Revolution and Peace, 1972), 32.

92 Machado, *In Search of a Usable Past*, 87.

93 Senem Üstün, 'Turkey and the Marshall Plan. Strive for Aid', *The Turkish Yearbook of International Relations* XXVII (1997): 39–40.

94 See Harris, *Troubled Alliance*, 31–44; 'Memorandum Conversation between Turkish Foreign Minister and Heads of ECA Paul Hoffman and Averell Harriman, Turkish Embassy Paris, 1 February 1950', in *Turkey. Principal Policies and Problems in the Relations of the United States with Turkey*, ed. United States Department of State (Washington, DC, 1950), 1225–25. Available online http://digital.library.wisc.edu/1711.dl/FRUS.FRUS1950v05 (accessed 30 January 2017).

95 Third year: $50 million, two-thirds as grants; final year: 70 million. Machado, *In Search of a Usable Past*, 86–87; Üstün, 'Turkey and the Marshall Plan', 34–37.

96 Memo Nielsen to Colonel John L. Tappin, Assistant to Milton Katz, 27 May 1949. NARA, RG 469, entry 1028, box 2.

97 See Price, *The Marshall Plan and Its Meaning*, 273.

98 See Machado, *In Search of a Usable Past*, 88–89; Üstün, 'Turkey and the Marshall Plan', 42–43, 49–51.

99 Memo Film Unit to Projects Control Officer, 10 July 1951. NARA, RG 469, entry 947, box 32.

100 Memo Philip Mackie to Stuart Schulberg, 17 April 1951. NARA, RG 469, entry 947, box 32.

101 See Üstün, 'Turkey and the Marshall Plan', 39–40.

102 Machado, *In Search of a Usable Past*, 94.

103 G.C.d'Olive, Information Officer, ECA Turkey, to Stuart Schulberg, 25 June 1951. NARA, RG 469, entry 947, box 32. The Turkish representatives also demanded cuts to *The Marshall Plan at Work in Turkey*, produced by Bill Mellor for the film unit; the scenes they objected to showed a beggar woman making an indecent gesture and a coal miner's dining hall with a girl dancing.

104 Dennis Clarke to Stuart Schulberg, 7 July 1951. NARA, RG 469, entry 947, box 32.

105 Memo Film Unit to Contracts Unit, Contracts Clarke & Hornby, 10 July 1951. NARA, RG 469, entry 947, box 32.

106 *Yusef and His Plough* (Yusuf ve Sabanı), *The Village Tractor* (Köy Traktörü), *Turkish Harvest*. It appears that *Control of Water* (Turkish title: Suyun Kontrolü) was never screened outside of Turkey. *Care of Tractors* (Turkish: Traktör Bakımı largely an edited version of the *Village Tractor*) was completed, but distribution outside Turkey could not be verified. The title of the sixth film produced by Clarke & Hornby remains unknown.

Chapter 3

1   See Jessica Gienow-Hecht, 'Culture and the Cold War in Europe', in *The Cambridge History of the Cold War*, ed. Leffler and Westad, Vol. 1.

2   George C. Marshall, Speech at Harvard University, 5 June 1947. Transcript available online: http://www.oecd.org/general/themarshallplanspeechatharvarduniversity5june1947.htm (accessed 30 January 2017).

3   Hardach, *Der Marshall-Plan*, 29–31.

4   Report by Secretary Marshall on the Fourth Meeting of the Council of Foreign Ministers in Moscow from 10 March to 24 April 1947, 28 April 1947. Available online: http://avalon.law.yale.edu/20th_century/decade23.asp (accessed 30 January 2017).

5   Hitchcock, 'The Marshall Plan and the Creation of the West', 87, 283.

6   Ibid., 90–91.

7   Carew, 'The Politics of Productivity and the Politics of Anti-Communism', 84–86.

8   Initially, all four Allies had been involved in the discussion of a currency reform, but the United States and Britain gradually excluded the Soviets. See Gunther Mai, *Der Alliierte Kontrollrat in Deutschland: 1945–1948. Alliierte Einheit – deutsche Teilung?* (München: Oldenbourg, 1995), 279–304.

9   Buchheim, *Die Wiedereingliederung Westdeutschlands*, 55–61.

10 Report to the National Security Council, NSC-68, 12 April 1950, 6. Truman Library, President's Secretary's File, Truman Papers. Available online: https://www.trumanlibrary.org/whistlestop/study_collections/coldwar/documents/pdf/10-1.pdf (accessed 30 January 2017).

11 'NSC-68, 1950', Office of the Historian, State Department. Available online: https://history.state.gov/milestones/1945-1952/NSC68 (accessed 30 January 2017).

12 James A. Huston, *Outposts and Allies. U.S. Army Logistics in the Cold War, 1945–1953* (Cranbury, London: Associated University Presses, 1988), 137.

13 Lundestad, 'Empire by Invitation?' 53.

14 See Hardach, *Der Marshall-Plan*, 128–30, 237; Ellwood, 'Italian Modernisation', 38.

15 While some sectors of the West Germany industry were also affected by the shortages of raw material, the West German economy profited from this rearmament boom, as the demands for steel and German-produced machine parts grew. See Tony Judt, *Postwar. A History of Europe since 1945* (London: Vintage, 2010), 152; Werner Abelshauser, 'Deutsche Wirtschaftspolitik zwischen europäischer Integration und Weltmarktorientierung', in *Das Bundeswirtschaftsministerium in der Ära der Sozialen Marktwirtschaft*, ed. Werner Abelshauser (Oldenbourg: De Gruyter, 2016), 492–94.

16 Gerhard Peters and John T. Woolley, 'Harry S. Truman, Statement by the President upon Signing the Mutual Security Act. October 10, 1951', *The American Presidency*

Project. Available online: http://www.presidency.ucsb.edu/ws/?pid=13944 (accessed 30 January 2017).

17 Mutual Security Act. Public Law 165, Sec. 503, 10 October 1951.

18 Greece and Turkey, although not as yet NATO members (they joined NATO officially on 18 February 1952), received, together with Iran, an additional sum of $396 million in military assistance.

19 Mutual Security Act. Public Law 165, Sec. 503, 10 October 1951.

20 See Hardach, *Der Marshall-Plan*, 133.

21 In autumn 1951, the film unit cancelled several projects and contracts with filmmakers as result of budget cuts. This concerned, for example, the film series *One-Two-Three*. See Stuart Schulberg to Victor Vicas, 8 October 1951. DFI, Nachlass Victor Vicas.

22 The Italian Information Division suspended film production from November 1951. Review of Activities, Information Division Italy, June 1948 to December 1950 (no date, presumably 1951). NARA 469, entry 303, box 2.

23 USIS was criticized as ineffective and came under close scrutiny under the new administration of President Eisenhower. On 1 August 1953, President Eisenhower created the US Information Agency (USIA), which pooled together all the foreign information services of the State Department, the MSA and the Defence Department. See Tobia, *Advertising America*, 103–6.

24 Eugene Rachlis to H. Fite, 27 May 1952. NARA, RG 469, entry 947, box 32; Nils Nilson to Rachlis, 14 March 1952. NARA, RG 469, entry 947, box 32.

25 See, for example, Joseph Carter, Information Division Italy, to Andrew Berding, MSA Washington, 28 May 1952. NARA, RG 469, entry 303, box 2.

26 Minutes, HICOG – ECA Motion Picture Conference, Paris, 30 November to 1 December 1950. NARA, RG 59, entry 5323, box 9.

27 Ibid.

28 See Hogan, *The Marshall Plan*, 380–81.

29 Official Country Plan for the USIE Program France, January 1952. NARA, RG 84, entry 2462, box 13. See also Ellwood, *Italian Modernisation*, 38.

30 See Hitchcock, 'The Marshall Plan and the Creation of the West', 157.

31 Policy Statement, Information Office ECA/MSA Mission to Netherlands, 1952 (no precise date). NARA, RG 469, entry 1335, box 9.

32 Helen and Peter Rathvon, Motion Picture Survey, conducted between 6 February and 26 March 1951, 29. NARA, RG 59, entry 5323, box 24; A. Sims, HICOG, to Richard R. Brown, Policy Statement for the 1952 Film Program, 2 February 1951. NARA, RG 59, entry 5323, box 9. See Theo Blank, 'Der härteste Schädel in Bonn', *Der Spiegel*, 10 December 1952, 6–13; Dieter Krueger, 'Der "Koreaschock" 1950', in *Korea – ein vergessener Krieg?: Der militärische Konflikt auf der koreanischen Halbinsel 1950–1953 im internationalen Kontext*, ed. Bernd Bonwetsch and Matthias Uhl (München: Oldenbourg, 2012).

33 USIS Austria, Country Action Plan, 21 July 1954. NARA, RG 469, entry 337, box 59.

34 Memo, MSA film unit Paris to all missions, 16 October 1952. NARA, RG 469, entry 1335, box 9. At least the missions in West Germany and the Netherlands were interested enough to produce synchronized versions. MSA Information Office West Germany, Quarterly Report, 1 January to 31 March 1953. NARA, RG 469, entry 1203, box 6.

35 The film's director, Peter Hopkinson, and cinematographer, John Baxter Peters, collaborated on two other MP films commissioned by the film section in Paris: *North Sea Harbor* (1951) and *The Ruhr* (1952). All three films were produced by Cinetone Studios in Amsterdam and exist in two different versions: one extended, approximately half-hour long version for the *Strength for the Free World*-series, which was to be screened on US television, and a second, shorter version intended for a European audience. A memo from the film section indicates that *The Smiths and the Robinsons* and *The Ruhr* had already been produced with two different audiences in mind. See Memo MSA film unit Paris to all missions, 16 October 1952. NARA, RG 469, entry 1335, box 9.

36 Ina Zweiniger-Bargielowska, *Austerity in Britain. Rationing, Controls, and Consumption, 1939–1955* (Oxford: Oxford University Press, 2000), 227.

37 The aim was to recruit 125,000. By February 1952, however, only 28,120 men had joined the volunteer force. See Stephen Michael Cullen, *In Search of the Real Dad's Army: The Home Guard and the Defence of the United Kingdom, 1940–1944* (Barnsley: Pen & Sword Military, 2011), 199–200.

38 Richard Massingham, *BFI Screenonline*. Available online: http://www.screenonline .org.uk/people/id/521707/ (accessed 30 January 2017).

39 *What a Life!* (1948), Dir. Michael Law, UK: Public Relationships Films.

40 Kieron Webb, 'What a Life!' in *Land of Promise. The British Documentary Movement 1930–1950*, ed. British Film Institute (London: BFI, 2008), 57.

41 Report on MSA Information Division Turkey, February 1953. NARA, RG 469, entry 1335, box 48; see also Linda Risso, '"Don't Mention the Soviets!" An Overview of the Short Films Produced by the NATO Information Service between 1949 and 1969', *Cold War History* 9, no. 4 (2009): 501–12.

42 Linda Christenson, 'Whitsun Holiday', *Marshall Plan Filmography MPF*, 2002. Available online: http://www.marshallfilms.org (accessed 26 January 2017).

43 Greg Castillo, *Cold War on the Home Front. The Soft Power of Midcentury Design* (Minneapolis, London: University of Minnesota Press, 2010), 27.

44 Ibid., 26–28; S. Jonathan Wiesen, *West German Industry and the Challenge of the Nazi Past, 1945–1955* (Chapel Hill, NC; London: University of North Carolina Press, 2001), 145–58.

45 See, for example, Minutes HICOG – ECA/OSR Motion Picture Conference Paris, 30 November to 1 December 1950. NARA, RG 59, entry 5323, box 9.

46 Mutual Security Agency, *Catalogue of Documentary Films* (1 September 1952), Appendix A, 104.

47 Often listed as USIS production (the MSA was abolished in summer 1953), it was supervised by the last head of the ECA/MSA, Al Hemsing.

48 On the representation of Boula, see Maria Fritsche, 'Der filmische Blick im Museum. Dekonstruktion des Eigenen und Fremden im US-amerikanischen Informationsfilm Wie die Jungen sungen (R: Georg Tressler, 1954)'. *Österreichische Zeitschrift für Volkskunde* 114, no. 3 (2011).

49 Tode, 'Die Grenze als zentrales Motiv', 459.

50 Walter Doyle, ECA Denmark, to Stuart Schulberg, 15 February 1951. NARA, RG 469, entry 1152, box 2.

51 Draft 'Way for Europe'. NARA, RG 469, entry 1335, box 2.

52 The head of the Special Media Section Eugene Rachlis sent the outlines and commentary scripts for both films to ECA Netherlands on 18 October 1950, to determine their interest. NARA, RG 469, entry 1335, box 2.

53 Philip Stapp to Nils Nilson, 18 December 1951. NARA, RG 469, entry 947, box 33.

54 Walter Ridder, Deputy Director Information Division, to Office of General Counsel, ECA, 2 January 1951. NARA, RG 469, entry 947, box 33.

55 Philip Stapp to Nils Nilson, 18 December 1951. NARA, RG 469, entry 947, box 33.

56 Nils Nilson to Larkins, 23 November 1951. NARA, RG 469, entry 947, box 33.

57 Since there are at least three different versions of *Without Fear* in circulation, it is difficult to ascertain which one was the final, approved version. A comparison of the different versions reveals that the commentary to the middle part of the film, which describes the communist regime, was modified several times. Thus two versions speak of 'dictatorship', while one refers to the 'all-powerful, totalitarian state'. Only one of the three versions uses the terms 'police state' or 'dictators'. NARA holds two versions. A third version was part of the BBC 4 series 'Animated Nations' (2005), 13.

58 Philip Stapp to Nils Nilson, 18 December 1951. NARA, RG 469, entry 947, box 33.

59 Paul R. Porter to Mr. Sumner, W. M. Larkins and Co Ltd., 31 January 1952; Murray Gartner, Office of General Counsel, to Walter Ridder, 7 January 1952. NARA, RG 469, entry 947, box 33.

60 Nils Nilson to W.K. Stewart, Contract Unit, 7 May 1952. NARA, RG 469, entry 947, box 34.

61 Quarterly Report, 1 October to 31 December 1952, MSA Information Office West Germany. NARA, RG 59, entry 5323, box 18.

62 Thordur Einarsson, ECA Iceland, to William R. Auman, MSA Denmark, 3 November 1952. NARA, RG 469, entry 1153, box 1; Sigurjón Baldur Hafsteinsson and Tinna Grétarsdóttir, 'Screening Propaganda: The Reception of Soviet and American Film Screenings in Rural Iceland, 1950–1975', *Film History* 23, no. 4 (2011): 361–62.

63 Evaluation of Audience Reactions to 'Without Fear', Report no. 175, HICOG (no precise date, 1953). NARA, RG 306, entry 1005, box 5.

64 Ibid.

65 Hans Bagge, 'Kommunister og Marshallfilms', *Søro Amtstidende*, 11 July 1950, partly cited in 'Marshallfilmene som optakt til en uamerikansk komité', *Land og Folk*, 14 July 1950.

66 Walter Doyle, ECA Denmark, to Stuart Schulberg, 15 February 1951. NARA, RG 469, entry 1152, box 2.

67 Christian Alsted, '1949 – En epoke kuliminirer', in *Kortfilmen og staten*, ed. Christian Alsted and Carl Nørrested (Copenhagen: Eventus, 1987), 282.

68 Vibeke Sørensen, *Denmark's Social Democratic Government and the Marshall Plan, 1947–1950* (Copenhagen: Museum Tusculanum Press, University of Copenhagen, 2001), 321–24.

69 Alsted, '1949 – En epoke kuliminirer', 282. The following report refers to nine films: Motion Picture Unit, Plan of Action, 30 June 1950 through 31 December 1950. NARA, RG 469, entry 1029, box 18.

70 The film committee was given the title *Ministeriernes Filmudvalg* in 1944. See Lars-Martin Sørensen, *Dansk film under Nazismen* (Copenhagen: Lindhardt og Ringhof, 2014), 337; Lars-Martin Sørensen, 'En svækket stat forstærker sin propaganda', in *Sculpting the Past*, ed. Det Danske Filminstitut (Copenhagen: Lindhardt og Ringhof, 2014). Available online: http://www.sculptingthepast.dk/Temaer/Besaettelsen/En-svaekket-stat.aspx (accessed 30 January 2017).

71 Draft of Contract between the US Government, Represented by the ECA, and the Danish Government Film Committee, January 1950, 7. NARA, RG 469, entry 1029, box 15.

72 The MFU withdrew from its role as producer before the production actually started, giving the official reason that it could not agree to be responsible for a foreign state. The withdrawal of the MFU allowed filmmakers more independence. See Alsted, '1949 – En epoke kuliminirer', 283.

73 Ebbe Neergaard, Leksikon for det 21. århundrede. Available online: http://www.leksikon.org/art.php?n=1836 (accessed 30 January 2017).

74 Thomas Durrance, ECA Denmark, to Lothar Wolff, 26 May 1950. NARA, RG 469, entry 1152, box 2; Sørensen, *Denmark's Social Democratic Government*, 321–24, 336–38.

75 John Poulsen, 'Dokumentarfilmens Godfather', *Arbejderen*, 5 August 2014. Available online: http://arbejderen.dk/anmeldelse/dokumentarfilmens-godfather (accessed 30 January 2017).

76 Lisbeth Richter Larsen, 'Regeringens Beskæftigelses-filmudvalg og Ministeriernes Filmudvalg (1941–1966)', Det Danske Filminstitut. Available online: http://www.dfi.dk/FaktaOmFilm/Filminstitutionernes-historie/Institutionerne/Regeringens-Beskaeftigelsesudvalg-og-Ministeriernes-Filmudvalg.aspx (accessed 30 January

2017); see Lars-Martin Sørensen, 'Theodor Christensen – Pioner, Polemiker, Propagandist', *Kosmorama*, no. 253 (2014). Available online: http://www .kosmorama.org/Artikler/Theodor-Christensen.aspx; C. Claire Thomson and Mary Hilson, 'Beauty in Bacon: "The Pattern of Co-operation" and the Export of Postwar Danish Democracy', *Kosmorama*, no. 255 (2014). Available online: http://www .kosmorama.org/Artikler/Beauty-in-Bacon.aspx (accessed 30 January 2017).

77 Protocol of MFU meeting, 31 May 1950, cited by Alsted, '1949 – En epoke kuliminirer', 284–85.

78 Bagge, 'Kommunister og Marshallfilms'.

79 *Berlingske Tidende*, cited by Walter Doyle, ECA Denmark, to Stuart Schulberg, 15 February 1951. NARA, RG 469, entry 1152, box 2.

80 See Alsted, '1949 – En epoke kuliminirer', 286.

81 The debate over the Danish MP films was reignited in February 1952, when the press got wind of the fact that the ECA had forced the Danish government to pay back the money it had taken from the counterpart funds to cover its share of the production costs. 'Amerikansk repressalie mod 6 danske kortfilm', *Land og Folk*, 9 February 1952; 'Dyr form-fejl', *Social-Demokraten*, 10 February 1952.

82 Stuart Schulberg to Walter Doyle, 26 February 1951. NARA, RG 469, entry 1152, box 2. The producers of *Caroline, the Cow* altered the commentary four times, but the ECA information officer withheld his final approval. He rewrote the commentary, which the supervisory team and the film committee of the Danish Agricultural Department rejected as too propagandistic. In the end, the Danish mission accepted the original commentary. Alsted, '1949 – En epoke kuliminirer', 289; Walter Doyle, ECA Denmark, to Stuart Schulberg, 15 February 1951. NARA, RG 469, entry 1152, box 2.

83 Though initially planned for distribution in other European countries, it is unclear whether *Kyndbyværket* was ever shown outside Denmark. See Kyndby-Krogstrup, 'En Marshall-Film af Kyndbyværket', *Frederiksborg Amts Avisa*, 18 November 1950.

84 Stuart Schulberg to Walter Doyle, 26 February 1951. NARA, RG 469, entry 1152, box 2.

85 Informational Guidance, Director of Information Washington, 16 January 1952. NARA, RG 84, entry 2462, box 33.

Chapter 4

1 Sec. 102 (a), Economic Cooperation Act of 1948.

2 See Price, *The Marshall Plan and Its Meaning*, 153.

3 Elliott Vanveltner Converse, *Rearming for the Cold War, 1945–1960* (Washington, DC: Historical Office, Office of the Secretary of Defense, 2011), 97–98.

4   Official Country Plan for the USIE Program France, January 1952. NARA, RG 84, entry 2462, box 13. See also Hogan, The Marshall Plan, 380–81; Judt, *Postwar*, 152; Ellwood, 'Italian Modernisation', 38.

5   De Grazia, *Irresistible Empire*, 358; Judt, *Postwar*, 152. Abelshauser points to the adverse effects of rearmament boom on West Germany, such as coal shortages and electricity cuts. Abelshauser, 'Deutsche Wirtschaftspolitik', 492–93.

6   Letter from Bartlett Harvey, ECA Program Review Officer, 19 June 1951. NARA, RG 469, entry 1335, box 9.

7   I use the film's French title to avoid confusion with the MP film *Productivity – Key to Plenty*.

8   Memo ECA film unit (no date, first half of 1951). NARA, RG 469, entry 947, box 34.

9   Kuisel, *Seducing the French*.

10 Ibid., 75; McKenzie, *Remaking France*, 153.

11 See Price, *The Marshall Plan and Its Meaning*, 331.

12 McKenzie, *Remaking France*, 152.

13 Sheri Berman, *The Primacy of Politics: Social Democracy and the Making of Europe's Twentieth Century* (New York: Cambridge Univ. Press, 2006), 179.

14 Berghahn, 'The Marshall Plan', 30.

15 Kuisel, *Seducing the French*, 72; McKenzie, *Remaking France*, 152–53.

16 Maier, 'The Politics of Productivity', 613.

17 Ibid., 615.

18 Informational Guidance, Director of Information Washington, 16 January 1952. NARA, RG 84, entry 2462, box 33.

19 Price, *The Marshall Plan and Its Meaning*, 333.

20 See, for example, Kuisel, *Seducing the French*, chapter 4.

21 See Price, *The Marshall Plan and Its Meaning*, 107–8, 336.

22 De Grazia, *Irresistible Empire*, 347.

23 For the ECA Labor Information programme, see McKenzie, *Remaking France*, 147–83.

24 Bent Boel, *The European Productivity Agency and Transatlantic Relations, 1953– 1961*, Vol. 4 (Copenhagen: Museum Tusculanum Press, 2003); Anthony Carew, 'The Anglo-American Council on Productivity (1948–52): The Ideological Roots of the Post-War Debate on Productivity in Britain'. *Journal of Contemporary History* 26, no. 1 (1991).

25 Reichert, 'Film und Rationalisierung'; Ramón Reichert, 'Die Filme des "Österreichischen Produktivitätszentrums" 1950–1987: Ein Beitrag zur Diskussion um den Film als historische Quelle'. *Relation. Beiträge zur vergleichenden Kommunikationsforschung* 7, no. 1+2 (2000).

26 For the French productivity centre, the *Centre français de productivité*, see Robert Gardellini, *Produktivität und französische Wirtschaft*. (Wiesbaden: Springer, 1965), 16. Also Kuisel, *Seducing the French*, 73–74.

27 History of ECA Mission Netherlands (no date, *ca.* 1952). NARA, RG 469, entry 1335, box 9.

28 In West Germany, the Rationalisierungskuratorium der Deutschen Wirtschaft (RKW), whose predecessor had already been founded in 1921, functioned as a national productivity centre since 1950. See *Amerika Dienst*, Vol. 4, no. 24/C (195), 1–2; Christian Kleinschmidt, 'Entwicklungshilfe für Europa. Die European Productivity Agency und das US Technical Assistance and Productivity Program', *Themenportal Europäische Geschichte* (2008). Available online: http://www.europa .clio-online.de/2008/Article=328 (accessed 25 July 2016).

29 Austria, Belgium, Denmark, France, Germany, the Netherlands, Iceland, Italy, Sweden, Switzerland and the United Kingdom. Norway set up an NPC in 1953.

30 Boel, *European Productivity Agency*, 36; Richard H. Pells, *Not Like Us. How Europeans Loved, Hated, and Transformed American Culture since World War II* (New York: Basic Books, 1997), 57.

31 See Boel, *European Productivity Agency*, 37; David Ellwood, 'The Marshall Plan and the Politics of Growth', in *Shaping Postwar Europe. European Unity and Disunity 1945–1957*, ed. Peter M.R. Stirk and David Willis (London: Pinter Publishers, 1991), 24; Ellwood, 'Italian Modernisation', 42.

32 Confidential Report ECA Information Officers Conference, Paris, 25 October 1949. NARA, RG 469, entry 1031, box. See also McKenzie, *Remaking France*, 153; Kuisel, *Seducing the French*, 75–76.

33 Memo, ECA Program Planning Officer to all information officers, 7 September 1951. NARA, RG 469, entry 1335, box 10.

34 Official Country Plan for the USIE Program France, January 1952. NARA, RG 84, entry 2462, box 13. However, it is important to note that scepticism towards productivity did not necessarily equate to rejection: many workers appreciated certain aspects of productivity that facilitated work processes or gave them a bonus. Even communist union members were by no means all opposed to productivity, as Brian McKenzie has found. See McKenzie, *Remaking France*, 172.

35 Ibid., 153; Kuisel, *Seducing the French*, 84–87, 89–90.

36 See Ellwood, 'Politics of Growth', 24. Ellwood, 'Italian Modernisation', 42; Boel, *European Productivity Agency*, 38.

37 Cited by Price, *The Marshall Plan and Its Meaning*, 108.

38 The rejection of American culture and the strong anti-American sentiments in post-war Europe have been analysed in a number of important studies. For an overview, see, for example, Alexander Stephan (ed.), *The Americanization of Europe. Culture, Diplomacy, and Anti-Americanism after 1945* (New York; Oxford: Berghahn, 2006).

39 Judt, *Postwar*, 220.

40 Official Country Plan for the USIE Program France, January 1952. NARA, RG 84, entry 2462, box 13.

41 See, for example, Price, *The Marshall Plan and Its Meaning*, 334, 342; Alexander Stephan, 'Cold War Alliances and the Emergence of Transatlantic Competition', in *The Americanization of Europe. Culture, Diplomacy and Anti-Americanism after 1945*, ed. Alexander Stephan (New York, Oxford: Berghahn, 2006), 14–15; Ellwood, 'Propaganda of the Marshall Plan', 230; Kuisel, *Seducing the French*; Pells, *Not Like Us*, 156–63; Wagnleitner, *Coca-Colonization and the Cold War*; Uta. G. Poiger (2000). *Jazz, Rock, and Rebels: Cold War Politics and American Culture in a Divided Germany* (Berkeley, London: University of California Press); Uta G. Poiger, 'American Music, Cold War Liberalism, and German Identities', in *Transactions, Transgressions, Transformations*, ed. Fehrenbach and Poiger.

42 Telegram Program Planning Officer at ECA Paris to all information officers, 7 September 1951. NARA, RG 469, entry 1335, box 10.

43 Telegram Head of ECA Paris to all missions, 7 September 1951, ibid.

44 Thomas Wilson, Confidential Report ECA Information Officers Conference, Paris, 25 October 1949. NARA, RG 469, entry 1031, box 1.

45 Survey of West German factory workers on the effectiveness of productivity and training films, Office of Public Affairs, HICOG, June 1953. NARA, RG 306, entry 1005, box 5. According to a survey of 179 workers who were shown a number of films over a prolonged length of time, the majority preferred films detailing specific work processes relevant to their specific field of work. Only a few questioned the rationale of productivity as such.

46 Confidential Report ECA Information Officers Conference, Paris, 25 October 1949. NARA, RG 469, entry 1031, box 1.

47 Minutes Regional Meeting of Information Officers, January 1949. NARA, RG 469, entry 1029, box 4.

48 Confidential Report ECA Information Officers Conference, Paris, 25 October 1949. NARA, RG 469, entry 1031, box 1.

49 Informational Guidance, Director of Information Washington, 16 January 1952. NARA, RG 84, entry 2462, box 33.

50 Between 1949 and 1951. Judt, *Postwar*, 97.

51 Price, *The Marshall Plan and Its Meaning*, 97–98, 333.

52 Judt, *Postwar*, 257–58; Barry J. Eichengreen, *The European Economy since 1945* (Princeton, NJ: Princeton University Press, 2007), 116.

53 See Bonifazio, *Schooling in Modernity*, chapter 4, for a more detailed analysis of how publicly sponsored information films tackled these modernization projects.

54 Jacques Colin in *La France made in USA* (2007), [TV documentary] Dir. Bob Swaim. France: Arte France.

55 Esposito, *America's Feeble Weapon*, 94–95; Kuisel, *Seducing the French*, 75.

56 Tressler, Interview.

57 'En virkelig trist formiddag', *Information*, 1 June 1951; 'Dansk Saglihed – fremmed Fantasi', *Berlingske Tidene*, 1 June 1951.

58 'Lidet obbyggelige Genopbygnings-Film', *Nationaltidende*, 1 June 1951; 'Dansk Marshall-dokumentarfilm', *Social-Demokraten*, 1 June 1950; 'Filmisk tak for Marshall-hjælpen til Danmark', *Social-Demokraten*, 8 June 1951; 'De første danske Marshall-film', *Politiken*, 1 June 1951.

59 Sørensen, *Denmark's Social Democratic Government*, 247.

60 'Fire kortfilm om økonomi', *Social-Demokraten*, 25 September 1952; 'Brugsfilm', *Nationaltidende*, 25 September 1952; 'Bacongrise med venusmaal', *Politiken*, 25 September 1952. See also Alsted, En epoke kuliminirer, 290.

61 'The Streamlined Pig', *Film User*, 7, no. 75 (1953).

62 'The Extraordinary Adventures of One Quart Milk'. *Film User* 6, no. 68 (1952).

63 Pierre Grimblat in *La France made in USA* (2007), [TV documentary] Dir. Bob Swaim. France: Arte France.

64 See, for example, Erica Carter, 'Alice in the Consumer Wonderland: West German Case Studies in Gender and Consumer Culture', in *West Germany under Construction. Politics, Society, and Culture in the Adenauer Era*, ed. Robert G. Moeller (Ann Arbor: University of Michigan Press, 1997); Erica Carter, 'How German Is She? Postwar West German Reconstruction and the Consuming Woman', in *Social History, Popular Culture, and Politics in Germany* (Ann Arbor: University of Michigan Press, 1997); David F. Crew, 'Gender, Media and Consumerism in Germany, 1920s–1950s', *Journal of Social History* (1998); Rebecca J. Pulju, *Women and Mass Consumer Society in Postwar France* (Cambridge: Cambridge University Press, 2011).

65 Memo Jean Joyce, ECA Washington, 23 April 1951. NARA, RG 469, entry 1031, box 2; also Pulju, *Women and Mass Consumer Society*, 12, 60.

66 Film script and contract. NA INF 6/36.

67 De Grazia, *Irresistible Empire*, 419.

68 See Pulju, *Women and Mass Consumer Society*, 64.

69 Official Country Plan for the USIE Program France, January 1952. NARA, RG 84, entry 2462, box 13.

70 Nielsen to Joyce, 3 May 1951. NARA, RG 469, entry 1031, box 2.

71 Mullen to Nielsen, 24 April 1951, ibid.

72 De Grazia, *Irresistible Empire*, 347.

73 See Ellwood, 'Politics of Growth', 22.

74 Kuisel, *Seducing the French*, 72–74; Esposito, *America's Feeble Weapon*, 94–95; Ellwood, 'Italian Modernisation', 42.

75 Giles Scott-Smith, *Networks of Empire. The US State Department's Foreign Leader Program in the Netherlands, France, and Britain 1950–70* (Brussels: Peter Lang, 2008), 145.

76 Berman, *The Primacy of Politics*, 177–83.

77 Ellwood, 'Politics of Growth', 20, McKenzie, *Remaking France*, 172.

78 Carew, 'The Anglo-American Council on Productivity (1948–52)', 79.

79 Federico Romero, *The United States and the European Trade Union Movement, 1944–1951* (Chapel Hill: University of North Carolina Press, 1992), 187.

80 Ellwood, 'Politics of Growth', 20; Kuisel, *Seducing the French*, 79–80. Members of communist unions were categorically excluded from these trips. See McKenzie, *Remaking France*, 174.

81 The English title *A Day's Work* was later changed to *A Tough Day*. Memo Motion Picture Section, 13 August 1951. NARA, RG 469, entry 947, box 32.

82 Quarterly Report, MSA West Germany, 1 January to 31 March 1953. NARA, RG 469, entry 1203, box 6; on reception in France, see Memo Wilson to Kaplan, 1 February 1952. NARA, RG 84, entry 2462, box 36.

83 Berman, *The Primacy of Politics*, 181–84.

84 See Carew, 80; Romero, *European Trade Union Movement*, 191–200.

85 On the reception of the film in France, see McKenzie, *Remaking France*, 167.

86 Romero, *European Trade Union Movement*, 177; De Grazia, *Irresistible Empire*, 347.

87 Production papers and contracts. NA INF 6/34.

88 Hoffman, cited by Price, *The Marshall Plan and Its Meaning*, 122.

Chapter 5

1   1949 Amendments to the Economic Cooperation Act § 102(a). See David M. Crawford, 'United States Foreign Assistance Legislation, 1947–1948'. *The Yale Law Journal* 58, no. 6 (1949): 871–922.

2   See Lundestad, 'Empire by Invitation?', 38.

3   Berghahn, 'The Marshall Plan', 33–34.

4   See Lundestad, 'Empire by Invitation?', 38; Schwartz, 'European Integration', 172; Hogan, *The Marshall Plan*, 194–95.

5   See Lundestad, 'Empire by Invitation?', 37–38.

6   Draft speech, Paul Hoffman, 29 July 1949. NARA, RG 469, entry 1028, box 2.

7   Hardach, *Der Marshall-Plan*, 165.

8   Confidential Report, Information Officers Meeting, 12–16 September 1949. NARA, RG 469, entry 1029, box 4.

9   Ibid.

10 Curt Cardwell, *NSC 68 and the Political Economy of the Early Cold War* (New York: Cambridge University Press, 2011), 128–59.

11 See Hogan, *The Marshall Plan*, 191, 222–23; Hardach, *Der Marshall-Plan*, 163–65.

12 See Schwartz, 'European Integration', 178, 184.

13   Milton Katz, from June 1949 deputy head of ECA Europe, informed the Information Officers about the change. See Protocol Information Officers Meeting Paris, 24–25 October 1949, Statement Roscoe Drummond, Director Information Division. NARA, RG 469, entry 1029, box 4.

14   Hardach, *Der Marshall-Plan*, 164.

15   Lundestad, 'Empire by Invitation?', 39; Hogan, *The Marshall Plan*, 190.

16   See Hardach, *Der Marshall-Plan*, 164; Statement Roscoe Drummond, Minutes Information Officers Meeting Paris, 24–25 October 1949. NARA 469, entry 1029, box 4; Memo Nielsen to William Stone, Dept. of State, 13 October 1949. NARA, RG 469, entry 1028, box 2.

17   Statement Roscoe Drummond, Minutes Information Officers Meeting Paris, 24–25 October 1949. NARA 469, entry 1029, box 4.

18   See also Bruch et al., 'Werben für die Integration', 194.

19   Frank Norall, Minutes, Regional Information and Labor Information Officers Conference, London, 4 April 1950. NARA, RG 469, entry 1029, box 14.

20   Hogan, *The Marshall Plan*, 273.

21   Thomas Schwartz, 'European Integration', 172; Hogan, *The Marshall Plan*, 271.

22   Confidential Report ECA Information Officers Conference, Paris, 25 October 1949. NARA, RG 469, entry 1031, box 1.

23   Bronislaw Geremek, 'The Marshall Plan and European Integration', in *The Marshall Plan. Lessons Learned for the 21st Century*, ed. Sorel and Padoan, 48.

24   Hogan, *The Marshall Plan*, 272.

25   Hardach, *Der Marshall-Plan*, 167–68.

26   Hogan, *The Marshall Plan*, 273.

27   See Hardach, *Der Marshall-Plan*, 167–68.

28   Geremek, 'The Marshall Plan and European Integration', 46–48; Judt, *Postwar*, 156; Berghahn, 'The Marshall Plan', 35.

29   Judt, *Postwar*, 153–55; Geremek, 'The Marshall Plan and European Integration', 48.

30   Elmer D. Graper, 'American Influence on the Attitudes of Western Europe', *Annals of the American Academy of Political and Social Science* 278 (1951): 12–22, 15.

31   Friendly to Harriman, 2 November 1948. NARA, RG 469, entry 1029, box 4. See also Frank Shea, Summary of Meeting, 24–25 October 1949. NARA, RG 469, entry 1029, box 4.

32   Report Eric Stern, Main Findings. Attached to Memo from Stern to Roscoe Drummond, 19 January 1950. NARA, RG 469, entry 1035, box 1.

33   Friendly to Harriman, 2 November 1948. NARA, RG 469, entry 1029, box 4. Frank Shea, Summary of Meeting 24–25 October 1949. NARA, RG 469, entry 1029, box 4.

34   Confidential Report ECA Information Officers Conference, Paris, 25 October 1949. NARA, RG 469, entry 1031, box 1.

35 Ibid. As for the freedom the information officers enjoyed, see, for example, Hall, Interview.

36 Confidential Report ECA Information Officers Conference, Paris, 25 October 1949. NARA, RG 469, entry 1031, box 1.

37 Ibid.

38 Statement Roscoe Drummond, Minutes Information Officers Meeting Paris, 24–25 October 1949. NARA 469, entry 1029, box 4.

39 Fernand Braudel, *The Mediterranean and the Mediterranean World in the Age of Philip II*, Vol. 1 (New York: Harper & Row, 1972), 18.

40 Bruch, 'Die Visualisierung des europäischen Raumes', 509.

41 Many information films sought to present Europe as a natural unity. See Tode, 'Die Grenze als zentrales Motiv', 469.

42 Bonifazio, *Schooling in Modernity*, 165.

43 Bruch et al., 'Werben für die Integration', 207.

44 Nielsen to Norall and Wolff, 14 March 1950. NARA, RG 469, entry 1031, box 2.

45 *Films et Documents* described the film as a geographical lesson on transatlanticism: 'une leçon de géographie sur "Qu'est-ce qu'un transatlantique"'. *Film et Documents* 16, no. 87 (1955): 616.

46 McKenzie, *Remaking France*, 167.

47 See also Tode, 'Die Grenze als zentrales Motiv', 447–51; Bruch and Clemens, 'Die filmische (Re-)Konstruktion', 492–93.

48 The call to remove these artificial barriers, however, does not extend to Eastern Europe. For what separates communist from capitalist Europe is not a national but an ideological barrier, which not even the much-heralded European 'freedom of spirit' can conquer.

49 Bruch, 'Die Visualisierung des europäischen Raumes', 509–11.

50 See also Bonifazio, *Schooling in Modernity*, chapter 4.

51 See Mehring, 'The Promises of "Young Europe": Cultural Diplomacy, Cosmopolitanism, and Youth Culture in the Films of the Marshall Plan', *European Journal of American Studies* 7, no. 2 (2012). Available online: http://ejas.revues .org/9701 (accessed 28 January 2017).

52 See also Bruch et al., 'Werben für die Integration', 81.

53 See, for example, Price, *The Marshall Plan and Its Meaning*, 98, 113, 117.

54 *Monthly Film Bulletin* 20, no. 233, 93.

55 *Drifters* (1929), [Documentary film] Dir. John Grierson, UK: Empire Marketing Board Film Unit.

56 Lothar Wolff to Charles Moffly, 19 November 1949. NARA, RG 469, entry 1030, box 8.

57 Lothar Wolff to Clark Dowsley, ECA Athens, 22 September 1949. NARA, RG 469, entry 1030, box 5.

58 Roland Barthes, *Mythologies* (1972; London: Vintage Classics, 2000), 66.

59 Telegram Nedville Nordness to Lothar Wolff, July 19, 1949. NARA, RG 469, entry 1030, box 12.

60 *The Film User*, no. 77 (1953), 146.

61 'Lidet opbyggelige Genopbygnings-Film', *Nationaltidene*, 1 June 1951; 'Dansk Saglighed – fremmed Fantasi', *Berlingske Tidene*, 1 June 1951; 'Skandinavisk Marshall-Film har Premiere', *Berlingske Aftenavis*, 24 January 1951; 'Filmisk tak for Marshall-hjelpen til Danmark', *SocialDemokraten*, 8 June 1951; 'Forpasset Chance', *Ekstra Bladet*, 1 June 1951.

62 Stuart Schulberg to Dowsley Clark, ECA Greece, 19 June 1950. NARA, RG 469, entry 1030, box 5.

63 Wolfgang Schmale, 'Geschlechtergeschichte Europas – ein "anderer" Blick auf die Geschichte Europas', *Historische Mitteilungen* 28 (2016): 145–61, 151.

64 Genn also spoke the commentary for the *Changing Face of Europe* series. See Bruch et al., 'Werben für die Integration', 203.

65 Ibid., 217.

66 See also Gabriele Clemens, 'Von der Venus von Milo bis zu Jean Monnet – Narrative der europäischen Integration', in *Werben für Europa*, ed. Clemens, 401–38.

67 I analysed an eighteen-minute version spoken in US English from NARA and a twelve-minute German version from the virtual film archive of the German Historical Museum, http://www.dhm.de/filmarchiv/virtuelles-filmarchiv/

68 See also Clemens, 'Europa – nur ein gemeinsamer Markt?', 54.

69 For visions about new forms of living in modern Europe, see Bruch et al., 'Werben für die Integration', 211.

70 Bonifazio, *Schooling in Modernity*, 113.

71 Letter Stuart Schulberg to Victor Vicas regarding the series *1-2-3: A Monthly Review from Europe*, 20 November 1950. DIF, Nachlass Victor Vicas.

Chapter 6

1 Anthony W. Hodgkinson and Rodney E. Sheratsky, *Humphrey Jennings. More than a Maker of Films* (Hanover, London: University Press of New England, 1982), 92.

2 Caleb Crain, 'Surveillance Society. The Mass-Observation Movement and the Meaning of Everyday Life', *The New Yorker*, 2006. Available online: http://www.newyorker.com/magazine/2006/09/11/surveillance-society (accessed 13 January 2017).

3 Kevin Jackson, 'Humphrey Jennings (1907-1950)', in *Land of Promise. The British Documentary Movement 1930-50*, ed. British Film Institute (London: BFI, 2008), 78.

4 Kevin Jackson, 'Dim Little Island', in *Land of Promise*, ed. British Film Institute, 58.

5   Stuart Schulberg, 'Making Marshall Plan Movies', *Film News*, 1951, 10, 19.

6   Hemsing, 'The Marshall Plan's European Film Unit', 273.

7   They had this in common with the journalists of the American sponsored newspaper *Neue Zeitung* in post-war Germany. See Gienow-Hecht, *Transmission Impossible*.

8   The only female filmmakers were the animator Joy Batchelor and the English documentarist Diane Pine, who directed *Men and Machines* (1951). During the war she had worked for the Crown Film Unit and was assistant director to Humphrey Jennings on *The Silent Village* (1943) – a memorial to the Nazi massacre in Lidice in 1942.

9   Peter Cowie, *Swedish Cinema, from Ingeborg Holm to Fanny and Alexander* (Stockholm: Swedish Institute, 1985), 186–87.

10 Alessandra Cori, *Il cinema di Romolo Marcellini: tra storia e società dal colonialismo agli anni'70* (Recco: Le Mani, 2009); Longo, 'Between Documentary and Neorealism', 23–24. Bonifazio, *Schooling in Modernity*, 14, 26. For the ideological continuity in Marcellini's filmmaking, see Bonifazio's illuminating analysis of Marcellini's documentary *Ten Years of Our Life* (Dieci anni della nostra vita, 1953), 179–84.

11 Daniel J. Leab, *Orwell Subverted: The CIA and the Filming of Animal Farm* (University Park: Pennsylvania State University Press, 2007), 76–84.

12 Peter Nau, 'Ein Fond von Schwermut. Wie der Regisseur Victor Vicas die fünfziger Jahre verwandelt hat', *Süddeutsche Zeitung*, 4 March 1999. DFI, Bio V8 Vav-Vis.

13 'Lothar Wolff', *Variety*, 5 October 1988, 158.

14 Tressler, Interview.

15 Ellis, *John Grierson*, 74–109; Barsam, *Nonfiction Film*, 89–90, 95–97, 98–106; Ian Aitken, 'The British Documentary Film Movement', in *The British Cinema Book*, ed. Robert Murphy (London: Palgrave Macmillan, 2009), 177–79.

16 'Shell's Pioneering Films', *Shell Global*. Available online: http://www.shell.com/inside-energy/shells-pioneering-films.html (accessed 30 January 2017). See also Swann, 'The Little State Department: Washington and Hollywood's Rhetoric of the Postwar Audience', in *Hollywood in Europe. Experiences of a Cultural Hegemony*, ed. David W. Ellwood and Rob Kroes (Amsterdam: VU University Press, 1994), 107; Colin Burgess, 'Sixty Years of Shell Film Sponsorship, 1934–94', *Journal of British Cinema and Television* 7, no. 2 (2010): 213–31.

17 A detailed filmography is available online: http://www.halasandbatchelor.co.uk.

18 Longo, 'Between Documentary and Neorealism', 23–24. Bonifazio, *Schooling in Modernity*, 14, 26.

19 The Eastman Museum in Rochester, New York, published a detailed biography of Wolff. Available online: https://eastman.org/lothar-wolff-collection-1926-1987. For *The March of Time*, see Barsam, *Nonfiction Film*, 163–65; Erik Barnouw,

Documentary. A History of the Non-Fiction Film. 2nd rev. edn (New York; Oxford: Oxford University Press, 1993), 121–22.

20 See letters and memos regarding information jobs in NARA, RG 469, entry 1029, box 1.

21 Stuart Schulberg to Henri Claudel, Ministère des Affaires Etrangères, 11 October 1950. NARA, RG 469, entry 1034, box 1.

22 Between 1932 and 1934 John Ferno was a member of the Communist Vereeniging van Arbeiders Fotografen, which sought to document proletarian culture. All biographical information on John Fernhout is taken from the online dossier of the Dutch photo museum: 'John Fernhout (1913–1987). Fotograaf en Cameraman', nederlands fotomuseum. Available online: http://collectie.nederlandsfotomuseum .nl/nl/fotografie-dossiers-2015/95-john-fernhout-1913-1987-fotograaf-en -cameraman (accessed 24 January 2017).

23 John Fernhout, Report of the Activities of the Film Unit of the R.V.D. from November 1944 until June 1945, 31 July 1945. Beeld & Geluid, F 100 John Fernhout.

24 '"Broken Dykes." Generally released', *The Spectator*, 9 August 1945, 11. Available online: http://archive.spectator.co.uk/article/10th-august-1945/11/the-cinema (accessed 13 January 2017).

25 Paul Rotha, *Documentary Film*. 3rd edn (London: Faber and Faber, 1963), 313; 'Biographical Note. Lothar Wolff Collection', Eastman Museum. Available online: https://eastman.org/lothar-wolff-collection-1926-1987 (accessed 13 January 2017).

26 *Tree of Life* (1971), *They Want to Live* (1973), *The Longest Wave* (1974). See Solange De Boer, 'John Fernhout', *Fotolexicon* 17, no. 33 (2000). Available online: http:// journal.depthoffield.eu/vol17/nr33/f01nl/en (accessed 24 January 2017).

27 Rotha, *Documentary Film*, 313.

28 Bruch et al., 'Werben für die Integration', 225.

29 Freedland's interest remained with the topic. He was involved in the production of *The Smuggler's Banquet* (Belgium/Germany 1952), which was the first fiction film of the famous Belgian documentarist Henri Storck. See Gabriele Clemens and Jeanpaul Goergen, 'Will Europe Unite? Filmaktivitäten der Europabewegung', in *Werben für Europa*, ed. Clemens, 174–82.

30 Dalin, 'Dansk dokumentarfilms far'.

31 Sørensen, 'Theodor Christensen'.

32 De Vries, 'When Amsterdam Went UPA'.

33 Martin Pickles, 'What Is Animation? Bob Godfrey in Conversation', *Vertigo Magazine*, no. 23 (2009). Available online: http://www.vertigomagazine.co.uk/ showarticle.php?sel=bac&siz=1&id=1127 (accessed 24 January 2017).

34 For the work and influence of Peter Sachs, see 'The Lost Continent. Exploring the Art and History of British Animation', 26 January 2012. Available online: http://ukanimation.blogspot.no/2012_01_01_archive.html (accessed 24 January 2017).

35 Interview with Dick Taylor in *Animation Nation. Part One: The Art of Persuasion* (2005), [TV documentary] Dir. & Prod: Merryn Threadgould, Alastair Laurence & Tuppence Stone, UK: BBC 4.

36 *Animation Nation. Part One: The Art of Persuasion.*

37 Price, *The Marshall Plan and Its Meaning*, 249.

38 Waldemar Nielsen, cited by ibid, 246.

39 See Press Release, ECA France, 27 March 1951. AN, F60 ter, 392; 'Biographical Note', Helen Paul Kirkpatrick Papers 1930–1998, Five Colleges Archives & Manuscript Collections. Available online: http://asteria.fivecolleges.edu/findaids/sophiasmith/mnsss36_bioghist.html (accessed 24 January 2017).

40 'TIME Chief Frank Shea Speaks here on Monday', *Proscript* 31, no. 4, 16 October 1952, 1.

41 Department of State, *Foreign Service List* (Washington, DC: Office of Public Affairs, 1952), 111; 'Walter T. Ridder, 72, Retired News Executive. Obituary', *The New York Times*, 18 March 1990. Available online: http://www.nytimes.com/1990/03/18/obituaries/walter-t-ridder-72-retired-news-executive.html (accessed 24 January 2017).

42 Berding continued his career in information and public relations, first as a deputy director of the USIA and in 1957 as Assistant Secretary of State for Public Affairs. 'World Affairs Speaker Named', *Toledo Blade*, 13 February 1963, 29. For Berding, see also Ellwood, 'Italian Modernisation', 29.

43 See Longo, 'Between Documentary and Neorealism', 30; see also 'Frank Gervasi, Author and Correspondent, 81. Obituary', *The New York Times*, 22 January 1990. Available online: http://www.nytimes.com/1990/01/22/obituaries/frank-gervasi-author-and-correspondent-81.html (accessed 24 January 2017).

44 'John H. Secondari', in *Encyclopedia of Television*, ed. The Museum of Broadcast Communications. Available online: http://www.museum.tv/eotv/secondarijo.htm (accessed 24 January 2017).

45 'Lothar Wolff', *Variety*, 5 October 1988, 158; Mae Tinee, '"Question 7" Born of "Luther" Film', *Chicago Daily Tribune*, 14 January 1962, W11.

46 Al Friendly to Colonel Gordon E. Textor, OMGUS, 20 April 1949. NARA, RG 469, entry 1029, box 7. Also: Friendly to Textor, 24 May 1949. NARA, RG 469, entry 1029, box 1.

47 'Lothar Wolff', *Variety*, 5 October 1988, 158; Mae Tinee, '"Question 7" Born of "Luther" Film', *Chicago Daily Tribune*, 14 January 1962, W11.

48 Wilson to Friendly, 9 May 1949. NARA, RG 469, entry 1029, box 1.

49 Nuremberg was initiated by Pare Lorentz. See Barnouw, *Documentary*, 175.

50 *Aus einem Deutschen Leben* (Death is My Trade, 1977), Dir. Theodor Kotulla, FRG: Iduna Film GmbH & Westdeutscher Rundfunk.

51 Al Hemsing, ECA Film Unit Paris, 1951–1955. Interview conducted by Robert
    Amerson, 18 April 1989. Foreign Affairs Oral History Collection, Association for
    Diplomatic Studies and Training, Arlington, VA. Available online: http://www.adst
    .org/OH%20TOCs/Hemsing,%20Albert%20E.toc.pdf (accessed 24 January 2017).

52 *Il Tesoro di Rommel* (Rommel's Treasure, 1955), Dir. Romolo Marcellini,
    Italy: Imperial Film and Translux; *La donna piùbella del mondo* (Beautiful but
    Dangerous, 1955), Dir. Robert Z. Leonard, Italy/France: G.E.S.I. Cinematografica
    and Sédif Productions.

53 Longo, *Documentary and Realism*, 19–22, 30–33; 'John H. Secondari', in
    Encyclopedia of Television.

54 W. Nielsen, Memo, The Information Program of the ECA in Europe, cited by Price,
    The Marshall Plan and Its Meaning, 246.

55 The ECA information offices spent $20 million annually on their propaganda
    efforts. Ibid., 245.

56 Minutes Information Officers Meeting Paris, 24–25 October 1949. NARA, 469,
    entry 1029, box 4.

57 Hall, Interview.

58 Minutes Information Officers Meeting Paris, 24–25 October 1949. NARA, 469,
    entry 1029, box 4.

59 In January 1949, the ECA employed a total of 2,926 personnel. See Hardach, *Der
    Marshall-Plan*, 96.

60 ECA (ed.), *A Report on Recovery Progress and United States Aid* (Washington, DC:
    ECA, 1950), 178.

61 Waldemar Nielsen, cited by Price, *The Marshall Plan and Its Meaning*, 246. This
    number does not include the contracted filmmakers.

62 See Hemsing, 'The Marshall Plan's European Film Unit', 271.

63 'Biographical Note', Helen Paul Kirkpatrick Papers 1930–1998, Five Colleges
    Archives & Manuscript Collections. Available online: http://asteria.fivecolleges.edu/
    findaids/sophiasmith/mnsss36_bioghist.html (accessed 24 January 2017).

64 See Hardach, *Der Marshall-Plan*, 96.

65 Memo Nielsen to Friendly, 3 February 1949. Friendly to Ehrlich, 21 February 1949.
    NARA, RG 469, entry 1029, box 1.

66 ECA Information Overseas, 5 June 1948, 1. NARA, RG 469, entry 1029, box 7.

67 Price, *The Marshall Plan and Its Meaning*, 246.

68 Memorandum Frank Shea to Information Officers, 10 November 1949. NARA, RG
    469, entry 1029, box 4. Correspondences and memos indicate that the information
    officers on the ground felt that their ideas and concerns were taken up by the ECA
    headquarters in Paris. See, for example, Dowsley Clark, ECA Greece, to Roscoe
    Drummond, 14 September 1949. NARA, RG 469, entry 1030, box 5.

69 See Letter Frank Norall to Dowsley Clark, ECA Greece, regarding payment of
    transport for John Ferno, 24 April 1950. Clark informs Lothar Wolff on 22 May

1950 that payment for Gallo's transport and equipment in Greece will be deducted from his fee. Memo W.K. Bryan, ECA Greece, to M.E. Pitts, ECA Paris, 12 April 1950. NARA, RG 469, entry 1222, box 2.

70 Minutes, HICOG – ECA Motion Picture Conference, Paris, 30 November to 1 December 1950. NARA, RG 59, entry 5323, box 9.

71 This was for example the case with a film on the German and French steel and coal industry, for which John Ferno was hired to produce an outline. Memo Eugene Rachlis, 17 October 1950. NARA, RG 469, entry 947, box 34.

72 See, for example, subcontracts Victor Vicas Films with G. Regnier (director), J. Dupont (assistant director), J. Fogel, E. Sechan (cinematographers) for the series *1-2-3*. DFI, Nachlass Victor Vicas.

73 Contract ECA-OSR-50-59 with Editorial Film Productions for *The Marshall Plan at Work*, 17 February 1950. NARA, RG 469, entry 1222, box 2.

74 Contract ECA-OSR-466 with Victor Vicas for *1-2-3. The Marshall Plan in Action*, 24 January 1951. DFI, Nachlass Victor Vicas.

75 The Public Health Division returned the script for Doctor for *Ardaknos* with a four-page list of suggestions and corrections, which were incorporated in the final script. Kathryn Walter, Public Health Division to Wolff, 17 February 1950; Wolff to Clark, 21 February 1950. NARA, RG 469, entry 1222, box 2.

76 Cited by Bruch et al., 'Werben für die Integration', 205.

77 Wolff, Rough Outline for a Picture on Naoussa's Spinning Plant, 20 December 1949; Wolff to Cark, First Outline Corinth Canal, 17 February 1950; Wolff to Cark, 26 May 1950; Clark to Wolff, 27 February 1950. NARA, RG 469, entry 1222, box 2.

78 Wolff to Charles Moffly, 19 November 1949. NARA, RG 469, entry 1030, box 8. Longo argues that Secondari was very keen to have his name listed in the titles. See Longo, 'Between Documentary and Neorealism', 29.

79 James L. Shute to Dowsley Cark, 9 June 1950. NARA, RG 469, entry 1222, box 2. See also Longo, 'Between Documentary and Neorealism', 28–29.

80 ECA Standard Contract with Herman van der Horst, Annex Section 4 Approval, 25 January 1952. NARA, RG 469, entry 1335, box 9.

81 Clark to Wolff, 22 May 1950. NARA, RG 469, entry 1222, box 2.

82 Tressler, Interview.

83 Stuart Schulberg to Walter Doyle, ECA Denmark, 26 February 1951. NARA, RG 469, entry 1152, box 2.

84 Hemsing, 'The Marshall Plan's European Film Unit', 273.

85 Schulberg, Proceedings, HICOG – ECA Motion Picture Conference, Paris, 30 November to 1 December 1950. NARA, RG 59, entry 5323, box 9.

86 Longo, 'Between Documentary and Neorealism', 24, also 28–29.

87 Edmundson to Drummond, 1 May 1950. NARA, RG 469, entry 1030, box 12.

88 See press clippings, Beeld & Geluid, H104, Horst, Herman van der; EYE, File 103 Herman van der Horst; EYE, File 181–1 Cannes.

89 Van der Horst to Nilson, 20 April 1952; Kilbon to Nilson, 6 May 1952; Nilson to Van der Horst, 8 May 1952. NARA, RG 469, entry 1335, box 9.

90 Nilson to Kilbon, 8 May 1952. NARA, RG 469, entry 1335, box 9.

91 Barsam, *Nonfiction Film*. 1st edn, 225.

92 For *Corinth Canal*, Ferno received a budget of $15,000, 3,000 of which were his salary. See Van Rens, 'Een Nederlander filmt voor Europe', 71; 'Les films du plan Marshall', 212–13.

93 John Grierson, 'The Nature of Propaganda', in *Grierson on Documentary*, ed. Hardy Forsyth (1942; London: Faber and Faber, 1979), 109–10; Grierson, 'The Bright Example', 188–89; Barsam, *Nonfiction Film*, 115, 152. Aitken, 'British Documentary', 178–79.

94 Tressler, Interview.

95 Cited by Bonifazio, *Schooling in Modernity*, 18.

96 Grierson, 'The Bright Example', 189.

97 John Grierson, cited by Ellis, *John Grierson*, 181.

98 See Aitken, 'British Documentary', 177.

99 My translation. Tressler in Lukas Maurer, 'Kleine Wirklichkeiten. 'Über den Filmemacher Georg Tressler', in *Halbstark. Georg Tressler: zwischen Auftrag und Autor*, ed. Robert Buchschwenter and Lukas Maurer (Wien: Filmarchiv Austria, 2003), 15.

100 Hemsing, 'The Marshall Plan's European Film Unit', 273.

Chapter 7

1   See Longo, 'Between Documentary and Neorealism', 22–23.

2   ECA Information Division Paris, *Economic Cooperation Administration 2nd Year. Overseas Information Program* (Paris: Georges Lang, 1950), 3.

3   Not all of these records survived. The distribution and attendance figures are very well documented for West Germany, Austria, Greece, France and partly Italy. Attendance records for MP film screenings in the other MP countries are scarce or non-existent.

4   Greece, Semi-Annual Report to Congress, 19 December 1949. NARA, RG 59, entry 5323, box 25.

5   Report of HICOG Film program, 15 March 1951. NARA, RG 59, entry 5323, box 1.

6   Report for the Month of July on ECA Information Activities, Trieste, 3 August 1949. NARA, RG 469, entry 1030, box 8.

7   Review of Activities, Information Division Italy, June 1948 to December 1950 (no date, presumably 1951). NARA, RG 469, entry 303, box 2.

8   Quarterly Report, Information Division MSA France (second quarter 1952), 28
    June 1952. NARA, RG 84, entry 2462, box 33.
9   Information Activities in the First Quarter of 1953; Information Activities in the
    Second Quarter of 1953, High Commissioner for Austria. NARA, RG 469, entry
    1203, box 6.
10 Quarterly Report, Information Office MSA West Germany, 1 July to 30 September
    1952. NARA, RG 469, entry 1203, box 6.
11 Information Activities in the Second Quarter of 1953, Public Affairs Division,
    High Commissioner for Austria. NARA, RG 469, entry 1203, box 6; The IIA and
    Communications in Italy, 1950–1952. An Analysis of Semi-Annual Evaluation
    Reports, Bureau of Social Science Research, March 1953. NARA, RG 306, entry
    1007A, box 33.
12 Daniela Treveri Gennari and John Sedgwick, 'Memories in Context: The Social
    and Economic Function of Cinema in 1950s Rome', *Film History* 27, no. 2 (2015):
    76–104, 79.
13 Jostein Gripsrud, 'Film Audiences', in *Oxford Guide to Film Studies*, ed. John Hill
    and Pamela Church Gibson (Oxford, New York: Oxford University Press, 1998),
    207.
14 Annette Kuhn, *An Everyday Magic. Cinema and Cultural Memory* (London: I.B.
    Tauris, 2002), 4.
15 See, for example, Sue Harper, 'A Lower Middle-Class Taste-Community in the
    1930s: Admissions Figures at the Regent Cinema, Portsmouth, UK', *Historical
    Journal of Film, Radio and Television* 24, no. 4 (2004): 565–87; Sue Harper and
    Vincent Porter, 'Moved to Tears: Weeping in the Cinema in Postwar Britain', *Screen*
    37, no. 2 (1996): 153–73; Robert James, 'Cinema-Going in a Port Town, 1914–1951.
    Film Booking Patterns at the Queens Cinema, Portsmouth', *Urban History* 40, no.
    2 (2013): 315–35; Trevor Griffiths, *The Cinema and Cinema-Going in Scotland,
    1896–1950* (Edinburgh: Edinburgh University Press, 2012).
16 See, for example, Kuhn, *An Everyday Magic*; Daniela Treveri Gennari, '"If You Have
    Seen It, You Cannot Forget!": Film Consumption and Memories of Cinema-Going
    in 1950s Rome', *Historical Journal of Film, Radio and Television* 35, no. 1 (2015):
    53–74; Hafsteinsson and Grétarsdóttir, 'Screening Propaganda'.
17 See, for example, John Sedgwick, *Popular Filmgoing in 1930s Britain. A Choice of
    Pleasures* (Exeter: University of Exeter Press, 2000); Joseph Garncarz, *Hollywood
    in Deutschland: zur Internationalisierung der Kinokultur 1925–1990* (Frankfurt
    am Main: Stroemfeld, 2013); Joseph Garncarz, *Wechselnde Vorlieben: über die
    Filmpräferenzen der Europäer 1896–1939* (Frankfurt am Main: Stroemfeld, 2015);
    Treveri Gennari and Sedgwick, 'Memories in Context'.
18 HICOG Report 173 (no date, *c.*1952/53). NARA, RG 306, entry 1005, box 5.
19 HICOG Report 234, 26 May 1956. NARA, RG 306, entry 1005, box 8.
20 HICOG Report 183, June 1953. NARA, RG 306, entry 1005, box 5.

21 See, for example, Frank Mehring, 'Propaganda für Demokratie. Die Filme des Marshallplans. Radiofeature', *Deutschlandfunk*, 8 February 2005. Available online: http://ejas.revues.org/9701 (accessed 30 January 2017).

22 Greece, Semi-Annual Report to Congress, 19 December 1949. NARA, RG 59, entry 5323, box 25.

23 Hafsteinsson and Grétarsdóttir, 'Screening Propaganda', 367–68.

24 Survey Motion Pictures in Greece (*ca.* 1950). NARA, RG 306, entry 1007A, box 27.

25 Richard Brower, USIS Greece to Maurice Rice, Director of USIE, 8 August 1952. NARA, RG 496, entry 1223, box 3.

26 Indicated by later dubbing reports.

27 The IIA and Communications in Italy, 1950–1952. An Analysis of Semi-Annual Evaluation Reports, Bureau of Social Science Research, March 1953. NARA, RG 306, entry 1007A, box 33.

28 Minutes Films Officers Conference, Munich, 19–21 November 1952. NARA, RG 59, entry 5323, box 14.

29 Quarterly Report, MSA Information Office Western Germany, 1 July to 30 September, 1952. NARA, RG 59, entry 5323, box 18.

30 Information Activities in the Second Quarter of 1953, Public Affairs Division, High Commissioner for Austria. NARA, RG 469, entry 1203, box 6.

31 Airgram MSA Norway to State Department, 18 April 1953. NARA, RG 469, entry 947, box 33.

32 Sedgewick, *Popular Filmgoing in 1930s Britain*.

33 Information Activities in the Second Quarter of 1953, Public Affairs Division, High Commissioner for Austria. NARA, RG 469, entry 1203, box 6; Quarterly Reports 1952, MSA West Germany. NARA, RG 59, entry 5323, box 18; Airgram MSA Norway to State Department, 18 April 1953. NARA, RG 469, entry 947, box 33; Report MSA Film Section Activities 1952. NARA, RG 469, entry 1335, box 9; Monthly Activities Report, Special Media Section, 15 September to 15 October 1950. NARA, RG 469, entry 1029, box 18.

34 Inga Millar, ECA Norway, to Patricia Sussmann, Film Unit Paris, 20 July 1951. NARA, RG 469, entry 947, box 33.

35 Thordur Einarsson, ECA Iceland, to William R. Auman, MSA Denmark, 3 November 1952. NARA, RG 469, entry 1153, box 1. See also Hafsteinsson and Grétarsdóttir, 'Screening Propaganda', 361–62.

36 Waldemar Nielsen to Colonel John L. Tappin, Assistant to Milton Katz, 27 May 1949. NARA, RG 469, entry 1028, box 2.

37 Patricia Sussmann to Nils Nilson, 13 March 1953. NARA, RG 469, entry 1223, box 3.

38 Victoria De Grazia, 'Visualizing the Marshall Plan', in *Images of the Marshall Plan in Europe*, ed. Bischof and Stiefel, 30.

39 Thomas Hodges to Waldemar Nielsen, 22 November 1949. NARA, RG 469, entry 1035, box 1.

40 Hans L. Zetterberg, 'The Start of Modern Public Opinion Research', in *The SAGE Handbook of Public Opinion Research*, ed. Wolfgang Donsbach and Michael W. Traugott (Los Angeles, London: SAGE, 2008), 112.

41 Thomas Hodges to Waldemar Nielsen, 27 February 1950. NARA, RG 469, entry 1031, box 2.

42 Contract between ECA and Eric Stern, 2 December 1949. NARA, RG 469, entry 1031, box 2.

43 Thomas Hodges to Bill Auman, 30 November 1949. NARA, RG 469, entry 1035, box 1.

44 Report Eric Stern, Main Findings – Holland, 7; Main Findings – Norway, 3 (no date, presumably November 1949). NARA, RG 469, entry 1035, box 1; Eric Stern, Media Impact Study Netherlands, carried out in December 1950 by Nederlandse Stichting voor Statistieck, The Hague. The survey was based on a controlled and representative sample of 2,000 adults. NARA, RG 306, entry 1007A, box 36.

45 Eric Stern, Media Impact Study Italy, carried out December 1950 by Instituto per le Ricerche Statistiche el'analisi dell Opinione Pubblica, Milano. The survey was based on a controlled and representative sample of 2,548 adults. NARA, RG 306, entry 1007A, box 34.

46 Eric Stern, Main Findings – France (no date, presumably November 1949). NARA, RG 469, entry 1035, box 1.

47 Memo Thomas Hodges to Bill Auman, 30 November 1949. NARA, RG 469, entry 1035, box 1.

48 Schlesinger to Al Friendly, 9 September 1948. NARA, RG 469, entry 1030.

49 Stern to Roscoe Drummond, 19 January 1950. NARA, RG 469, entry 1035.

50 Memo Thomas Hodges to Bill Auman, 30 November 1949. Eric Stern, Main Findings – France (no date, presumably November 1949). NARA, RG 469, entry 1035, box 1.

51 Ibid. On the French opposition against the MP, see Bossuat, *La France, l'aide américaine,* 396, 401; Kuisel, *Seducing the French*, 72–76.

52 Telegram Ministère des Affaires Etrangères to SGCI and other ministries, 16 October 1949; Telegram Ministère des Affaires Etrangères, 13 December 1949. AN, F 60ter 381.

53 Secrétaire SGCI to Président du Conseil, 12 November 1948. AN, F 60ter 381.

54 Eric Stern, Main Findings – France (no date, presumably November 1949). NARA, RG 469, entry 1035, box 1.

55 Eric Stern to Roscoe Drummond, 19 January 1950. NARA, RG 469, entry 1035, box 1.

56 See especially chapter 3 of Kuisel, *Seducing the French*.

57 Secrétaire SGCI to Président du Conseil, 12 November 1948. AN, F 60ter 381.

58 Kuisel, *Seducing the French*; McKenzie, *Remaking France*.

59 Reuss to Friendly, 25 February 1949. NARA, RG 469, entry 1029, box 7.

60 Eric Stern, Media Impact Study, West Germany, carried out September 1950 by Institut für Demaskopie, Allensbach. The survey was based on a controlled and representative sample of 2,500 people in the three Western zones and in West Berlin. NARA, RG 306, entry 1007A, box 29.

61 Eric Stern, Media Impact Study, West Germany, carried out November 1950 by Institut für Demaskopie, Allensbach. NARA, RG 306, entry 1007A, box 30.

62 Siegfried Kracauer, Appeals to the Near and the Middle East. Prepared for the Bureau of Social Research, Columbia University. May 1952. NARA, RG 306, entry 1007A, box 24.

63 No name is mentioned, but it was presumably Joseph Zigman. Report of Trip to US, Chief Documentary Film Unit, HICOG, 1 November 1950. NARA, RG 59, entry 5323, box 9.

64 Ibid.

65 Siegfried Kracauer, Appeals to the Near and the Middle East. Prepared for the Bureau of Social Research, Columbia University. May 1952. NARA, RG 306, entry 1007A, box 24.

66 On the role of religion in shaping the cultures of seeing and the development of visual media, see, for example, Karl Kaser, *Andere Blicke: Religion und visuelle Kulturen auf dem Balkan und im Nahen Osten* (Wien, Köln, Weimar: Böhlau, 2013).

67 The report, conducted on behalf of the ECA by Vergil D. Reed, was based on the analysis of all previously conducted ECA studies, surveys, reports and interviews with ECA staff. NARA, RG 469, entry 1034, box 1.

68 Vergil D. Reed, Report, 2 September 1950, 5. NARA, RG 469, entry 1034, box 1.

69 Waldemar Nielsen to Thomas K. Hodges, ECA Research Unit, 4 October 1950. Some information officers questioned the validity of some of the findings about the Europeans' stance towards the MP. See Roscoe Drummond, Administrator's Staff Meeting, 24 September 1950. NARA, RG 469, entry 1034, box 1.

70 The French communist trade union federation had established *cinéclubs* in many factories. These cinemas also showed Hollywood films that presented the United States in a critical light, such as *Grapes of Wrath* or *Citizen Kane*. See McKenzie, *Remaking France*, 166.

71 M.H. Wiborg, 'Marshall Plan (Side-lights)', attached to letter from American Embassy, 28 September 1949. NARA, RG 469, entry 1028, box 1.

72 Description and Assessment of US Information Services in France, US State Department, 1 October 1952. NARA, RG 84, entry 2462, box 13.

73 Helen and Peter Rathvon, Motion Picture Survey, conducted between 6 February and 26 March 1951, 29. NARA, RG 59, entry 5323, box 24.

74 Rob Kroes, *Photographic Memories: Private Pictures, Public Images, and American History* (Hanover, NH: University Press of New England, 2007), 160.

75 Minutes, HICOG – ECA Motion Picture Conference, Paris, 30 November to 1 December 1950. NARA, RG 59, entry 5323, box 9.

76   Minutes Films Officers Conference, Munich, 19–21 November 1952. NARA, RG
     59, entry 5323, box 14.
77   Henry McNulty, ECA Belgium, to Stuart Schulberg, 18 October 1950. NARA, RG
     469, entry 1034, box 1.
78   The IIA and Communications in Italy, 1950–1952. An Analysis of Semi-Annual
     Evaluation Reports, Bureau of Social Science Research, March 1953. NARA, RG
     306, entry 1007A, box 33.
79   R. Weening to K. Kilban, MSA Netherlands, 6 October 1952. NARA, RG 469, entry
     1335, box 9.
80   Helen and Peter Rathvon, Motion Picture Survey, conducted between 6 February
     and 26 March 1951, 3. NARA, RG 59, entry 5323, box 24.
81   The IIA and Communications in Italy, 1950–1952. An Analysis of Semi-Annual
     Evaluation Reports, Bureau of Social Science Research, March 1953. NARA, RG
     306, entry 1007A, box 33.
82   Review of Activities, Information Division Italy, June 1948 to December 1950 (no
     date, presumably 1951). NARA 469, entry 303, box 2.
83   Ibid.
84   Policy Statement, Information Office, ECA/MSA Mission to Netherlands (1952, no
     exact date). NARA, RG 469, entry 1335, box 9.

Chapter 8

1   Hemsing, 'The Marshall Plan's European Film Unit', 274.
2   Grierson was critical of the commercial distribution of documentaries, believing
    that the cinema's demand for 'a maximum in novelty' and spectacle had a
    corruptive influence. John Grierson, 'Progress and Prospect', in *Grierson on
    Documentary*, ed. Hardy Forsyth (1949; London: Faber and Faber, 1979), 198–99;
    see also Ellis, *John Grierson*, 243.
3   Memorandum of meeting between the Secretary of State and the Economic
    Cooperation Administrator, 24 May 1948. NARA, RG 469, entry 1029, box 2.
4   Memo W. Nielsen to William Stone, Dept. of State, 13 October 1949. NARA, RG
    469, entry 1028, box 2.
5   James W. Brown, Productivity and Technical Assistance Division, Report on visit to
    Norway and Sweden, 14–22 July 1952. NARA, RG 469, entry 1203, box 6.
6   Cultural Liaison of Iceland and the Soviet Union MIR was founded in 1950 in
    Reykjavik. Hafsteinsson and Grétarsdóttir, 'Screening Propaganda', 363.
7   Andrew Berding, cited in a letter by Roscoe Drummond to Robert Mullen, 8
    September 1949. NARA, RG 469, entry 1031, box 2.
8   Tressler, Interview.

9 Some MP films were circulating up to four years in the non-theatrical circuit. Minutes of the Films Officers Conference, Munich, 19–21 November 1952. NARA, RG 59, entry 5323, box 14.

10 Review of Activities, Information Division Italy, June 1948 to December 1950 (no date, presumably 1951). NARA, RG 469, entry 303, box 2.

11 Hemsing, 'The Marshall Plan's European Film Unit', 274.

12 Ralph Weening, Information Office The Netherlands, to Patricia Sussmann, Film Unit Paris, 13 July 1951. NARA, RG 469, entry 1335, box 6. In 1951, the Dutch ECA information office was put in charge of the film programme for neighbouring Belgium and was assigned a motion picture specialist.

13 Herman van der Horst secured commercial distribution rights for *Shoot the Nets!* for the Benelux states and Great Britain, later also for Indonesia and the Dutch West Indies. See Contract ECA-NL-13, 4 July 1950 and Amendment No. 1, 22 July 1953. Beeld & Geluid, H104.

14 Contract MSA-E-87 between Twentieth Century Fox and MSA, 2 April 1952. Various amendments were made to extend the contract. NARA, RG 469, entry 947, box 33.

15 Monthly Activities Report, Special Media Section, 15 September to 15 October 1950. NARA, RG 469, entry 1029, box 18.

16 Monthly Activities Report, Special Media Section, 29 July to 11 August 1950. NARA, RG 469, entry 1029, box 18.

17 Norbert Aping, *The Final Film of Laurel and Hardy: A Study of the Chaotic Making and Marketing of Atoll K.* (Jefferson, NC, London: McFarland, 2008), 14.

18 Monthly Activities Report, Special Media Section, 15 September to 15 October 1950. NARA, RG 469, entry 1029, box 18.

19 Minutes of the Films Officers Conference, Munich, 19–21 November 1952. NARA, RG 59, entry 5323, box 14.

20 Monthly Activities Report, Special Media Section, 15 September to 15 October 1950. NARA, RG 469, entry 1029, box 18.

21 Study of Audience Reactions to *Without Fear*, Report No. 175, HICOG, no precise date (*ca.* 1953 or earlier). NARA, RG 306, entry 1005, box 8.

22 Memo Bent Demer, ECA Denmark, 6 December 1948. NARA, RG 469, entry 1030, box 2.

23 James W. Brown, Productivity and Technical Assistance Division, Report on Visit to Norway and Sweden, 14–22 July 1952. NARA, RG 469, entry 1203, box 6.

24 Thomas Hodges, Research and Analysis Section, to Bill Auman, 30 November 1949. NARA, RG 469, entry 1035, box 1.

25 James W. Brown, Productivity and Technical Assistance Division, Report on visit to Norway and Sweden, 14–22 July 1952. NARA, RG 469, entry 1203, box 6.

26 See Letter Frank R. Shea, Field Branch, to George Gaskill, ECA Germany, 29 June 1949. NARA, RG 469, entry 1031, box 1.

27 Pierre Sorlin, *European Cinemas, European Societies 1939–1990* (New York, London: Routledge, 1991), 89; Neil Sinyard, 'British Film in the 1950s', *BFI Screenonline*. Available online: http://www.screenonline.org.uk/film/id/1147086/ (accessed 27 October 2016). For the number of cinemas, see Alan Burton and Steve Chibnall, *Historical Dictionary of British Cinema* (Lanham, Toronto, Plymouth, UK: The Scarecrow Press, 2013), 158.

28 Zoë Druick, 'At the Margins of Cinema History: Mobile Cinema in the British Empire', *Public*, no. 40 (2012): 118–25; Ellis, *John Grierson*, 96.

29 Ellis, *John Grierson*, 242–44.

30 The other three films were *Adventure in Sardinia*, *Village without Water* and *My Trip Abroad*. Report on MSA Film Section Activities 1952. NARA, RG 469, entry 1335, box 9. Van der Horst's distribution contract with Nederland is archived at Beeld & Geluid, H104.

31 MSA Netherlands, Report of Non-commercial Distribution of 16 mm films January through March 1952; Report on MSA Film Section Activities 1952. NARA, RG 469, entry 1335, box 9.

32 HICOG administered the US occupation zone, but its information activities spanned across the whole territory of the newly created Federal Republic of Germany.

33 See Letter Frank R. Shea, Field Branch, to George Gaskill, ECA Germany, 29 June 1949. NARA, RG 469, entry 1031, box 1.

34 A Report of the Film Program of the Office of the US High Commissioner for Germany, 15 March 1951. NARA, RG 59, entry 5323, box 1.

35 USIS Film Program in Germany, Office of Public Affairs, State Department, 1 August 1954. NARA, RG 469, entry 1203, box 10.

36 Numbers for 1951. Axel Schildt, *Zwischen Abendland und Amerika. Studien zur westdeutschen Ideenlandschaft der 50er Jahre* (München: Oldenbourg, 1999), 169–70.

37 Werner Sollors regularly attended film screenings for children organized by a US cultural centre in Frankfurt. He recalls mainly seeing informational and educational documentaries. Sollors, cited by Mehring, 'Propaganda für Demokratie'; see also Hein-Kremer, *Die amerikanische Kulturoffensive*.

38 A Report of the Film Program of the Office of the US High Commissioner for Germany, 15 March 1951. NARA, RG 59, entry 5323, box 1.

39 USIS Film Program in Germany, Office of Public Affairs, State Department, 1 August 1954. NARA, RG 469, entry 1203, box 10.

40 See Quarterly Report, MSA Information Office Western Germany, 1 October to 31 December 1952, 18. NARA, RG 59, entry 5323, box 18.

41   According to German statistics, the number of screens in West Germany in 1950
     was almost 4,000, with 487 million tickets sold. See http://www.filmportal.de/
     thema/die-1950er-jahre. *Der Spiegel* wrote of 3,895 cinemas in 1950: 'Kino, das
     grosse Traumgeschäft', *Der Spiegel*, 6 September 1950. Available online: http://www
     .spiegel.de/spiegel/print/d-44449216.html (accessed 26 January 2017).

42   Minutes HICOG – ECA Motion Picture Conference, Paris, 30 November to 1
     December 1950. NARA, RG 59, entry 5323, box 9.

43   Statement John Scott, Film Distribution Officer, HICOG. Ibid.

44   Quarterly Report, MSA Information Office Western Germany, 1 October to 31
     December 1952. NARA, RG 59, entry 5323, box 18.

45   See Kaser, *Andere Blicke*, 222. Siegfried Kracauer, Appeals to the Near and the
     Middle East. Prepared for the Bureau of Social Research, Columbia University. May
     1952. NARA, RG 306, entry 1007A, box 24.

46   Memo Waldemar Nielsen, 27 May 1949. NARA, RG 469, entry 1028, box 2.

47   Longo, 'Between Documentary and Neorealism', 11; Elaine Mancini, *Struggles of the
     Italian Film Industry during Fascism, 1930–1935* (Ann Arbor, MI: UMI Research
     Press, 1985), chapter 26.

48   Sorlin, *European Cinemas*, 89–92; Treveri Gennari and Sedgwick, 'Memories in
     Context', 83–88; Treveri Gennari, 'If You Have Seen It, You Cannot Forget!', 56.

49   Dario Edoardo Vigano, 'The Roman Catholic Church, Cinema and the "Culture
     of Dialogue". Italian Catholics and the Movies after the Second World War', in
     Moralizing Cinema. Film, Catholicism and Power, ed. Daniela Biltereyst and Daniela
     Treveri Gennari (New York, London: Routledge, 2014), 37–40.

50   Bureau of Social Science Research, Draft Survey Mass Media of Communication in
     Italy, USIA (no date, presumably 1952/53). NARA, RG 306, entry 1007A, box 33;
     Sorlin, *European Cinemas*, 89, 92.

51   Victoria De Grazia, 'Mass Culture and Sovereignty: The American Challenge to
     European Cinemas, 1920–1960', *The Journal of Modern History* 61, no. 1 (1989):
     82.

52   In 1951, 60 per cent of the gross box-office receipts were derived from US films.
     Bureau of Social Science Research, Draft Survey Mass Media of Communication in
     Italy, USIA (no date, presumably 1952/53). NARA, RG 306, entry 1007A, box 33.

53   Review of Activities, Information Division Italy, June 1948 to December 1950 (no
     date, presumably 1951). NARA 469, entry 303, box 2.

54   Telegram, MSA Information Office Rome, 9 April 1952. NARA, RG 469, entry 947,
     box 32.

55   Plan of Action, 30 June to 31 December 1950, Motion Picture Unit. NARA, RG 469,
     entry 1029, box 18.

56   Telegram, MSA Information Office Rome, 9 April 1952. NARA, RG 469, entry 947,
     box 32.

57 Review of Activities, Information Division Italy, June 1948 to December 1950 (no date, presumably 1951). NARA 469, entry 303, box 2.

58 Bureau of Social Science Research, Draft Survey Mass Media of Communication in Italy, USIA (no date, presumably 1952/53). NARA, RG 306, entry 1007A, box 33.

59 The IIA and Communications in Italy, 1950–1952. An Analysis of Semi-Annual Evaluation Reports, Bureau of Social Science Research, March 1953. NARA, RG 306, entry 1007A, box 33.

60 Report USIS Bologna, May 1951, cited by The IIA and Communications in Italy, 1950–1952. An Analysis of Semi-Annual Evaluation Reports, Bureau of Social Science Research, March 1953. NARA, RG 306, entry 1007A, box 33.

61 Ibid.

62 Ibid.

63 Hayward, *French National Cinema*, 49.

64 A study conducted on behalf of the US embassy in Paris identified 5,999 16-mm theatres (of which one-third were mobile units) in 1953, of which 4,470 operated commercially and 1,529 non-commercially. A Study of Theatrical Distribution in France, submitted to the State Department by the US embassy in France, 18 May 1953. NARA, RG 84, entry 2462, box 13.

65 The import of dubbed foreign films was limited to 186 films (121 from the United States) in 1948; in November 1952 the quota was reduced to 138 foreign films (90 US films). Films shown in their original versions did not fall under the quota, but could only be played at thirty cinemas in France. A Study of Theatrical Distribution in France, submitted to the State Department by the US embassy in France, 18 May 1953. NARA, RG 84, entry 2462, box 13.

66 Ibid.

67 Plan of Action, 30 June to 31 December 1950, Motion Picture Unit; Monthly Activities Report, Special Media Section, 15 September to 15 October 1950. NARA, RG 469, entry 1029, box 18.

68 A Study of Theatrical Distribution in France, submitted to the State Department by the US embassy in France, 18 May 1953. NARA, RG 84, entry 2462, box 13.

69 Foreign Service Inspection Report, Foreign Service Post Paris, December 1951. NARA, RG 84, entry 2462, box 13.

70 Information Activities Report, MSA France, 10 March 1952. NARA, RG 84, entry 2462, box 13.

71 Foreign Service Inspection Report, Foreign Service Post Paris, December 1951. NARA, RG 84, entry 2462, box 13.

72 Pascal Laborderie, 'Le voile sacré. Un film d'éducation populaire dans le réseau du cinéma éducateur laïque', in *L'image dans l'histoire de la formation des adultes*, ed. Françoise Laot (Paris: l'Harmattan, 2010), 31–32.

73 Information Activities Report, MSA France, 10 March 1952; Quarterly Report, MSA France, period ending 30 June 1952. NARA, RG 84, entry 2462, box 13.

74 Memo Mondial Films, H. Kaplan to L.S. Brady, 6 November 1953. NARA, RG 84, entry 2462, box 13. The contract was renewed, but came again under scrutiny in 1955. Audit report of Mondial Films Documentaire, 18 May 1955, USIA. NARA, RG 306, no entry no: Office of the General Council, Copyright Unit, Rights and Permission Files, box 58.

75 Bossuat, *La France, l'aide américaine*, 396, 401.

76 Wilson, Interview; Bossuat, *La France, l'aide américaine*, 401.

77 Telegram, Ministère des Affaires Etrangères to SGCI and other Ministries, 16 October 1949. AN, F 60ter 381. See also Bossuat, *La France, l'aide américaine*, 398–99.

78 The plan included, among other things, the production of three films per month(!). Bossuat, *La France, l'aide américaine*, 399.

79 Patricia Sussmann, Report on Film Distribution in Greece, 13 March 1953. NARA, RG 469, entry 1223, box 3.

80 Arthur Diggle, Labor Information Officer Greece, to Boris Scherbak, MSA Paris, 3 June 1952. NARA, RG 469, entry 1223, box 3.

81 Karalis, *A History of Greek Cinema*, 32, 50.

82 Achilleas Hadjikyriacou, *Masculinity and Gender in Greek Cinema, 1949–1967* (New York, London: Bloomsbury, 2013), 71.

83 Report by American Embassy on Motion Picture Entertainment 35 mm, 19 December 1949. NARA, RG 469, entry 1030, box 5.

84 Patricia Sussmann, Report on Film Distribution in Greece, 13 March 1953. NARA, RG 469, entry 1223, box 3.

85 Memo Arthur Diggle, Labor Information Greece, to Dowsley Clark, MSA Information Greece, 1 July 1952. NARA, RG 496, entry 1223, box 3.

86 Arthur Diggle, Labor Information MSA Greece, to Mary-Emma Pioda, Productivity Division MSA Paris, 19 May 1952. Ibid.

87 Semi-Annual Report to Congress, Greece, 19 December 1949. NARA, RG 59, entry 5323, box 25. Also various memoranda in NARA, RG 469, entry 1223, box 3, file Films, 1 of 2.

88 See report by US Embassy report on visual education and 16 mm equipment in Greece, 16 September 1949. NARA, RG 469, entry 1030, box 5.

89 Arthur Diggle, Labor Information MSA Greece, script for USIS Athens radio broadcast, 20 April 1953. NARA, RG 496, entry 1223, box 3; Memo Martin O'Harrell, Labor Information Athens to Dowsley Clark, Information Division Paris, 27 September 1951; Memo John Gatsos, Field Representative Thessaly, 15 October 1951. NARA, RG 469, entry 1223, box 3.

90 Memo Martin O'Harrell, Labor Information office Athens to Dowsley Clark, Information Division Paris, 27 September 1951; Memo John Gatsos, Field Representative Thessaly, 15 October 1951. NARA, RG 496, entry 1223, box 3.

91 Richard Brower, USIS Greece to Maurice Rice, Director of USIE, 8 August 1952. NARA, RG 496, entry 1223, box 3.

92 Memo Basil Glossotis, 23 October 1951. NARA, RG 496, entry 1223, box 3.

93 Memo Basil Glossotis, 8 November 1951. NARA, RG 496, entry 1223, box 3.

94 Thanos Boilis, Mobile Unit Operator, to Richard Brower, USIS Greece, 3 June 1953. NARA, RG 496, entry 1223, box 3.

95 Ibid.

96 Memo, Richard Brower, USIS Greece, to Robert McCoy, Labor Division MSA, 5 June 1953. NARA, RG 496, entry 1223, box 3.

97 Frank Norall to Waldemar Nielsen, 28 March 1950. NARA, RG 469, entry 1029, box 18.

98 According to a study of the International Motion Picture Service, the number of film programmes in Europe rose from 20,718 in the period July to September 1950 to 63,721 in the period October to December 1951; the ECA programmes increased from 1,628 to 5,065 over the same period. See Bureau of Social Science Research, Report for International Information Administration, State Department, July 1952, Appendix, Table IIIB. NARA, RG 306, entry 1007A, box 34.

99 Bureau of Social Science Research, Report for International Information Administration, State Department, 25 July 1952 NARA, RG 306, entry 1007A, box 34.

100 Ibid., 20, 23.

101 Review of Activities, Information Division Italy, June 1948 to December 1950 (no date, presumably 1951). NARA 469, entry 303, box 2.

102 See, for example, Telegram ECA Italy, 18 August 1950. NARA, RG 469, entry 1029, box 17; The America House Evaluated. A Study of the Effectiveness of the US Information Centers in Germany, Report no. 181, 17 July 1953. NARA, RG 59, entry 5320, box 1.

103 ECA Information Division Paris, *Economic Cooperation Administration 2nd Year.*

Conclusion

1 Milward, *The Reconstruction of Western Europe*, 90–91.

2 Hemsing, 'The Marshall Plan's European Film Unit', 269.

3 Milward, *The Reconstruction of Western Europe*, 113–23.

4 Ellwood, 'The 1948 Elections in Italy'; Saunders, *The Cultural Cold War*, 68, 91.

5 Milward, *The Reconstruction of Western Europe*, 123.

6 International Evaluation Staff (IEV): Averoff Prison Project, Greece, Athens, 11 May 1953. NARA, RG 306, entry 1007A, box 28.

7 HICOG Film Branch, Monthly Synchronisation Report, November 1952. NARA, RG 59, entry 5323, box 14.

8   See Pells, *Not Like Us*, 195.

9   See, for example, Volker Berghahn, *Transatlantische Kulturkriege: Shepard Stone, die Ford-Stiftung und der europäische Antiamerikanismus* (Stuttgart: Franz Steiner Verlag, 2004), 360.

10 For a concise overview of the development of the term Americanization, see Gassert, 'Amerikanismus', 532–38; For a scholarly discussion of the concept of Americanization, see Kuisel, 'Americanization for Historians'; Pells, *Not Like Us*, 158–63, 192–94; Doering-Manteuffel's understanding of Americanization is much narrower and akin to cultural imperialism. Anselm Doering-Manteuffel, 'Amerikanisierung und Westernisierung'. *Docupedia-Zeitgeschichte* (2011). Available online: http://docupedia.de/zg/Amerikanisierung_und_ Westernisierung?oldid=84584 (accessed 30 January 2017).

11 For a thorough analysis of the debate on American influence, see Gienow-Hecht, 'Shame on US?'

12 See De Grazia, *Irresistible Empire*, 554; Kuisel, *Seducing the French*; Pells, *Not Like Us*; Wagnleitner, *Coca-Colonisation*.

13 Cited by Price, *The Marshall Plan and Its Meaning*, 108.

14 Jan Logemann, 'European Imports? European Immigrants and the Transformation of American Consumer Culture from the 1920s to the 1960s', *Bulletin of the German Historical Institute* 52, Spring (2013); Volker R. Berghahn, 'The Debate on "Americanization" among Economic and Cultural Historians', *Cold War History* 10, no. 1 (2010): 110.

15 See Gassert, 'Amerikanismus', 532; see also Kuisel, 'Americanization for Historians', 510.

16 Pells, *Not Like Us*, 11, 21.

17 Doering-Manteuffel, *Amerikanisierung und Westernisierung*; Berghahn, *Transatlantische Kulturkriege*, 16; also Axel Schildt, 'Sind die Westdeutschen amerikanisiert worden? Zur zeitgeschichtlichen Erforschung kulturellen Transfers und seiner gesellschaftlichen Folgen nach dem Zweiten Weltkrieg', *Aus Politik und Zeitgeschichte* 2000, no. 50 (2000): 3–10; Axel Schildt and Arnold Sywottek, '"Reconstruction" and "Modernization": West German Social History during the 1950s', in *West Germany under Construction. Politics, Society, and Culture in the Adenauer Era*, ed. Robert G. Moeller (Ann Arbor: University of Michigan Press, 1997); Günter Bischof and Anton Pelinka, *The Americanization/Westernization of Austria* (New Brunswick, NJ.: Transaction Publishers, 2004); Holger Nehring, '"Westernization": A New Paradigm for Interpreting West European History in a Cold War Context', *Cold War History* 4, no. 2 (2004).

18 De Grazia, *Irresistible Empire*, 229; Heide Fehrenbach, 'Persistent Myths of Americanization: German Reconstruction and the Renationalization of Postwar Cinema 1945–1965', in *Transactions, Transgressions, Transformations*, ed. Fehrenbach and Poiger, 102–3.

19   See Wagnleitner, *Coca-Colonisation*, 267–68, 289. Paul Swann, 'The Little State
       Department', 177–81.

20   Until the First World War, Italy and France had been the world's largest film exporters.
       See De Grazia, *Irresistible Empire*, 63–65. By 1925, the United States had achieved
       control over the film market in many European countries: the market share of
       Hollywood films in 1925 was 66 per cent in Italy, 77 per cent in France and a whopping
       95 per cent in Britain. Only in Germany was Hollywood's market share much lower,
       shrinking to 31.3 per cent after the introduction of sound. See Guback, 'Hollywood's
       International Market', 294; Thomas J. Saunders, *Hollywood in Berlin. American Cinema
       and Weimar Germany* (Berkeley: University of California Press, 1994), 222.

21   De Grazia, 'Mass Culture and Sovereignty', 75. European attempts to defy
       Hollywood's economic and cultural dominance in the interwar years remained
       largely unsuccessful. See Higson and Maltby, 'Film Europe', 4; Guback, 'Hollywood's
       International Market', 297.

22   Wagnleitner, *Coca-Colonisation*, 279–83.

23   Many European governments sought to prevent Hollywood from withdrawing
       their locally earned box-office returns and converting them into US dollars, since
       they suffered an acute dollar shortage on account of trade imbalance. Swann, 'The
       Little State Department', 182.

24   For the desire to revive national film culture and protect it against Hollywood, see
       Fehrenbach, 'Persistent Myths of Americanization', 90–92.

25   OMGUS paid for the distribution costs and used the revenues of impounded and
       rereleased German films to cover the costs. See Wagnleitner, *Coca-Colonisation*,
       288–89, 295; Ulrike Halbritter, 'Der Einfluss der Alliierten Besatzungsmächte auf
       die österreichische Filmwirtschaft und Spielfilmproduktion in den Jahren 1945
       bis 1955' (Master thesis, University of Vienna, Wien, 1993), 29–32; Goergen,
       'Orientierung und Ausrichtung', 38.

26   On the MPEA and its powerful position in Europe, see Guback, 'Hollywood's
       International Market', 299–301; Wagnleitner, *Coca-Colonisation,* 285–86; Sarah
       Street, *British National Cinema* (London, New York: Routledge, 1997), 14–15, 20;
       Hayward, *French National Cinema*, 26–27.

27   The head of the OMGUS motion picture unit in Austria, Eugen Sharin, previously
       an export manager for various Hollywood studios, worked hard to establish the
       most favourable conditions for Hollywood. Already in September 1945 he was able
       to report that the Austrian market was virtually conquered: 'a beautiful, unequalled,
       monopolistic opportunity for the dissemination of information, to say nothing of
       doing some business in the Motion Picture field'. Sharin, 22 September 1945, cited
       by Wagnleitner, *Coca-Colonisation*, 311.

28   Hollywood sought to curb competition from European film industries and tried
       to undermine OMGUS' efforts to revive the German film industry. Fehrenbach,
       'Persistent Myths of Americanization', 88–89.

29 Ibid., 87–88.

30 Beth Burchard, 'Hollywood Stars Speak German!', *HICOG Information Bulletin*, May 1950, 42; Wagnleitner, *Coca-Colonisation*, 320–21.

31 Swann, 'The Little State Department', 188–92.

32 The MPEA distributed the OMGUS newsreel *Welt im Film*, but then replaced it with its own newsreel. Wagnleitner, *Coca-Colonisation*, 316–17.

33 Hollywood films made up 61 per cent of the total days of exhibition in Western Europe in 1951, with the highest percentage in Ireland (80 per cent) and Belgium and Denmark (75 per cent), and the lowest in France and Switzerland (50 per cent). Wagnleitner, *Coca-Colonisation*, 295.

34 Higson and Maltby, 'Film Europe', 21; Fehrenbach and Poiger, 'Americanization Reconsidered', xx.

35 Sorlin, 'European Cinemas', 98. See Garncarz, 'Hollywood in Germany'. Garncarz, 'Hollywood in Deutschland'; Garncarz, 'Wechselnde Vorlieben'; Fehrenbach, 'Persistent Myths of Americanization', 88; Maria Fritsche, *Homemade Men in Postwar Austrian Cinema: Nationhood, Genre and Masculinity* (New York, Oxford: Berghahn Books, 2013), 23–27; Hayward, *French National Cinema*, 27. Jennifer Fay, *Theatres of Occupation. Hollywood and the Reeducation of Postwar Germany* (Minneapolis, MN: University of Minneapolis Press, 2008); Patrick Merziger, 'Americanised, Europeanised or Nationalised? The Film Industry in Europe under the Influence of Hollywood, 1927–1968', *European Review of History: Revue européenne d'histoire* 20, no. 5 (2013): 802–4; Saunders, *Hollywood in Berlin*, 1994.

36 Research Department of the Foreign Office, The Film Situation in all the Zones of Germany, 5 May 1946. NARA, RG 260, entry 260 (A1), box 266.

37 Higson and Maltby, 'Film Europe', 20.

38 See, for example, Garncarz, 'Hollywood in Germany', 100; Heide Fehrenbach, *Cinema in Democratizing Germany: Reconstructing National Identity after Hitler* (Chapel Hill: University of North Carolina Press, 1995), 165–68.

39 Ellwood, 'Propaganda of the Marshall Plan', 226; Ellwood, 'Film and the Marshall Plan', 67.

Sources

Primary Sources

Archival Sources – text records

National Archives and Records Administration, College Park, MD, USA (NARA)

RG 59 Department of State
RG 84 Foreign Service Post Files
RG 260 United States Occupation Headquarters & OMGUS
RG 306 US Information Agency
RG 469 US Foreign Assistance Agencies

National Archives, London-Kew, UK (NA)

FO Foreign Office
INF Ministry of Information
T Treasury

British Film Institute, London, UK (BFI)

Information film companies and filmmakers
Trade papers and film magazines

Archives Nationales, Paris-Pierrefitte, France (AN)

F 60 President du Conseil
F 60ter Le Secrétariat général du Comité interministériel pour les questions de coopération économique européenne (SGCI)

Centre national du cinéma et de l'image animée, Paris, France (CNC)

Dossiers de Commission de Classification – visa d'exploitation

Bundesarchiv, Koblenz, Germany (BA)

B 145 Presse und Informationsdienst der Bundesregierung
B 146 Bundesministerium für den Marshallplan, Abt. Öffentlichkeitsarbeit
B 168 Bundeszentrale für politische Bildung
Z 14 Der Berater für den Marshallplan beim Vorsitzer des Verwaltungsrates des Vereinigten Wirtschaftsgebietes

Deutsches Filminstitut, Frankfurt, France (DFI)

Nachlass Victor Vicas
Pressclippings archive, trade papers and magazines

Forschungsstelle für Zeitgeschichte, Hamburg, Germany (FZH)

Vorlass Heiner Ross Re-education & Film

Beeld & Geluid, Hilversum, The Netherlands

Files John Fernhout, Ytzen Brusse, Herman van der Horst
Press clippings archive

EYE Filmmuseum, Amsterdam, The Netherlands

File Herman van der Horst
File Cinetone Studios

Det Danske Filminstitut, Copenhagen, Denmark

Press clippings archive
Danish MP films

Wienbibliothek, Vienna, Austria

Press clippings archive

Filmmuseum, Vienna, Austria

Trade papers and film magazines

Oral History Interviews

Dixon, Ben Franklin. Officer of Greek Affairs, US State Department. Interview
conducted by Charles Stuart Kennedy, 31 October 1990. Foreign Affairs Oral

History Collection, Association for Diplomatic Studies and Training, Arlington, VA. Available online: www.adst.org.

Hall, Lawrence. ECA Information Division Paris 1948–1950, ECA Turkey 1950–1953. Interview conducted by Hans Tuch, 23 August 1988. Foreign Affairs Oral History Collection, Association for Diplomatic Studies and Training, Arlington, VA. Available online: www.adst.org.

Hemsing, Al. ECA Film Unit Paris 1951–1955. Interview conducted by Robert Amerson, 18 April 1989. Foreign Affairs Oral History Collection, Association for Diplomatic Studies and Training, Arlington, VA. Available online: www.adst.org.

Kirkpatrick, Helen. Head of Information Division, ECA France. Interview conducted by Ann Kasper, 4 April 1990, Session 2. Washington Press Club Foundation – Oral History Collection. Available online: http://beta.wpcf.org/oralhistory/kirk2.html

Tressler, Georg. Austrian filmmaker. Interview conducted by Linda and Eric Christenson, Berlin, 15 February 2004.

Warren, James C. Economic analyst at ECA Athens 1950–1954. Interview conducted by Charles Stuart Kennedy, 22 March 2001. Foreign Affairs Oral History Collection, Association for Diplomatic Studies and Training, Arlington, VA. Available online: www.adst.org.

Wilson, Thomas W., Information Officer ECA UK. Interview conducted by Charles Stuart Kennedy, 30 October 1996. Foreign Affairs Oral History Collection, Association for Diplomatic Studies and Training, Arlington, VA. Available online: www.adst.org.

TV documentaries

Animation Nation. Part One: The Art of Persuasion (2005), [TV documentary] Dir. & Prod: Merryn Threadgould, Alastair Laurence & Tuppence Stone, UK: BBC 4.

The Cold War (1998), [TV documentary series], Prod. Jeremy Isaacs, USA: CNN.

La France made in USA (2007), [TV documentary] Dir. Bob Swaim. France: Arte France.

Websites/online databases

Halas and Batchelor: http://www.halasandbatchelor.co.uk.

Helen Paul Kirkpatrick Papers 1930–1998, Five Colleges Archives & Manuscript Collections: http://asteria.fivecolleges.edu/findaids/sophiasmith/mnsss36_bioghist.html

John Fernhout, Nederlands fotomuseum: http://collectie.nederlandsfotomuseum.nl/nl/fotografie-dossiers-2015/95-john-fernhout-1913-1987-fotograaf-en-cameraman

John H. Secondari, Encyclopedia of Television, The Museum of Broadcast Communications: http://www.museum.tv/eotv/secondarijo.htm

Marshall Plan Filmography, created by Linda Christenson for the George C. Marshall
Foundation, 2002: http://www.marshallfilms.org
Shell Film: http://www.shell.com/inside-energy/shells-pioneering-films.html.
Lothar Wolff Collection, Eastman Museum: https://eastman.org/lothar-wolff-
collection-1926-1987

Printed government publications and catalogues

Archivo Centrale Dello Stato, United States Information Service di Trieste. Catalogo des
fondo cienmatografico (1941–1966). Roma, 2007.
Department of State, Office of Public Affairs (ed.), Foreign Service List. Washington,
DC, 1952.
ECA (ed.), A Report on the Recovery Progress and United States Aid. Washington, DC,
1950.
ECA Service d'Information Mission spéciale en France (ed.), La presse française et le
Plan Marshall. Paris: Chaix-Paris, 1949.
ECA Information Division Paris (ed.), Economic Cooperation Administration 2nd
Year. Overseas Information Program. Paris: Georges Lang, 1950.
Economic Cooperation Administration ECA (ed.),. Catalogue of Documentary Films.
1951.
Interfilm Hamburg (ed.), Tonfilmkatalog. Hamburg: British Information Services, 1951.
Landes-Film-Dienst für Jugend und Volksbildung in West Berlin E.V. (ed.), Europa im
Film. Informationsfilme – 16mm, Ton – der Landes-Film-Dienste für Jugend und
Volksbildung in der Bundesrepublik und West Berlin, no date.
Landesjugendausschuss Hessen (ed.), Schmaltonfilmnachweis (Dokumentar-, Kultur-
und Unterrichtsfilme) für die Bildungsarbeit in Jugendgruppen, no date.
USIS Film-Abteilung Hamburg (ed.), Liste der im Filmarchiv verfügbaren Filme, 1953.
Mutual Security Agency MSA (ed.), Catalogue of Documentary Films. Mutual Security
Agency, 1952.
Ministerpräsident des Landes Nordrhein-Westfalen – Landeszentrale für politische
Bildung (ed.), Europa in Film und Bild. Catalogue. Edited by Bungter, Eduard and
Hendrik Otten. Düsseldorf, 1969.
Staatliche Landesbildstelle Hamburg (ed.), Filmkatalog. Hamburg, 1959.
The Marshall Plan. US Economic Assistance under the European Recovery Program.
April 3, 1948–June 20, 1952. Statistics of Marshall Aid payments. Compiled by
Statistics & Reports Division, Agency for International Development, 17 November
1975. Available online: http://pdf.usaid.gov/pdf_docs/Pdacs197.pdf (accessed 30
January 2017).

Bibliography

Abelshauser, Werner. *Wirtschaft in Westdeutschland 1945–1948: Rekonstruktion und Wachstumsbedingungen in der amerikanischen und britischen Zone* Stuttgart: DVA, 1975.

Abelshauser, Werner. 'Der Kleine Marshallplan. Handelsintegration durch innereuropäische Wirtschaftshilfe 1948–1950'. *Geschichte und Gesellschaft,* Sonderheft 10 (1984): 212–24.

Abelshauser, Werner. 'Kriegswirtschaft und Wirtschaftswunder. Deutschlands wirtschaftliche Mobilisierung für den Zweiten Weltkrieg und die Folgen für die Nachkrieszeit'. *Vierteljahreshefte für Zeitgeschichte* 47, no. 4 (1999): 503–38.

Abelshauser, Werner. 'Deutsche Wirtschaftspolitik zwischen europäischer Integration und Weltmarktorientierung'. In *Das Bundeswirtschaftsministerium in der Ära der Sozialen Marktwirtschaft,* edited by Werner Abelshauser, 482–581. Oldenbourg: De Gruyter, 2016.

Aitken, Ian. 'The British Documentary Film Movement'. In *The British Cinema Book,* edited by Robert Murphy, 177–84. London: Palgrave Macmillan, 2009.

Alsted, Christian. '1949 – en epoke kuliminirer'. In *Kortfilmen og staten,* edited by Christian Alsted and Carl Nørrested, 269–97. Copenhagen: Eventus, 1987.

Aping, Norbert. *The Final Film of Laurel and Hardy. A Study of the Chaotic Making and Marketing of Atoll K.* Jefferson, NC; London: McFarland, 2008.

Arkes, Hadley. *Bureaucracy, the Marshall Plan, and the National Interest.* Princeton, NJ: Princeton University Press, 1972.

Barnouw, Erik. *Documentary. A History of the Non-Fiction Film.* 2nd rev. ed. New York; Oxford: Oxford University Press, 1993.

Barsam, Richard Meran. *Nonfiction Film. A Critical History.* 1st ed. New York: Dutton, 1973.

Barsam, Richard Meran. *Nonfiction Film. A Critical History.* Revised and expanded ed. Bloomington: Indiana University Press, 1993.

Barthes, Roland. *Mythologies.* 1972. London: Vintage Classics, 2000.

Becker-Döring, Claudia. 'Öffentlichkeitsarbeit für den Marshallplan in Westdeutschland am Beispiel von ECA-Dokumentarfilmen'. University of Hamburg, Hamburg, 1998.

Belmonte, Laura A. *Selling the American Way. U.S. Propaganda and the Cold War.* Philadelphia: University of Pennsylvania Press, 2013.

Benz, Wolfgang (ed.). *Deutschland unter alliierter Besatzung 1945–1949/55.* Berlin: Akademie Verlag, 1999.

Bergfelder, Tim. 'National, Transnational or Supranational cinema? Rethinking European Film Studies'. *Media, Culture & Society* 27, no. 3 (2005): 315–31.

Berghahn, Volker. 'Zur Amerikanisierung der westdeutschen Wirtschaft'. In *Vom Marshallplan zur EWG. Die Eingliederung der Bundesrepublik Deutschland in die westliche Welt*, edited by Ludolf Herbst, Bührer Werner and Hanno Sowade, 227–53. München: Oldenbourg, 1990.

Berghahn, Volker. *Transatlantische Kulturkriege: Shepard Stone, die Ford-Stiftung und der europäische Antiamerikanismus.* Stuttgart: Franz Steiner Verlag, 2004.

Berghahn, Volker R. 'The Marshall Plan and the Recasting of Europe's Postwar Industrial Systems'. In *The Marshall Plan. Lessons Learned for the 21st Century*, edited by Eliot Sorel and Pier Carlo Padoan, 29–41. Paris: OECD, 2008.

Berghahn, Volker R. 'The Debate on "Americanization" among Economic and Cultural Historians'. *Cold War History* 10, no. 1 (2010): 107–30.

Berghahn, Volker. *American Big Business in Britain and Germany. A Comparative History of Two 'Special Relationships' in the 20th Century.* Princeton, NJ: Princeton University Press, 2014.

Berman, Sheri. *The Primacy of Politics: Social Democracy and the Making of Europe's Twentieth Century.* New York: Cambridge University Press, 2006.

Bernays, Edward. *Propaganda.* 1928. With an Introduction by Mark Crispin Miller. Brooklyn, NY: IG Publishing, 2005.

Bischof, Günter, and Anton Pelinka. *The Americanization/Westernization of Austria.* New Brunswick, NJ: Transaction Publishers, 2004.

Bischof, Günter, and Dieter Stiefel (eds.). *Images of the Marshall Plan in Europe: Film, Photographs, Exhibits, Posters.* Innsbruck: Studienverlag, 2009.

Boel, Bent. *The European Productivity Agency and Transatlantic Relations, 1953–1961.* Vol. 4, Copenhagen: Museum Tusculanum Press, 2003.

Bonifazio, Paola. *Schooling in Modernity. The Politics of Sponsored Films in Postwar Italy.* Toronto: University of Toronto Press, 2014.

Bonifazio, Paola. 'United We Drill: ENI, Films, and the Culture of Work'. *Annali d'italianistica* 32 (2014): 329–50.

Bossuat, Gérard. *La France, l'aide américaine et la construction européenne, 1944–1954.* Vol. 1, Paris: Ministère de l'Économie et des Finances, 1997.

Braudel, Fernand. *The Mediterranean and the Mediterranean World in the Age of Philip II.* Vol. 1, New York: Harper & Row, 1972.

Bruch, Anne. 'Die Visualisierung des europäischen Raumes'. In *Werben für Europa. Die mediale Konstruktion europäischer Identität durch Europafilme*, edited by Gabriele Clemens, 507–30. Paderborn: Ferdinand Schöningh, 2016a.

Bruch, Anne. 'Karten, Dia- und Organigramme – Die Visualisierung des europäischen Raumes und seiner politischen Ordnung'. In *Werben für Europa. Die mediale Konstruktion europäischer Identität durch Europafilme*, edited by Gabriele Clemens, 507–30. Paderborn: Ferdinand Schöningh, 2016b.

Bruch, Anne, and Gabriele Clemens. 'Die filmische (Re-)Konstruktion des Europäer'. In *Werben für Europa. Die mediale Konstruktion europäischer Identität durch Europafilme*, edited by Gabriele Clemens, 489–506. Paderborn: Ferdinand Schöningh, 2016.

Bruch, Anne, Gabriele Clemens, Jeanpaul Goergen, and Thomas Tode. 'Das Werben für die Integration Europas in den Marshallplan-Filmen'. In *Werben für Europa. Die mediale Konstruktion europäischer Identität durch Europafilme*, edited by Gabriele Clemens, 191–226. Paderborn: Ferdinand Schöningh, 2016.

Bruzzi, Stella. *New Documentary. A Critical Introduction*. 2nd ed. London; New York: Routledge, 2006.

Buchheim, Christoph. *Die Wiedereingliederung Westdeutschlands in die Weltwirtschaft 1945–1958*. München: Oldenbourg, 1990.

Bührer, Werner. *Westdeutschland in der OEEC: Eingliederung, Krise, Bewährung 1947–1961*. München: Oldenbourg, 1997.

Burgess, Colin. 'Sixty Years of Shell Film Sponsorship, 1934–94'. *Journal of British Cinema and Television* 7, no. 2 (2010): 213–31.

Burk, Kathleen. 'The Marshall Plan: Filling in Some of the Blanks'. *Contemporary European History* 10, no. 2 (2001): 267–94.

Burton, Alan, and Steve Chibnall. *Historical Dictionary of British Cinema*. Lanham; Toronto; Plymouth, UK: The Scarecrow Press, 2013.

Cardwell, Curt. *NSC 68 and the Political Economy of the Early Cold War*. New York: Cambridge University Press, 2011.

Carew, Anthony. 'The Anglo-American Council on Productivity (1948–52): The Ideological Roots of the Post-War Debate on Productivity in Britain'. *Journal of Contemporary History* 26, no. 1 (1991): 49–69.

Carew, Anthony. 'The Politics of Productivity and the Politics of Anti-Communism: American and European Labour in the Cold War'. In *The Cultural Cold War in Western Europe, 1945–1960*, edited by Giles Scott-Smith and Hans Krabbendam, 73–91. London: Frank Cass, 2003.

Carter, Erica. 'Alice in the Consumer Wonderland: West German Case Studies in Gender and Consumer Culture'. In *West Germany under Construction. Politics, Society, and Culture in the Adenauer Era*, edited by Robert G. Moeller, 347–71. Ann Arbor: University of Michigan Press, 1997a.

Carter, Erica. *How German Is She? Postwar West German Reconstruction and the Consuming Woman*. Ann Arbor: University of Michigan Press, 1997b.

Castillo, Greg. *Cold War on the Home Front. The Soft Power of Midcentury Design*. Minneapolis; London: University of Minnesota Press, 2010.

Clemens, Gabriele. 'Umerziehung durch Film. Britische und Amerikanische Filmpolitik in Deutschland 1945–1949'. In *Mediale Mobilmachung II: Hollywood, Exil, Nachkriegszeit*, edited by Harro Segeberg, 243–71. München: Ferdinand Schöningh Verlag, 2004.

Clemens, Gabriele. 'Europa – nur ein gemeinsamer Markt? Die Öffentlichkeitsarbeit für den europäischen Integrationsprozess am Beispiel der Europafilme zwischen Marshallplan und Römischen Verträgen 1947–1957'. In *Vom gemeinsamen Markt zur europäischen Unionsbildung. 50 Jahre Römische Verträge 1957–2007*, edited by Michael Gehler, 45–62. Wien; Köln; Weimar: Böhlau, 2009.

Clemens, Gabriele. 'Von der Venus von Milo bis zu Jean Monnet – Narrative der europäischen Integration'. In *Werben für Europa. Die mediale Konstruktion europäischer Identität durch Europafilme*, edited by Gabriele Clemens, 401–38. Paderborn: Ferdinand Schöningh, 2016.

Clemens, Gabriele (ed.). *Werben für Europa. Die mediale Konstruktion europäischer Identität durch Europafilme*. Paderborn: Ferdinand Schöningh, 2016.

Converse, Elliott Vanveltner. *Rearming for the Cold War, 1945–1960*. Washington, DC: Historical Office, Office of the Secretary of Defense, 2011.

Cori, Alessandra. *Il cinema di Romolo Marcellini: tra storia e società dal colonialismo agli anni'70*. Recco: Le Mani, 2009.

Cowie, Peter. *Swedish Cinema, from Ingeborg Holm to Fanny and Alexander*. Stockholm: Swedish Institute, 1985.

Crawford, David M. 'United States Foreign Assistance Legislation, 1947–1948'. *The Yale Law Journal* 58, no. 6 (1949): 871–922.

Crew, David F. 'Gender, Media and Consumerism in Germany, 1920s–1950s'. *Journal of Social History* (1998): 395–402.

Cromwell, William C. 'The Marshall Plan, Britain and the Cold War'. *Review of International Studies* 8, no. 4 (1982): 233–49.

Cronin, James E. 'The Marshall Plan and Cold War Political Discourse'. In *The Marshall Plan: Fifty Years After*, edited by Martin Schain, 281–93. New York: Palgrave, 2001.

Cull, Nicholas John. '"The Man Who Invented Truth": The Tenure of Edward R. Murrow as Director of the United States Information Agency during the Kennedy Years'. In *Across the Blocs. Cold War Cultural and Social History*, edited by Patrick Major and Rana Mitter, 23–48. London; Portland, OR: Frank Cass, 2004.

Cullen, Stephen Michael. *In Search of the Real Dad's Army: the Home Guard and the Defence of the United Kingdom, 1940–1944*. Barnsley: Pen & Sword Military, 2011.

Dalin, Steen. 'Dansk dokumentarfilms far'. *filmmagasinet ekko* (2014). Available online: http://www.ekkofilm.dk/artikler/dansk-dokumentarfilms-far/

De Boer, Solange. 'John Fernhout'. *Fotolexicon* 17, no. 33 (2000). Available online: http://journal.depthoffield.eu/vol17/nr33/f01nl/en

De Grazia, Victoria. 'Mass Culture and Sovereignty: The American Challenge to European Cinemas, 1920–1960'. *The Journal of Modern History* 61, no. 1 (1989): 53–87.

De Grazia, Victoria. *Irresistible Empire: America's Advance through Twentieth-Century Europe*. Cambridge, MA: Belknap Press of Harvard University Press, 2005.

De Grazia, Victoria. 'Visualizing the Marshall Plan'. In *Images of the Marshall Plan in Europe: Film, Photographs, Exhibits, Posters*, edited by Günter Bischof and Dieter Stiefel, 25–37. Innsbruck: Studienverlag, 2009.

De Vries, Jan Willem. 'When Amsterdam Went UPA: Dutch Modern Cartoons in the 1950s' (2013). Available online: http://www.cartoonbrew.com/cartoon-modern/when-amsterdam-went-upa-dutch-modern-cartoons-in-the-1950s-90904.html (accessed 24 January 2017).

Dingemans, Ralph, and Romme Rian. *Nederland en het marshall-plan, een bronnenoverzicht en filmografie 1947–1953*. Den Haag: Algemeen Rijksarchief, 1997.

Doering-Manteuffel, Anselm. 'Amerikanisierung und Westernisierung'. *Docupedia-Zeitgeschichte* (2011). Available online: http://docupedia.de/zg/Amerikanisierung_und_Westernisierung?oldid=84584

Druick, Zoë. 'At the Margins of Cinema History: Mobile Cinema in the British Empire'. *Public*, no. 40 (2012): 118–25.

Dyer MacCann, Richard. 'Film and Foreign Policy: The USIA, 1962–67'. *Cinema Journal* 9, no. 1 (1969): 23–42.

Eichengreen, Barry J. *The European Economy since 1945*. Princeton, NJ: Princeton University Press, 2007.

Eitzen, Dirk. 'When Is a Documentary? Documentary as a Mode of Reception'. *Cinema Journal* 35, no. 1 (1995): 81–102.

Ellis, Jack C. *John Grierson. Life, Contributions, Influence*. Carbondale, IL: Southern Illinois University Press, 2000.

Ellis, Jack C., and Betsy A. McLane. *A New History of Documentary Film*. 2nd ed. New York; London: Continuum, 2006.

Ellwood, David. 'The American Challenge and the Origins of the Politics of Growth'. In *Making the New Europe. European Unity and the Second World War*, edited by Michael Leonard Smith and Peter M. R. Stirk, 184–99. London; New York: Pinter Publishers, 1990.

Ellwood, David. 'The Marshall Plan and the Politics of Growth'. In *Shaping Postwar Europe. European Unity and Disunity 1945–1957*, edited by Peter M.R. Stirk and David Willis, 15–26. London: Pinter Publishers, 1991.

Ellwood, David. *Rebuilding Europe: Western Europe, America and Postwar Reconstruction*. London; New York: Longman, 1992.

Ellwood, David. 'The Impact of the Marshall Plan on Italy; the Impact of Italy on the Marshall Plan'. In *Cultural Transmission and Receptions: American Mass Culture in Europe*, edited by Rob Kroes, Robert W. Rydell and Doeko F.J. Bosscher, 100–24. Amsterdam: VU University Press, 1993a.

Ellwood, David. 'The 1948 Elections in Italy. A Cold War Propaganda Battle'. *Historical Journal of Film, Radio and Television* 13, no. 1 (1993b): 19–33.

Ellwood, David. '"You too can be like us." Selling the Marshall Plan'. *History Today* 48, no. 10 (1998): 33–39.

Ellwood, David. 'Italian Modernisation and the Propaganda of the Marshall Plan'. In *The Art of Persuasion. Political Communication in Italy from 1945 to the 1990s*, edited by Luciano Cheles and Lucio Spinoza, 23–48. Manchester, NH: Manchester University Press, 2001.

Ellwood, David. 'The Propaganda of the Marshall Plan in Italy in a Cold War Context'. *Intelligence & National Security* 18, no. 2 (2003): 225–36.

Ellwood, David. 'Film and the Marshall Plan'. In *Images of the Marshall Plan in Europe: Film, Photographs, Exhibits, Posters*, edited by Günter Bischof and Dieter Stiefel, 61–68. Innsbruck: Studienverlag, 2009.

Ellwood, David. *The Shock of America. Europe and the Challenge of the Century*. 1st ed. Oxford: Oxford University Press, 2012.

Esposito, Chiarella. *America's Feeble Weapon. Funding the Marshall Plan in France and Italy, 1948–1950*. Westport, CT: Greenwood Press, 1994.

Fay, Jennifer. *Theatres of Occupation. Hollywood and the Reeducation of Postwar Germany*. Minneapolis, MN: University of Minneapolis Press, 2008.

Fehrenbach, Heide. *Cinema in Democratizing Germany: Reconstructing National Identity after Hitler*. Chapel Hill: University of North Carolina Press, 1995.

Fehrenbach, Heide. 'Persistent Myths of Americanization: German Reconstruction and the Renationalization of Postwar Cinema 1945–1965'. In *Transactions, Transgressions, Transformations: American Culture in Western Europe and Japan*, edited by Heide Fehrenbach and Uta G. Poiger, 81–108. Oxford; New York: Berghahn, 2000.

Fehrenbach, Heide, and Uta G. Poiger. 'Americanization Reconsidered. Introduction'. In *Transactions, Transgressions, Transformations. American Culture in Western Europe and Japan*, edited by Heide Fehrenbach and Uta G. Poiger, xiii–xxxiv. New York: Berghahn Books, 2000.

Fluck, Winfried. 'The Americanization of Modern Culture: A Cultural History of the Popular Media'. In *Romance with America? Essays on Culture, Literature, and American Studies*, edited by Laura Bieger and Johannes Voelz, 239–67. Heidelberg: Winter, 2009.

Fritsche, Maria. 'Der filmische Blick im Museum. Dekonstruktion des Eigenen und Fremden im US-amerikanischen Informationsfilm Wie die Jungen sungen (R: Georg Tressler, 1954)'. *Österreichische Zeitschrift für Volkskunde* 114, no. 3 (2011): 349–66.

Fritsche, Maria. *Homemade Men in Postwar Austrian Cinema: Nationhood, Genre and Masculinity*. New York; Oxford: Berghahn Books, 2013.

Fuchs, Eckhardt, Anne Bruch, and Michael Annegarn-Gläß. 'Educational Films: A Historical Review of Media Innovation in Schools'. *Journal of Educational Media, Memory, and Society* 8, no. 1 (2016): 1–13.

Gaddis, John Lewis. *The Cold War. A New History*. New York: Penguin Press, 2005.

Gardellini, Robert. *Produktivität und französische Wirtschaft*. Wiesbaden: Springer, 1965.

Garncarz, Joseph. 'Hollywood in Germany. The Role of American Films in Germany, 1925–1990'. In *Hollywood in Europe. Experiences of a Cultural Hegemony*, edited by David W. Ellwood and Rob Kroes, 94–135. Amsterdam: VU University Press, 1994.

Garncarz, Joseph. 'Hollywood in Deutschland: zur Internationalisierung der Kinokultur 1925 – 1990'. Frankfurt am Main: Stroemfeld, 2013.

Garncarz, Joseph. *Wechselnde Vorlieben: über die Filmpräferenzen der Europäer 1896–1939*. Frankfurt am Main: Stroemfeld, 2015.

Gassert, Philipp. 'Amerikanismus, Antiamerikanismus, Amerikanisierung'. *Archiv für Sozialgeschichte* 39 (1999): 531–61.

Gendrault, Camille. 'Coproductions between France and Italy during the Post-war Period: The Building Up of a Transnational Audience?' In *Transnational Cinema in Europe*, edited by Manuel Palacio and Jörg Türschmann, 61–76. Zürich; Berlin: LIT, 2013.

Geremek, Bronislaw. 'The Marshall Plan and European Integration'. In *The Marshall Plan. Lessons Learned for the 21st Century*, edited by Eliot Sorel and Pier Carlo Padoan, 43–50. Paris: OECD, 2008.

Gienow-Hecht, Jessica. 'Shame on US? Academics, Cultural Transfer, and the Cold War: A Critical Review'. *Diplomatic History* 24, no. 3 (2000): 465–94.

Gienow-Hecht, Jessica C.E. *Transmission Impossible. American Journalism as Cultural Diplomacy in Postwar Germany, 1945–1955*. Baton Rouge: Louisiana State University Press, 1999.

Gienow-Hecht, Jessica C.E. 'Culture and the Cold War in Europe'. In *The Cambridge History of the Cold War*, edited by Melvyn P. Leffler and Odd Arne Westad, 398–419. Cambridge: Cambridge University Press, 2010a.

Gienow-Hecht, Jessica C.E. 'What Are We Searching For? Culture, Diplomacy, Agents, and the State'. In *Searching for a Cultural Diplomacy*, edited by Jessica C.E. Gienow-Hecht and Mark C. Donfried, 5–12. New York: Berghahn Books, 2010b.

Gimello-Mesplomb, Frédéric. 'The Economy of 1950s Popular French Cinema'. *Studies in French Cinema* 6, no. 2 (2006): 141–50.

Girvin, Brian. 'Ireland and the Marshall Plan: A Cargo Cult in the North Atlantic?' In *Explorations in OEEC History*, edited by Richard T. Griffiths, 61–71. Paris: Organisation for Economic Co-operation and Development, 1997.

Goergen, Jeanpaul. 'Blick nach vorne: Re-orientation-Filme unter HICOG 1949–1952'. In *Schuld und Sühne? Kriegserlebnis und Kriegsdeutung in deutschen Medien der Nachkriegszeit (1945–1961)*, edited by Ursula Heukenkamp, 415–28. Amsterdam: Rodopi, 2001.

Goergen, Jeanpaul. 'Orientierung und Ausrichtung. Die amerikanische Dokumentarfilmproduktion "Zeit im Film 1949–1952"'. In *Lernen Sie diskutieren! Re-education durch Film: Strategien der westlichen Alliierten nach 1945*, edited by Heiner Ross, 33–54. Berlin: Cinegraph Babelsberg, Berlin-Brandenburgisches Centrum für Filmforschung, 2005.

Goergen, Jeanpaul. 'Verbreitung der Europafilme in der Bundesrepublik'. In *Werben für Europa. Die mediale Konstruktion europäischer Identität durch Europafilme*, edited by Gabriele Clemens, 337–54. Paderborn: Ferdinand Schöningh, 2016.

Graper, Elmer D. 'American Influence on the Attitudes of Western Europe'. *Annals of the American Academy of Political and Social Science* 278 (1951): 12–22.

Grierson, John. 'First Principles of Documentary (1932–1934)'. In *Nonfiction Film: Theory and Criticism*, edited by Richard Barsam, 19–30. New York: Dutton, 1976.

Grierson, John. 'The Nature of Propagand'. 1942. In *Grierson on Documentary*, edited by Hardy Forsyth, 101–10. London: Faber and Faber, 1979.

Grierson, John. 'Documentary: The Bright Example'. 1947. In *Grierson on Documentary*, edited by Hardy Forsyth, 187–93. London: Faber and Faber, 1979.

Grierson, John. 'Progress and Prospect'. 1949. In *Grierson on Documentary*, edited by Hardy Forsyth, 194–202. London: Faber and Faber, 1979.

Griffiths, Trevor. *The Cinema and Cinema-Going in Scotland, 1896–1950*. Edinburgh: Edinburgh University Press, 2012.

Gripsrud, Jostein. 'Film Audiences'. In *Oxford Guide to Film Studies*, edited by John Hill and Pamela Church Gibson, 202–11. Oxford; New York: Oxford University Press, 1998.

Guback, Thomas. 'Hollywood's International Market'. In *Film Theory. Critical Concepts in Media and Cultural Studies*, edited by K.J. Shepherdson, Philip Simpson and Andrew Utterson, 293–311. London: Routledge, 2004.

Hadjikyriacou, Achilleas. *Masculinity and Gender in Greek Cinema, 1949–1967*. New York; London: Bloomsbury, 2013.

Hafsteinsson, Sigurjón Baldur, and Tinna Grétarsdóttir. 'Screening Propaganda: The Reception of Soviet and American Film Screenings in Rural Iceland, 1950–1975'. *Film History* 23, no. 4 (2011): 361–75.

Hahn, Brigitte. *Umerziehung durch Dokumentarfilm? Ein Instrument amerikanischer Kulturpolitik im Nachkriegsdeutschland (1945–1953)*. Berlin: Lit Verlag, 1993.

Hahn, Brigitte. 'Dokumentarfilm im Dienste der Umerziehung. Amerikanische Filmpolitik 1945–1953'. In *Lernen Sie diskutieren! Re-education durch Film: Strategien der westlichen Alliierten nach 1945*, edited by Heiner Ross, 19–32. Berlin: Cinegraph Babelsberg, Berlin-Brandenburgisches Centrum für Filmforschung, 2005.

Halbritter, Ulrike. 'Der Einfluss der Alliierten Besatzungsmächte auf die österreichische Filmwirtschaft und Spielfilmproduktion in den Jahren 1945 bis 1955'. Master thesis, University of Vienna, Wien, 1993.

Hardach, Gerd. *Der Marshall-Plan. Auslandshilfe und Wiederaufbau in Westdeutschland 1948–1952*. München: dtv, 1994.

Harper, Sue. 'A Lower Middle-Class Taste-Community in the 1930s: Admissions Figures at the Regent Cinema, Portsmouth, UK'. *Historical Journal of Film, Radio and Television* 24, no. 4 (2004): 565–87.

Harper, Sue. 'Fragmentation and Crisis: 1940s Admissions Figures at the Regent Cinema, Portsmouth, UK'. *Historical Journal of Film, Radio and Television* 26, no. 3 (2006): 361–94.

Harper, Sue, and Vincent Porter. 'Moved to Tears: Weeping in the Cinema in Postwar Britain'. *Screen* 37, no. 2 (1996): 153–73.

Harris, George S. *Troubled Alliance. Turkish-American Problems in Historical Perspective, 1945–1971*. Washington, DC: American Enterprise Institute for Public Policy Research, Hoover Institution on War, Revolution and Peace, 1972.

Hayward, Susan. *French National Cinema*. London; New York: Routledge, 1993.

Hediger, Vinzenz, and Patrick Vonderau. *Films that Work. Industrial Film and the Productivity of Media*. Amsterdam: Amsterdam University Press, 2009.

Heffelfinger, Elizabeth. 'Foreign Policy, Domestic Fiction: Government-Sponsored Documentaries and Network Television Promote the Marshall Plan at Home'. *Historical Journal of Film, Radio and Television* 28, no. 1 (2008): 1–21.

Hein-Kremer, Maritta. *Die amerikanische Kulturoffensive. Gründung und Entwicklung der amerikanischen Information Centers in Westdeutschland und West-Berlin 1945–1955*. Köln: Böhlau, 1996.

Hemsing, Albert. 'The Marshall Plan's European Film Unit, 1948–1955. A Memoir and Filmography'. *Historical Journal of Film, Radio and Television* 14, no. 3 (1994): 269–97.

Higson, Andrew. 'The Limiting Imagination of National Cinema'. In *Cinema and Nation*, edited by Mette Hjort and Scott MacKenzie, 63–74. London; New York: Routledge, 2000.

Higson, Andrew. 'The Concept of National Cinema'. In *The European Cinema Reader*, edited by Catherine Fowler, 132–42. London: Routledge, 2002.

Higson, Andrew, and Richard Maltby. '"Film Europe" and "Film America": An Introduction'. In *'Film Europe' and 'Film America'. Cinema, Commerce and Cultural Exchange 1920–1939*, edited by Andrew Higson and Richard Maltby, 1–31. Exeter: University of Exeter Press, 1999.

Hitchcock, William I. *The Struggle for Europe. The Turbulent History of a Divided Continent, 1945–2002*. New York: Anchor Books, 2004.

Hitchcock, William I. 'The Marshall Plan and the Creation of the West'. In *The Cambridge History of the Cold War*, edited by Melvyn P. Leffler and Odd Arne Westad, 154–74. Cambridge; New York: Cambridge University Press, 2010.

Hodgkinson, Anthony W., and Rodney E. Sheratsky. *Humphrey Jennings. More Than a Maker of Films*. Hanover; London: University Press of New England, 1982.

Hogan, Michael J. *The Marshall Plan: America, Britain, and the Reconstruction of Western Europe 1947–1952*. Cambridge, UK; New York: Cambridge University Press, 1987.

Huston, James A. *Outposts and Allies. U.S. Army Logistics in the Cold War, 1945–1953*. Cranbury; London: Associated University Presses, 1988.

Jackson, Kevin (ed.). *The Humphrey Jennings Film Reader*. Manchester: Carcanet, 1993.

Jackson, Kevin. 'Dim Little Island'. In *Land of Promise. The British Documentary Movement 1930–1950*, edited by British Film Institute, 58. London: BFI, 2008a.

Jackson, Kevin. 'Humphrey Jennings (1907–1950)'. In *Land of Promise. The British Documentary Movement 1930–1950*, edited by British Film Institute, 77–79. London: BFI, 2008b.

James, Robert. 'Cinema-Going in a Port Town, 1914–1951. Film Booking Patterns at the Queens Cinema, Portsmouth'. *Urban History* 40, no. 2 (2013): 315–35.

Jarvie, Ian. 'The Postwar Economic Foreign Policy of the American Film Industry: Europe 1945–1950'. *Film History* 4, no. 4 (1990): 277–88.

Jarvie, Ian. 'The Cold War and the Movie Industry'. *Historical Journal of Film, Radio and Television* 28, no. 2 (2008): 241–47.

Jeffreys-Jones, Rhodri. 'Eternal Vigilance? 50 Years of the CIA'. In *Studies in Intelligence*, edited by Rhodri Jeffreys-Jones and Andrew Christopher, 21–40. London; Portland: Cass, 1997.

Judt, Tony. *Postwar. A History of Europe since 1945*. London: Vintage, 2010.

Karalis, Vrasidas. *A History of Greek Cinema*. New York: Continuum, 2012.

Kaser, Karl. *Andere Blicke: Religion und visuelle Kulturen auf dem Balkan und im Nahen Osten*. Wien; Köln, Weimar: Böhlau, 2013.

Kindleberger, Charles P. *Marshall Plan Days*. 1987. Abingdon: Routledge, 2010.

Koppes, Clayton R., and Gregory D. Black. 'What to Show the World: The Office of War Information and Hollywood, 1942–1945'. *The Journal of American History* 64, no. 1 (1977): 87–105.

Krige, John. *American Hegemony and the Postwar Reconstruction of Science in Europe*. Cambridge, MA; London: MIT, 2006.

Kroes, Rob. *If You've Seen One, You've Seen the Mall. Europeans and American Mass Culture*. Urbana: University of Illinois Press, 1996.

Kroes, Rob. *Photographic Memories: Private Pictures, Public Images, and American History*. Hanover; New Hampshire: University Press of New England, 2007.

Kroes, Rob, Robert W. Rydell, and Doeko F.J. Bosscher. 'Introduction'. In *Cultural Transmission and Receptions: American Mass Culture in Europe*, edited by Rob Kroes, Robert W. Rydell and Doeko F.J. Bosscher, vii–xii. Amsterdam: VU University Press, 1993.

Krueger, Dieter. 'Der "Koreaschock" 1950'. In *Korea – ein vergessener Krieg?: Der militärische Konflikt auf der koreanischen Halbinsel 1950–1953 im internationalen Kontext*, edited by Bernd Bonwetsch and Matthias Uhl, 167–76. München: Oldenbourg, 2012.

Kuhn, Annette. *An Everyday Magic. Cinema and Cultural Memory*. London: I.B. Tauris, 2002.

Kuisel, Richard. 'Commentary. Americanization for Historians'. *Diplomatic History* 24, no. 3 (2000): 509–15.

Kuisel, Richard F. *Seducing the French. The Dilemma of Americanization*. Berkeley; Los Angeles, CA: University of California Press, 1993.

Kuisel, Richard F. 'The French Cinema and Hollywood. A Case Study of Americanization'. In *Transactions, Transgressions, Transformations: American Culture in Western Europe and Japan*, edited by Heide Fehrenbach and Uta G. Poiger, 208–23. Oxford; New York: Berghahn, 2000.

Kunczik, Michael, and Eva Johanna Schweitzer. 'The Use of Public Opinion Research in Propaganda'. In *The SAGE Handbook of Public Opinion Research*, edited by Wolfgang Donsbach and Michael W. Traugott, 104–12. Los Angeles, CA; London: SAGE, 2008.

Laborderie, Pascal. 'Le voile sacré. Un film d'éducation populaire dans le réseau du cinéma éducateur laïque'. In *L'image dans l'histoire de la formation des adultes*, edited by Françoise Laot, 31–48. Paris: l'Harmattan, 2010.

LaFeber, Walter. *America, Russia, and the Cold War, 1945–2002.* 10th ed. New York: McGraw-Hill, 2003.

Leab, Daniel J. *Orwell Subverted: The CIA and the Filming of Animal Farm.* University Park: Pennsylvania State University Press, 2007.

Lippmann, Walter. *Public Opinion.* 1922. New York; London: Free Press Paperbacks, 1997.

Loewy, Ronny. 'Atrocity Pictures. Alliierte Filmaufnahmen aus den befreiten Konzentrations- und Vernichtungslagern'. In *Lernen Sie diskutieren! Re-education durch Film: Strategien der westlichen Alliierten nach 1945,* edited by Heiner Ross, 89–96. Berlin: Cinegraph Babelsberg, 2005.

Logan, Philip C. *Humphrey Jennings and British Documentary Film: A Re-assessment.* Farnham: Ashgate, 2011.

Logemann, Jan. 'European Imports? European Immigrants and the Transformation of American Consumer Culture from the 1920s to the 1960s'. *Bulletin of the German Historical Institute* 52, no. Spring (2013): 113–33.

Longo, Regina M. 'Between Documentary and Neorealism: Marshall Plan Films in Italy (1948–1955)'. *California Italian Studies* 3, no. 2 (2012a): 1–45. Available online: http://escholarship.org/uc/item/0dq0394d#page-1

Longo, Regina M. 'Marshall Plan Films in Italy 1948–1955: Cinema as Soft Power'. PhD thesis, University of California, Santa Barbara, 2012b.

Lundestad, Geir. 'Empire by Invitation? The United States and Western Europe, 1945–1952'. *Journal of Peace Research* 23, no. 3 (1986): 263–77.

Lynch, Frances M.B. *France and the International Economy. From Vichy to the Treaty of Rome.* London; New York: Routledge, 1997.

Machado, Barry. *In Search of a Usable Past. The Marshall Plan and Postwar Reconstruction Today.* Lexington, VA: George C. Marshall Foundation, 2007.

Machado, Barry. 'A Usable Marshall Plan'. In *The Marshall Plan. Lessons Learned for the 21st Century,* edited by Eliot Sorel and Pier Carlo Padoan, 51–68. Paris: OECD, 2008.

Mai, Gunther. *Der Alliierte Kontrollrat in Deutschland: 1945–1948. Alliierte Einheit – deutsche Teilung?* München: Oldenbourg, 1995.

Maier, Charles S. 'The Politics of Productivity: Foundations of American International Economic Policy after World War II'. *International Organization* 31, no. 4 (1977): 607–33.

Maier, Charles S. 'Alliance and Autonomy: European Identity and U.S. Foreign Policy Objectives in the Truman Years'. In *The Truman Presidency,* edited by Michael J. Lacey, 273–98. Cambridge: Woodrow Wilson International Center for Scholars, 1989.

Maier, Charles S. 'The World Economy and the Cold War in the Middle of the Twentieth Century'. In *The Cambridge History of the Cold War,* edited by Melvyn P. Leffler and Odd Arne Westad, 44–66. Cambridge; New York: Cambridge University Press, 2010.

Maier, Charles S., and Günter Bischof. *The Marshall Plan and Germany. West German Development within the Framework of the European Recovery Program.* New York; Oxford: Berg, 1991.

Mancini, Elaine. *Struggles of the Italian Film Industry during Fascism, 1930–1935*. Ann Arbor, MI: UMI Research Press, 1985.

Maurer, Lukas. 'Kleine Wirklichkeiten. Über den Filmemacher Georg Tressler'. In *Halbstark. Georg Tressler: zwischen Auftrag und Autor*, edited by Robert Buchschwenter and Lukas Maurer, 11–30. Wien: Filmarchiv Austria, 2003.

McKenzie, Brian Angus. *Remaking France: Americanization, Public Diplomacy, and the Marshall Plan*. New York: Berghahn, 2005.

Mehring, Frank. 'Propaganda für die Demokratie? Deutschland und das 'Neue Europa' in den Filmen des Marshallplans' (2005). Available online: http://www.dhm.de/filmarchiv/film-im-kontext/propaganda/

Mehring, Frank. 'The Promises of "Young Europe": Cultural Diplomacy, Cosmopolitanism, and Youth Culture in the Films of the Marshall Plan'. *European Journal of American Studies* 7, no. 2 (2012). Available online: http://ejas.revues.org/9701

Merziger, Patrick. 'Americanised, Europeanised or Nationalised? The Film Industry in Europe under the Influence of Hollywood, 1927–1968'. *European Review of History: Revue européenne d'histoire* 20, no. 5 (2013): 793–813.

Miller, Mark Crispin. 'Introduction'. In Edward Bernays. *Propaganda*. 1928, 9–33. Brooklyn, NY: IG Publishing, 2005.

Milward, Alan S. *The Reconstruction of Western Europe, 1945–51*. Berkley; Los Angeles, CA: University of California Press, 1984.

Milward, Alan S. 'Was the Marshall Plan Necessary?' *Diplomatic History* 13, no. 2 (1989): 231–53.

Nehring, Holger. '"Westernization": A New Paradigm for Interpreting West European History in a Cold War Context'. *Cold War History* 4, no. 2 (2004): 175–91.

Nichols, Bill. 'The Voice of Documentar'. In *Movies and Methods. An Anthology*, edited by Bill Nichols, 258–73. Berkeley; London: University of California Press, 1985.

Osgood, Kenneth A. 'Propaganda'. In *Encyclopedia of American Foreign Policy*, edited by Alexander DeConde et al., 239–54. New York: Charles Scribner's Sons, 2002.

Pells, Richard H. *Not Like Us. How Europeans Loved, Hated, and Transformed American Culture since World War II*. New York: Basic Books, 1997.

Pfister, Eugen. *Europa im Bild: Imaginationen Europas in Wochenschauen in Deutschland, Frankreich, Großbritannien und Österreich 1948–1959*. Göttingen: V&R unipress, 2014.

Pharo, Helge. 'Norway, the United States and the Marshall Plan, 1947–52'. In *Explorations in OEEC History*, edited by Richard T Griffiths, 73–85. Paris: Organisation for Economic Co-operation and Development, 1997.

Philipsen, Ingeborg. 'Out of Tune: The Congress for Cultural Freedom in Denmark 1953–1960'. In *The Cultural Cold War in Western Europe, 1945–1960*, edited by Giles Scott-Smith and Hans Krabbendam, 237–53. London: Frank Cass, 2003.

Pickles, Martin. 'What Is Animation? Bob Godfrey in Conversation'. *Vertigo Magazine*, no. 23 (2009). Available online: http://www.vertigomagazine.co.uk/showarticle.php?sel=bac&siz=1&id=1127

Poiger, Uta G. *Jazz, Rock, and Rebels: Cold War Politics and American Culture in a Divided Germany*. Berkeley; London: University of California Press, 2000.

Pollard, Robert A. *Economic Security and the Origins of the Cold War, 1945–1950*. New York: Columbia University Press, 1985.

Pommerin, Reiner. 'The United States and the Armament of the Federal Republic of Germany'. In *The American Impact on Postwar Germany*, edited by Reiner Pommerin, 15–33. Providence: Berghahn Books, 1997.

Price, Harry B. *The Marshall Plan and Its Meaning*. Ithaca, NY: Cornell University Press, 1955.

Pulju, Rebecca J. *Women and Mass Consumer Society in Postwar France*. Cambridge: Cambridge University Press, 2011.

Purdue, A.W. 'The Transformative Impact of World War II'. *European History Online (EGO)*, (2016). Available online: http://www.ieg-ego.eu/purduea-2016-en.

Rainer, Christiane, and Dieter Stiefel. '"Helping People to Help Each Other". Die Marshallplanfilme fuer Österreich'. In *Besetzte Bilder. Film, Kultur und Propaganda in Österreich 1945–1955*, edited by Karin Moser, 409–37. Wien: Filmarchiv Austria, 2005.

Rajak, Svetozar. 'The Cold War in the Balkans, 1945–1956'. In *The Cambridge History of the Cold War*, edited by Melvyn P. Leffler and Odd Arne Westad, 198–220. Cambridge; New York: Cambridge University Press, 2010.

Reeves, Nicholas. 'Film Propaganda and Its Audience: The Example of Britain's Official Films during the First World War'. *Journal of Contemporary History* 18, no. 3 (1983): 463–94.

Reeves, Nicholas. *The Power of Film Propaganda. Myth or Reality?* London: Cassell, 1999.

Reichert, Ramón. 'Die Filme des "Österreichischen Produktivitätszentrums" 1950–1987: Ein Beitrag zur Diskussion um den Film als historische Quelle'. *Relation. Beiträge zur vergleichenden Kommunikationsforschung* 7, no. 1+2 (2000): 69–128.

Reichert, Ramón. 'Film und Rationalisierung. Die Produktivitätsfilme des ÖPWZ während des European Recovery Program'. *Blätter für Technikgeschichte* 62 (2000): 45–111.

Reichert, Ramón. 'Marshallplan und Film: Intermedialität, narrative Strategien und Geschlechterrepräsentation'. In *Besetzte Bilder. Film, Kultur und Propaganda in Österreich 1945–1955*, edited by Karin Moser, 439–73. Wien: Filmarchiv Austria, 2005.

Reichert, Ramón, 'Culture and Identity Politics: Narrative Strategies in Austrian Marshall Plan Movies'. In *Images of the Marshall Plan in Europe: Film, Photographs, Exhibits, Posters*, edited by Günter Bischof and Dieter Stiefel, 129–38. Innsbruck: Studienverlag, 2009.

Risso, Linda. '"Enlightening Public Opinion": A Study of NATO's Information Policies between 1949 and 1959 Based on Recently Declassified Documents'. *Cold War History* 7, no. 1 (2007): 45–74.

Risso, Linda. "'Don't Mention the Soviets!" An Overview of the Short Films Produced by the NATO Information Service between 1949 and 1969'. *Cold War History* 9, no. 4 (2009): 501–12.

Romero, Federico. *The United States and the European Trade Union Movement, 1944–1951*. Chapel Hill: University of North Carolina Press, 1992.

Rosenberg, Emily S. *Spreading the American Dream: American Economic and Cultural Expansion, 1890–1945*. 1st edn. New York: Hill and Wang, 1982.

Rotha, Paul. *Documentary Film*. 3rd ed. London: Faber and Faber, 1963.

Rother, Rainer. 'Selling Democracy – Winning the Peace'. In *Selling Democracy. Winning the Peace*, edited by Rainer Rother, 6–11. Berlin: 55. Internationale Filmfestspiele Berlin, 2005.

Saunders, Frances Stonor. *The Cultural Cold War. The CIA and the World of Arts and Letters*. New York: The New Press, 2000.

Saunders, Thomas J. *Hollywood in Berlin. American Cinema and Weimar Germany*. Berkeley: University of California Press, 1994.

Schildt, Axel. *Zwischen Abendland und Amerika. Studien zur westdeutschen Ideenlandschaft der 50er Jahre*. München: Oldenbourg, 1999.

Schildt, Axel. 'Sind die Westdeutschen amerikanisiert worden? Zur zeitgeschichtlichen Erforschung kulturellen Transfers und seiner gesellschaftlichen Folgen nach dem Zweiten Weltkrieg'. *Aus Politik und Zeitgeschichte* 2000, no. 50 (2000): 3–10.

Schildt, Axel, and Detlef Siegfried. *Deutsche Kulturgeschichte: die Bundesrepublik – 1945 bis zur Gegenwart*. München: Hanser, 2009.

Schildt, Axel, and Arnold Sywottek. '"Reconstruction" and "Modernization": West German Social History during the 1950s'. In *West Germany under Construction. Politics, Society, and Culture in the Adenauer Era*, edited by Robert G. Moeller, 413–43. Ann Arbor: University of Michigan Press, 1997.

Schmale, Wolfgang. 'Geschlechtergeschichte Europas – ein "anderer" Blick auf die Geschichte Europas'. *Historische Mitteilungen* 28 (2016): 145–61.

Schreurs, Rik. 'A Marshall Plan for Africa? The Overseas Territories Committee and the Origins of European Co-Operation in Africa'. In *Explorations in OEEC History*, edited by Richard T. Griffiths, 87–98. Paris: Organisation for Economic Co-operation and Development, 1997.

Schröder, Hans-Jürgen. 'Marshall Plan Propaganda in Austria and Western Germany'. In *The Marshall Plan in Austria*, edited by Günter Bischof, Anton Pelinka and Dieter Stiefel, 212–46. New Brunswick, NJ; London: Transaction Publishers, 2000.

Schröder, Hans-Jürgen. 'Informationskampagnen zum Marshall-Plan'. *Orientierungen zur Wirtschafts- und Gesellschaftspolitik*, no. 112 (2007): 43–48.

Schröder, Hans-Jürgen. 'Visualizing the Marshall Plan in Western Germany: Films, Exhibits, Posters'. In *Images of the Marshall Plan in Europe: Film, Photographs, Exhibits, Posters*, edited by Günter Bischof and Dieter Stiefel, 69–86. Innsbruck: Studienverlag, 2009.

Schwartz, Thomas. 'European Integration and the "Special Relationship". Implementing the Marshall Plan in the Federal Republic'. In *The Marshall Plan and Germany. West German Development within the Framework of the European Recovery Program*, edited by Charles S. Maier and Günter Bischof, 171–215. New York; Oxford: Berg, 1991.

Scott, Ian S. '*Why We Fight* and *Projections of America*. Frank Capra, Robert Riskin, and the Making of World War II Propaganda'. In *Why We Fought: America's Wars in Film and History*, edited by Peter C. Rollins and John E. O'Connor, 242–57. Lexington: University Press of Kentucky, 2008.

Scott Lucas, W. 'Beyond Freedom, Beyond Control: Approaches to Culture and the State-Private Network in the Cold War'. In *The Cultural Cold War in Western Europe, 1945–1960*, edited by Giles Scott-Smith and Hans Krabbendam, 53–72. London: Frank Cass, 2003.

Scott-Smith, Giles. *The Politics of Apolitical Culture: The Congress for Cultural Freedom and the Political Economy of American Hegemony 1945–1955*. London; New York: Routledge, 2002.

Scott-Smith, Giles. *Networks of Empire. The US State Department's Foreign Leader Program in the Netherlands, France, and Britain 1950–70*. Brussels: Peter Lang, 2008.

Sedgwick, John. *Popular Filmgoing in 1930s Britain. A Choice of Pleasures*. Exeter: University of Exeter Press, 2000.

Shaw, Tony. *British Cinema and the Cold War. The State, Propaganda, and Consensus*. London; New York: I.B. Tauris, 2006.

Shaw, Tony. *Hollywood's Cold War*. Edinburgh: University of Edinburgh Press, 2007.

Simon, Herbert A. 'Birth of an Organization: The Economic Cooperation Administration'. *Public Administration Review* 13, no. 4 (1953): 227–36.

Smith, Bruce Lannes. 'Propaganda'. *Encyclopædia Britannica*. Available online: https://global.britannica.com/topic/propaganda

Sørensen, Lars-Martin. 'Theodor Christensen – Pioner, Polemiker, Propagandist'. *Kosmorama*, no. 253 (2014). Available online: http://www.kosmorama.org/Artikler/Theodor-Christensen.aspx

Sørensen, Lars-Martin. *Dansk Film under Nazismen*. Copenhagen: Lindhardt og Ringhof Forlag, 2014.

Sørensen, Lars-Martin. 'En svækket stat forstærker sin propaganda'. In *Sculpting the Past*. Det Danske Filminstitut, 2014. Available online: http://www.sculptingthepast.dk/Temaer/Besaettelsen/En-svaekket-stat.aspx.

Sørensen, Vibeke. *Denmark's Social Democratic Government and the Marshall Plan, 1947–1950*. Copenhagen: Museum Tusculanum Press, University of Copenhagen, 2001.

Sorlin, Pierre. *European Cinemas, European Societies 1939–1990*. New York; London: Routledge, 1991.

Spagnolo, Carlo. 'Reinterpreting the Marshall Plan: The Impact of the European Recovery Programme in Britain, France, Western Germany and Italy (1947–1952)'.

In *The Postwar Challenge: Cultural, Social, and Political Change in Western Europe, 1945–58*, edited by Dominik Geppert, 275–98. Oxford: Oxford University Press, 2003.

Stephan, Alexander. 'Cold War Alliances and the Emergence of Transatlantic Competition: An Introduction'. In *The Americanization of Europe. Culture, Diplomacy, and Anti-Americanism after 1945*, edited by Alexander Stephan, 1–20. New York; Oxford: Berghahn, 2006.

Stephan, Alexander (ed.). *The Americanization of Europe. Culture, Diplomacy, and Anti-Americanism after 1945*. New York; Oxford: Berghahn, 2006.

Street, Sarah. *British National Cinema*. London; New York: Routledge, 1997.

Swann, Paul. 'The Little State Department: Washington and Hollywood's Rhetoric of the Postwar Audience'. In *Hollywood in Europe. Experiences of a Cultural Hegemony*, edited by David W. Ellwood and Rob Kroes, 176–95. Amsterdam: VU University Press, 1994.

Theien, Iselin. 'Velferd eller moralisme? Regulering av forbruk i et historisk perspektiv'. *Tidsskrift for samfunnsforskning*, no. 4 (2011): 529–41.

Thompson, Kristin. 'The End of the "Film Europe" Movement'. In *History on/and/in Film*, edited by Tom O'Regan and Brian Shoesmith, 45–56. Perth: History and Film Association of Australia, 1987.

Thomson, C. Claire, and Mary Hilson. 'Beauty in Bacon: "The Pattern of Co-operation" and the Export of Postwar Danish Democracy'. *Kosmorama*, no. 255 (2014). Available online: http://www.kosmorama.org/Artikler/Beauty-in-Bacon.aspx.

Thys, Marianne. 'Idéologies. Les Films du Plan Marshall'. In *Mémoires du Monde. Prologue de Jean-Louis Jean-Louis Comolli*, edited by Marianne Thys, 225–40. Crisnée; Bruxelles: Cinémathèque de la Fédération Wallonie-Bruxelles, 2011.

Tobia, Simona. *Advertising America. The United States Information Service in Italy (1945–1956)*. Milano: LED, 2008.

Tode, Thomas. 'Die Grenze als zentrales Motiv der Europafilm-Rhetorik'. In *Werben für Europa. Die mediale Konstruktion europäischer Identität durch Europafilme*, edited by Gabriele Clemens, 439–69. Paderborn: Ferdinand Schöningh, 2016.

Treveri Gennari, Daniela. '"If You Have Seen It, You Cannot Forget!": Film Consumption and Memories of Cinema-Going in 1950s Rome'. *Historical Journal of Film, Radio and Television* 35, no. 1 (2015): 53–74.

Treveri Gennari, Daniela, and John Sedgwick. 'Memories in Context: The Social and Economic Function of Cinema in 1950s Rome'. *Film History* 27, no. 2 (2015): 76–104.

Üstün, Senem. 'Turkey and the Marshall Plan. Strive for Aid'. *The Turkish Yearbook of International Relations* XXVII (1997): 31–52.

van Rens, Noël. 'Een Nederlander filmt voor Europe. TERUG NAAR HUIS van John Fernhout'. *Jaarboek Mediageschiedenis* 7 (1995): 63–90.

van Rens, Noël. 'Les films du plan Marshall: 1948–192. La naissance de l'Europe dans l'image'. In *L' âge d'or du documentaire. Europe: Années cinquante. Grande-Bretagne,*

Belgique, Pays-Bas, Danemark, Norvège, Suède Europe, edited by Roger Odin, 187–226. Paris; Montréal: l'Harmattan, 1998.

Vigano, Dario Edoardo. 'The Roman Catholic Church, Cinema and the "Culture of Dialogue". Italian Catholics and the Movies after the Second World War'. In *Moralizing Cinema. Film, Catholicism and Power*, edited by Daniela Biltereyst and Daniela Treveri Gennari, 35–48. New York; London: Routledge, 2014.

Wagner, Peter. *Mythos Marshall-Plan. Das europäische Weideraufbauprogramm in der deutschen öffentlichen Meinung 1947-1952*. Pfaffenweiler: Centaurus Verlagsgesellschaft, 1996.

Wagnleitner, Reinhold. *Coca-Colonisation und Kalter Krieg. Die Kulturmission der USA in Österreich nach dem Zweiten Weltkrieg*. Wien: Verlag für Gesellschaftskritik, 1991.

Wagnleitner, Reinhold. *Coca-Colonization and the Cold War: The Cultural Mission of the United States in Austria after the Second World War*. Chapel Hill: University of North Carolina Press, 1994.

Wagnleitner, Reinhold. 'American Cultural Diplomacy, the Cinema and the Cold War in Central Europe'. Working Paper. Minneapolis: University of Minnesota, Center for Austrian Studies. Available online: http://hdl.handle.net/11299/5697

Webb, Kieron. 'What a Life!' In *Land of Promise. The British Documentary Movement 1930-1950*, edited by British Film Institute, 57. London: BFI, 2008.

Weckel, Ulrike. *Beschämende Bilder. Deutsche Reaktionen auf alliierte Dokumentarfilme über befreite Konzentrationslager*. Stuttgart: Steiner, 2012.

Wheeler, George S. *Die Amerikanische Politik in Deutschland (1945-1950)*. Berlin: Kongress-Verlag, 1958.

Whelan, Bernadette. 'Marshall Plan Publicity and Propaganda in Italy and Ireland, 1947-1951'. *Historical Journal of Film, Radio and Television* 23, no. 4 (2003): 311–28.

Whitfield, Stephen J. *The Culture of the Cold War*. Baltimore: Johns Hopkins University Press, 1991.

Wiesen, S. Jonathan. *West German Industry and the Challenge of the Nazi Past, 1945-1955*. Chapel Hill, NC; London: University of North Carolina Press, 2001.

Wilford, Hugh. 'Calling the Tune? The CIA, the British Left and the Cold War, 1945-1960'. In *The Cultural Cold War in Western Europe, 1945-1960*, edited by Giles Scott-Smith and Hans Krabbendam, 41–50. London: Frank Cass, 2003.

Winston, Brian. '"The Last Refuge of a Scoundrel": Propaganda in eine Kulture, die Propaganda ablehnt'. In *Die Kamera als Waffe. Propagandabilder des Zweiten Weltkrieges*, edited by Rainer Rother and Judith Prokasky, 255–66. München: edition text + kritik, 2010.

Woller, Hans. 'Zur Demokratiebereitschaft in der Provinz des amerikanischen Besatzungsgebiets: aus den Stimmungsberichten des Ansbacher Oberbürgermeisters an die Militärregierung 1946-1949'. *Vierteljahreshefte für Zeitgeschichte* 3, no. 2 (1983): 335–64.

Zetterberg, Hans L. 'The Start of Modern Public Opinion Research'. In *The SAGE Handbook of Public Opinion Research*, edited by Wolfgang Donsbach and Michael W. Traugott, 104–12. Los Angeles, CA; London: SAGE, 2008.

Zimmermann, Peter, and Kay Hoffmann. *Geschichte des dokumentarischen Films in Deutschland, Drittes Reich, 1933–1945*. Vol. 3, Stuttgart: Reclam, 2005.

Zweiniger-Bargielowska, Ina. *Austerity in Britain. Rationing, Controls, and Consumption, 1939–1955*. Oxford: Oxford University Press, 2000.

Names and Film Title Index

Acheson, Dean 76, 132
Adventure in Sardinia 54, 187–8, 210, 220, 241
Air of Freedom 67, 85–7, 241
All My Ships 95–7, 165, 175, 241
And So They Live 162
Animal Farm 90, 159
Appian Way, The 56, 242
Aquila 28, 38, 43–4, 242
As the Young Ones Sing 87–8, 116, 139, 174, 242
Asseo, Jacques 100, 249, 251, 252
Assignment for Europe 242

Batchelor, Joy 90, 110, 159, 161, 166, 251
Beautiful but Dangerous 169
Belgium - A Year of Progress 242
Berding, Andrew 54–5, 98, 104, 109, 168, 176, 207–8
Bernays, Edward 12, 190
Bigger Potato Crops 30, 35, 242
Breakthrough 32, 53, 149, 153–5, 160, 187, 242
Bull's Eye for Farmer Pietersen 30, 114–15, 187, 242

Calabria 242
Care of Tractors 242
Caroline, the Cow 97, 118, 242, 277 n.82
Changing Face of Europe, The 30, 49, 55, 64, 81, 108, 135–6, 139, 149, 152, 157, 173, 178, 210, 242–3, 285
Christensen, Theodor 95–6, 165, 175, 241
Ciampino aeroporto d'Europa 243
City out of Darkness 35, 67, 210, 243
Clark, Dowsley 59–60, 174
Clarke & Hornby 69, 71, 252
Clarke, Dennis 71
Clay, Lucius 64–5
Clearing the Lines (The Changing Face of Europe, no. 5) 243
Concerning Dairy Production 33–4, 117, 243
Control of Water 69, 243

Corinth Canal 59–60, 143, 150–1, 162–3, 173, 184, 187–8, 243
Cotton 56, 243
Council of Europe, The 139, 164, 243

Dalrymple, Ian 157, 173, 242, 243
Death is My Trade 169
Diary of Timothy, A 157
Doctor for Ardaknos, A 162, 173, 243
Don Camillo and Peppone 94, 211
Drifters 144
Drummond, Roscoe Falk, Lauritz 133–4, 170–1, 197
Dunkirk to Dunkerque (A Tale of Two Cities) 244

E comme Europe 139–41, 148, 159, 244
Edmundson, Charles 176
Egan, Convery 67
Ehrlich, Blake 172
Eisenhower, Dwight D. 76, 198
Emilia 114, 218, 244
ERP in Action 35, 49, 108, 186, 244
Europe Looks Ahead 244
European Labor Day 244
Evans, Joseph 53
Expert Services 121–2, 244
Extraordinary Adventures of One Quart Milk, The 119, 120, 244

Farm in Four Countries, A 115, 162, 244
Ferno (Fernhout), John 31, 59–60, 150, 159, 161–4, 173, 177, 187, 213, 243, 244, 246, 248
Fires Were Started 157
Flaherty, Robert 165
400 Million, The 162
Free City 144, 146, 159, 173, 244
Freedland (Friedland), George 141, 165, 246, 250
Friendly, Al 44–5, 52, 65–6, 73, 77, 91, 133, 168–9, 172, 193, 217

Gallo, Vittorio 59, 173, 176, 178, 242, 243, 244, 245, 246, 251, 252
Genn, Leo 54, 151
Gervasi, Frank 31, 53–5, 146, 168–9, 175
Glossotis, Basil 223
Good Life, The (The Changing Face of Europe, no. 6) 140, 157, 238, 243
Grierson, John 12, 26, 160, 178, 205
Grimblat, Pierre 119, 244

Halas, John 159, 161, 166, 251
Halas and Batchelor 90, 110, 159, 161, 165–6
Hall, Lawrence 170, 223
Handicraft Town 27–8, 45, 111, 159, 182, 244
Hansl and the 200,000 Chicks 33, 245
Harriman, Averell W. 25, 78, 133, 171, 190
Hasty Heart, The 211
Hemsing, Albert 5, 23–4, 168–9, 174, 205, 229
Henry's Story 63, 143, 210, 245
Hidden Power 58, 245
Hidden Treasures 245
Hides for Tomorrow 66, 210, 245
Hodges, Thomas 134
Hoffman, Paul G. 21, 25, 76–7, 107, 127, 130–3, 142, 171, 234
Home we Love, The 245
Hour of Choice, The 54, 81, 136–40, 155, 159, 185, 245
Hugo and the Harp 245
Hugo and the House of Europe 67, 245
Hugo in the Circus 245

I Went Back 33, 54, 151, 246
Ideas at Work 127, 185, 188, 246
Independent People, An 246
Invisible Link, The 115, 149–50, 164, 187, 246
Island Odyssey 143, 188, 246
Italy Today 246

Jennings, Humphrey 157–9, 243
Jensen, Bjørn Frank 66, 166, 245
Jungle that Was, The 40, 63, 187–8, 252

Kirkpatrick, Helen 61, 167, 171
Kracauer, Siegfried 39, 195–6

Kurland, David 59–60, 146, 173–4, 248, 253
Kyndbyværket 97, 246

Land of Apulia 56–7, 114, 246
Land Redeemed 30, 56, 114, 246
Larkins Studio 90, 166, 175
Legg, Stuart 54, 136, 159, 161, 245
Let's Be Childish 116, 139, 141–2, 165, 188, 246
Liberty 63, 134, 138, 246
Life and Death of a Cave City 58, 155, 173, 247
Lippman, Walter 12, 160, 190, 258
Liquid Force 62, 149, 247
Liquid Sunshine 27, 143, 247
Listen to Britain 157
Living Stream, The 32, 148–9, 159, 188, 210, 247

Machines at Work 111, 247
Mack, Harald 66, 166, 245
Mackie, Philip 70, 82, 249–51, 254
Marcellini, Romolo 144, 159, 161, 176, 178, 182, 244, 246–7, 250, 252
March of Time, The 161, 168
Marketing 121–2, 247
Marshall Plan at Work in Austria, The 247
Marshall Plan at Work in Belgium (and Luxembourg), The 247
Marshall Plan at Work in Denmark, The 247
Marshall Plan at Work in France, The 247
Marshall Plan at Work in Great Britain, The 247–8
Marshall Plan at Work in Greece, The 248
Marshall Plan at Work in Holland, The 140, 248
Marshall Plan at Work in Ireland, The 248
Marshall Plan at Work in Italy, The 248
Marshall Plan at Work in Norway, The 248
Marshall Plan at Work in Turkey, The 248
Marshall Plan at Work in Western Germany, The 248
Marshall, George C. 2, 12, 73–4, 86
McCloy, John 66
McNulty, Henry 201
Men and Machines (The Changing Face of Europe, no. 4) 29, 81–2, 84, 243

Men at Work 27–8, 56, 248
Mill Town 60, 173–4, 217, 248
Miner's Window, The 162–3, 248
Miracle of Cassino, The 249
Mitterrand, Robert 62
Monnet, Jean 132–3
Montana 210
Mullen, Robert 123
My Trip Abroad 249

Neergaard, Ebbe 95–7
Nielsen, Waldemar (Wally) 55, 69, 136, 170, 172
Nilson, Nils 71, 90, 168–9, 176–7
No Way Back 164
Norall, Frank 131
North Sea Harbour (Strength for the Free World) 249
Norway, Nation on Skis 53
Nuremberg 169

Oldest Enemy, The 249
1-2-3: A Monthly Review from Europe 49, 149, 153, 162, 232, 254
Our Drawings 249
Over to You 29, 126, 249

Piece of Coal, A 55, 249
Porter, Paul 90
Power for All (The Changing Face of Europe, no. 1) 149, 242
Power for Peace 84, 249
Price, Harry 13, 102, 167, 172
Productivité (Productivity) 100–2, 110, 249
Productivity - Key to Progress 121–2, 185, 188, 249
Project for Tomorrow 33, 116–17, 164, 249
Promise of Barty O'Brien, The 26, 250
Provence - terre de peuplement 62, 250

Rachlis, Eugene 79
Rádvanyi, Géza von 148, 159, 244
Railroads 27, 250
Rathvon, Peter 67–8, 197–9, 202
Reed, Vergil D. 197
Renaissance agricole 62, 250
Report from Britain 54, 250
Return from the Valley 29, 33, 60, 162–3, 186, 250

Reuss, Henry S. 193
Rice and Bulls 30, 62, 113–14, 117, 210, 250
Ridder, Walter 65, 167
Rigaux, Jean 119
Ring, Bjørn 66, 166, 245
River Without Borders 220
Rommel's Treasure 169
Roos, Jørgen 95, 118, 252
Roosevelt, Franklin D. 12, 17, 103, 161, 190
Ruhr, The 250
Rural Sardinia 114, 250

Sachs, Peter 90, 166, 253
Sarrut, Andre 100, 249, 252
Schlesinger, Arthur Jr. 191, 294
School for Colonels 84, 250
Schulberg, Stuart 49, 65–7, 79, 97, 151, 158, 161, 164, 168–9, 175, 200–1
Schuman, Robert 132, 198
Secondari, John 54, 59, 145, 168–9, 173, 176, 244, 247
Seed Is Sown, A 251
Sentinels of Bronze (Sentinelle di bronzo) 159
Shea, Frank 167, 193
Ship is Born, A 28, 31, 56, 145–6, 251
Shoemaker and the Hatter, The 89–90, 110–11, 139, 155, 159, 166, 184, 187–8, 202, 220, 251
Shoot the Nets! 144–5, 159, 176, 184, 187–8, 210, 213, 251
Silkmakers of Como, The 58, 112, 251
Simplification 251
Smiths and the Robinsons, The 30, 81–5, 251
Smoke 66, 251
Somewhere to Live (The Changing Face of Europe, no. 3) 30, 140, 152, 155, 243
Spanish Earth 162
Spiro, Julian 55, 178, 242, 254
Stalin, Joseph 12, 74–5, 86, 145
Stapp, Philipp 89–90, 245, 252, 253
Steady 245
Storm over Italy 251
Story of a Rescue 26, 40, 100, 210–11, 251
Story of Koula, The 1, 30, 33, 59, 116–17, 173, 186, 188, 251
Story of Mahmoud, The 33, 63, 114, 232, 251

Streamlined Pig, The 30, 95, 97, 118–19, 188, 232, 252

Sucksdorff, Arne 32, 148–9, 159, 247*Symphony of a City (Människor i stad)* 159

Talking to the Italians 182, 252
300.000.000 Mouths (The Changing Face of Europe, no. 2) 242
Three Cities 85, 252
Three Coins in a Fountain 169
Tomorrow We Live 56, 252
Toonder, Marten 66, 165–6, 245
Tough Day, A 124, 246
Transatlantic 252
Traudl's New Kitchen Garden 252
Treasure of the Rhône 35, 62, 149, 252
Tressler, Georg 43, 52, 87, 117–18, 160–1, 174, 178–9, 242, 243, 245, 249, 252
Trieste to Lampedusa 252
Trip in Sicily 55, 252
Truman, Harry S. 3, 8, 16–18, 58, 73–7, 236–7
Turkish Harvest 69, 252
Twenty Hours a Day 252
Two Counts 55, 145, 252

Van der Horst, Herman 32, 144, 159, 176–7, 213, 245, 250, 251
Vicas, Victor 124, 160–1, 164–5, 243, 246, 249, 254

Victory at Thermopylae 30, 35, 60, 113, 187, 217, 253
Village that Wouldn't Die, The 29, 62, 253
Village Tractor, The 69–71, 114, 253
Village Without Water 27, 35, 40–1, 45, 188, 253
Village Without Words 38, 57, 146–7, 253

Walcheren 30, 163, 246
Wallace, Graham 157, 242, 243
We and the Others 66, 184, 253
Wessex Films 64, 135, 157
What a Life! 83
Whitsun Holiday 85, 253
Why We Fight 161
Wiborg, Mary Hoyt 197
Wilson, Thomas W. 53, 109, 134, 169
Without Fear 31, 85, 89–90, 92–4, 139, 166, 185, 188, 211, 253
Wolff, Lothar 43, 59, 96, 145, 159–61, 163, 168–9, 244
Work Flow 253

Years of Decision, The 253
Yusef and his Plough 30, 33, 69–70, 116–17, 253

Zinc Valley 27, 55, 253

Subject Index

Africa 63, 87, 159, 162, 188
agriculture. *See individual countries;*
    Marshall Plan; productivity
aid 51–2, 58, 73–5, 145, 163, 203, 227, 233
    See also Marshall Aid
Allied Forces. *See* Germany; OMGUS
Americanization 7–8, 10, 20, 48, 107,
    233–40
audience
    numbers 183–4, 208, 219, 225–7
    preferences 26, 33, 40, 94, 181, 185–9,
        199–200, 204, 237–8
    reception 181–90, 193–7, 199–205
    social make up 117, 184–5, 187, 196,
        200, 203, 238
    See also film exhibition
Austria 3, 6, 9, 13, 49–52, 65, 81, 98, 105,
    160–1, 169, 183–4, 187, 190, 192,
    197, 199, 210, 235–8, 240
    film production 30, 33–5, 43, 87–8,
        115–17, 149, 174–5, 178–9

Belgium 3, 9, 40, 51, 63, 98, 176, 200, 209–11
Berlin 67, 75, 85–7

Catholic Church 107, 139, 216, 219, 234
censorship 59, 97, 172
Central Intelligence Agency (CIA) 13–14,
    52, 74, 159, 235
cinema. *See* film exhibition
Cold War
    escalation 20, 30, 68, 75, 79, 85, 89
    impact on Marshall Plan 2, 10–11,
        17–18, 73–81, 84–7, 93, 95–6, 98
    and MP propaganda 2, 10–11, 18–19,
        73, 81, 89, 93–4, 96–7
    See also Korean War; propaganda;
        rearmament
communism/communists
    and European trade unions 14–15, 32,
        52, 58, 100, 105–6, 123–6, 207, 221,
        230

fear of communism 4, 12, 14, 17, 36,
    74, 76, 85, 89–90, 92–4, 98, 188–9,
    211, 221, 235
and the Marshall Plan 3–5, 9, 12–19,
    25, 74, 85, 190
as theme in MP films 19, 25, 28–33,
    36–7, 44, 86–7, 95–6, 100
    See also propaganda; Soviet Union
consumer 29, 102, 107–10, 120–2, 190,
    233–5, 239
cultural transfer 1–2, 5, 7–11, 13–15,
    19–20, 26, 32, 48, 54, 65, 68, 70–1,
    80, 88, 107, 110, 136–7, 139, 151,
    156, 158, 162, 165–70, 172, 196,
    200, 203–5, 212, 224, 230, 233–8,
    240
culture. *See* propaganda; OMGUS; USIS

defence. *See* Korean War; rearmament
Denmark 3, 9, 30, 50, 89, 94–7, 113, 118,
    148–9, 165–6, 190, 212

East Germany. *See* Berlin; Germany
Eastern Europe 3, 14, 32, 85–7, 126,
    135–8, 156, 238
ECA. *See* Economic Cooperation
    Administration
Economic Cooperation Administration
    (ECA)
    organizational structure 5, 21–2, 24
    policies 5, 7–8, 25, 43, 45, 47, 52, 55,
        69, 73, 79, 89–90, 95, 98–9, 125,
        127, 132, 158, 170–3, 178, 189, 192,
        194–5, 197–8, 204, 225, 230–3, 239
    powers/tasks 52–3, 55, 64, 78, 106, 108,
        121, 123–4, 196
    relations with OMGUS 13, 15, 64–7,
        168–9, 175, 177, 235
    relations with State Department 10, 15,
        45, 55, 61, 67–8, 76, 78, 106, 131–3,
        170, 172, 185, 190, 197, 213, 226,
        230, 239

See also Information Division
economy. *See* Europe
electricity 30, 115, 148–50, 154, 215
Europe
    economy 3–4, 15–16, 32, 51, 64, 73–4,
        77, 99–100, 130, 203, 229
    film industry 6, 48, 54, 59, 67, 69, 97,
        158, 160, 169, 175–6, 184–5, 216,
        222
    and the Marshall Plan 1–2, 5, 15–16,
        19, 36, 43, 73, 75, 99, 190, 198
    relations with US 11, 15–16, 18–19,
        32, 36, 63, 68, 70–1, 76, 99, 105,
        129–38, 169–70, 176–7, 179, 192–3,
        195, 198, 218, 224, 229–40
    as theme in MP films 2, 6–8, 19–20, 23,
        26–7, 29–32, 38–9, 47–9, 65, 81, 99,
        118, 139–45, 148–60, 163–73, 178,
        181, 188, 205, 207, 209–12, 215, 226
    trade 63, 80, 104–8, 110, 113, 127
    See also Americanization; audience;
        European integration
European integration/unification
    European resistance against 133–4,
        138–9, 142, 153, 156, 189, 203–4,
        225
    and Germany 65–6, 68, 94, 98, 129,
        187, 199
    term/concept 27, 30, 104, 131–2, 134,
        156
    as US policy aim 3, 20, 38, 49, 66, 76,
        110, 127, 129–31, 142, 153, 155–6,
        225, 239
European Recovery Programme (ERP).
    See Marshall Plan
exchange programmes 104–6, 126–7
    See also trade unions; productivity

Film, aims 5, 11, 18–19, 24–5, 30, 32, 36,
    44, 80–1, 85, 89, 109–10, 115, 123,
    153, 233, 238
    animation film 26, 32, 34, 66, 89–91,
        94, 100–2, 110, 118, 139, 159–60,
        165–6, 175, 177, 187–8, 210–11
    documentary 1, 9, 12, 25–7, 29–31,
        33–4, 38, 40, 43–4, 48, 53–6, 60,
        65–6, 68–9, 81–2, 85, 87, 95–7,
        112, 118–19, 121–2, 126–7, 136–8,
        143–6, 148, 150–3, 157–65, 169,

        174–9, 182, 184, 187–8, 195, 198–9,
        205–6, 209–10, 212–13, 215–16,
        225, 231, 239
    fiction film 26, 33, 44, 82, 124, 160,
        164–5, 177, 201, 232
    newsreels 176, 183, 199, 207, 231,
        236–7
    sound 31–2, 38–40, 119, 137, 152
    visual style 6–8, 11, 19–20, 21–2, 26,
        28, 30–4, 36–9, 42–5, 56, 80, 89,
        91–3, 101–2, 110, 118–19, 125,
        139–41, 143–9, 156, 179, 196, 202
    voice-over 32, 34, 39–42, 91, 118–19,
        146, 149, 151, 175
film distribution
    commercial/theatrical 68, 157–8,
        172, 176, 183, 188–9, 197, 204–5,
        209–11, 214–17, 219–21, 224–5
    cooperation with local agencies 90,
        116, 126–7, 140–2, 172–4, 211–12,
        237
    cooperation with USIS 206–7, 214–15,
        217–26
    non-commercial/non-theatrical 158,
        183, 186, 205–9, 211, 213–14, 217,
        222, 224–5
film exhibition
    cinemas 2, 59, 163, 183–5, 188, 197,
        202, 207–9, 212–17, 219–20, 222,
        224, 237–8
    mobile film units 14, 43, 117, 143, 160,
        183, 195, 206–8, 213–20, 222–3
    open air screenings 182, 208, 216, 218,
        222
    See also audience
filmmakers 2, 6–10, 19–20, 25, 37–8,
    42–5, 47–8, 52–4, 59–60, 64, 67,
    78, 85, 89–90, 94–7, 117–18, 143,
    151, 153, 156, 157–62, 164–5, 167,
    169, 172–3, 175–9, 181, 196, 213,
    216–17, 231–2, 238–9
film officers. *See* Information Division
film production
    dubbing 10, 52, 181, 212, 232
    financing 47–54, 71, 96, 177, 210, 237
    locally initiated productions 7, 20, 43,
        47–9
    organization 49–52
    output 54–71

See also filmmakers; France; Germany; Great Britain; Greece; Information Division; Italy
film reception. *See* audience
France
communists 9, 18, 49, 60–1, 74, 106, 117, 123, 125, 193, 197, 220–1
economy 60, 74, 81, 129
film distribution/exhibition 63–4, 117, 138–40, 143, 148–9, 183, 191, 210–11, 214, 219–20
film production 50, 60–4, 100–2, 111, 113–14, 118–20, 122, 124–5, 138–42, 149
French government and ECA 71, 100, 105, 107, 113–14, 138, 190, 192, 222
opposition to Marshall Plan policies 98, 100, 106, 192–3, 197–8, 215, 221

gender. *See* men; women
Germany
economy 16, 64–5, 73–4, 98, 129
and European integration 81, 130–1, 139, 190, 199, 200
film distribution/exhibition 68, 85–6, 94, 139, 143, 148, 155, 160, 164, 183–5, 187, 194–5, 210–11, 213–14, 219, 221
film production 13, 50, 64–8, 85–7, 169, 175
Nazism/Nazi dictatorship 13, 58, 61, 64–5, 83, 140, 154, 164–6, 168, 175, 201, 237
See also OMGUS; Soviet Union
Great Britain
economy 51, 53, 73, 75, 103, 106, 130
film distribution/exhibition 36, 54, 83–4, 110, 140–1, 157, 183–4, 187, 189, 191, 200, 208, 210–13, 219–21
film production 48, 53–4, 64, 69, 71, 82–4, 89–90, 110–11, 121–2, 126–7, 136, 151–2, 157, 161, 166
Greece
agriculture 1, 60, 113
civil war 58, 73–4, 163, 221–2
communism 9, 18, 49, 58, 73–4, 223, 230–1
economy 73–4, 113, 167, 221
film distribution/exhibition 9, 30, 33, 113, 140, 143, 146, 150, 183–6,

188–9, 196, 208, 211, 215, 217, 222, 224
film production 48–50, 55, 58–60, 71, 113, 150–1, 222
opposition to Marshall Plan policies 58–9

High Commissioner of Germany (HICOG) 10, 66–8, 85, 87, 94, 195–6, 213–15, 232, 235
Hollywood
cooperation with ECA 161, 168, 210, 216, 219
cooperation with US government 20, 55, 68, 235–7, 239
influence in Europe 47–8, 234–6, 238

Iceland 3, 9, 49, 51, 93, 135, 186, 188, 207, 224
industry. *See* Europe; productivity; work
Information Division
collaboration/conflicts with USIS 10, 13–15, 22, 24, 54, 68, 78, 108, 170–1, 181, 183, 185, 190, 197, 203, 206–7, 214–15, 217–27, 231
country missions 5, 10, 22–4, 33, 43, 45, 47–9, 52, 71, 78, 93, 107, 133, 146, 159, 171–2, 181, 184–5, 189, 195, 201, 203, 206, 209, 225, 232
film unit 5, 23–4, 43, 47, 49, 52–5, 67, 69–71, 78–9, 87, 89–90, 95, 157–8, 160–4, 166, 168–9, 171–3, 175–6, 183, 189, 194–7, 200–4, 217, 222–3, 239
information officers 2, 7–8, 19–20, 22, 25, 42, 45, 48, 54, 61, 70, 78–9, 87, 94, 97–8, 104, 107–9, 111, 119, 133–4, 156, 158, 161, 167, 169–73, 175–6, 179, 181, 187, 189, 195–6, 198–201, 205, 227, 230, 239
policy/strategy 5, 7, 13, 36, 47, 61, 69, 79, 89, 98, 104–5, 108–9, 123, 126, 136, 167–8, 190, 204, 207, 215, 225–7, 239
role/tasks 22–4, 26, 44–5, 48–9, 52, 55, 62, 65–6, 90, 132–3, 170–2, 181, 192–7, 199, 202–3
See also Economic Cooperation Administration; film production; propaganda
Ireland 3, 9, 26, 49–52, 55, 165

Italy
  agriculture 30, 40, 55–6, 113–14, 203
  communists 9, 49, 58, 74, 81, 123, 230
  elections 54–5, 230
  fascism 12, 159, 161, 176, 201, 215–16
  film distribution/exhibition 6, 30, 32,
    36, 38, 40, 71, 111, 140, 143, 145–6,
    155, 159, 182–3, 185, 187, 191,
    201–2, 211, 214–19, 224–5, 233
  film production 26–8, 40–5, 50, 54–9,
    111–12, 114, 144–8, 155, 169, 173,
    176, 209, 215–16
  North-South divide 27, 41, 111, 114
  opposition to Marshall Plan policies
    98, 106

Korean War 5, 8, 20, 24, 29–30, 36, 73,
  75–7, 79–80, 84, 99, 201–3, 220,
  222, 225, 232

labour. *See* trade unions; work/workers
liberalism
  as basis of US foreign policy 12, 65,
    103, 124, 171, 178, 233, 235–6, 238
  versus communism 12, 18, 74, 85,
    87–8, 93, 103, 124, 126, 164,
    229–30, 235, 238
  and the Marshall Plan 11–13, 15–19,
    25, 29, 37, 74, 99–100, 120, 166,
    229–30, 233
  as theme in MP films 32, 43, 65, 85–90,
    92–3, 122, 126, 138, 164, 175, 233
  See also European integration; US
    government
Luxembourg 3, 9, 22

marketing 12, 119, 121–2, 190, 197
Marshall Aid
  allocation 4, 16, 18, 22, 25, 27, 29,
    30–1, 51–3, 65, 68, 70–1, 75, 86,
    96, 98, 113–14, 143, 147, 154, 198,
    229–30
  counterpart funds 50–3, 56, 59–60,
    62–3
  funding of anti-Communist forces 25,
    31, 52, 75, 178
  technical assistance 40, 58, 77, 104–7,
    115–17, 126–7
Marshall Plan
  aims/motives 2, 7, 11, 16, 18, 25, 36,

    52, 68, 93, 99, 103, 133, 177–9, 192,
    194, 198, 204, 225, 231–2, 239
  criticism of 18, 58, 61, 90, 100, 106,
    131, 203, 221
  impact 5, 8, 11, 16, 20, 70, 79, 185, 190,
    192–6, 202–3, 211, 226–7, 229–31,
    233, 239–40
  measures 2, 4, 11, 37, 45, 76, 94, 106–7,
    123–4, 130–1, 147, 202–3, 209, 212,
    227, 231, 236, 238
  See also Economic Cooperation
    Administration; US government
media. *See* propaganda; USIS
men/masculinity 27–9, 34, 56, 69, 108,
  114–16, 120, 123, 154, 158, 171,
  182, 197, 204
Movie theatre. *See* film exhibition
Mutual Security Agency (MSA) 5, 24–5,
  78, 84, 87, 90, 109, 158, 162, 168,
  187, 190, 202, 220, 222, 233
Mutual Security Programme 24, 77, 98

NATO. *See* North Atlantic Treaty
  Organization
Netherlands 3, 9, 29–30, 32, 40, 50, 63,
  81, 99–100, 113, 115, 133, 140, 144,
  159, 163, 189, 190–1, 204, 213
North Atlantic Treaty Organization
  (NATO) 18–19, 68, 76–7, 81, 84,
  187, 222
Norway 3, 9, 32, 50, 53, 148–9, 153–5, 188,
  190–1, 206, 212

OEEC. *See* Organisation for European
  Economic Co-operation
Organisation for European Economic
  Co-operation (OEEC) 3, 62, 68, 70,
  105–6, 130
Overseas Military Government (OMGUS)
  re-education 13, 65, 168, 175, 236–7
  relations with ECA 10, 13–15, 64–7,
    168–9, 175, 177, 235
  See also ECA; Germany

Portugal 3, 9, 49, 51–2, 63, 215
productivity
  agriculture 25, 30, 33, 55, 62–3, 95,
    113–19, 197, 229
  concept 4, 6, 8, 11, 13, 20, 26–7,
    31–8, 44, 58, 78, 86, 91, 94–5,

97–8, 100–5, 108–13, 120–7, 130–1,
133–4, 150–3, 161, 199, 203, 219,
222, 232–40
and industry 4, 16, 25, 27–32, 50–1,
53, 56, 60, 64, 66, 68, 80–1, 86, 95,
100–2, 104–10, 112, 118–26, 154–5,
164, 192, 197, 212, 223, 229, 234–5
and Korean War 29–30, 77
productivity programmes 56, 95, 113,
115, 206–11, 214
resistance against 58, 98, 106–7, 123,
232
as theme in MP films 11, 30–1, 36,
53–4, 58, 80, 100–2, 108–27, 150,
185, 188, 212
propaganda
aims 1–2, 4–11, 15, 18–20, 109, 134,
179, 227
communist/Soviet propaganda 12–13,
21, 25, 44, 86, 89, 96–7, 109, 193,
197, 199, 230, 240
impact 71, 81, 94, 107, 120, 123, 131,
142, 158, 161–2, 167, 170, 190–1,
211–13, 215–18, 231, 233, 240
strategies 21–4, 26, 29, 32, 35, 45,
48–50, 53–4, 58, 61–2, 64, 68–9, 73,
93, 171, 177, 181–2, 185, 189–99,
201–6, 209, 220–2, 225–6, 236–9
term 11–14
See also film; Information Division;
USIS

rearmament 20, 77–81, 84–5, 98–9, 198–9,
203–4, 232
See also Cold War
river. *See* water

Schuman Plan 132, 198
Second World War 17, 84, 103–4, 144,
150, 152–3, 161, 167, 213, 219,
233–5, 240
ship/shipping 1, 31, 38, 60, 62–3, 79, 138,
143–8, 150–1
Smith-Mundt-Act of 1948 14
Social Democracy. *See* welfare state
Soviet Union
cultural activities in Europe 197, 207,
216, 218, 220
and Germany 73–5, 129
and the Marshall Plan 3, 17, 51, 229

relations with the US 58, 74–6, 202,
235
See also propaganda
Spain 135
State Department. *See* US State
Department
Sweden 3, 9, 49–51, 148–9, 159
Switzerland 3, 9, 22, 49, 51, 149, 210–11

technical assistance 4, 40, 58, 77, 104,
106–7, 126, 234
See also Marshall Aid
trade. *See* Europe; liberalism
trade unions
communist trade unions 14–15, 32, 52,
58, 100, 105–6, 123–6, 207, 221, 230
non-communist, "free" trade unions
14–15, 32, 52, 105, 123, 125–6, 222,
225, 230
opposition to MP 58, 61, 100, 106, 203,
221
and productivity 32, 58, 100, 105–6,
123–6, 183, 203, 206–7, 230
Trieste 3, 22, 43–4, 50, 55, 85, 144–5, 159,
183, 209
Truman Doctrine 3, 17, 58, 73–5
Turkey 3, 9, 48, 50, 51–2, 63, 68–71, 73,
113, 116, 137, 188–9, 195–6, 208,
212, 215, 224

unemployment 18, 27–8, 58, 60, 74, 77, 93,
95, 98, 124–5, 153, 203
United States (US)
anti-communism 14–15, 25, 31, 52,
67, 74–5, 79, 85, 87, 90, 94, 98, 126,
164, 166, 178, 185, 188, 199, 202,
211
Cold War 17–18, 20, 30–1, 68, 71,
73–5, 77–81, 85–6, 89
US opposition to Marshall Plan 10,
18, 77, 79, 131, 171, 179, 185, 193,
201–4
See also Europe; US government
United States Information Service (USIS)
cooperation/conflicts with ECA 14–15,
22, 24, 183, 185, 190, 197, 206
cultural activities 15, 54, 203, 207, 214
film distribution/exhibition 36,
68–9, 108, 181, 186, 202, 207, 214,
217–27, 231

role/tasks 14, 22, 78, 170–1, 181, 201, 215, 230

US Army 22, 51, 54, 160–1, 164, 177, 236. *See also* OMGUS

US government
  foreign policy 8, 14–15, 24, 74–8, 103, 106, 132–3, 230, 235
  relations with European governments 39, 61, 67, 126, 131–2, 190
  See also ECA; Hollywood; rearmament; US State Department

US State Department
  cooperation with ECA 15, 45, 54–5, 61, 67–8, 78, 170, 185, 190–1, 197–8, 226, 230, 235, 239
  United States Information Agency (USIA) 5, 10, 24–5, 78, 220

USIA. *See* United States Information Agency

USIS. *See* United States Information Service

Vienna 87, 152, 160, 174

water 27, 35, 38, 40–2, 45, 60, 69, 135, 146, 148–51, 188

welfare state 18, 104, 123–4

West Germany. *See* Germany

Western Europe. *See* Europe

women/femininity
  as theme in MP films 29, 69, 120–3, 141, 155, 187, 197
  within ECA 108, 115, 121, 167, 171, 197, 203–4
  See also men; trade unions

work/workers
  as addressees of propaganda 2, 4–5, 17, 22, 24–5, 27–9, 52–4, 61, 70, 158, 160–6, 168, 171–3, 175, 177–9, 192–3, 197–8, 201–4, 221, 227
  handicraft versus mass production 100–2, 104–10, 112, 118, 121
  as theme in MP films 44, 61, 69, 91, 93, 100–1, 105, 111–13, 116, 123–7, 131–4, 138, 141, 144, 146–8, 154, 156, 158, 164, 166, 169, 182, 185, 187, 189, 195, 208, 222–3, 225, 233, 235–6, 238

Yugoslavia 74, 144–5